Chile Under Pinochet

Recovering the Truth

Mark Ensalaco

PENN

University of Pennsylvania Press

Philadelphia

10 9 8 7 6 5 4 3 2 1

Published by
University of Pennsylvania Press
Philadelphia, Pennsylvania 19104-4011

Library of Congress Cataloging-in-Publication Data

Ensalaco, Mark.
    Chile under Pinochet : recovering the truth / Mark Ensalaco.
        p.   cm. — (Pennsylvania studies in human rights)
    Includes bibliographical references (p.   –   ) and index.
    ISBN 0-8122-3520-7 (alk. paper). — ISBN 0-8122-1708-X (pbk. : alk. paper)
        1. Human rights — Chile — History.   2. Chile — Politics and
    government — 1973–1988.   3. Pinochet Ugarte, Augusto.   4. Political
    persecution — Chile.   5. Victims of state-sponsored terrorism — Chile.
    6. Disappeared persons — Chile.   7. Military government — Chile —
    History.   I. Title.   II. Series.
    JC599.C5E67   1999
    323.4'9'098309047 — dc21   99-32950
                                                                        CIP

To
Salvatore ("Chic") and Ruth,
my parents, who possessed that
quality of mercy
which is the leitmotiv of this book

Contents

Preface

In August 1991, just weeks before the eighteenth anniversary of the coup d'état that brought General Augusto Pinochet to power, the Vicariate of Solidarity announced the gruesome discovery of more than one hundred bodies in Santiago's General Cemetery. The bodies had been interred secretly between September and December 1973. In a few cases, two bodies were placed in a single coffin. After years of heartbreaking and meticulous work, the women and men of the Roman Catholic Church's human rights office finally had found some of the first of the more than two thousand Chileans "disappeared" by the Pinochet regime. General Pinochet had relinquished the presidency in 1990 after seventeen years as Chile's dictator, but was still commander of Chile's armed forces. After the discovery, Pinochet's nominal commander-in-chief, transitional President Patricio Aylwin, summoned the general to the Moneda palace to express his outrage. President Aylwin could do nothing more than this. Pinochet enjoyed complete impunity for crimes that he may have ordered or that were committed by the men he commanded. President Aylwin could not even force the former dictator into retirement. As a dour Pinochet emerged from the Moneda, a young television reporter suddenly thrust a microphone at him, and asked him to comment on the appalling fact that some caskets contained two bodies. Pinochet quipped coldly, "How very economical!" That cruel and cynical remark is the origin of this book.

I was in Chile as Visiting Professor at the Law School of the University of Concepción at the time, where I was conducting research on the reform of Pinochet's 1980 constitution, especially insofar as it involved the scheme of civil-military relations within the larger context of Chile's democratic transition. I had arrived in the country on the first of several visits over the following five years just after the publication of the Report of the National Commission on Truth and Reconciliation. Patricio Aylwin had created this presidential "truth commission" in 1990 as one of his first official acts, to provide an accounting of the human rights violations committed by the

Pinochet regime. The National Commission on Truth and Reconciliation produced its multi-volume report only months before Pinochet made his cruel, extemporaneous remark. I immediately realized that no study of Chile's negotiated return to democratic rule would be complete without an examination of the controversial and potentially disruptive matter of human rights. Then I had a second realization: that there was no comprehensive account of the human rights violations of the Pinochet dictatorship available in English to students or scholars. So I set out to write a political history of the repression and the official efforts to recover the truth about it.

I wrote the book with the conviction that students of Chilean history, Latin American politics, political violence, and human rights would benefit from a book about a tragic phase in the history of this important Latin American nation. There are many excellent books about the coup d'état that brought down Salvador Allende's socialist government, Pinochet's emergence as first among equals on the military junta, the neoliberal economic model implemented by the military government, the negotiated transition to democracy, and specific acts of repression, like the assassination of Orlando Letelier in Washington in 1976. But there was no complete history of the period that elucidated the repression. Students and scholars can pore over the English translation of the Report of the National Commission on Truth and Reconciliation, or the dozens of damning reports of the United Nations, the Organization of American States, Amnesty International, Americas Watch, and other human rights organizations. But these are not narrative accounts, nor do they explicate the human rights violations in terms of the politics of an authoritarian regime. General Pinochet's cruel remark convinced me of the need for a readable, complete, and narrative account of the human rights catastrophe that occurred in Chile.

This book is specifically about Chile under Pinochet, but it is intended as well as a case study of a repressive regime for students of authoritarianism and state terrorism. The Pinochet dictatorship was remarkable. During Pinochet's seventeen-year rule, the Chilean state was militarized, the judicial system was marginalized, power was vested in Pinochet as both armed forces commander-in-chief and chief of state, the secret police acted above and outside the law, and the most fundamental rights of thousands of Chileans were systematically violated. Political scientists were not sure how to characterize the regime. During the 1970s and early 1980s, experts in Latin American politics and comparative politics debated whether Chile under Pinochet was ruled by a Bureaucratic Authoritarian (BA) regime. The Pinochet regime differed from the BA regimes in Argentina, Brazil, and Uruguay, because Pinochet had emerged as the sole dictator. In the other countries of the Southern Cone, the military ruled as an institution and the presidency rotated among senior officers and between the different branches of the armed forces. The Pinochet regime, if not entirely different, was at best a hybrid personalistic dictatorship and BA regime. These were not merely academic debates. Political scientists were attempting to define the nature of the beast, to use an especially apt phrase, and to probe tensions in BA regimes in order to help prevent their consolidation and hasten their demise.

The Pinochet regime was a variant of a BA regime. Its distinctive features were discernible. But in an important sense the Pinochet regime had a generic quality. Like all authoritarian regimes, whether of the left or the right, the Pinochet regime was inherently repressive. The theoretical studies of the military dictatorships of the Southern Cone gave us an excellent understanding of the nature and internal dynamics of Bureaucratic Authoritarian regimes, but they rarely explained state terrorism as a function of politics or studied repression as a subject specifically deserving of attention. The documentation of repression was left to the human rights organizations, whose reports were often cited but seldom incorporated into political or historical analyses.

Repression was policy in Chile under Pinochet, just as it is policy in any authoritarian regime. General Pinochet's military government set out to transform Chile as a matter of policy. The extirpation of Marxism was a prerequisite of that transformation: indeed, on the night of the coup a member of the military junta announced the mission to extirpate Marxism from the Chilean body politic. Repression was a matter of state, and it was conducted relentlessly and ruthlessly. That is deserving of examination. This book is a case study of repression in an authoritarian regime: how the state was organized to repress, how the repression was carried out, who directed it, who suffered from it.

The book is also about the human rights movement that emerged in Chile in reaction to the repression. The human rights movement began to emerge almost immediately after the September 1973 coup d'état, and new organizations appeared at every critical phase in the evolution of the dictatorship. The movement was diverse and courageous. In many ways, the Chilean human rights movement was the most dynamic in Latin America. Again, there are several excellent books about the work of specific human rights organizations, especially the renowned Vicariate of Solidarity. But I recognized the need for a book that recounted how human rights organizations struggled to counteract the repression and ultimately to induce the return of democracy.

The struggle for human rights is essentially political. Human rights activism, which someone once described as the "mobilization of shame," is intended to influence the political calculations of policy-makers. State terrorism was policy in Chile. The human rights movement sought to change that policy by forcing those who made it to recalculate costs and benefits. But because politics is ultimately about power, the human rights movement was at a tremendous disadvantage. The disparity of political power between those bent on killing their enemies with no regard for world opinion and those concerned with protecting human rights with no fear of the personal or professional consequences was vast.

Finally, the book is about the importance of truth, justice, the rule of law, and human rights in democratic transitions. The politics of human rights is an integral part of the politics of democratic transition. The book is specifically about the policy of accountability of the government of Patricio Aylwin, but it is also intended to serve as a case study of the moral, political, and legal dilemmas of a transitional government vis-à-vis the guardians of the old order and the families of their victims. President Aylwin had very few precedents to guide him and formidable challenges to confront. His policy, summed up in the phrase "the whole truth and justice to the extent possible," has been the subject of considerable debate in the human rights community. Some of its most vocal advocates have gone on to advise truth and reconciliation commissions in countries as different as El Salvador and South Africa. Others were left disappointed and angry at the apparent timidity of the policy. The subtitle of the book, *Recovering the Truth*, emphasizes the importance of recovering the truth as a measure of partial justice, regardless of whether the full measure of justice is possible.

The human rights policy of transitional governments has not been a major focus of the political science literature on democratic transitions. But if democracy is defined in terms of the rule of law as well as free and fair elections, democratic governments must make a good faith effort to do justice by the victims of a previous authoritarian regime in order to complete the transition to democracy. This book relates the efforts of one democratic government to balance the moral imperatives to do justice against the harsh political realities that constrained its actions. Reconciling the virtue of justice and the virtue of prudence was how President Aylwin expressed the dilemma.

The book is based primarily on an examination of the documentary record, although the later chapters contain interview material. I have treated the documents themselves as artifacts whose production is part of the story I narrate. The Report of the National Commission on Truth and Reconciliation is the most dramatic example of this. Also important are the carefully documented contemporaneous reports of the International Commission of Jurists, Amnesty International, Americas Watch, the Inter-American Human Rights Commission, and the United Nations Human Rights Commission. The publication of these reports was made possible by the Chilean human rights organizations, the Committee for Peace, the Vicariate of Solidarity, the Foundation for Social Assistance of the Christian Churches, the Chilean Human Rights Commission, the Commission on the Defense of the Rights of the People, and others. Testimony in U.S. congressional hearings likewise forms part of the documentary record.

Internal communications and public communiqués of the Movement of the Revolutionary Left, produced at a moment when the secret police was disappearing its leaders, give a fascinating depiction of an organization on the brink of destruction. The official responses of the armed forces and police and the Chilean Supreme Court of Justice to the Report of the National Commission on Truth and Reconciliation reveal that two of Chile's most important institutions adamantly refused to acknowledge the truth that President Aylwin had hoped would facilitate national reconciliation. Finally, Augusto Pinochet's memoir, *Camino recorrido*, contains the general's own recollections. Although they do not reveal secrets that could prove culpability, they reveal a view of the world, a perception of enemies, and a disdain for the international community that are well worth the space given to the ghostwritten memoir. To be fair to general Pinochet, I thought it right that he should speak for himself. Notably, his own words often proved the point of his critics.

Chapter 1, "The Victors and the Vanquished," introduces readers to the most important actors in the process of ideological polarization that culminated in the coup d'état in 1973. For students of Latin American politics, it is an introduction to the often bewildering array of political parties, especially the parties of the left. After the military overthrew socialist president Salvador Allende, these actors became either the victors or the vanquished. The following chapters chronicle the assault of the armed forces and secret police on the vanquished parties of Chile's once dynamic left.

Chapter 2, "An Invented War," describes the violence in the first months of the military regime. This was the most violent period of the seventeen-year dictatorship, if the violence is measured in terms of the number of those swept up by the armed forces, interrogated in places like the National Stadium, tortured, and killed. The chapter depicts the armed forces waging an invented war and violating the "laws and customs of war" in the process.

Chapter 3, "The New Order," describes the salient features of the Pinochet regime: the militarization of the state, the marginalization of the judicial system, the fusion of the powers of commander-in-chief and chief executive, and the ascendancy of Pinochet's secret state police, the Directorate for National Intelligence, or DINA. It also profiles the founder and director of the DINA, whose inordinate power was due to Pinochet's unwavering support, a fact that allows for the imputation of the dictator's personal culpability. Finally, the chapter reviews the genesis of the human rights organizations and describes the human rights activism and humanitarian action in which they engaged. Chile's dynamic human rights movement, which emerged in reaction to the atrocities committed by the military and secret police, constituted the very antithesis of the Pinochet regime.

Chapter 4, "A War of Extermination," chronicles the second phase of the repression, the destructive campaign to extirpate the parties of the left. The DINA and the air force's Joint Command perfected the terrible and terrifying practice of "disappearance," introduced in modern times by the Nazis.

In successive waves, these agencies "disappeared" the cadre of the Movement of the Revolutionary Left, then the Socialists, then the Communists. The chapter examines the sequence of events that are a "disappearance," and the awful legacy of thousands of "disappeared."

Chapter 5, "The Court of World Opinion," examines the synergy between international human rights organizations and the human rights organizations that emerged in Chile. It describes the negotiations that led up to the fact-finding missions of the International Commission of Jurists, Amnesty International, and the Inter-American Human Rights Commission, and summarizes their reports and findings. The chapter also narrates an episode that took place while the Organization of American States General Assembly was meeting in Santiago, when a group of courageous Chilean attorneys denounced the "new primitivism" into which their country was descending and forced the Chilean legal profession to examine its conscience.

Chapter 6, "A War of Resistance," describes the consolidation of Pinochet's hold on power and his imposition of a new constitution to legitimate his rule. It also describes the next phase of the political violence, characterized by the violent suppression of street protests by the police and a campaign of bombings and assassinations launched by the armed left. The chapter recounts two of the most horrific crimes of the dictatorship, the throat-slashing of three communists and the immolation of two young protesters, as well as the failed attempt to assassinate General Pinochet. The street protests and the violence of the armed left, as forms of resistance, had a negligible effect on Pinochet. But their failure to produce an immediate transition altered the strategy of the opposition.

Chapter 7, "The Peaceful Way to Democracy," analyzes the efforts of the United States, the United Nations, and the domestic opposition to influence the internal political dynamics of Chile and the relative ineffectiveness of diplomatic pressures to affect the course of events. It also chronicles the inception of the process of the democratic transition, a process that acquired momentum only after the moderate opposition decided to adhere to the dictator's rules. The moderate opposition, led by the Christian Democrats, managed to defeat Pinochet in a plebiscite on his continued rule in 1988, but the decision to abide by Pinochet's terms resulted in a negotiated transition with important consequences for justice afterward.

Chapter 8, "Recovering the Truth," examines the mandate, work, and findings of the National Commission on Truth and Reconciliation, the presidential "truth commission" created by President Patricio Aylwin as one of his first official acts. The chapter explores the moral, political, and legal dilemmas facing Aylwin, who as a transitional head of state had to address the grim legacy of the human rights violations of the past without imperiling the democratic transition. Justice was not possible in Chile, if by justice was meant prosecution, for both legal and political reasons. President Aylwin settled on a policy of accountability expressed in a memorable phrase: "the whole truth and justice to the extent possible."

Chapter 9, "The Politics of Human Rights," presents the reactions to the truth commission report of the Chilean armed forces and Carabineros, the Supreme Court of Justice, and the families of the "disappeared." The armed forces and Supreme Court of Justice categorically rejected the findings, conclusions, and recommendations of the National Commission on Truth and Reconciliation, a fact with disturbing implications for democracy. The families of the victims lamented the inability of the National Commission on Truth and Reconciliation to breach the wall of impunity and recover the whole truth. The chapter goes on to describe the ineffectual efforts to discover the fate and whereabouts of the "disappeared," once the mandate of the Truth and Reconciliation Commission ran out. The chapter, and the book, conclude with the episode surrounding Manuel Contreras's incarceration for his guilt in the Letelier/Moffitt murders in Washington, and some remarks about the extent of "possible justice."

In my own judgment, the "disappearances" define the political legacy of the Pinochet regime, and the inability of the democratic government to compel the armed forces to disclose information about the "disappeared" marked the imperfect democratic transition. The failure to prosecute the guilty because of debilitating political and legal constraints has disturbing implications in terms of the rule of law, and the anguish of the families of the "disappeared" constitutes a perpetual injustice. General Pinochet, having ceded the presidency to Patricio Aylwin, held the renascent democracy hostage in order to preserve the military's — and his own — impunity. President Aylwin, in order to safeguard the democracy and promote national reconciliation, balanced political judgments against moral instincts. The families of the victims, especially the families of the "disappeared," were left in the breach. This was the state of affairs in Chile in 1995 at the end of Patricio Aylwin's abbreviated term in office as transitional president. This book is about the political forces and historical processes that produced that situation beginning on September 11, 1973.

a testimony that might one day call attention to the terrible secret she was living through, so that the world would know about this horror that was taking place parallel to the peaceful existence of those who did not want to know, who could afford the illusion of a normal life, and of those who could deny that they were on a raft adrift in a sea of sorrow, ignoring, despite all evidence, that only blocks away from their happy world there were others, these others who live or die on the dark side.

— Isabel Allende, *The House of the Spirits*

Chapter 1
The Victors and the Vanquished

> We come here to pray for the future of Chile. We ask the Lord that there
> be neither victors nor vanquished among us.
> — Cardinal Raúl Silva Henríquez

September 11, 1973

President Salvador Allende began to receive disturbing reports of troop
movements in and around Santiago late on the night of September 10. His
advisors placed calls to senior military officers for explanations, but their
answers were evasive or deceptive. Chile was plunged in the midst of a profound political crisis, and the breakdown of its vaunted democracy seemed
inevitable and imminent.[1] These rumors could be the first reports of an
impending coup d'état.

But the main elements of the Chilean navy had left the port of Valparaíso
on the evening of September 10 to rendezvous with a U.S. task force for
maneuvers, leading Allende to believe that the threat of a coup had departed temporarily with the fleet. Nonetheless, the embattled president told
confidants that he would announce a date for a national plebiscite at noon
the next day. He gave a very different speech instead. Once out to sea, naval
officers opened secret orders instructing them to return to port, isolate
Valparaíso, and set in motion a previously drawn up national security plan.
The military was indeed mounting a coup to depose Salvador Allende's
Popular Unity government.

Allende's presidency, now in its third year, had been tense and conflictive
from the onset. But over the past year attitudes had hardened and events
had spun out of control. In October 1972 the independent truckers' association went on strike to forestall a possible takeover of the transportation
industry by the socialist president. The *paro* paralyzed an already ailing
economy and led to confrontations between government opponents and
supporters. The independent truckers ended the action only when Allende
invited the senior military commanders into his cabinet, initiating a process

by which the armed forces were drawn into a worsening political conflict, and themselves became politicized.

Allende's leftist coalition had fared well in mid-term congressional elections held in March 1973, but the results revealed a sharply polarized country. In April bus owners went on strike and were soon followed by copper miners. In late May the Supreme Court openly charged Allende with "illicitly interfering with the proper exercise of judicial power," a situation that implied the "preemptory or imminent rupture of the country's legality."[2] At the end of June, a Santiago tank regiment mutinied. This so-called *tancazo* failed to spark a general uprising, but it was a prelude to the September coup. The armed forces commander-in-chief, General Carlos Prats, personally confronted the rebels and convinced them to stand down, but Prats's tenure as commander of the armed forces would be curtailed as a result. In July a cascading series of events led even the most optimistic observers to believe that a coup was inevitable. On July 2 the General Comptroller's Office ruled against the president in his bid to implement only those portions he approved in an important piece of legislation. In that same week, both houses of the Chilean Congress passed a joint resolution reiterating the Supreme Court's allegations about the government's illegal conduct. On July 25 the independent truckers declared another strike and this time vowed to immobilize the transportation industry until Allende resigned. The following night Allende's naval aide-de-camp was assassinated. The extreme right Fatherland and Liberty paramilitary organization accused the extremist Movement of the Revolutionary Left of the murder, and vice versa. Chile was lurching toward a disaster.

If there was a possibility of avoiding a breach of Chile's democratic traditions, it depended on negotiations between Allende's coalition government and the leadership of Chile's center-right Christian Democratic party. The Roman Catholic prelate, Cardinal Raúl Silva Henríquez, issued the call for negotiations in the third week of July. The cardinal had his differences with Allende, especially over the socialist president's initiatives in public education, but he could foresee the coming tragedy and attempted to avert it. In the years to come Cardinal Silva would come to personify the movement against the repression that was the hallmark of the military regime that ousted Allende.

The negotiations between Allende and the Christian Democrats, then led by Patricio Aylwin, began on July 30. By mid-August they were suspended without an agreement that might have solved the mounting crisis.[3] In the meantime Allende formed a new cabinet, his ninth in less than three years. To lessen tensions, Allende again resorted to the expedient of appointing the most senior military officers to cabinet posts.[4] This new "National Security Cabinet" was short-lived. General Prats was forced to resign on August 23, and the other officers in the government abandoned the cabinet as well. The men who replaced them would lead the coup and direct the junta a few short, tension-filled weeks later.

The day of the cabinet resignations, the Chilean lower house passed a resolution that could easily be interpreted as a justification for the coup d'état if not an actual call to arms. By a nearly two to one margin, the Chamber of Deputies passed a resolution castigating Allende for having disregarded the courts, and the comptroller general for having encouraged illegal seizures of productive property and for having supported the formation and arming of extremist groups. The resolution contained specific language directed at the soldiers in the cabinet, urging them to "put an immediate end to all the de facto situations listed above which violate the constitution and the law."[5]

As the nation's independence day celebrations on September 18–19 approached, the only option left to Allende was to convoke a plebiscite on his government and the peaceful transformation to socialism it was attempting to implement. For their part, the senior leaders of the armed forces had to review their options. The exact date when those officers opted for military intervention, or even when many coup leaders began making contingency plans, is still a matter of considerable debate. It is certain that a declaration was drafted and signed by service chiefs on September 9. It is also known that Allende announced to confidants on the evening of September 10 that he would announce a date for a plebiscite the following day. Instead, on the morning of the eleventh, Allende awoke to the news of the rebellion of the navy in Valparaíso, and quickly departed for the Moneda palace, arriving a few minutes before 8 a.m. A quarter of an hour later Allende went on the radio to report the actions in Valparaíso. The only hope was that this was an isolated action, like the *tancazo*, the rebellion of the tank squadron at the end of June. In fact, that same squadron was again en route to the seat of government. The army and air force had not made their intentions known, and units of the national police, or carabineros, were still standing guard in front of the Moneda. "Confirmed reports indicate that the navy has rebelled in Valparaíso," Allende said, then calmly added, "Santiago is billeted and normal." Then he expressed the only hope his government possessed. "I hope that the soldiers of the Fatherland respond positively and that they defend the constitution and the law."[6]

When the high command of the armed forces and carabineros broadcast their first edict just before 8:30 a.m., it was clear that they were united in a concerted effort to depose Allende's government. Edict No. One, read by a military spokesman, said, in part:

First, the President of the Republic must immediately surrender his office to the armed forces and carabineros of Chile.

Second, the armed forces and carabineros are united in order to begin the historic and responsible mission to fight for the liberation of the Fatherland, and to prevent our country from falling beneath the marxist yoke.[7]

Presidential advisors and cabinet ministers rushed to their posts during the slowly transpiring coup. But defense of the Moneda, or of the government, was futile. Defense Minister Orlando Letelier was arrested when he reached the Defense Ministry, across the street from the Moneda. His personal saga would become one of the most widely known of the dictatorship. After his arrest Letelier was imprisoned, then exiled, and finally assassinated in Washington in an operation that would lead the FBI to develop damaging information about the military regime. Other Allende ministers and aides, like Interior Minister Carlos Briones and physician Enrique París, managed to enter the palace. Hours later, with the palace in flames, they would surrender themselves through the side entrance of the palace on Morandé Street in the final moments of the military siege of the seat of government. Many would be taken to military installations and later transferred to remote and desolate Dawson Island in the frigid Strait of Magellan. París and the young members of Allende's special detachment of bodyguards would be taken to a military installation from which they were subsequently disappeared.

Allende's final address to the nation was transmitted sometime before 10 a.m. via Radio Magallanes. The air force had not yet been able to locate and destroy its secret antenna. The impromptu speech was impassioned. "I will not resign," he pledged, and after castigating the military high command he concluded with a dramatic coda. "These are my last words, and I have the certainty that my sacrifice will not be in vain. I have the certainty that, at least, it will be a moral lesson that will castigate felony, cowardice and treason."[8]

In the ensuing fighting, the air force fulfilled its threat to attack the building by air with rockets launched from British-made Hawker-Hunter jets. At 1 p.m. ground forces began cautiously to advance toward the palace under sniper fire from adjacent buildings. The images of the aerial attack are now part of Chile's national history, even if interpretations of its meaning are controversial. Twenty years later national television aired a documentary, "El Once veinte años después" — The Eleventh Twenty Years Later. Chileans would see some of those same images again and would see some images for the first time: those of Salvador Allende's lifeless body, slumped on a sofa, dead of a self-inflicted gunshot wound.

A week after the coup, Cardinal Raúl Silva Henríquez appealed for tolerance and mercy. The cardinal customarily says the Te Deum Mass of Thanksgiving on September 18, Chile's independence day. The junta had coveted the church's blessing, but Cardinal Silva was wary of being manipulated. In the previous year he had made his opposition to some of Allende's policies known, but he had also called for dialogue between Allende and the Christian Democrats to prevent a national catastrophe. Instead of the customary Te Deum, the cardinal said a mass of reconciliation, but refused to celebrate it at a military installation.[9]

The cardinal solemnly reminded his listeners that Chileans "love liberty."

"During long years of our life as a nation we have made enormous sacrifices to obtain it, to conserve it, to promote it," he said, and there "exists within us a love of and respect for the law." Then he directed his remarks to those who he acknowledged "had taken on their shoulders the heavy responsibility of guiding our destinies."

"We ask the Lord that among us there be neither victors nor vanquished."[10]

The plea went unheeded. The victors of September 11 gave no quarter to the vanquished.

The Vanquished

Salvador Allende, the candidate of the Popular Unity (UP) coalition of leftist parties, was elected president on September 4, 1970. It was his third bid for the office. The election returns gave him only a slim plurality, 36.2 percent of the vote. Former president Jorge Alessandri, running as an independent, was a close second with 34.9 percent of the ballots. Christian Democrat Radomiro Tomic finished third with 27.8 percent. Congress would have to ratify Allende's election, an act which was pro forma until 1970. But Allende was an avowed Marxist committed to transforming Chile into a socialist state. Allende's supporters would note that both he and Christian Democrat Tomic were committed to profound change; thus their combined vote total validated the assertion that Chileans demanded reform, perhaps even revolution. His opponents could claim that nearly two-thirds of Chilean voters had voted for someone other than Allende. Legislators could have selected Alessandri.

Popular Unity's goal, articulated in a document dubbed the "Basic Program," was the peaceful transition to socialism.[11] It entailed the extension of agrarian reform begun as part of President Eduardo Frei's "Revolution in Liberty," the nationalization of the copper industry, and the creation of a socialized sector of the economy. This was far more revolutionary than anything before proposed, because the underlying objective was not merely to reform property relations but to transform them fundamentally along socialist lines. The implementation of the Popular Unity program was announced to be "the beginning of the construction of socialism," a gradual, peaceful, and supposedly irreversible process.

Allende was convinced that the transformation could be accomplished within the confines of Chile's constitutional democracy, a "via pacífica." But members of his own coalition, and indeed of his own party, were not convinced that revolution could be legislated. Implementing the program would be difficult, not only because of opposition to some or all of it, but because of the factiousness of the Popular Unity coalition.

Popular Unity was a coalition of Marxist and progressive parties and party factions. Two parties dominated it, Allende's own Socialist Party (PS) and the Communist Party of Chile (PC). The progressive, non-Marxist Radical

Party (PR), once Chile's major political force, also joined in making the Popular Unity's electoral victory possible. The Radicals split after a year of the Popular Unity government, with the Marxist-leaning members forming the Radical Left Party (PIR). The PR remained in the coalition until April 1972. Three smaller coalition members, the Movement for Unitary Popular Action (MAPU), the Independent Popular Action party (API), and the Christian Left (IC), were the products of schisms within the Christian Democratic Party (PDC). The Christian Left entered the coalition in 1971.

Allende had been among the most prominent figures in the Socialist Party for decades. A physician by training, he had served as minister of health, and in the Chilean Senate he had been president of Chile's upper house. Allende represented the social democratic faction of a party prone to factionalism. The party, formed in 1933 through the convergence of a number of leftist organizations, contained an array of political and ideological tendencies.[12] Independent Marxists, Trotskyists, and anarcho-sindicalists were represented in the party. The Cuban revolution led to the emergence of another faction, Guevarists, advocating armed struggle as the only effective means to power.[13]

Allende would have to contend with this more militant faction of his party throughout his presidency. The most staunch advocate of armed struggle was Carlos Altamirano, the PS secretary general. At the party's twenty-second Party Congress, held in 1967, Altamirano's faction managed to have the PS declared Marxist-Leninist.[14] The party line would ultimately clash with Popular Unity's notion of a peaceful way to socialism, asserting that "revolutionary violence is inevitable and legitimate." "Only by destroying the bureaucratic and military apparatus of the bourgeois state," the party affirmed, "is it possible to consolidate the Socialist revolution."[15] On the very eve of the formation of the Popular Unity Coalition in October 1969, the PS was still calling for a Revolutionary Front that excluded non-Marxist parties and casting doubt on the efficacy of a peaceful road to socialism.

The Socialist party would incur a heavy cost for its bellicosity. Altamirano managed to evade capture after the coup, but was unable to return to his country until 1991. He was a changed man. Other party leaders were imprisoned or forced into exile. The party's determined effort to establish an "internal front" to sustain the credibility that only results from maintaining a presence in the country met with fierce repression. But, when democracy returned to Chile the PS was an indispensable partner in the coalition of parties dominated by the Christian Democrats. A new generation of Socialist party leaders would then face a different challenge — how to press for an accounting of the human rights violations that had occurred during the dictatorship without appearing to be engaging in dangerous brinkmanship.

The Communist party, led by General Secretary Luis Corvalán, was more amenable to a broad-based coalition and the via pacífica advocated by Allende. The PC can trace its origin to 1912 with the emergence of the Socialist Workers party (POS). A decade later the POS became the Chilean Communist party at the behest of Moscow and the Comintern, and attached itself to the Third International.[16] Thereafter its fidelity to the Moscow line was unambiguous. The PC was committed to the formation of electoral coalitions with all progressive forces, and to coming to power by that means. The party enjoyed representation in congress as early as 1941, and by 1970 it could boast of nearly a quarter of a million members.

From the earliest days of the Cold War, the PC sought to bring center-left parties into a coalition. That position, originally stated at the party's tenth General Congress in 1956, was reiterated with minor changes in 1969, a full decade after the Cuban revolution.[17] The PC leadership believed, as did Allende, that the Chilean left had failed in its previous attempts to gain power in 1958 and 1964 because the electoral coalitions did not include progressive, non-Marxist parties, especially the once mighty Radical Party.[18] Allende and his Communist allies were determined to correct that error, making the Popular Unity the left's last, best chance to come to power via elections.

The PC exercised considerable influence within the Popular Unity government.[19] As an indication of the affinities of Allende and the Communists, the Socialist president appointed a Communist finance minister in June 1972. It was a significant move, given the centrality of economic measures for the UP program. Communist leaders exhibited greater moderation than the Socialists as the country moved towards the March 1973 midterm elections, and the political crisis entered its final phase. The Communist campaign theme, "consolidate and continue advancing," was answered by a discordant and provocative call from the Socialists to "advance without compromise."[20]

The PC did not resist the military when it moved against Allende. Instead, Luís Corvalán, the party's secretary general, and much of the party leadership went underground on September 11. Corvalán evaded capture by the intelligence services until the end of the month. He was released from detention in December 1976 in exchange for the Russian dissident Victor Buskovsky. The PC was not a priority on the military's list for destruction, and the party's moderation continued for some time after the coup. In its first official statement after the coup, issued in September, the PC blamed the disaster on the UP's political isolation, which it attributed to provocative, militant actions of the "ultra left." But the experience of the dictatorship hardened the Communist Party. The very month Corvalán was traded for the Russian intellectual, the Chilean intelligence services disappeared the Party's Central Committee. A more militant, confrontational mood came over exiled leaders.

In its first party plenary after the coup, held in 1977, the PC adopted a critical position about the Allende experiment. Subsequently, the party's leadership openly acknowledged that it had committed a serious error by not acquiring the paramilitary capacity to defend Allende's incipient revolution.[21] From there it was a small step to a call for armed resistance. When the Sandinistas toppled the Somoza dictatorship in Nicaragua in 1979, some PC leaders became convinced that all means, including armed struggle, were justified and required to bring down the dictatorship. The result was the formation of the Manuel Rodríguez Patriotic Front, which appeared on the scene in 1984 and nearly assassinated Pinochet two years later.

The moderation of the Chilean Communist party and Latin America's traditional left generally drove many young Marxists into the ranks of guerrilla organizations beginning in the mid-1960s.[22] The orthodoxy of Moscow-line Communist and Socialist parties appeared to be a formula for timidity. The victory of the Cuban revolution, and the mystique of Che Guevara, led directly to the emergence of Latin America's "ultra-left."

The initial manifestation of this trend in Chile was the Marxist Revolutionary Vanguard (VRM), formed in 1962. The VRM attracted the young Trotskyists languishing in the conservative parties of the traditional left. Having abandoned or been expelled from the PS or PC, they gravitated to the VRM, which rapidly became a forum for discussions about the need for a conspiratorial, revolutionary organization that would unify the left. The defeat of Salvador Allende's FRAP electoral coalition in 1964 and the U.S. invasion of the Dominican Republic the following year reinforced their beliefs about the necessity of armed struggle and their determination to engage in it. It became clear that socialist revolution could not be made at the polls, and that the United States was prepared to employ military force if necessary to impede revolutionary change. "The true path," announced the magazine *El Rebelde*, is "the workers to power, by reason AND by force."[23]

However, the VRM was not a conspiratorial, clandestine organization per se. Those who took seriously the discussions about the need for such an organization were eager to go farther, and in July 1965 they announced the formation of the Movement of the Revolutionary Left (MIR).[24] The operative word was "revolutionary." The MIR's Declaration of Principles, drafted at its constituent assembly, was an indictment of the conservativism of the traditional left, and a call to popular insurrection.

"The MIR is being organized to be the Marxist-Leninist vanguard of the working class and the oppressed strata of Chile," it proclaimed. "The MIR, guided by the principles of the struggle of class against class, uncompromisingly combats the exploiters and rejects any strategy tending to soften the struggle." By that the young revolutionaries meant the reformism advocated by the listless leadership of the traditional left. "The bureaucratic directorates of the traditional parties of the Chilean left," the document alleged, "defraud the hopes of the workers; instead of struggling to overthrow the bourgeoisie, they limit themselves to proposing reforms to the capitalist system."[25] Communist party leaders in particular responded harshly, accusing the MIR of irrationality and adventurism, and condescendingly offered to welcome MIRistas back into the party if they could exhibit party discipline.[26] The rhetorical skirmishes between the MIR and the PC would continue right up to the moment the military ended Allende's dream of a socialist Chile.

Despite the rhetoric the MIR, too, remained little more than a radical discussion group until its Third Congress in 1967. In elections held that year, the movement's senior leadership positions were filled by a close circle of radicalized students from the University of Concepción. Miguel Enríquez became the movement's general secretary, while his brother Edgardo and their brother-in-law Juan Bautista Van Schowen were elected to MIR's all-important Political Commission. All had attended the university; indeed Miguel and Edgardo Enríquez were the children of the university's rector, who would later serve as Allende's Minister of Education. Van Schowen, the nephew of an army flag officer, earned his medical degree at Concepción. The surgeon turned revolutionary became the editor of the MIR's polemical *El Rebelde* in 1968.[27] Another senior leader, Andrés Pascal Allende, was President Allende's nephew.

The leadership change set the MIR on a reckless course of action that did much to precipitate the coup. Miguel Enríquez became the movement's principal theoretician, and produced countless revolutionary manifestos and some highly perceptive analyses of Chile's political situation, an activity he continued until his death in late 1974. As the movement's leader and organizer, he was determined to turn the MIR into a potent revolutionary organization capable of the armed struggle to which it was rhetorically committed. For one thing, the MIR went underground after violent incidents with the national police, or Carabineros.[28]

Enríquez insisted that the MIR become more combative and its cadres more hardened. Each of the organization's four principal components maintained a tight structure of insulated cells of no more than five cadres.[29] Contact between cells operating in the same vicinity was prohibited for reasons of security.[30] Some members were disillusioned by the absence of opportunities for internal debate that went with the militarism of the party and, after the election of Allende, some abandoned the MIR.[31] That should not have mattered because the MIR was never intended to be a mass party. Even so, the ranks of the MIR swelled in the three years between the election of Salvador Allende and the coup, from 2,000 to 5,000 members.[32] The rapid increase in membership had a devastating effect on the supposedly clandestine organization. Despite the tight cell structure, the military's intelligence services infiltrated the organization prior to the coup. The military and security forces would prove able to decimate the MIR within two years; some of its most ferocious persecutors had been former MIRistas.

Enríquez concentrated on preparing disciplined cadres for several related tasks, all very alarming to the Carabineros and the armed forces. Enríquez directed the MIR to intensify efforts to assume leadership of popular organizations. This would put thousands of workers and peasants at the MIR's disposal for the inevitable confrontation. Meanwhile, MIRistas would engage in street agitation for the purpose of provoking violence. Most important, the MIR would dedicate itself to "special tasks," a designation that meant bank robberies and kidnappings to fund the organization.[33]

The MIR boasted of these actions in its publications, *Punto final* and *Rebelde*. "The Revolutionary Movement of the Left," said a typical communiqué, "reports to the people that its 'Rigoberto Zamora Command' expropriated the Banco Nacional de Trabajo." "The money belongs to the workers," it proclaimed, "and not to the thieves who had robbed it from the workers." Thus, "the MIR will return the money to the workers by investing in arms and by organizing the armed apparatus necessary to return to the workers what the owners have robbed from them. That is, by creating a government of workers and peasants that will build socialism in Chile."[34]

The candidacy of Salvador Allende posed as many problems for the MIR as the MIR later posed for President Salvador Allende. The Movement's original Declaration of Principles rejected the premise of Allende's candidacy. "The MIR rejects the theory of a 'Peaceful Way,'" the Movement had declared in 1965, "because it disarms the proletariat politically." The MIR's founders were prescient. The vía pacífica was a dead end "because the bourgeoisie will resist it, to the point of totalitarian dictatorship or civil war before it will cede power peacefully."[35]

The election of Salvador Allende in 1970 dramatically altered the complexion of Chilean politics, but it did not assuage the skepticism of the members of the MIR's Political Commission. On the contrary, their own predictions about the inevitable reaction of the bourgeoisie lent urgency to their preparations. Enríquez saw two immediate tasks that, as it turned out, worked at cross-purposes. The first was to protect President Allende, the second was to infiltrate the armed forces.[36]

The MIRistas were excellent recruits for Allende's elite detachment of bodyguards, commonly know as the Group of the President's Friends.[37] But it was madness to believe that a lightly armed security detail could protect the president if combat broke out, as became apparent when armored units assaulted the Moneda on September 11. In a televised interview given two decades later, a senior MIR leader would claim that a MIR special forces team was positioned to rescue Allende from the Moneda before the converging army units fully secured the perimeter; Allende would have then rallied armed workers to defend the revolution from the industrial belts around Santiago.[38] The president refused the MIR's offer, according to the MIR leader; instead, Allende committed suicide, while his bodyguards surrendered themselves to vengeful soldiers and were later killed.

Nothing could have been more provocative than a conspiracy to infiltrate the armed forces. There is considerable debate as to whether the MIR intended to organize cells in the various branches, but the service commanders were understandably alarmed by even a hint of subversive activity in the ranks. The navy claimed to have uncovered a plot to stage a mutiny in the fleet at the end of the first week of August, and arrested 23 sailors.[39] Enríquez denied the allegations, but such plotting would not have been out of character. In the aftermath of the coup, the air force put almost one hundred officers and airmen, including a general, on trial for alleged contacts with the subversive movement. Only the possible loss of the monopoly of arms concerns armed forces' high commands more than the existence of conspiracies to incite insubordination within their ranks. The armed forces had to contemplate both contingencies. So, if the possible infiltration of the armed forces was part of the high command's rationale for mounting the coup, the MIR's effort to undermine the armed forces worked against its efforts to protect the president.

The MIR presented a vexing problem for Allende. He had to appear to distance himself from the MIR without entirely alienating it. But the MIR rejected UP's commitment to operating within the framework of legal norms, and its rural organization, the Revolutionary Peasants Movement (MIR-MCR), organized land occupations and violent confrontations between campesinos and landowners.[40] The Revolutionary Workers Front (MIR-FTR) likewise staged work stoppages in the industrial belts ringing Santiago. Allende repudiated these actions, but neither rural landowners nor urban industrialists were convinced that Allende would act decisively to restore order or to protect property rights. For Allende and his advisors, the violence was an inconvenience. "Allende and his minister of interior repeatedly and publicly condemned land occupations, urging the campesinos to allow the government to proceed with its program of orderly expropriation without the daily pressure of armed confrontations and the negative implications for production of permanent conflict in the countryside."[41] What Allende and his cabinet viewed as inconvenient militancy, his opponents viewed as an attack on property.

The MIR's predictions about a coup were accurate. If the Movement had committed a fatal error, Enríquez wrote, it was the passivity shown after the June 29 *tancazo*. Revolutionary momentum, if it had existed at all, was lost at that point. From the onset of the Popular Unity government, Enríquez had worked to establish a network of safe-houses to enable MIRistas to elude capture. The members of the Political Commission did not flee the country on September 11. "The MIR does not exile itself," one public announcement boasted. Instead, Enríquez set out to unify the left in an "anti-fascist front" and to prevent the consolidation of the military regime. Success required that the MIR survive.

The Movement's experience with clandestine life enabled its leadership to elude security for a while after the coup. But only for a while. Juan Bautista Van Schowen, the physician turned revolutionary, would be captured and disappeared in December 1973. Miguel Enríquez would die in a fire fight less than a year later and his brother would be disappeared in neighboring Argentina. Andrés Pascal Allende, the president's nephew, narrowly escaped death when the security forces closed in on the few surviving members of the Political Commission in a farm house in late 1975. Wounded, he managed to flee the country with the help of a sympathetic embassy. In the interim, much of the rank and file of the MIR militant organization would be killed.

The Chilean left, which had been victorious at the polls in September 1970, was rapidly vanquished by the Chilean armed forces three years later. Esoteric, ideological debates among the PS, the PC, and the MIR were symptomatic of the Latin American left, but the subtle distinctions articulated in communiqués and manifestos meant nothing to the Chilean military once it set out to extirpate Marxism from the country. The armed forces rapidly arrested Allende loyalists, especially those occupying positions in agencies responsible for the land reform and the state takeover of industry. In the countryside, vengeful landowners moved violently against the beneficiaries of the agrarian reforms to regain their expropriated properties. The military moved aggressively against the MIR in order to secure its monopoly of arms, and the security forces systematically decapitated the leadership of the PS and PC in successive waves. The toll was horrendous, according to the presidential truth commission.[42] More than 400 socialist leaders and militants were killed or disappeared by the military regime over the next seventeen years; 384 MIRistas were abducted, disappeared and killed; 353 Communist party members lost their lives.

The Victors

Immensely powerful actors were arrayed against Allende, and they had a staunch ally in the Nixon administration in the United States. Salvador Allende's election came less than three years after legendary guerrilla leader Ernesto "Che" Guevara had been killed in neighboring Bolivia while attempting to create, in his words, "One, Two, Three, Many Vietnams."[43] Times were not propitious for the election of a socialist, even one pledged to a peaceful transition to socialism.

According to a U.S. Senate inquiry into U.S. involvement in Chilean affairs, the United States attempted first to block the confirmation of Allende's election and then to destabilize his government and ultimately to remove him by force.[44] An amateurish attempt on October 22, 1970 to abduct the commander of the armed forces, General René Schneider, was the most dramatic example of the plotting. Schneider, a committed constitutionalist, resisted his assailants and was fatally wounded.[45] Allende's election was confirmed by the Chilean congress by a vote of 153 to 35 on October 24, the day before Schneider succumbed to his wounds. But the congress voted to confirm the Marxist president-elect only after he signed a Statute of Guarantees drafted by the leadership of the Christian Democratic party.

The Christian Democratic Party (PDC) was the pivotal actor in the events that led up to the coup, until the armed forces actually intervened. The PDC was formally registered in 1957, but its inspiration and inception both can be traced back decades to the National Falange. National Falange was formed in 1938 by progressive lay Catholics like Eduardo Frei, Radomiro Tomic, and Bernardo Leighton, after they were expelled from the Conservative party for their reformist ideas. Each would play a prominent role in the Chilean political life in the years to come.

The Falange drew its support from segments of the middle class disaffected by the conservativism of the traditional parties. Its inspiration derived from the social teaching of the Catholic Church, especially the social encyclicals Rerum Novarum and Quadragesimo Anno.[46] The Catholic Church rejected Marxist dogma outright, but it was critical of unfettered, liberal capitalism as well. The notion of a "third way" — neither socialist nor capitalist — found wide appeal.

The PDC's rise was swift. In the 1961 congressional elections, the first in which the PDC ran candidates under that name, the party garnered 16 percent of the vote. Three years later Eduardo Frei won the presidency, and in off year elections in 1965 the PDC's share of the congressional vote increased to just over 41 percent.[47] The PDC was on the way to becoming Chile's dominant political force. But the party would also become a microcosm of Chilean society and would suffer from its ideological afflictions. Before the party was a decade old it would be pulled in different directions by leaders who interpreted the vague notion of a "third way" to mean different things.

Frei's program, heralded as "Revolution in Liberty," was genuinely progressive, and its accomplishments, including agrarian reform and the nationalization of the copper industry, were substantial. But the program was not revolutionary. Frei was instinctively inclined toward capitalism rather than socialism, for which reason his 1964 campaign benefited substantially from covert U.S. support. The United States recognized a dangerous trend. Political momentum was with the left, and the Johnson and then Nixon administrations acted to forestall an Allende victory.

The radicalization of the 1960s, however, also affected the PDC. The party's standard bearer in the historic 1970 election was Radomiro Tomic, a founder of the PDC and the leader of its left wing. By now the PDC's vision of a just society came to be termed "communitarian socialism," but even that did not satisfy some on the party's left wing. Dissidents abandoned the party in 1969 to form the MAPU, a small player in the Popular Unity coalition. The following year Tomic finished third in the presidential elections, behind Allende and the aging ex-president Arturo Alessandri. The outcome revealed how polarized Chilean politics had become. Tomic's communitarian socialism was not radical enough for a third of the electorate, while another third felt safe with the candidate of the antiquated right. For his part, Tomic declared that Allende's leadership was essential to "the unity of the people."[48]

A year later the PDC suffered more defections when young members formed the Christian Left and entered Allende's governing coalition. The new defection rendered the PDC an essentially conservative party, centered around the leadership of former president Frei. As a result, the PDC would lose the ability to mediate a political crisis that ultimately led to military intervention. The PDC's presidency changed four times between Allende's election and the coup that deposed him, and with each change the party became more hostile to the Popular Unity government.

All that was in the future. In September 1970 the PDC was still a pivotal actor. Congress had to confirm Allende's election, and the Christian Democrat deputies controlled the necessary votes. Conservatives within the party were profoundly concerned about Allende's commitment to the parliamentary strategy, a not unreasonable concern given the party line of the president-elect's own Socialist party. The PDC could have blocked Allende's confirmation; indeed, that was the hope of the Nixon administration. One scenario had the PDC joining with the right to select former president Alessandri, who would immediately resign and call for new elections. Frei would then be permitted to run for reelection. But Frei would not approve the stratagem.

Nonetheless the PDC demanded assurances before it would confirm a socialist president. Those assurances came in the form of a Statute of Guarantees, drafted by Christian Democrat leaders Tomic, Renán Fuentealba, Juan Hamilton, Jaime Castillo, and Luis Maira. By signing the document, Allende pledged to respect, among other things, the rights of all political parties, the right to private education (meaning the Catholic Church's role in providing it), and the monopoly of arms, chain of command, and non-political character of the armed forces. Allende did not hesitate to sign the statute; he was merely pledging to respect principles implicit in the idea of a peaceful road to socialism. Allende may have been motivated by tactical considerations as well. Revolutionary theorist Régis Debray would later quote Allende as asserting that his assent to the guarantees was necessary for him to assume power.[49]

The PDC leadership was rapidly convinced that Allende was violating the agreement. Within a year of his inauguration, some Christian Democrat legislators were drafting bills and constitutional amendments aimed at controlling the Marxist head of state, and they were voting to impeach his ministers.[50] Allende's tactics, and the perception that Allende could not control, and even tolerated, extremist violence, drove the Christian Democrats from constructive to outright opposition. The congress's hesitancy to move ahead with the creation of a social area of property prompted Allende to circumvent the legislature. Allende's legal advisor, Eduardo Novoa, urged the president to use obscure legal provisions that authorized the chief executive to requisition a plant if production was not maintained. The president would appoint a manager to oversee operations; although legal title had not been transferred as if the government had purchased controlling interest in the property, the plant was effectively state-run if not state-owned. The Christian Democrats in the congress objected that the legislature's prerogatives were being usurped. Worse still, Allende moved to requisition many factories that had not been on his original list of properties to be acquired in the wake of owner lockouts to protest Popular Unity policies. Many properties were requisitioned after the devastating October 1972 strike that brought contending sides to the brink of violent confrontation. Sometimes the loss of production was due to MIR-instigated worker take-overs, giving the appearance that Allende was permitting an extremist organization to act outside the law, then using the law to transform Chile into a socialist state.

The escalating violence also convinced moderate opponents that Allende was violating the Statute of Guarantees. The assassination of former Frei Interior Minister Pérez Zujovic in June 1971 by leftist extremists hastened the PDC's move toward confrontation.[51] Allende denounced the murder, but the perception that Chile was descending into a spiral of violence was becoming widespread. The July 1973 assassination of Allende's own naval attaché further contributed to that belief. By the time the negotiations between the government and the Christian Democrats broke down, former president Frei considered a coup d'état not only inevitable, but the only solution to the crisis. The PDC-sponsored nonbinding congressional resolution condemning the government illegalities gave the military what cover it needed to mount it.

The removal of Allende should have been a victory for the Christian Democrats, but it would be seventeen years before the party could revel in it. The party's senior leadership, beginning with Frei, was tragically mistaken about the military's intentions, as quickly became apparent. The week after the coup Frei was seated on the dais together with other former heads of state as Cardinal Silva said the mass of reconciliation and appealed to the victors to have mercy on the vanquished. But an angry Frei refused to shake hands with Chile's new leaders, the four officers who comprised the military junta, because the military had closed congress without informing him and thus foreclosed the possibility that he would assume the presidency of the junta.[52] The PDC would wander in the political wilderness for nearly a decade before the party moved openly into opposition to the dictatorship, initiating the gradual transition back to civilian rule.

The PDC did not suffer the severity of the repression directed against the PS, the PC, and the MIR. While the parties of the left were declared illegal, the PDC was declared in indefinite recess and its assets confiscated. That changed in 1977, when the PDC, too, was declared disbanded by the government. The security forces, however, did not systematically target PDC leaders for disappearance or murder. An important exception was the attempt on the life of Bernardo Leighton in Italy in 1975. Leighton, who brought the first habeas corpus action before a Chilean court after the coup, vehemently opposed a draft statement expressing the PDC's official line that the coup was inevitable.

It did not take long for the PDC to recognize the repressiveness of the military regime. Jaime Castillo, who helped draft the Statute of Guarantees in 1970, became an indefatigable human rights defender. In 1976 Castillo and five associates would scandalize their colleagues in the legal profession by denouncing abuses before OAS ministers gathered in the Chilean capital. In 1978, after returning from the first of his two exiles, Castillo became director of the Chilean Human Rights Commission. He would be named to the presidential commission to document the repression after the transition to democracy in 1990. Eventually Frei, too, would publicly denounce the military's human rights practices. Two years after the coup, Frei, who neither anticipated nor condoned the bloodshed committed by the military afterward, published *The Mandate of History*, in which he criticized the regime's repression.[53]

The PDC, however, did eventually emerge as the political victor. When in 1989 Pinochet was finally compelled by dint of his own constitution to call competitive elections, the PDC's candidate was in the most advantageous position to win. The PDC was by the mid-1980s a member of the Concertación de los Partidos para la Democracia, an opposition coalition that included the Socialists but excluded the Communists. But there was no realistic possibility that the coalition would select a Socialist as its candidate. The logical choice was Christian Democrat Patricio Aylwin, the very man who had led the PDC in failed negotiations with Allende in the fateful final weeks of his government.

Patricio Aylwin's election in December 1989 was predictable. The Christian Democrats emerged from the dictatorship as Chile's single most important party, and their hold on power was comfortable despite electoral laws that gave right-wing parties disproportionate representation in both chambers of the legislature. Aylwin was elected to serve a shortened, four-year term, but was succeeded by a fellow Christian Democrat, Eduardo Frei (son of the former president), in 1995. Both would have to confront the grim legacy of the crimes committed by the previous regime, but the political context in which they found themselves severely limited their range of action. The struggle for human rights in Chile, therefore, would continue well after the negotiated transition to democracy that occurred in 1990.

Historically, the Chilean right consisted of a number of small parties. In 1966 they banded together to form the National Party to reverse their declining electoral fortunes. The right was adamantly opposed to the Popular Unity program, but its political clout was weak. The National Party and the Radical Democratic Party (which broke from the Radicals when the PR joined the Popular Unity coalition) controlled only 43 seats, too few to block Allende's confirmation in 1970. The right opposed Popular Unity's legislative initiatives, with the notable exception of the nationalization of the copper industry. As the political crisis became acute, the right entered into an electoral alliance with the PDC to contest the important March 1973 congressional elections. The formation of the Democratic Confederation, or CODE as the alliance was called, indicated that Chilean politics had become polarized.

The overthrow of Allende was a victory for the Chilean right, which endorsed the military's pronunciamento. If the PDC hoped for a relatively brief period of military rule, the National Party hoped the military would stay on. The National Party was not shocked by the junta's decree declaring non-Marxist parties in indefinite recess; on the contrary, it went so far as to disband voluntarily. The notion of putting an end to politics was one that fit squarely with the thinking of a party that had seen its electoral fortunes steadily decline to the point where it could not block the confirmation of a Marxist president. The National party president, Sergio Onofre Jarpa, would be called on by Pinochet to serve as interior minister in 1983, at a critical moment of the dictatorship when the appearance of dialogue with the opposition became necessary. When democracy returned to Chile in 1990, the political landscape had changed dramatically. The National party would be revived in the form of the Party of National Renovation (RN), but it was not the political heir of the regime. A new generation of technocrats emerged and formed the Independent Democratic Union (UDI). The UDI was formed under the tutelage of Jaime Guzmán, the brilliant lawyer who is widely credited with being the leading ideologue of the Pinochet regime. Although they are natural allies in opposition to the governing Concertación, tensions exist between them. Nevertheless, both the RN and UDI are the political beneficiaries of an election code promulgated by the regime. The system it creates virtually guarantees to RN and UDI candidates a disproportionate number of seats in the congress in Chile's new democracy. The new constitutional scheme is nearly ideal for the political right, even if the Christian Democrats are in the Moneda and socialists hold minor cabinet positions.

The most vehement and effective opposition to the Popular Unity program was mounted by the associations of entrepreneurs. Allende's dream of transforming Chile into a socialist society directly impinged on the economic interests of these associations, or *gremios empresariales*.[54] There were two principal associations, representing thousands of enterprises. One, the Confederation of Production and Commerce (CPC), represented the large industries and was immensely powerful.[55] The large firms whose interests the CPC represented benefited enormously from the military's seizure of power, especially after Pinochet embraced neo-liberalism.

The associations within the Council of Small and Medium-Sized Business (CPME) caused Allende the most serious problems. Four gremios in particular exacted a high economic price. The independent truck owners had every reason to suspect that the Popular Unity government would requisition their vehicles, since transportation is vital to any economy. They launched the massive strike that in October 1972 led to confrontation and violence and left the impression that Chile was on the brink of civil war. They ended their action only after Allende brought the military into his cabinet in early November. The association of microbus and taxi owners had much in common with the truckers, except that its members transported people, not goods. Its strikes were equally effective in paralyzing the Chilean economy. The National Association of Retailers was alarmed by the government's rationing of supplies. A one-day strike in September 1972 was a sign of things to come. Finally, the Confederation of Professionals of Chile brought together middle- and upper-middle-class doctors, pharmacists, nurses, teachers, and even commercial pilots. They, too, could have a tremendous impact on the economy and the everyday lives of Chileans. All four organizations staged work stoppages throughout July, August, and September 1973, leading the armed forces finally to intervene.

These organizations and others like them had a common aversion to the socialism propounded by Popular Unity, and they viewed the military's intervention as salvation. But they did not have identical interests. Their differences became apparent in the early years of the Pinochet dictatorship.[56] Those affiliated with CPC became vocal advocates of an open economy, guided by neo-liberal economic policies. Those associated with the CPME had a quite different vision, and they were threatened by the neo-liberals advocating the economic law of the jungle almost as much as they were by socialists bent on requisitioning their property. They envisioned and pressed for a corporativist society in which the gremios would be officially recognized and possess privileged access to the state; the state in turn would protect them and their economic interests. If the neo-liberals were emulating Milton Friedman, the neo-corporatist gremialists were idolizing Francisco Franco.

The victory of Chilean entrepreneurs was far and away the most dramatic. The economic model in place in Chile serves the entrepreneurs well, and it matters little that Christian Democrats are in power or that socialists are coalition partners with the PDC. If the military's mission was to fundamentally transform Chilean society, to depoliticize it, and to leave key decisions to the market rather than the politicians, it has succeeded.

The Chilean right also had its extremists. To counteract what they believed to be the left's attempt to impose totalitarianism in Chile, the children of Chile's well-to-do formed Fatherland and Liberty (Patria y Libertad,

PL). Fatherland and Liberty was a paramilitary movement with fascist inclinations and a corporativist vision of society. The ultra-right PL was the perfect counterpart to the ultra-left MIR. If the MIR's actions were intended to generate revolutionary consciousness among the masses and to provoke the inevitable class struggle, Fatherland and Liberty's actions were intended to create a generalized fear of chaos and thereby to prompt average Chileans to welcome military intervention. The economic and psychological impact of Fatherland and Liberty's campaign was considerable. Allende even alluded to the sabotage campaign in his famous final speech on the morning of the coup. Fatherland and Liberty militants had engaged in a systematic campaign to destroy electric towers and oil pipelines and sabotage industrial machinery, all of which aggravated the economic situation caused by the gremialists' economic actions.

Fatherland and Liberty formally disbanded soon after the military seized power, but its members took part in the repression that followed. Fatherland and Liberty identified and denounced sympathizers of the Popular Unity government, especially in areas where military commanders did not believe their mission was to round up everyone who supported the deposed government.[57] When the military junta in late 1973 took the fateful decision to create a new intelligence agency to extirpate Marxism, the military recruited heavily among former Fatherland and Liberty militants. The overthrow of Allende was a victory for Fatherland and Liberty, because its raison d'être had been to provoke military intervention. Pinochet did not grant Fatherland and Liberty its dream of a quasi-fascist Chile in which Fatherland and Liberty would be an integral part of a civic-military movement. But the military regime did afford its members, as agents of the regime's security forces, the opportunity to persecute and kill the hated communists.

The Chilean armed forces and Carabineros, as institutions, were reluctantly drawn into the crisis that culminated on September 11, 1973, although some officers favored action from the moment of Allende's election. For the high command to contemplate a coup, the armed forces and police had to pass through their own process of radicalization. In fact, the composition of the high command had to be changed three times before the service commanders acceded to intervention. The commanders who made the final decision, and later composed the junta, had been at their posts less than a month when the unthinkable occurred. The process of radicalization was set in motion by others, but when the military acted the deep-seated culture of anti-bolshevism among its men and officers provided the motivation for a human rights catastrophe.

The Chilean right and the Nixon administration feared the inauguration of Allende and understood that the military could prevent it. That was the rationale behind the attempted kidnapping of General Schneider in October 1970. By the time a Santiago armored unit rebelled in June 1973, at the prompting of Fatherland and Liberty leaders, it was clear that segments of the armed forces had been radicalized. In the meantime, senior officers were being brought into Allende's cabinets because politicians could not resolve the political and ideological differences that divided them. Behind all this was the abiding fear of the men and officers of Chile's three armed services and its militarized police that, as the political situation deteriorated, the armed forces would became politicized, infiltrated by leftists, and eventually drawn into a civil war with the irregular forces of a parallel army.

The opposition to Allende had urged the armed forces to intervene for three years. When the senior commanders finally moved against the leftist government the armed forces of Chile were heralded as victors and their commander-in-chief as savior. The high command has dramatized its action. September 11 had been made a national holiday, on par with the Day of the Glories of the Army celebrated on September 19.

Military men gained a prominence and notoriety long denied them.[58] In 1969, the commander of Santiago's Tacna regiment ordered his troops into the streets to protest the low wages and poor living conditions of the troops. This isolated rebellion was eerily suggestive of the actions that would take place four years later, but they did little more than anger President Eduardo Frei, then in his final year in office. The pronunciamento of September 11 changed all that, and no one benefited more from this than the armed forces commander-in-chief, General Augusto Pinochet. A mystique had grown up around the man.

Pinochet became the embodiment of the Chilean military and everything that was thought to be great about it. In the midst of debates about possible reforms to the constitution the regime had imposed in 1980, the army high command went so far as to assert that verbal attacks on Pinochet were tantamount to attacks on the substance of the constitution and vice versa. Pinochet and his supporters are not modest about the dictator's role in the country's economic success. Had it not been for the armed forces' "patriotic and decisive action," the Ministry of Defense claimed after the return to democracy, Chile would not be in a position "to move forward in justice and democracy."[59] The assertion came in the armed forces' combined responses to the official report of a presidential truth commission into the human rights violations committed during the dictatorship.

After September 11, the nation's destiny was determined by a military junta, over which Pinochet presided with considerable skill. The state became militarized, and the armed forces' budgets increased dramatically.[60] But as the regime evolved tensions between branches arose. Pinochet's dual role as executive/commander-in-chief made him first among equals and nullified the original intent of the coup plotters to rule collectively.[61] A rift opened between the armed forces and the government staffed by soldiers. A far more dangerous rift opened between the armed forces and the secret police set up by the junta over the objections of some senior officers. The agency, the Directorate for National Intelligence (DINA), would wage a covert war of extermination against the Chilean left that led to international condemnation of the military government's treatment of its citizens.

Pinochet shrewdly dissolved the agency when it had outlived its purpose, but tremendous harm had been caused. The human toll had been horrific, and the societal effects — in terms of the physical and psychological scars resulting from the calculated practice of repression — linger. The harm is aggravated by the high command's continuing refusal to acknowledge the human rights violations, or even to disclose the fate and whereabouts of thousands of its victims. The armed forces' victory was achieved at a tremendous cost.

Chapter 2
An Invented War

> It was a completely invented war.
> — Laura Novoa, National Commission on Truth and Reconciliation

A Chance at Combat

The Chilean nation's motto, "By Reason or Force," was never more apropos than on September 11. Politics had become a deadly serious business during the three years of Allende's Popular Unity government, although the origin of the crisis can be traced back much farther. Political discourse verged on irrationality, and the failure of reason inevitably meant that the victors would be those who possessed sufficient force to overwhelm their political enemies. This was the logic of war.

Armed forces exist to wage war, and once the Chilean military was drawn into the political conflict the men and officers of the armed forces reacted just as their indoctrination and training had prepared them to react. The high command still claims that Chile was at war.[1] The air attack and ground assault on the Moneda palace certainly gave the impression of a country at war. Whether or not the armed forces genuinely believed that they had launched a preemptive strike in an impending civil war, in retrospect three things are certain. First, the armed forces rapidly took complete control of the country, and the paramilitary formations of the MIR, Socialist, and Communist parties were powerless to prevent it. So, if there were an impending civil war, the armed forces immediately won it.[2] Second, the armed forces would not declare a quick victory. Because the war the high command anticipated failed to materialize, the high command would have to invent it. Senior officers had trained for combat, and whether they were in a war or not, they were not about to suspend their war-winning operations. Third, even if it had been true that Chile was at war, the armed forces' conduct in that war violated the laws and customs of armed conflict as codified in the Geneva Conventions of 1949.

Because Chile had not been at war since the War of the Pacific at the end of the nineteenth century, none of the commanders who ordered their troops to depose Allende had commanded men in combat. So when the military high command ordered troops into action on September 11 it had a once-in-a-lifetime opportunity to employ many of its weapons and tactics. Transcripts of the recorded VHF radio communications between senior officers on the day of the coup reveal the attitudes and emotions of career soldiers engaged in a one-sided battle — deep antipathy, even hatred, toward officials of the besieged government.[3]

Army General Augusto Pinochet directed operations on September 11 from his position at the army communications center at Peñalolén on the outskirts of the capital. The focal point of the operations was, obviously, the Moneda palace. President Allende's surrender and departure from Chile aboard an air force jet was the immediate objective of the high command. Pinochet, with this chance at combat, monitored the dramatic negotiations even while he maneuvered units into position for an air and ground assault on the building in which Allende was barricaded with his security detachment and close advisors. Admiral Patricio Carvajal was on the scene relaying information to Pinochet from the Ministry of Defense building diagonally across from the besieged Moneda in the city center. It was Carvajal who, together with two other officers, had visited Pinochet on the night of the ninth to inform him that the navy intended to move against Allende on the eleventh. The day after the coup, Carvajal would return to the Ministry of Defense as the military regime's new defense minister. Now it fell to Carvajal to inform Pinochet that Allende refused to surrender without a fight. Pinochet reacted angrily to news of Allende's intransigence.

Pinochet: "Correct. It means that at 11:00 they're [the jet fighters are] going up, and they're going to see what happens."

Carvajal: "By evacuating the Moneda it is easier to attack it."

Pinochet: "Once it's bombed, we assault it with [the Buin regiment] and with the Infantry School [troops]. Brady has to be told [General Herman Brady, commander of the Army's Second Division]."

Pinochet then has to inquire about the deployment of troops around the Moneda, and he is especially concerned about the disposition of the Carabineros. The Director General of the Carabineros, José María Sepulveda, was inside the palace and loyal to Allende. General Mendoza had gone to the Carabinero headquarters to effect a barracks coup to ensure the adherence of the police force to the coup d'état.

Pinochet: "Are the tanks arriving? Have the Infantry School [troops] arrived?

Carvajal: "The non-commissioned officers, with Commander Canessa, the Tacna artillery regiment, and the armored units. The Carabineros withdrew. We saw them leaving the Moneda."

Pinochet: "Correct. Mendoza controls the Carabineros?"

Carvajal: "Correct. Mendoza controls the Carabineros. He told me that the head-quarters of the Carabineros, the building, is neutralized. No one has fired, nothing, from the building."

Pinochet: "Copy. Another thing, Patricio. At 11:00 in the morning on the dot the Moneda has to be attacked, because that guy is not going to surrender."

Carvajal: "The Moneda is already being attacked. It is surrounded and being attacked with a lot of force. So, I think that soon they're going to be able to take it."

Later Pinochet inquires about the whereabouts of several socialist leaders and Allende advisors who have left the Moneda, including Edgardo Enríquez, father of the MIR leader.

Pinochet: "Patricio, Augusto here speaking to you. Tell me, Mr. Altamirano and this other one, Enríquez, Where are they? Have they found them or are they escaping?"

Carvajal: "I don't have any information about where they are."

Pinochet: "It's advisable to give the intelligence services of the three branches the mission of finding them and taking them prisoner. These guys are escaping, they are real snakes."

One last time Carvajal informs Pinochet that inside the palace they are willing to negotiate, but victory is within Pinochet's grasp, and the general will hear nothing of it.

Pinochet: "Unconditional surrender! There is nothing to negotiate! Unconditional surrender!"

Carvajal: "Very well, copy. Unconditional surrender, [meaning] that he be taken prisoner, offering him only that his life be respected, let's say."

Pinochet: "His life and physical integrity, and right away he's going to be sent elsewhere!"

The air force did not attack the Moneda at 11:00 as planned. The fighter-bombers were running low on fuel and were forced to return to Concepción to take on more. But they did attack Allende's residence. Just before the attack on the seat of government, Pinochet communicated the following to Carvajal.

Pinochet: "We can't appear to be weak of character by accepting a period of discussions with these people, because we can't accept time-frames or discussions; [discussions] mean dialogue, they mean weakness. . . . Mr. Tohá, Mr. Almeyda, all those filthy people who want to ruin the country, they should catch them, and that plane you have ready, Up! without clothes, just what they have! Out."

The exchanges are revealing. They convey the hatred Pinochet and much of the officer corps had for members of the Popular Unity government.[4] They are noteworthy too, for how Pinochet's rage became policy. Each of the men he named in these exchanges suffered arrest, mistreatment, exile, or death. The intelligence services did, as Pinochet advised, track down and arrest Edgardo Enríquez, Allende's education minister. Enríquez was sent to remote Dawson Island as a prisoner of war. Over the next two years Enríquez suffered the loss of two sons and his son-in-law, all members of the MIR's Political Commission. Altamirano, the Socialist leader, managed to evade capture and was unceremoniously smuggled into exile. But the intelligence services did not end their hunt for him. Altamirano was tracked, first to Mexico City and then to Madrid, by an American-born assassin, Michael Townley, who had orders to kill him and a number of Socialist, Communist, and even Christian Democratic leaders.[5] Altamirano was fortunate that Townley never found an opportunity to eliminate him; others were not so fortunate.

José Tohá had served as interior minister, then as defense minister, and was now a senior political advisor of the Popular Unity coalition. The high command had a special loathing for him, because as interior minister Tohá permitted the MIR and other paramilitary formations to operate. Tohá was not put on board a plane and sent into exile; instead he was imprisoned on Dawson Island where the harsh conditions destroyed his health. He died on March 15, 1974 in a military hospital, having committed suicide according to the military spokesman. An official investigation would later reject that explanation. Clodomiro Almeyda was also arrested and imprisoned on Dawson Island. International efforts to free him and other Popular Unity officials finally led to his release and exile. In exile Almeyda vied for control of the Socialist party with Altamirano and came to embody the hard-line of the party.

Pinochet never abandoned the idea that people such as these ought to be put on a plane with only the clothes on their backs. He must have thought it a special indignity for individuals whom the security forces could not simply liquidate. In 1976 the general ordered that two leading human rights activists, Jaime Castillo and Eugenio Velasco, be picked up and driven directly to Santiago's international airport with only the clothes they had on. And, just as the general had wanted with the others, they were up, without so much as a change of clothes.

The men who stood by Allende in the Moneda were treated cruelly when the one-sided battle was concluded. Around 2 p.m., with the palace in flames, Allende ordered his ministers, advisors, and bodyguards to abandon the building through the side entrance on Morandé Street across from the Ministry of Public Works in the cramped government center. As they filed out, Allende disappeared into the ornate Independence Room and killed himself. Below on the street, his advisors and bodyguards were made to lie face down and motionless on the sidewalk, where they remained for some four hours before being taken to regimental headquarters of the Tacna

Regiment, one of the units involved in the assault. Some were later transported to one of the detention sites reserved for leading Popular Unity officials. Others were disappeared.

One of those disappeared was Enrique París, a physician, advisor to Allende, and member of the central committee of the Communist party. His case, described in a later chapter, stands out as one of the few that made its way through the Inter-American human rights system. The Inter-American Human Rights Commission, after adhering to the time-consuming procedures intended to produce a friendly settlement, would resolve that París was a victim of the repression practiced by Chile's new government.

The young men in Allende's security detail also disappeared after surrender. Some fifteen of them had managed to enter the palace with the president and, in the dramatic morning hours of the standoff, were photographed at his side brandishing light arms and even a few shoulder-held anti-tank weapons. Three more members of the squad were arrested outside the palace as they attempted to come to Allende's defense, as was Enrique Contreras, son of the president's private secretary and lover. Allende had ordered them to cease resisting even as troops were securing the first floor of the building; otherwise, he told them, there would be a massacre. But surrender did not mean safety, because their captors were of no mind to give quarter. These men, most in their mid-twenties, were viewed as extraordinarily dangerous. They were armed and had put up resistance. Indeed, sniper fire around Constitution Plaza had killed four soldiers. If there was any substance to the high command's worst fears—that a parallel army existed in Chile—then the men of Allende's security detail were its elite corps. The high command was not about to take the risk of affording these men the treatment required by the armed forces' own code of justice, much less the Geneva Conventions. Sometime on the twelfth, according to witnesses, the men of Allende's security detachment were transported by truck to the Tacna Regiment's post in Peldhue. The unavoidable inference is that all were executed and secretly buried at that location.[6]

The military has never adequately explained its reasons for employing these modern weapons to carry out a coup d'état. Allende could have been detained at his residence by a special forces team in a bloodless coup if the military had moved up its actions by a matter of hours. The armored ground assault and the aerial attack on the Moneda constituted excessive force, risked collateral damage to surrounding buildings (including the U.S. Embassy), and caused enduring trauma to the national psyche. The high command perhaps reasoned that a ferocious assault would strike fear into the mind of anyone who might resist the coup. Indeed, one of the edicts broadcast by radio in the early hours of the coup warned that the armed forces would quell any attempted resistance with the same force with which they attacked the Moneda. Or the junta may have needed a dramatic show of force to substantiate the claim that Chile was threatened by well-armed subversives and to justify subsequent actions.[7] An equally plausible explanation is that once a war had been begun none of the senior commanders wanted to miss their chance to employ their most advanced and destructive weapons in combat. The navy had no enemy ships to sink, but marines went into action in Valparaíso and Talcahuano. Air force officers are pilots before all else; the eleventh was General Leigh's only chance at directing close ground support for attacking tanks and infantry in battle. And Pinochet, commanding an army that had not seen action for close to a century, could not pass up an opportunity to direct troop movements and demand unconditional surrender from a besieged and defeated enemy.

War Without Mercy

Soon after Pinochet became army chief of staff in early 1972, he ordered the armed forces' national security plan to be revamped. The existing plan, which involved static defense of government installations and industrial facilities, was faulty. The best defense, Pinochet reasoned, was a good offense.[8] On September 11 Pinochet, who was now in command of the army and the Chilean armed forces, ordered the revised plan put into action. Santiago was divided into security zones, and entire regions of the national territory fell under the operational command of field commanders. Chile was declared at war, and armed forces and police set out to secure their assigned military objectives. The capture of the president was the first priority. Neutralization of the radicalized State Technical University, the industrial sectors, and the shanty-towns of the capital was the next urgent matter. Finally there was the need to pacify the remainder of the national territory, especially the south, where the MIR was active, and the north, where military commanders anticipated the most serious problems. It turns out that there was no real danger.[9]

Radical students, militant workers, and even armed leftist guerrillas were woefully unprepared for the final confrontation when it arrived. The intelligence operatives of the Communist party had been able to confirm that the coup was being mounted in the pre-dawn hours; the headline of the party newspaper appearing on the morning of the eleventh instructed "everyone to his combat post."[10] Students at the State Technical University assembled there for the purpose of deploying in the industrial belts and putting up resistance. Members of the armed formations of the Socialist and Communist parties made their way there as well. But Allende did not sound the battle cry in his radio addresses, and although there was sporadic fighting in Santiago and elsewhere in the country, there was no effective, sustained, or organized resistance.

Military and carabinero units descended on the campus of the State Technical University early on the morning of the eleventh. The army did not gain control of the campus until the next morning, however, and sporadic, ineffective fire was exchanged throughout the night.[11] The university rector, Enrique Kirberg, and the president of the students' association, Osiel Núñez, were detained in the operation along with some 600 students. Kirberg's itinerary was identical to those of other prominent Allende supporters: after being detained briefly at a military installation, he was banished to Dawson Island on the twenty-second. Nuñez was tortured, but his life was spared. From the National Stadium he was eventually sent to a public jail and then into exile. But other young radicals were less fortunate and began an odyssey experienced by hundreds in the ensuing days. They were transported first to Chile Stadium and then transferred to the larger National Stadium on the fourteenth. All were brutally interrogated, many were executed.

The industrial belts of Los Cerrillos and Vicuña MacKenna Avenues fell within the operational zone of the Old Guard regiment, stationed at Los Andes. The regiment's troops deployed in the area at 7 a.m on September 11, well before the armored units involved in the siege of the Moneda palace arrived to take up their positions, even before General Pinochet was at his command post at Peñalolén. There was intense fighting at a few locations, most notably the Sumar plant and the Indumet factories. Ineffective, uncoordinated fighting around the Sumar plant continued until at least the thirteenth. There was also fighting in the capital's shanty-towns. The raid on the Indumet factory on the eleventh cost the life of three carabineros; six more were killed in confrontations at the La Legua shanty-town. As was the case with the four soldiers killed attempting to storm the Moneda palace, the deaths of these men would be avenged several-fold in the raids that followed.

In the days and weeks to follow, factories in the zone and numerous shanty-towns were raided in massive combined search and destroy operations.[12] But the purpose of the operations was no longer to suppress armed resistance: henceforth the arrests and executions were intended to sweep up the left's most capable workplace and shanty-town organizers. The situation in Chile bordered on the chaotic, and the loss of life, although exaggerated in the first international reports, was tragically high. In the vast majority of cases the violence could not reasonably be justified by military necessity — to employ the language of the Nuremberg principles.

Chileans and scores of foreigners met their death in one of several scenarios. Many of those swept up in massive factory or shanty-town raids were summarily executed or transported to the National Stadium, where they were executed within a few hours or days. Known Popular Unity supporters were individually sought, arrested in their homes or on the street, interrogated, and executed. Sometimes the intelligence services did not have to hunt the person at all — an astounding number of Chileans dutifully turned themselves in at a military checkpoint or police station after they heard their names broadcast over the radio. Some were caught on the streets by army patrols during the curfew hours and killed on the spot. Others, including a number of children, were struck dead by stray bullets.[13]

Six days after the coup the army troops supported by carabineros raided the Elecmetal factory. The plant had just resumed operations as the capital struggled to return to normal. The raid lasted less than an hour. The soldiers were looking for Víctor Toro, director of the MIR-MPR, and other MIRistas. They did not find Toro, but five other men were violently boarded on trucks commandeered on the property, taken to an unknown location, and executed. Their bodies were discovered the following day. There was hardly time enough to interrogate these men, suggesting either that they had been denounced by fellow employees or that their political affiliation had been ascertained from one or more of the thousands of detainees in the Chile and National Stadiums or at other sites. The same thing happened at the Sumar factory, the scene of fighting the day after the coup. On the twenty-third soldiers returned with a list, took three men into custody, and took them away. Their bodies were left beside the highway leading out of the capital.

The shanty-town raids followed a similar pattern. In another combined operation on September 20, army and air force troops and carabineros moved against the La Bandera shanty-town. A number of persons were taken to the soccer field. When the dawn-to-dusk operation was over the raiders took four men with them. The body of only one of the men was discovered.

Elements of the Buin regiment, famous for its action on the eleventh, returned to action later in the month. On the twenty-third they swept down on the Roosevelt shanty-town in the vicinity of Santiago's Conchalí district. They took five men prisoner. The bodies of four of the men were found discarded on the Panamerican highway, that of the fifth on the Bulnes bridge over the Mapocho River.

On three separate nights soldiers attached to the Yungay regiment descended on San Juan de Dios Hospital in the capital. They arrested seven men and executed them between September 15 and 19. Most were staff members; one was a medical student, one a labor leader among staff members, another a Catholic priest who was director of personnel. All seven were executed, but only five of them turned up at the Medical-Legal Institute. The action had an unintended impact. The hierarchy of the Catholic Church was slowly becoming convinced that the armed forces were committing atrocities. The murder of Father Joan Alsina, one of a few Catholic clerics killed in the first wave of the repression, caused the scales to fall from the eyes of all but the most incredulous.

On the last day of September troops of this same Yungay regiment conducted an operation in the Santiago Pino shanty-town. When it was over six residents were dead. According to a military source, the men were taken prisoner after a failed attempt to ambush the troops. The troops summarily executed the men, in conformity with a military edict authorizing troops to kill "in the act" anyone attempting to put up resistance.

Authority to shoot on sight Chileans who violated the dusk-to-dawn curfew established the junta's absolute control over the streets of Santiago and the villages in the farthest corners of the narrow country. The curfew served another purpose: it gave the security forces the opportunity to conduct nocturnal abductions and to dispose of bodies without being seen. Curfew violations cost many Chileans their lives. Two days after the coup, Fernando Flores was shot dead in the presence of his daughter, some three hours after the curfew had taken effect. Flores was on an errand to buy bread, and either did not take the curfew seriously or was in desperate need of food. Two days later, Humberto Valenzuela was shot dead in the Conchalí district of metropolitan Santiago, an area assigned to the Buin regiment. He was shot as soon as he stepped from his house, also to run errands. That same day, Juan Fernando Vásquez was shot and gravely wounded. The fifteen-year-old boy had not violated the 6 p.m. curfew, which was still half an hour off, when carabineros shot him. He died on the fifteenth, one of nearly fifty victims of political violence in Chile under the age of 16. On the twelfth, fourteen-year-old Luis Retamal was struck dead by bullets fired by air force personnel patrolling his neighborhood. His father noticed the patrol and sent his teenage son, who was playing outside the home, inside. When the boy appeared on his balcony to see what was happening on the street, a bullet struck and instantly killed him.

Inside the Arena

As in all wars, the scale of operations created tremendous logistical and public relations problems up and down the chain of command. The military had to confine many thousands of suspected subversives, it had to interrogate them, and in hundreds of cases it had to dispose of their bodies. Military commanders solved the logistical problems with relative ease; the public relations problems were more vexing. For their part, representatives of international human rights organizations confronted the same set of facts, but viewed them from an entirely different vantage point: this was a humanitarian crisis.

Thousands of Chileans fled to foreign embassies seeking asylum; hundreds of foreign nationals made their way to their embassies. The flood of refugees and asylum seekers was an unwelcome public relations problem for the regime and a desperate humanitarian problem for humanitarian organizations and foreign governments. There are innumerable compelling stories of persons who had every reason to believe that harm would befall them if the military had caught up with them before they could make it to the safety of foreign embassies. Luis Maira, a Christian Democrat who had joined the Christian Left in the first year of the Popular Unity government, eluded capture and made his way to the Mexican embassy. Maira had been one of the drafters of the Statute of Guarantees, signed by Allende as a precondition for congressional confirmation of his presidential victory in 1970. He had few illusions about the armed forces' adherence to constitutional guarantees of civil and political rights, unlike a tragic number of his colleagues who surrendered to the military as ordered when their names were broadcast over radio. In exile Maira became a prolific author and would eventually write a penetrating critique of Pinochet's 1980 constitution. The military wanted to be rid of many of these people, and in most cases simply banishing them would solve its problem. In other cases, being rid of a hunted subversive meant something more sinister, and even when a person did make it out of the country he had every reason to fear assassination.[14]

Some embassies made heroic efforts to provide safe haven. Coups are endemic to Latin America, so Latin American governments have a long-standing practice of opening their embassies to those who are unfortunate enough to be counted among the vanquished rather than the victors. European governments were also receptive to asylum-seekers. The Italian and Swedish embassies were especially accommodating. Some 4,000 Chileans sought asylum by the end of 1973, and the military government granted safe conduct documents in all but 500 cases, according to Amnesty International. But in December the junta hardened its policy with respect to asylum. First the junta expelled the Swedish ambassador; then it informed other European diplomats that it would no longer entertain their requests for safe passage out of Chile.[15] Almost a year later, in November 1974, the secret police cast the lifeless body of Lumi Videla, a member of the Movement of the Revolutionary Left, over the wall into the Italian embassy compound. This was a not-so-subtle message that henceforth only dead subversives would enter foreign embassies. Security around foreign embassies was tightened as well.

The detention of many thousands of suspected leftists, Chilean and foreign, presented a problem of another order. To solve the logistical problem, the military commandeered Santiago's sports facilities. The Chile Stadium and the much larger National Stadium complex were pressed into service as makeshift internment camps and interrogation centers. The most notorious site was the National Stadium, where prisoners held at the smaller Chile Stadium were moved in October. By all accounts, prisoners arrived en masse from smaller detention sites and jails aboard buses and military trucks. The conditions of confinement were horrendous. The soccer stadium and the adjoining velodrome had an enormous 80,000-person capacity, but apart from the locker rooms, showers, lavatories, and administrative offices there was no place to house the prisoners. The gated tunnels leading to the stands and the open air arena were hurriedly converted into sleeping areas. Protection from the wind and the cold was nonexistent. Initially prisoners were confined to these sealed-off passageways. It was only in the second week that prisoners were allowed to mill about in the stands of the arena during daytime.

Amnesty International, citing the military government, the Catholic Church, the International Commission of Jurists, and the Red Cross as sources, reported that as many as 50,000 prisoners were taken prisoner throughout Chile in the first weeks after the coup. The Chilean foreign minister set the number at 10,900 through the end of October. An unspecified number of those, he said, had been released. The Red Cross, however, counted some 7,000 detainees at the National Stadium alone as of September 22.[16] The confinement of so many persons, virtually all without charge, left the junta with a serious public relations problem. What was worse, atrocities were occurring in the arena.

Teams of intelligence officers were detailed to the arena to extract information and to make life or death judgments about a prisoner's dangerousness. The teams worked efficiently and around the clock, interrogating as many as two to three hundred prisoners each day in the adjacent velodrome.[17] Prisoners were tortured in dressing rooms and lavatories, and scores were taken away for execution. The military interrogators had collaborators. Disaffected former leftists circulated among prisoners identifying union leaders, shanty-town agitators, and leftist militants. One collaborator, a mysterious hooded man, has become immortalized by his depiction in the Costa-Gavras film *Missing*. The man, Juan Muñoz Alarcón, confessed his involvement to the Catholic Church's human rights defender, the Vicariate of Solidarity, in 1977. He was murdered within a few weeks of confiding his secret. Personal rancor motivated him as much as anything else, he admitted.

The Chilean interrogation squads had foreign assistance as well. The war against Marxism was by now a regional, even a hemispheric effort. The Brazilian coup had been staged almost a decade earlier, and the Brazilian military regime would be the first to grant diplomatic recognition to the Chilean junta; Uruguay's democracy was in the final stages of disintegration; and Argentina, which had a brief spell of military dictatorship in the mid-1960s, would fall under the harshest of the Southern Cone military regimes in March 1976. The militaries were sharing information, and the Brazilians were well along the learning curve. Amnesty International and other human rights organizations established the presence of Brazilians in the National Stadium. According to Amnesty International, a group of Brazilian experts arrived in mid-October to assist the Chileans and to direct the interrogation of Brazilian nationals. Amnesty International even established the identity of the team leader and described the man, Alfredo Poeck, as a known "torture specialist in Brazil."[18] After the arrival of the Brazilians, torture techniques became noticeably more sophisticated.

Executions at the Chile and National Stadiums began within 48 hours of the coup, after sufficient time to interrogate the first wave of prisoners had elapsed, and perhaps after a command decision had come down. Human rights investigators have yet to uncover a document or directive stating the reason some prisoners were executed and others were spared. There are logical inferences about the calculations involved: the dangerousness versus prominence of a prisoner. But a variety of factors, including the capriciousness of interrogators, probably came into play.[19]

The executions created another logistical and public relations problem: the disposal of the bodies. Bodies were rarely turned over to families for burial; rather, army and police patrols and stadium executioners simply left the dead by the side of the road or dumped them in the Mapocho River running through the heart of the city. Many of the bodies that were found were either claimed at the Medical-Legal Institute or taken from there or other hospitals and emergency clinics for clandestine burial. Many of those secretly interred were buried at Lot 29 of the General Cemetery. The method was expeditious, callous in the extreme—and violated the Geneva Conventions of 1949.[20]

Sócrates Ponce had been one of those captured by army troops at the Indumet factory on September 11.[21] He was transported to the Tacna regiment, and to Chile Stadium, on the twelfth. The next day his name was read over the public address system at the sport facility, and he was ordered to present himself. He had been selected for execution. His body was found on a street corner a short distance from the stadium the following morning. Gregorio Mimica, who had been arrested on the campus of the State Technical University, was briefly held at Chile Stadium and then released. On the fourteenth, an army patrol went to his house to arrest him again. He has not been seen alive since. Víctor Jara, the renowned folk-singer, was also arrested at the State Technical University. He was taken to the Chile Stadium and severely beaten. According to witnesses, Jara was put in line with others to be taken to the larger National Stadium. His face was swollen and bruised and both his wrists were broken. Jara never arrived at the National Stadium; his body was discovered by residents of one of Santiago's shanty-towns, literally riddled with bullets.

Hernán Cea was also at his place of work, a textile plant in the contested industrial belt, on the morning of the eleventh. He was arrested there and brought to Chile Stadium. On the fifteenth, Cea became combative with a guard, who promptly shot him dead. But Cea's body was not found on the side of the road; he would be one of scores of victims whose bodies turned up in Lot 29 of the General Cemetery.

The wife of Carlos Castro located her husband's body, and saw that it was taken to the Medical-Legal Institute, on her own. Castro and a friend were detained by a military patrol near curfew on the fifteenth. The soldiers evidently executed them, soon thereafter, at another location. Witnesses had observed the arrest but knew nothing about where the men had been taken or what had happened to them. Castro's wife began to search for him. By now, Chileans knew enough to search the banks of the rivers when their loved ones did not turn up at the Medical-Legal Institute. Castro's widow found her husband's remains under a thin layer of sand on the shore of the Mapocho River. The body of the other man was never found.

The disposal of bodies in rivers or at sea made recovery almost impossible, and it created a terrifying spectacle. The sight of bloated bodies drifting down the river toward the sea, or washed up on shore, deepened the mood of terror in the capital. Whether the bodies were cast into the river merely to dispose of them or to terrorize is not easy to ascertain. Elsewhere in the country victims were taken to riversides. In Osorno, for example, victims were made to kneel on the bridge of the Pilmaquén River so that the force of the bullet that struck and killed them would propel them into the river to be swept downstream and out to sea by the current. Incredibly, one of the intended victims, a woman who served as major of Entre Lagos, survived to report the massacre. The bodies were never recovered.[22] The method, in this case, seems to have been intended to conceal the crime.

It is conceivable that the spectacle of a body floating by multiple witnesses was staged for effect: there are wild estimates of the number of killed in the first weeks after the coup, and the sight of bodies rushing by aghast witnesses added to the perception of countless victims. One body observed by five, ten, twenty persons could easily be mistakenly counted as five, ten, twenty different victims. There were almost certainly fewer bodies carried by the rivers than anecdotal evidence would suggest, and the estimates as to how many Chileans suffered this indignity are part of an enduring controversy. Ironically, an inflated body count served the purpose of the junta. If the larger political purpose of the repression was to instill a culture of terror among Chileans to facilitate the long-term transformation of Chile's socioeconomic and political systems, the generalized belief that thousands perished would be beneficial. Insistence on elevated figures, while adding to the monstrousness of the regime, would do more harm than good to the human rights movement in Chile.

What were logistical and public relations problems for the military constituted a humanitarian emergency for international humanitarian and human rights organizations. The International Committee of the Red Cross (ICRC) wanted immediate access to these sports arenas and other known detention sites. An inspection by the ICRC was all the more important because the junta made it known that, until the Red Cross visited detention sites, no other organizations would be permitted to visit them. The Geneva-based humanitarian organization quickly assembled an inspection team, but its entry into Chile from neighboring Argentina was delayed a full week, until the junta reopened the borders.[23] The team did not gain access to detention sites until September 25. It was never permitted to inspect interrogation centers. The Red Cross kept on file in Geneva the names of all prisoners it was able to interview. Moreover, it distributed tens of thousands of blankets and mattresses, boxes of powdered milk, and medicines.[24]

By December the junta understood the necessity to create a bureau to process these people and to respond to the inquiries of desperate families and determined human rights and humanitarian organizations. Accordingly, the junta set up the National Executive Secretariat for Prisoners (SENDET) to reduce the massive number of detainees. But SENDET was an agency without authority. Though it existed to process prisoners, Amnesty International lamented that it could not supply information relating to prisoners held in military barracks. In fact, the officer in charge of the new agency admitted that information about prisoners did not cross his desk for up to three weeks after an arrest had been made.[25]

Not all those held in the stadiums and the other detention sites were Chileans. The military had a xenophobic hatred of the thousands of foreign nationals who had been attracted to Chile by Allende's socialist experiment. The defense and interior ministries were reporting that as many as 13,000 foreign nationals were in Chile at the time of the coup, many with evil intentions. Depending on which agency was leveling the allegations, between 3,000 and 13,000 (all known foreign nationals!) were Marxist mercenaries present in the country to participate in the Popular Unity government's planned armed takeover. The international response to the xenophobia was immediate. Two days after the coup, the United Nations High Commissioner for Refugees contacted the foreign minister to state the UNHCR's concerns. By the end of October the junta had decided to rid itself of this particular problem as well. The interior ministry, headed by General Oscar Bonilla, authorized the temporary formation of a National Committee for Aid to Refugees. By November, when an Amnesty International delegation visited Chile, the number of foreigners detained had decreased dramatically, at least in the National Stadium, from more than four hundred to just twenty.[26] It was possible to influence the military government's behavior, sometimes.

Vengeance in the Countryside

In outlying areas vengeance killings, often with the participation of civilians, were especially gruesome. Townships like Lonquén and Paine were sites of terrible atrocities. On October 7 fifteen campesinos were abducted by carabineros on Maipo Island. Eleven of them were from just three families. The men were last seen alive, being taken away, lying face down in a small truck owned by the man on whose farm the men had been employed. Their bodies would be discovered five years later in an abandoned lime kiln in nearby Lonquén. Family members made an effort to locate the men through the courts, but the Carabineros responded to the habeas corpus petition by asserting that the men had been taken to the National Stadium. Given what is known now about what became of missing persons last seen in the National Stadium, that information was itself distressing. In fact the men were never taken there: they were transported to the lime oven at Lonquén.[27]

In 1978, after the worst of the repression had passed and Pinochet was comfortably in power, the Catholic Church's human rights office was anonymously informed that victims were hidden at Lonquén. A delegation was sent to the site and made the gruesome discovery. The discovery prompted the reopening of the case. Now carabineros involved in the abduction of the men claimed that they had stopped at Lonquén on the way to Santiago because one of the men admitted that a cache of weapons had been hidden in the very place the bodies of the men would be discovered. When the carabineros arrived with their prisoners supposedly to confiscate the concealed weapons, they were ambushed, according to their version of events. Somehow, none of the carabineros and none of their attackers were killed, wounded, or captured, but all the prisoners died in the exchange of fire. The carabineros claimed to have panicked and deposited the bodies in the lime kiln, fearful of the reaction of the families back home. Of course there is no accounting of any weapons recovered from the place, despite the fact that the regime meticulously documented weapons allegedly confiscated from subversive groups; indeed, Pinochet's memoir lists the quantity, type, and manufacture of weapons the armed forces and Carabineros claim to have come across throughout the years of the dictatorship.

To the south of the capital, on the highway leading to Rancagua, the traveler passes through Buin, then Paine. There army troops and police, with the assistance of property owners, went on a spree of revenge killings. The victims were farmers and members of the agricultural cooperatives that had sprung up during the Allende years. The killings began two days after the coup and continued through November. Initially, victims were abducted one at a time, usually at their homes. In one instance four persons surrendered themselves at the local police station, as ordered. Then in October infantry troops from the San Bernardo Regiment began making massive arrests at the collective farm camps. Thirteen persons were swept up on October 3, five on the thirteenth, twenty-seven from three different cooperatives on the sixteenth, six more on the twentieth. All were executed. The toll was remarkable. Sixty persons in all were murdered, for no reason other than that they had been beneficiaries of Allende's hated land reforms.

The Battle of Concepción

General Washington Carrasco, commander of the army's Third Division in Concepción, carried out his orders to occupy the government offices and detain subversives without incident on the morning of September 11. It turns out that only a small team of military engineers and telephone company employees was needed to cut off all telephone communications of Popular Unity officials and sympathizers. The communist governor of Concepción was arrested and would later die under torture. Then troops under General Carrasco's command began to round up the new regime's enemies.

The military had anticipated problems in and around Concepción, a provincial capital in Chile's Bio-Bio region, and in the Araucanía and Los Lagos regions further south. The University of Concepción was the birthplace of the MIR, and the organization was suspected of having a dangerous presence. Indeed, the university's former rector, Edgardo Enríquez, was now Allende's Minister of Education; his sons Miguel and Edgardo were members of the MIR's Political Commission; Miguel was MIR secretary general. Membership in the Communist and Socialist parties was substantial in the coal-mining towns of Lota and Coronel, as well as in coastal towns like Talcahuano, Penco, and Tomé, where the forestry and commercial fishing industries are found. It was the same in the forestry and lumber industries in the south around Temuco, Osorno, and Valdivia.

But the military presence was substantial as well. The headquarters of the army's Third Division was located only a mile or so from the campus of the University of Concepción. The navy also had a major presence nearby. The port at Talcahuano was home to the navy's Second Naval District. Chilean marines were stationed at Fort Borgoño, located on the sprawling Talcahauno base. The Seamen's Training School was located on Quiriquina Island, a short distance from where the Bio-Bio River empties into the Pacific. The situation around Concepción was so secure that the air force moved the fighter-bombers used in the action over Santiago to Concepción in the weeks before the coup to avoid sabotage in the capital. The military encountered no organized resistance in Concepción and suffered no combat casualties.

But more than 200 Chileans were killed by the military in the Bio-Bio region between September 11 and the end of the year. Twenty-nine were killed in Concepción province.[28] Hundreds more were arrested by army and navy units operating separately. Most of the detained were taken to the naval installations in Talcahuano and on Quiriquina Island. In October the International Committee of the Red Cross reported that 158 prisoners were being held at the Talcahuano naval base and another 522 on Quirquina Island. Nineteen foreign nationals were among them. The soccer stadium, close by the sprawling base of the army's Third Division, was used as well; the same ICRC report placed 589 prisoners there. The city jail in Concepción housed another 60 prisoners in the custody of either the army or the navy. Only a dozen had been sentenced by war tribunals. Conditions were crowded, and prisoners were tortured.

There were no confirmed reports of fire-fights in Concepción. As in the capital city, the death toll can be attributed solely to vengeance. The MIRistas, communists, and socialists in Concepción province and elsewhere were pursued, captured, and killed because the military believed the ideas they advocated were dangerous, even though the captured men themselves no longer posed any danger. José Castro and Ernesto Mardones, a MIRista, were arrested north of Concepción on September 14. They disappeared. Mardones's body was found on the banks of the Bio Bio River two months later; Castro's remains are still missing. Each day between September 18 and 21 there were deaths and disappearances. Socialist Arturo Villegas disappeared after arrest on the eighteenth; Héctor Rodríguez disappeared after being arrested with several suspected MIRistas the following day; Filipe Campos and Freddy Torres, both Ecuadorians, were found shot to death on the banks of the Bio Bio; José Constanzo was shot to death at the Fort Borgoño marine base on the twenty-first, allegedly after attempting to wrest a weapon from one of his guards.

One week later, on September 28, MIRista Ricardo Barra died at Fort Borgoño as a result of the torture he had suffered. He had been arrested by naval intelligence officers with three other men, all MIRistas. They were brought before a war tribunal on weapons charges. The tribunal pronounced lengthy prison sentences, but they did not live to serve them. The three were shot to death on October 9, allegedly while attempting to escape under cover of an ambush of their guards staged by unknown attackers.

Then there were the war tribunals. On October 21 a court martial sentenced four men to death for violation of the arms control law and for organizing armed groups. They were executed the following day and buried in the city cemetery. The families were not informed and only discovered the burial site in July 1990, after Chile's democratic transition. The navy conducted its own war tribunal at the end of the year. Fifty-two persons were tried and two sentenced to death. The commander of the Second Naval District upheld the sentences, and the two men, both communist militants, were executed five days before Christmas.

The battle of Concepción was supposed to be the battle with the boastful MIR. The air force and the army vied with each other to see which branch could inflict the most damage. Air force intelligence, the SIFA, had certain advantages. The SIFA had been aggressive in conducting weapons searches in the area, under the authority of the Arms Control Law enacted in 1972. In June 1973, a SIFA unit engaged in a fire-fight with members of the Communist party's Ramona Parra Brigade. At the end of August 1973, only weeks before the coup, the air force moved against a MIR training camp in Temuco and arrested 28 MIRistas.[29] Having rehearsed the operation in August, air force personnel rapidly rearrested, executed, and disappeared MIRistas in the province.

The air force's Helicopter Squadron 3, stationed at the Maquehua air force base in Temuco, earned a reputation for cruelty during the campaign. The army's Tucapel regiment competed with it. Thirty-nine persons were killed around Temuco in this initial phase of the repression. Nine of them were MIRistas, including Ambrosio Badilla Vasey, a member of the MIR's central committee. The Helicopter Squadron's reach extended farther south in the Los Lagos (or Lakes) region. The MIR's Revolutionary Peasant Movement was active in the area, and managed to stage some quixotic attacks on Carabinero checkpoints immediately after the coup. The intelligence services tracked them down. Sixteen were executed after a war tribunal in the city of Valdivia on October 3 and 4. Most were loggers working in the commercial forestry industry with ties to the MIR. Others were students at Austral University in Valdivia. The executions were a severe blow to the organization in the region. One of those executed, Fernando Krauss, was regional secretary for the MIR's Revolutionary Student Front. The prize catch of the operation, however, was the head of the MIR's Revolutionary Campesino Movement, José Gregario Liendo Vera, "Comandante Pepe." A week later, on October 9, the army executed seventeen more persons in the area. They were loggers, farmers, and peasant activists. The following day Helicopter Squadron 3 arrested sixteen employees of the same lumber and forestry complex where Comandante Pepe had worked and agitated. The prisoners were taken to a bridge over the Toltén River and executed.

Drumhead Justice

The lengths to which the high command in Santiago would go to invent a war became tragically apparent in October. For three weeks in October, even while the secretary general of the Inter-American Human Rights Commission was in Chile, army officers carrying special orders from General Pinochet were embarked on a helicopter tour dispensing drumhead justice.

The main character in the episode was army General Sergio Arellano Stark, although he has always protested his ignorance of the summary executions committed by members of his delegation. Accompanying him were Lieutenant Colonel Sergio Arredondo González, Majors Pedro Espinoza and Marcelo Moren Brito, and Lieutenants Armando Fernández Larios and Juan Chiminelli. Three of these officers, Majors Espinoza and Moren and Lieutenant Fernández, would later gain notoriety in the regime's secret police, the DINA. General Arellano did not make it into the intelligence circle.

Arellano had been one of the principal coup plotters. It was Arellano who visited Pinochet on the evening of September 8 to inform him that the plans for the impending coup were already drawn up. Now, three weeks later, Arellano left Santiago aboard a Puma helicopter at the head of a delegation specially authorized by the commander-in-chief to review the sentences handed down by the hastily convened war tribunals. The delegation would visit some seven cities and towns, convening and sometimes reconvening courts martial and handing down sentences more severe than local commanders had deemed warranted. Notably, some of these were the cities and towns where, according to his memoir of the coup, Pinochet had anticipated the most trouble. When the fateful tour concluded on October 19, 1973, the delegation had left at least 72 victims of summary executions in its wake.

The caravan of death, as some have called it, is paradigmatic of the first phase of the repression.[30] First, the episode indicated that the high command in Santiago was as frightened of not being at war as it was of actually being in one. Second, like the roundup and crackdown taking place in the capital, it signaled that the most important elements of the armed forces were intent not just on pacifying the country, but on exterminating the left. Third, the events of October revealed the military's proclivity to invoke laws and violate them at the same time. Fourth, those most prone to commit the violations, like those in the delegation, would become part of Pinochet's inner circle as officers in the notorious DINA. Finally, the hard-liners were so determined to extirpate Marxism from Chile that they were not deterred by the presence of human rights organizations in the country.

The arrival of Arellano's delegation aboard the Puma helicopter was a bad omen for political prisoners and sometimes for local commanders. The trail began in Chile's Seventh Region, where the delegation visited Talca and Cauquenes. Arellano's delegation arrived in Talca, south of Santiago, on Sunday September 30.[31] The delegation's first order of business was to relieve the local commander, Lieutenant Colonel Efraín Jaña, of his command, apparently for failing to immediately carry out orders to arrest the local governor. The man, a socialist, had attempted to flee the country and had shot and killed a policeman and a civilian before being captured. It was the only act of armed resistance in the area. The commander eventually brought the governor before a court martial and he was executed. Otherwise all was calm. Jaña later recounted in his interview with Chilean journalist Patricia Verdugo that, when Arellano asked how many casualties his unit had sustained, Jaña repeatedly had to tell him that, apart from this incident, there had been no trouble. Jaña later said that General Arellano scolded him: "Don't you realize we are at war?"[32]

Despite the relative calm in the province, some 25 persons were executed, some of them while purportedly attempting to escape. This would become part of a pattern. Arellano's delegation does not appear to have ordered any executions in Talca, but it was clear that a hard line was being set down. Over the next three weeks, dozens of Chileans would perish while the delegation was present or soon after it departed.

From Talca the Puma helicopter carried the delegation to nearby Cauquenes, also on September 30. Four socialists were executed there on October 4 while the delegation was still in the city. There is some doubt about the degree of the delegation's direct involvement, according to the official account published in 1991. Notably, the reason for such doubt is that the number killed, four, seemed to investigators to be low. In the incidents that would follow, the number would range from thirteen to twenty-six victims. From Caquenes the delegation continued south, visiting Temuco and Valdivia. Death sentences were also pronounced by war tribunals in these cities. The delegation's presence in the south was ominous. But it was in the north that Arellano's group left its mark.

The high command in Santiago was extremely concerned about the possibility of resistance, or sabotage, in the arid north. Chile's copper industry is centered there, a fact that presented a number of potential problems. The copper miners were organized, and leftist influence among them was strong. Explosives were used at mines like Chuquicamata, the world's largest open pit copper mine, and manufactured in Dupont's nearby ENAEX plant. The reasoning is clear. Leftists presumably had the motive to resist, the explosives gave them the means, and the mines presented them with the opportunity to commit sabotage. But apart from some inconsequential incidents no trouble developed, and local commanders took control of the situation with a minimum of violence.

The Puma helicopter touched in the north in the second week of October, and those aboard it went on a rampage. In rapid succession, the helicopter touched down in La Serena, Copiapó, Antofagasta, and Calama. Before the delegation returned to Santiago via Antofagasta, 68 persons had been executed — 68 murders committed within 72 hours.[33] All the victims were affiliated with the MIR, the Socialist and Communist parties, or leftist organizations like the MAPU. Local commanders were left to fabricate stories, falsify documents, and conceal the whereabouts of the victims. Sense of duty, concern for the armed forces as an institution, and worries about the local population prompted the local commanders to cooperate. Something unprecedented was happening in Chile.

The policy to eradicate the left by killing leftists required some finessing. The regime was obsessed with laws and legality. This was the rationale for the war tribunals, even though in many cases the death sentences were out of all proportion with the alleged action of the accused, due process was violated, and the law was applied retroactively. In a number of instances the publication of a public notice that there had been a war tribunal, and that executions were carried out in conformity with sentences handed down by it, was a complete fabrication. The other expedient used by the delegation was to resort to the so-called fugitive law. To commit illegalities masked as proper procedure, the delegation had merely to stage prisoner escapes.

The delegation arrived in La Serena on October 16. There fifteen prisoners were taken from the local jail to the facilities of Arica Regiment and executed. The area commander released a public notice of the executions the same afternoon. He reported that all had been brought before a war tribunal and sentenced to death for offenses ranging from obtaining weapons, to conducting training in guerrilla tactics and the use of explosives, to planning an attack on a local police station. The war tribunal was convened on special orders from Santiago and communicated by Arellano's delegation. It is not clear, however, whether a war tribunal was actually held. Even if one had been convened, the defendants were not afforded the right to an adequate defense. Also, the sentences were severe and the behavior of the war tribunals cruel.

A case in point. Roberto Guzmán, a MIRista, surrendered to authorities as ordered a week after the coup. On September 27 a war tribunal sentenced him to five years imprisonment for inciting miners to seize explosives. Arellano's delegation, however, took him from his cell along with fourteen other men on October 16. All were executed. In a cruel turn of events, Guzmán's sentence was reduced in 1975 to 541 days. Neither Guzmán's family nor the families of the other victims were able to obtain the bodies of their loved ones.[34]

Copiapó was the next destination on the group's itinerary. In the early morning hours of October 17 thirteen men were shot to death after having been taken from the local prison on the pretext that they were being transferred to La Serena, the small city from which the delegation had just arrived. The victims had not been sentenced to death by war tribunals; in fact they were supposedly en route to La Serena to have their sentences reviewed. The deaths were justified by the fugitive law. The armed forces implausibly alleged that the prisoners attempted a mass escape after the truck transporting them broke down. The following day four more leftists were executed, this time by a firing squad in the prison at Copiapó. The delegation was still present and the day before had searched the homes of the four victims. The families were informed that the men were to have been brought before a war tribunal, but no record of one has been produced. Like the others, their bodies were secretly interred, then removed to an unknown location. They have still not been recovered and restored to their families.

The punitive tour culminated with a spasm of violence between the early morning hours and the afternoon of October 19. Arellano arrived in Antofagasta from Copiapó on the morning of October 18. He was received by General Joaquín Lagos Osorio, commander of Chile's First Army Division. As such, General Lagos had operational command of the entire region, including Copiapó. With the militarization of the state accompanying the military takeover, Lagos assumed the region's governorship. General Lagos would have outranked Arellano by virtue of his longer service, had not Arellano been named by General Pinochet to head this extraordinary delegation.

According to General Lagos, Arellano's mission was to clarify matters relating to the administration of justice in this unprecedented situation. As in La Serena and Copiapó, a substantial number of prisoners were being held in the local jail, presumably for trial. In fact, Lagos later told journalist Patricia Verdugo, he had earlier been informed by General Oscar Bonilla, the regime's minister of interior, that the Bar Association of Antofagasta would be involved in the proceedings.

Unbeknownst to Lagos, Arellano's delegation was in reality dispensing drumhead justice. Shortly after midnight on October 19, members of the delegation took fourteen of the prisoners awaiting trial from the local jail and summarily executed them. Some of General Lagos's own troops had been ordered to participate, without his knowledge or consent. When Lagos saw Arellano off again around 8:30 that same morning he still had not learned of the massacre. In fact, he had not yet learned of what had occurred on the seventeenth in Copiapó, a city that also fell under his operational command. His subordinates informed him of the events and confessed to their part in it. They apparently believed Lagos was cognizant of Arellano's intent. Thereafter it fell to Lagos to draft a false announcement that the fourteen had been sentenced to death. The notices appeared in the press on three different days, a ploy intended to create the impression of three separate sets of executions.[35] The day after the executions, the Bar Association of Antofagasta, which Interior Minister General Bonilla had told Lagos would be taking up the matter of the prisoners, informed General Lagos that it would not become involved because of what had happened "the night before."

Meanwhile, Arellano's delegation was on the way to visit Calama. The enormous Chuquicamata copper mine was nearby. Among the delegation's victims this time were ten employees of the Dupont explosive manufacturing plant. Like Guzmán, who had been executed in Cauquenes, their access to explosives and their leftist leanings made them doubly dangerous. They were arrested on October 12 and eventually taken to a local jail in Calama. Sometime after four o'clock in the afternoon of October 19 they were boarded on a truck to be transferred to Antofagasta, supposedly to be tried there. All were murdered en route.

The crime was cruder than the one committed in Copiapó some nights earlier. For one thing, the official reason for the transfer was absurd. The men were supposedly being moved from Calama to Antofagasta to be tried, even though a war tribunal was set to be convened in Calama itself. The site of the massacre, moreover, lies off the main road to Antofagasta. Then there was the alleged escape attempt after the truck in which the men were being transported developed electrical problems. Despite the large contingent of soldiers guarding the prisoners, it was claimed that these men decided in unison to make a break and were shot to death for failing to obey orders to halt. Eyewitnesses, including soldiers from the local detachment who participated, belied the claims. The murders, they say, were committed with tremendous cruelty. Some were shot only to be wounded so as to prolong the suffering before they were finally dispatched. Some were said to have been shot to pieces. Curved knives, or corvos, of the kind used by Indian Gurkhas were used in some cases. And, as in the other cases, the bodies were never released to family members despite military assurances that they would be turned over.

In his sworn testimony some thirteen years after the events, General Lagos, commander of the First Army Division, recounted that he confronted Arellano about the crimes and even managed to bring them to the attention of General Augusto Pinochet, who passed through Antofagasta on October 20, the day the delegation terminated its trip. General Arellano has always protested his innocence.[36] Arellano maintained he knew nothing about the events, and attributed them to Lieutenant Colonel Arredondo, who, he said, acted on his own accord or under secret orders. Some knowledgeable observers believe that Pinochet dispatched Arellano, a potential rival, in order to "dirty his hands."[37] One member of the official presidential commission would even admit that Arellano left a "reasonable doubt" when he recounted his version of events many years later. Lieutenant Armando Fernández Larios has also maintained his innocence. Fernández Larios, who participated in the siege of the Moneda palace, later joined the DINA and confessed to his participation in the assassination of Orlando Letelier and Ronnie Moffitt in Washington in 1976. He claims only to have served as Arellano's bodyguard during the tour, although eyewitnesses claim he acted with extreme sadism in Calama, the final stop on the delegation's tour.

For his part, Pinochet is said to have told General Lagos that he never thought Arellano, or anyone in the delegation he had authorized, would undertake to commit such acts. But if Pinochet was shocked by the crimes he did not look into them, much less punish those responsible. On the contrary, members of the delegation were to find their way into the all-powerful DINA. Pedro Espinoza was assigned to the DINA when it was created the following month and eventually became its chief of operations. Marcelo Moren Brito also found his way into the DINA and eventually took charge of the infamous Villa Grimaldi detention site, which for survivors became synonymous with torture.

The crimes committed by Arellano's delegation should be placed in some perspective. The official presidential commission concluded that there were 22 cases of human rights violations resulting in death in the Coquimbo region; 15 of those were committed by Arellano's men in La Serena on October 16. The same is true of the Atacama region. Thirteen of the 19 murders committed in that part of Chile were committed in Copiapó on October 17.

Explaining the Atrocities

Even in retrospect it is difficult to define a single concept for what was occurring in Chile in the weeks between September 11 and the end of the year. Human rights defenders have a distinctively legal idiom, and the facts they would establish over the years left no doubt that the regime was committing human rights violations as international human rights law defines that term. The concept assigns culpability, but it does not explain motivation, and the question of motivation is important.

Vengeance, blind hatred, rage, and instinctive cruelty seem to have prompted the violence of the early weeks of the new order, for the most part. The brutality and the killings, in other words, were emotional reactions rather than cold, calculated acts — they were more like battlefield massacres than premeditated murders. That characterization is not intended to sound exculpatory. Rather, it is meant to contrast the crimes of these early weeks with the crimes committed in the years to follow. Those later crimes were far more systematic and premeditated. They were policy.

The crimes committed during the final weeks of 1973 were acts of vengeful, enraged, hateful, and cruel men. The radio transmissions between Pinochet and Carvajal in the first hours of the coup reveal that. Supporters of the Popular Unity were mistreated and more than a thousand of them were killed before the end of the year, because they were the "filthy people" who had brought misfortune on Chile. Their mistreatment was simple vengeance exacted by enraged soldiers, who were blinded by hate for communists by intensive indoctrination and made cruel by rigorous training.

The junta made unconvincing efforts to justify the coup. The most elaborate justification came in the form of a White Paper released in November. It outlined Plan Zeta, an alleged plot to assassinate senior military officers during the Independence Day celebrations on September 18 and 19. Plan Z has all the hallmarks of a fabrication, but it is nonetheless important. Dishonest police, it is often discovered, only frame suspects they believe to be guilty. The logic is the same. The supporters of Popular Unity were guilty, but those less discerning than the soldiers had to be convinced of the guilt. The conclusion drawn by the intelligence officers who supposedly discovered the document alleged to contain the "cruel and gory plan" known as Plan Z was straightforward.

The Unidad Popular and Salvador Allende, not satisfied with trampling upon the majority will of the country, with violating the substance and the form of the Constitution and the laws, with disregarding the condemnation and warnings of the other powers of the State, with ruining the country economically and financially, and with having sown and spread hate, violence and death throughout the nation, was prepared and ready to carry out this self-coup designed to conquer an absolute power based on force and crime, and installing the "people's dictatorship."[38]

The concluding passage of the White Paper is perhaps more revealing of the state of mind of the officers than of the intentions of Allende's supporters. And it explains the first wave of violence.

The coup d'état produced victims in every region of the country. Some were harder hit than others, of course. Metropolitan Santiago became a free fire zone; more than five hundred persons were killed before New Year's Day 1974. Another five hundred victims are known to have been amassed in the Bio-Bio, Araucanía, and Los Lagos regions to the south, where the army, air force, and police competed to inflict the most damage on the MIR. In the remaining nine regions, the dead number in the dozens rather than the hundreds. Even where there was no armed resistance, which was virtually all the cases, the armed forces and police were determined simply to kill their enemies.

In just three and a half months the military regime committed atrocities on a scale unprecedented in Chile's history as an independent republic. Because the military regime took precautions to conceal its crimes, some contemporary estimates of the number of deaths after the coup were wildly inflated. Thomas Hauser, whose book *Missing* became controversial for its accusations of U.S. complicity in the coup and in the disappearance of two North Americans, wrote that 15,000 were executed, without giving a time-frame.[39] Dinges and Landau gave a substantially lower figure in their exposé on the involvement of the DINA in the assassination of Orlando Letelier. "An army general later admitted," the authors write, "that at least 3,000 persons were killed, less than a dozen military officers and police person-nel." They added that the "U.S. Embassy and intelligence estimates at the time, for the same period, put the dead at around 5,000."[40] Nathaniel Davis, who was U.S. ambassador in Santiago at the time of the coup and thus privy to the U.S. Embassy estimates Dinges and Landau mention, noted in his 1985 book that "estimates of the number of people killed during and imme-diately after the coup vary from a low of 2,500 to a high of 80,000."[41] A U.S. State Department report dating from March 1974, cited by Amnesty Inter-national, gave a surprisingly high figure: 10,800 by the end of the year. This is the high end of the range of reliable estimates suggested by Nathaniel Davis. AI, for its part, stated that "more than 2,000 people are now known to have been executed in custody between 11 September and the end of De-cember 1973."[42]

A reasonably accurate accounting of the number killed in this period became possible only after the Chilean military returned to the barracks in 1990. More than 1,260 Chileans were killed from September 11 until the end of 1973, according to this official count.[43] Tens of thousands were ar-rested and detained without charge, charged with offenses that were not crimes when they were allegedly committed, denied due process of law, harassed, maltreated, tortured, and exiled. The scale of the calamity was unprecedented.

The worst had not passed. Agents of the Pinochet regime would murder another 600 Chileans over the next three years. But what had been indis-criminate repression for the first few months after the coup converted to state terrorism conducted in a permanent state of siege that ended only in 1977. In waves, the regime persecuted the MIR, the Socialists, then the Communists. The repression became more discriminating and methodical. Torture techniques were improved. More ominously, fewer bodies were being delivered to the Medical-Legal Institute; more were being "disap-peared" in a deliberate policy to conceal the crimes and to inflict psycholog-ical terror.

Chapter 3
The New Order

The fundamental mission [of the armed forces] is to make a prosperous nation out of a country in ruins. That is not a task for demagogues, nor will it be resolved in a matter of hours.

— General Augusto Pinochet

The Junta

Only hours after the body of Salvador Allende was removed from the charred Moneda palace, the men who had deposed him appeared on television to justify their actions and to declare their intentions. Until that moment they were obscure figures. Three of them had assumed the senior leadership positions of their respective services in the final weeks of August, when the National Security Cabinet collapsed under the weight of the truckers' strike. The fourth wrested control of his post on the morning of the coup, while his nominal commander stood beside Allende in the besieged Moneda. One of these men, army general Augusto Pinochet Ugarte, would soon dominate Chilean politics as no other figure in the nation's history.

Pinochet, then fifty-eight, assumed command of the army and the overall command of the armed forces on August 23, when General Carlos Prats resigned amid growing tensions between the Allende government and segments of the armed forces. Prats, who had been vilified by the families of the officers he commanded, could not tolerate any more abuse. The day before Prats submitted his resignation, Pinochet defended him when the Council of Generals met to decide what should be done for the good of the service.[1] General Prats and his wife Sofía were assassinated in exile in Buenos Aires on September 29, 1974. Pinochet vehemently denies having ordered the assassination of his predecessor and comrade-in-arms, but he did not launch an exhaustive investigation into the crime.

General Gustavo Leigh Guzmán took command of the air force two days before Pinochet assumed his post. Leigh's predecessor had been transportation minister, and his inability to settle the truckers' strike led to his resignation and Leigh's ascendance. Leigh was ambitious in the extreme and appeared to have a promising future. The very day that Leigh became air force commander, General Prats recorded in his diary that "a sluggish, ambitious, mediocre coup plotter has been replaced by another coup plotter [Leigh] who is intelligent, astute and ten times more ambitious."[2] In fact, Leigh had become involved in the movement to remove Allende well before Pinochet, he was articulate, and his anti-communist credentials were unquestioned. Leigh would be the first to openly announce the junta's intention to extirpate Marxism from Chile. But conflicts with Pinochet and an intense rivalry with the Directorate for National Intelligence, an agency that reported directly to Pinochet, led to his removal from the junta in July 1978. Leigh had had the audacity to criticize Pinochet's announced timetable for a return to a democratic rule. In March 1989 Leigh would narrowly survive an assassination attempt by armed militants of the very Communist party the general had sworn to destroy.

Admiral José Toribio Merino Castro became acting navy commander on August 31, less than ten days before he ordered his fleet to put out to sea, then to return to port surreptitiously to lead a revolution. Merino was, by most accounts, one of the most militant advocates of a coup to oust Allende. And it was Merino who first united a group of Chicago-trained economists to study economic reforms to be implemented after the seizure of power.

Carabinero Director General César Mendoza Durán did not even hold that position on the morning of the coup; indeed he was sixth in command. Once the carabineros guarding the Moneda were persuaded to abandon their posts prior to the aerial bombardment of the building, the militarized police corps suffered a leadership crisis that brought Mendoza into command and into the junta. Allende reserved especially harsh words for Mendoza in his last broadcast, alluding to him as a vile, crawling viper. Mendoza would be forced to resign after the revelation that agents of the Carabinero intelligence were guilty of the triple homicide of communist leaders in 1985. But before he departed he left his mark in the form of the so-called Ley de Mendoza (Mendoza law) that stipulated that carabineros convicted of human rights violations would serve their sentences in Carabinero installations.

When these men and other high-ranking officers began to conspire is a matter of controversy, but some facts are known. By most accounts with the exception of his own, Pinochet only reluctantly joined the plotters. General Sergio Arellano Stark, who a month after the coup would lead a delegation that summarily executed some seventy-two prisoners, visited Pinochet on the evening of September 8. He asked Pinochet to contact Air Force General Leigh, but Pinochet did not call. The following night Pinochet was again visited in his home, this time by two navy admirals, including Patricio Carvajal, and a captain. The men were bearing the coup declaration for Pinochet's signature.

The most cynical interpretations hold that Pinochet hedged his bets. The army commander had his wife transported to a military base in the Andes, a

short helicopter trip from the army telecommunications center at Peñalolén, his post on the day of the coup. Had the coup failed, goes the argument, Pinochet would have been able to flee the country over the Andes
with his wife. Or, if constitutionalists were to rise in defense of Allende's
government, Pinochet might even had made the pretense of leading constitutionalist officers in the counter-coup. Notably, General Cantuarias, the
commander of the base where Pinochet sent his wife for safeguarding, was
known to be an Allende sympathizer. He died under mysterious circumstances within weeks of the coup, while under arrest, allegedly by suicide.

The other version has Pinochet far more involved from the moment he
assumed command of the armed forces. Not surprisingly it is the version
found in Pinochet's memoir of the affair, entitled *El Día decisivo*.[3] But in one
sense this controversy, much like the one surrounding the circumstances of
Allende's death, was merely a rallying point for those who took different
sides during Chile's tragedy. Whether Pinochet took the lead in organizing
the coup is less relevant than the fact that he came to exercise inordinate
influence over the country's destiny, and presided over a concerted campaign of state terrorism.

These four men now constituted a junta and claimed extraordinary powers. But none of them had a clear sense of how long they would retain power
or to whom they would relinquish it. Instead, in their first appearance before the nation they spoke about patriotic duty, portrayed themselves as
reluctant warriors, and pledged themselves to the restoration of the rule of
law. The air force commander, however, set the tone for the events to follow.

Protocol dictated that Pinochet, as the senior commander of the country's oldest and largest armed service, speak first. His terse remarks provided no insight into the man or his intentions. "Patriotic duty compelled
the armed forces," he said, "to save the country from the acute chaos into
which the government of Salvador Allende was leading it." Then Pinochet
assured his listeners that he had no personal ambitions. "I have no preten-
sion to direct the Junta while it lasts," he said. "What we will do is rotate.
Now it is me, tomorrow it will be Admiral Merino, then General Leigh and
after him, General Mendoza. I don't want to appear to be an irreplaceable
person."[4]

Leigh spoke second and announced a crusade. The armed forces took
the extraordinary decision to intervene after "three years of bearing the
Marxist cancer," he said, and now the armed forces would undertake a "sad
and painful mission." "We understand the enormous responsibility that will
be on our shoulders, but we are certain and sure that the great majority of
the Chilean people is with us, that it is ready to fight communism, that it is
ready to extirpate it, whatever the cost."

The navy's commanding admiral came across as a humble officer who
would much rather be aboard ship carrying out his duties as a sailor. He
acknowledged that the armed forces had broken with a long and admirable

tradition. "Perhaps it is sad that a democratic tradition that was so long on this continent was broken." But he surmised, "we are sure that all Chile must understand the sacrifice this signifies for us, that it is easier for us, more sacred, to be at sea on our ships."

When the director general of the Carabineros spoke, it was as if he had not heard Leigh's declaration of war against communism. The Carabineros joined the junta he said, to "reestablish the rule of law which had been seriously ruptured." "It is not a question of crushing political or ideological currents, or of personal revenge, but as I said, of reestablishing public order and returning the country to the path of obeying the constitution, and the laws of the Republic." "It is the spirit of the junta," he reassured the listeners, "to return to the path of true legality."

These impromptu remarks left the impression that the period of military rule would be relatively brief, and that Chileans had nothing to fear from their new government. Leigh's impassioned remark about extirpating Marxism from Chile was more than counterbalanced by Mendoza's reassurances about the rule of law. Such notions would be dispelled a month after the coup, when Pinochet took to the television airwaves to announce that the armed forces' "fundamental mission to make a prosperous nation out of a country in ruins" would not be resolved "in a matter of hours," and then echoed Leigh's view that the military government was engaged in a "battle to extirpate evil from Chile at the root."[5] The military government would not tread the path of true legality, as Mendoza had pledged — it would tread a warpath.

The Regime

The new regime was exceptional, and not just by Chilean standards. The Chilean state was militarized, and Pinochet managed to fuse the offices of armed forces commander-in-chief and chief executive to become dictator of Chile. The judicial system was marginalized, with the acquiescence of the magistrates of the Supreme Court, and with catastrophic consequences for human rights. For a time a secret governmental agency acting above and outside the law went about extirpating Marxism from Chile and doing the dirty work that would enable the junta to dramatically transform Chile.

The junta immediately began to issue decree laws that militarized the Chilean state and authorized it to wage war. Decree Law No. 1, announced on September 11, invested in the four-man junta "supreme rule over the nation." Decree Law No. 5, issued the same day, announced that the junta would exercise all executive, legislative, and constitutive powers. Congress was closed, as Pinochet had publicly announced the night before. Political parties were declared in indefinite recess. Leftist political parties were banned altogether. Military officers were assigned to governmental posts. All but two cabinet posts, justice and education, went to high-ranking officers. Soldiers became intendentes, governors, and mayors. Eventually the military intervened in the universities as well.

Crucial to the regime's legal authority to conduct its war against subversion, and the courts' acquiescence to the regime, was a bewildering array of states of emergency. As one of its first acts after seizing power, the junta declared a state of siege "in the degree of external or internal war." The state of siege was routinely renewed, in some form, every six months until 1978.[6] States of emergency, including the state of siege, had been provided for by the Chilean constitution of 1925, which the junta declared it would respect unless circumstances dictated otherwise. Indeed, just prior to the coup, congress denied Allende the authority to declare a state of siege in the midst of the transportation strike. The new military leaders, having declared congress in recess, granted themselves such authority. Thereafter the junta expanded and systematized emergency measures before finally incorporating them into a new constitution in 1980. Those measures gave Pinochet, as president of the junta, sweeping authority to declare a state of siege "when there is an internal disturbance provoked by rebellious or seditious forces already organized or being organized whether openly or underground."[7]

The self-conferred authority to promulgate laws by decree was a hallmark of the regime. Decree laws provided legal cover for the military regime's policies and actions, but such laws were arbitrary and the security forces, which reported directly to Pinochet, simply ignored them. Ex post facto laws subjected the militants of leftist parties to sanctions ranging from loss of employment to exile and execution for their advocacy of now suppressed ideologies. Laws granting the secret police sweeping authority to detain were promulgated, and there were dozens of secret laws.[8] War councils, established to try officials or sympathizers of the Popular Unity, arbitrarily applied wartime rather than peacetime provisions of the military code of justice. In what constituted a systematic miscarriage of justice, thousands were deprived of liberty and hundreds were stood before firing squads. Sometimes the condemnation of the war council was complete fiction. Military patrols indiscriminately killed Chileans who violated the dusk-to-dawn curfew that permitted the security forces to roam freely and to transport detainees to a series of clandestine interrogation centers. The fugitive law (*ley de fuga*) provided the pretext for what was tantamount to summary execution of prisoners who were alleged to have attempted escape.

The decree laws were vague on the judicial system, and omitted any reference whatsoever to the General Comptroller's Office. Decree Law No. 1 stated that "the powers of the judicial branch remain fully in effect," but ominously noted that the junta would "respect the Constitution and the laws of the Republic, to the extent the present situation allows." In fact the junta would marginalize the judicial system, with tremendous consequences for the rights of Chileans and the integrity of the institution. The General Comptroller's Office possessed what amounted to judicial review under the

1925 constitution in effect on the day of the coup. The junta did not dissolve this institution, but neither did it heed it. It sent laws to the comptroller to be duly noted and published in the public record, but its oversight functions were almost entirely ignored. The Constitutional Tribunal, another body provided for by the 1925 constitution, was eliminated with the Congress. It had existed to resolve constitutional controversies arising from the balance of executive and legislative authorities; there being no separate executive and legislative branches under military rule, there would be no controversies to resolve, thus no need for a body to resolve them.

The fact that the junta did not close the courts did not mean it would respect the rule of law, however. It was a calculated move. The military government had every expectation that judges would not exert their authority to hinder it. The public utterances of the chief justices of the high court over the years confirmed that expectation. The day after the coup the four members of the junta visited the court under an armed escort. The president of the Supreme Court of Justice, Enrique Urrutia Manzano, could not contain his enthusiasm. "A few days ago," Urrutia reminded those in attendance, "our concerns were, precisely, [President Allende's] refusal to acknowledge the authority of our resolutions, in such a determined and progressive manner that the day that the courts would disappear was viewed as not far off." And, without courts, he warned, "there is no justice." Thus the president of the high court exclaimed his "most intimate satisfaction" with the junta's pledge to respect the rulings of the court without subjecting them to prior "administrative" review.[9] Representatives of virtually every human rights organization that would meet with Urrutia or his successors, José María Eyzaguirre and Israel Bórquez, expressed shock and dismay over the magistrates' disregard and even disdain for human rights. Only when Rafael Retamal assumed the presidency of the high court in 1984 did the court begin to recover its voice.[10]

The common practice of Chilean judges, following the lead of the high court, was to accept the police and security forces at their word at a moment in the country's history when they should have scrutinized official claims with the utmost care. Judges routinely and uncritically rejected habeas corpus petitions on the basis of official denials that the person named in the action was in detention. This abetted the secret police, which by early 1974 began to "disappear" the regime's enemies. When the authorities did acknowledge the detention of an individual on whose behalf the action was brought, the judges simply accepted the security force's version of events and their claim that the detention was legal. Rarely did the courts act on the increasing number of complaints of torture. When evidence of abuses was too solid to ignore, judges could simply declare themselves incompetent to hear cases on the grounds that the legal provisions of the state of siege were controlling law. There were very few judges who dared act independently, according to a survey conducted by the news magazine *APSI* shortly before the presidential elections in 1989. Judges and attorneys consulted by *APSI* could agree on only nine.[11]

Jorge Correa, a noted legal scholar who served as the secretary for the presidential commission established in 1991 to investigate the regime's human rights violations, explained the situation tersely. The junta chose not to intervene in the Supreme Court, he observed, "because the armed forces needed legitimate collaborators." Thus, Correa lamented, "it was the Supreme Court, composed of justices appointed by democratic presidents, that made no effort to protect human rights during the worst years of the dictatorship." The reasons for this are complex, but, Correa argued, legal formalism and, ironically, a misplaced belief in judicial independence permitted judges "to comfort themselves while they ignored the government's abuse of human rights."[12]

The abdication of the magistrates made the predicament of prisoners truly desperate. Those swept up by the security forces entered a parallel universe where the rule of law was absent and the doctrine of national security held sway. Suspected subversives were subjected to a lawless process in which interrogators applied time-tested intelligence-gathering techniques. Essentially, the secret police interrogators were in the business of compelling self-incrimination by means of torture, and they wielded nearly absolute power over life or death. An intelligence officer's final judgment as to a leftist's level of ideological indoctrination, basic military instruction, or specialized guerrilla training, and even the supposed degree of future dangerousness, meant either release or disappearance.

The constitutional power claimed by the junta was the most critical and disturbing matter. The junta pledged to respect the 1925 constitution, with the proviso that circumstances would have to dictate the extent to which that would be prudent. Of course, the decree laws churned out by the junta inevitably clashed with the constitution. To remedy that problem the junta issued a decree law in December of 1974 declaring, in effect, that the regime's decrees had the force of constitutional amendments whenever they conflicted with provisions of the 1925 constitution. That was a great expedient, but one that left Chile, in the words of an astute observer, in a "juridical Wonderland."[13] Pinochet understood that, in order to accomplish the armed forces' historic mission, a new scheme of things was necessary. Accordingly, he named a commission to draft a new constitution only a month after the coup. The commission worked on the project for more than seven years before producing a draft that Pinochet reviewed, revised, and finally submitted for a plebiscite in 1980.

The militarization of the Chilean state made it possible for the armed forces' commander-in-chief to acquire unrivaled control over a government staffed by soldiers, and thus over the destiny of the country. One of the first acts of the junta was to select Pinochet as its president, initiating the process by which Pinochet consolidated his power as both commander-in-chief and chief executive. That process was substantially complete by July 1978, when Pinochet succeeded in ousting air force commander Gustavo Leigh from the junta and from the armed forces. Nothing like Pinochetismo occurred in the other Southern Cone countries. In Brazil, Argentina, and Uruguay collegial rule by the armed forces was the rule. Not only did the presidency of the junta rotate among the ranking generals and admirals, policy initiatives were debated and eventually approved by all senior officers. This created a particular dynamic, especially in Brazil, where the important matter of presidential succession caused internal frictions.

The four officers who comprised the Chilean junta had apparently intended the presidency of the emergency government to rotate. In his very first public remarks, on the evening of the coup, Pinochet had given assurances that he had no personal ambitions. The other members of the junta, however, did not have the foresight to stipulate that arrangement in writing. Pinochet, in those same remarks, mentioned only a gentlemen's agreement. This enabled Pinochet to become an irreplaceable *caudillo*.

Pinochet's emergence is attributable to a number of factors, the most important being his manipulation of Chile's deeply rooted legacy of presidentialism, and the hierarchy of command.[14] By June 1974 Pinochet had acquired additional trappings of presidentialism. A decree law issued at the end of June 1974 stipulated that "executive power is exercised by the president of the junta" and made Pinochet "Supreme Chief of the Nation," a title dating back to the period immediately after Chile's independence from Spain. Another decree law, issued in December of the same year, bestowed upon Pinochet the formal title of President of the Republic. The other members of the junta did not block the move.[15]

The consequences of this maneuvering were far-reaching. As a member of the junta, Pinochet possessed what amounted to veto power over all legislative and policy initiatives, because decree laws were required to be approved unanimously. Soon Pinochet's executive staff came to be the locus of policymaking, and the role of the junta was gradually diminished until Pinochet controlled nearly absolute executive power. The other members of the junta were initially given responsibility over specific policy areas. But after the middle of 1976 there was no longer public mention of the other junta members as overseers of policy.[16] Perceptively, Leigh argued that Pinochet not be allowed to retain the power to vote in the junta, in an effort to introduce a check on the executive's inordinate and growing power. He failed.

As armed forces commander, Pinochet controlled promotions, retirement, and post assignments.[17] Pinochet promoted an inordinate number of young officers to the rank of colonel and general. These men were far younger than he and very much beholden to him. Those officers Pinochet could not simply force into retirement he transferred to posts where they could be less influential. The ouster of Leigh in July 1978 was the most important and visible maneuver, but it was not the only one of consequence.

In July 1974 Pinochet moved General Oscar Bonilla from ministry of interior to ministry of defense. As interior minister Bonilla enjoyed some public visability. And Bonilla had several differences with Pinochet, and some concerns about the growing influence of younger, ruthless officers assigned to the security forces. The move effectively silenced him. (Bonilla died a year later in a helicopter crash.) By the end of the first year of the military regime, three officers who had participated extensively in the coup passed into retirement. Three years later, only one other officer who had been involved remained on active duty.[18] More ominously, lesser ranking officers, like Colonels Manuel Contreras and Pedro Espinoza, gained inordinate power because of their positions in the regime's new intelligence agency.

DINA

The Directorate for National Intelligence, DINA, was already functioning when the junta formally created it at the end of 1973. DINA began its formal existence as a department within the National Executive Secretariat for the Detained (SENDET), a bureau established to eliminate the immense logistical and public relations problems of the overcrowded detention sites.[19] As such, DINA was charged with establishing interrogation procedures, classifying prisoners, and coordinating intelligence functions. In fact, some of the men who later became DINA personnel had been interrogating and classifying the thousands of prisoners held in the National Stadium and other detention sites from the very beginning. But the DINA's mission was not just to interrogate leftists — it was to eliminate them.

The DINA became an independent agency on June 14, 1974. According to article two of the decree law creating it, as published in the *Diario oficial*, the DINA would be "a military body of a technical and professional nature under the direct command of the Junta," whose mission would be "to produce the intelligence needed for policy formulation and planning and for the adoption of those measures required for the protection of national security and the development of the country."[20] But the version appearing in the *Diario oficial*, containing eight articles, was abridged. The content of articles nine through eleven would be published in a special annex with limited distribution to those with a need to know. Those articles authorized the DINA to conduct searches and make arrests. Its true mission, however, was to commit murder.

The driving force behind the creation of this new intelligence agency was Lieutenant Colonel Manuel Contreras, who would direct the DINA until Pinochet was pressured to disband it and to transfer operations to another agency in 1977.[21] Contreras was a looming figure in the Pinochet dictatorship. Contreras completed his officer training at the end of 1948 and was assigned to the army's combat engineering division as a lieutenant. He rose quickly through the ranks, serving in a number of routine posts, before taking charge of Chile's combat engineers and sappers. In 1960 Contreras was accepted at the prestigious War Academy, where Pinochet served as assistant director and professor of strategy. It was apparently then that Contreras gained the future dictator's confidence. But now Contreras saw a future for himself in intelligence, a section that lagged far behind infantry, artillery, combat engineering, and even cavalry in terms of training and professionalism. Contreras made intelligence his vocation and even returned to the academy to teach the subject in 1966. The following year he traveled to Fort Benning, Georgia for advanced training. He completed his advanced studies on the eve of Salvador Allende's election and served a stint in the General Staff before being put in charge of studies at the Engineering School at the Tejas Verdes base, located at the mouth of the Maipo River on the Pacific. In December 1972, by then Major Manuel Contreras assumed overall command of an army engineering regiment based at Tejas Verdes. According to troops posted there, Contreras began converting the base into a concentration camp and interrogation center on September 9, 1973, the same day that Pinochet signed the coup declaration.

Contreras had no trouble convincing Pinochet of the need for a new intelligence agency to fight subversion. In the second week of November, Pinochet arranged for Contreras to brief senior officers of the armed forces and Carabineros on his plans for one.[22] There was formidable opposition to the idea. For one thing, there was potential for inter-service rivalries, which later surfaced. The branches of the armed force each had their own intelligence sections, known by their acronyms SIM (army), SIN (navy), SIFA (air force), and SICAR (Carabineros). Their commanders were understandably concerned about the potential loss of status and the diversion of resources. And many senior officers, some with normal intelligence duties, foresaw a Gestapo in-the-making. General Bonilla, the regime's interior and later defense minister, expressed concerns, as did General Sergio Arellano (whom Pinochet sent north in October in the company of future DINA officers, possibly to "dirty his hands"), and Colonel (later General) Ordlanier Mena, head of army intelligence.[23] In 1975 Mena, now a general officer, would confront Pinochet with evidence that Contreras was keeping surveillance files on army personnel, confirming earlier suspicions about the danger DINA posed to the army. Pinochet resolved the matter in Contreras's favor by retiring Mena and posting him to Panama as ambassador. The concerns that the DINA would become the Chilean Gestapo were well founded but irrelevant and perhaps somewhat naive. A secret state police was exactly what Pinochet and Contreras needed to extirpate Marxism from Chile.

The placement of the DINA within the new prison bureau may have been a compromise, but it brought Contreras's dream closer to realization. In the first week of December Contreras moved the headquarters of the new agency from temporary quarters to a permanent location at 90 Marcoleta

Street, near Santiago's Plaza Italia. Contreras was already recruiting operatives from the various services, and government agencies were processing DINA's requests for information. DINA acquired a number of facilities in the metropolitan area, places like Londres 38, José Domingo Cañas, and Villa Grimaldi, once an elegant estate. These sites, known by various code names, would become infamous places of torture and death.

In June 1974, with the campaign to extirpate Marxism from Chile in full swing, the junta granted the DINA the autonomy Contreras had coveted. To assuage the fears of more senior officers, the DINA was supposed to answer to the junta and its agents were to be drawn from each of the branches. The reality turned out to be quite different, however. The DINA was accountable not to the junta but to Pinochet. Eventually air force commander Leigh would pull his men from the agency, in part because they were assigned staff rather than command duties. Afterward Leigh was determined to steal the DINA's thunder, first by making an overture to the MIR at the very moment the DINA was about to destroy it, and then by forming a combined operations section (known as the Joint Command) within SIFA, apparently in contravention of an order from Pinochet.

The DINA was an organization that was purposefully shrouded in mystery, but some things are known about it.[24] Its agents were recruited from the existing intelligence sections of the armed forces and police, and from the plainclothes detectives (*Investigaciones*). Members were also drawn from the extremist, right wing Fatherland and Liberty organization. Its militants were ready recruits and especially eager to participate in the annihilation of the left. (The U.S. ambassador in 1973, Nathaniel Davis, recalled that Patria y Libertad militants painted a single-word warning — "Djakarta" — in prominent places around Santiago in the weeks leading up to the coup. The allusion to the Indonesian capital was ominous. Communists had been systematically massacred in Java.)[25] Estimates of the number of agents vary, but it is believed that at the time of its dissolution in 1977 DINA employed some 4,000 agents and an extensive network of informants and collaborators.[26] Moreover, the agency was at least partially funded by an elaborate series of export-import firms and other enterprises. This made Contreras a man to be reckoned with, and possibly a threat to Pinochet himself.

The DINA was organized much like any intelligence service charged with conducting clandestine operations in addition to gathering intelligence. It consisted of four departments, Administration, Logistics, Archives and Documentation, and Operations. The Operations Department was charged with purging the left.

Operations was itself divided into two sections, Internal and Foreign Operations. The Internal Operations were conducted by three Brigades, the most important being the Metropolitan Intelligence Brigade (BIM). The BIM was composed of Special Groups with folkloric code names, and each Special Group operated a number of five-man Action Teams out of different locations in the capital. Each Special Group had a deadly mission: Caupolicán was charged with destruction of the MIR; Tucapel the Socialist party; Purén the Communist party. Only the code names of Caupolicán's Action Teams are known with any certainty: Hawk I and II, Vampire, and Tucan.[27]

The Internal Operations section inflicted the most harm, but the actions of the Foreign Operations section received the most attention. The attention was unwelcome and ultimately led to the demise of the agency. Manuel Contreras did not content himself with being the master of Chilean intelligence or the mastermind of the campaign against the Chilean left. Contreras wanted to be at the center of the regional intelligence community and made numerous overtures to his counterparts. The idea was code-named Operation Condor and was to involve the creation of a sort of INTERPOL for the purpose of tracking subversives. It is certain that the regional intelligence agencies shared information and arranged for the repatriation of known leftists who were arrested in neighboring countries.[28] Contreras also solicited the collaboration of anti-communist and neo-fascist organizations in Europe and North America.[29] But Contreras over-reached and miscalculated. A series of assassinations only drew greater attention to the dictatorship already on trial in the court of world opinion. The assassination of former commander-in-chief Carlos Prats (Pinochet's immediate predecessor) and his wife in Buenos Aires in 1974; the wounding of Christian Democrat leader Bernardo Leighton and his wife in Rome in 1975; and, perhaps especially, the assassination of Orlando Letelier and North American Ronnie Moffitt on Embassy Row in Washington in 1976 — these operations made DINA a well-known acronym.

Contreras and his chief lieutenant Pedro Espinoza would be indicted by a U.S. federal grand jury for having ordered the assassination of Orlando Letelier. The Chilean courts twice refused to extradite Contreras, who secretly transferred files out of the country to protect himself once he was forced from power. In the end, Pinochet would have to sacrifice the DINA and Contreras, under pressure from the international community and even from the armed forces.[30] Eventually the Chilean courts would be able to judge Contreras, but it would not be easy. That is a story that would play out years into Chile's democratic transition.

The Quality of Mercy

The military's pronunciamento of September 11 set in motion a destructive process that would obliterate thousands of Chileans over the next seventeen years. But the repression also moved many Chileans to manifest, at considerable personal and professional risk, that most admirable quality to which Cardinal Silva had appealed soon after the coup — mercy.

One of the truly remarkable legacies of Chile's dirty war was the emergence of one of Latin America's — and perhaps the world's — most renowned and capable human rights movements. The organizations that comprised the movement would be as diverse as their members were courageous. Members of the religious community, the families of the regime's victims, and figures from the centrist political parties would all become active in the campaign to counteract and ultimately end the repression. These organizations would adopt different but complementary approaches and initiate a range of programs of humanitarian action and human rights activism. They would provide direct material, medical, and psychological assistance to refugees, victims, and their families, and they would document, denounce, and publicize violations. In the process they would prompt international organizations to take up the cause of human rights in Chile and would compile a record of human rights violations that would be corroborated and authenticated by a presidential commission in 1991. By the time the regime finally ceded power in 1990, the movement had acquired invaluable institutional memory and political savvy and had produced a number of internationally renowned leaders in the cause of human rights, and a generation of committed and competent human rights defenders.

New human rights organizations emerged at nearly every critical juncture in the evolution of the regime or phase of the repression. The first was the Committee for Cooperation for Peace in Chile, which appeared at the end of 1973; in fact, the men and women who comprised the Committee for Peace began to act within days of the September coup. Working closely with the International Committee of the Red Cross and the UN High Commissioner for Refugees, the committee's intervention saved countless lives, especially in the first weeks of the military government. The Committee for Peace was replaced in 1975 by two separate organizations, the celebrated Vicariate of Solidarity and the equally effective Foundation for Social Assistance of the Christian Churches (FASIC). Next to emerge, out of necessity, were the Association of Families of the Detained-Disappeared and the Association of the Families of the Executed for Political Reasons. Both appeared in 1974. These were followed by the Chilean Human Rights Commission (1978), the Commission for the Rights of the People (1980), the National Commission Against Torture (1982), the Sebastian Acevedo Movement Against Torture (1983), and other lesser known entities. By 1985 some fifteen human rights groups were active in Chile.[31]

Chile's religious leaders initially discounted anecdotal evidence that the military was committing atrocities in the immediate aftermath of the coup. The sight of dozens of bloated bodies on the banks of the Mapocho River in the capital and the murder of Father Joan Alsina, a Spaniard, aboard a naval vessel led to their conversion.[32]

Chile's spiritual leaders awoke to a calamity. Thousands of Chileans and foreign nationals were being detained. Hundreds were executed. Many others sought refuge in foreign embassies. The religious leaders' instinct was to show mercy, but the tasks were enormous: locate detained persons, provide legal defense when release could not be obtained, arrange for safe passage out of the country and into exile, recover the bodies, find the disappeared, provide material assistance to the persecuted who were dismissed from their jobs. It would be an immense undertaking. After a rapid assessment of the emergency, the heads of the various denominations formed two ad hoc committees, one to take up the cases of the many hundreds of foreign nationals who had been attracted to Chile by Allende's experiment, the other for the thousands of Chileans at grave risk in this atmosphere of conquest.

This was the origin of the Committee for Cooperation for Peace in Chile, known commonly as the Committee for Peace, formally established in October 1973. Bishop Fernando Ariztía, the Auxiliary Bishop of Santiago, was instrumental in setting up the committee, with the firm backing of Cardinal Silva. Joining him in the effort was Lutheran Bishop Helmut Frenz, who provided initial financing for the committee on behalf of the World Council of Churches.[33] The committee was ecumenical, being comprised of the Catholic, Lutheran, and Methodist denominations, the Rabbinical Council of Chile, and the World Council of Churches. The churches, especially the Catholic Church, had opposed Allende but could not condone the barbarity that followed Allende's ouster. A number of renowned human rights activists joined this important effort, including José Zalaquett and Hernán Montealegre, to name just two of the most prominent Chileans who would work tirelessly at great risk until the regime ceded power some seventeen and a half years later.

Over the next two years, until the end of 1975, the Committee for Peace labored to counteract the repression the regime was practicing with increasing sophistication and efficiency. Pinochet was angry with the churches' response, but did not attempt a frontal assault on religious institutions, especially the Roman Catholic Church. This set his regime apart from the military clique in El Salvador, which a decade later targeted priests, nuns, religious, and even archbishops with almost no regard for public outrage. But Pinochet applied behind-the-scenes pressures. The dictator's demands that the committee be dissolved increased beginning in mid-May 1975. On May 15 a Mexican newspaper printed excerpts of a leaked internal document of the committee.[34] The publication of portions of the document, which depicted the violations occurring in Chile, caused an uproar. Regime supporters, led by Chile's leading daily *El Mercurio*, called for the committee's dissolution. Then, in November, the DINA tracked down the surviving senior leaders of the Movement of the Revolutionary Left on a farm outside the capital. In the ensuing firefight, one MIRista was killed and several others were wounded but managed to escape. The extremists made their way to a church where their wounds were treated; eventually, a priest affiliated with the Committee for Peace helped them flee the country. Finally, Pinochet had his chance to be rid of the meddlesome committee.

At the end of 1975 Pinochet wrote Cardinal Raúl Silva to suggest that he dissolve the committee. The Catholic cardinal, who had opposed Allende's attempt to reform the education system but who had also brokered negotiations in a attempt to stave off disaster, responded by warning Pinochet that "the measure recommended will probably result, both in Chile and above all abroad, in damage greater than that which it seeks to avoid."[35] It was an insightful prediction. The Committee for Peace was closed, but its work was not ended. Undeterred by the general, Cardinal Silva created the Vicaría de la Solidaridad and brought it under the authority — and protection — of the Roman Catholic Church. As if to underscore the point, Silva provided the Vicariate with facilities adjacent to the Catholic cathedral overlooking Santiago's Plaza de Armas and appointed Cristián Precht, the general secretary of the Committee for Peace, vicar of the new human rights organization.

The Vicariate began its work in January 1976 and, like its predecessor, responded to the human rights calamity with a comprehensive program of legal assistance and humanitarian aid. Priority was placed on legal defense. The Vicariate provided legal defense and tirelessly filed habeas corpus actions on behalf of family members. The indifference and sometimes hostility of the courts rendered effective defense nearly impossible, especially in the dictatorship's first decade. Nevertheless, legal action had some effect, if only to force the regime to respond. "One reason for the Vicaría's emphasis on legal response," Americas Watch reported in 1987, "is that the regime itself partakes of Chile's legalistic traditions."[36] The work was invaluable.

The Vicaría's work of documentation and analysis has not only served as an archival history of repression in Chile but has also provided a model for reliable, conservative methodology. The program of analysis records all cases undertaken by the Vicaría; these cases are the source of its published statistics on repression. The reports produced by the analysis program are an essential reference for human rights monitors in Chile and abroad and for such specialists as the UN Special Rapporteur on the Situation of Human Rights in Chile.[37]

Jaime Esponda, who headed the Vicariate's National Coordination section within its Legal Department before becoming the executive secretary of the Chilean chapter of Amnesty International, explained the historical and moral value of this undertaking. "The Vicariate intends to contribute to the full consolidation of human rights in the Chile of the future," he explained, "by placing at the disposal of the national community the documentary record of testimonies which, when they become known to future generations, should help to prevent us from ever again suffering so much pain and injustice."[38]

To that end, the Vicariate published a semi-monthly bulletin, *Solidaridad*, and a monthly report based on the habeas corpus and *amparo* actions in which it was engaged. The information gathered by the Vicariate also served as the basis for the monthly report the Chilean Human Rights Commission began producing in 1983. Non-Chilean human rights organizations, in turn, routinely incorporated the information contained in the Chilean Human Rights Commission's reports. Americas Watch and the International League for Human Rights published frequent reports based almost entirely on information from the Chilean organizations. Vicariate of Solidarity statistics and individual case histories found their way into Amnesty International country reports as well. The Vicariate also conducted a program of medical assistance. Its medical staff provided onsite emergency medical assistance to torture victims, some of whom were deposited in front of the cathedral by the security forces when they had finished interrogating them.[39]

The work of the Vicariate of Solidarity was exemplary. Unfortunately, Cardinal Juan Francisco Fresno, who had replaced Cardinal Silva in 1982, replaced the church's human rights office with a Vicariate for Social Concern within a year of Chile's democratic transition. But before the Vicariate discontinued its work it would announce the discovery of more than one hundred bodies in the capital's General Cemetery.

Three months after Cardinal Silva created the Vicariate for Solidarity, Lutheran Bishop Helmut Frenz followed his lead and formed the Foundation for Social Assistance of the Christian Churches (FASIC).[40] FASIC continued the work of the ad hoc committees established to attend to the needs of Chilean and foreign detainees in the large detention sites like the National Stadium, and of those seeking asylum in foreign embassies and attempting to leave the country. The Lutheran bishop was prompted by the promulgation of a decree law intended to empty the large detention sites like the National Stadium of political prisoners. FASIC's lawyers understood that the law was a public relations gesture intended to relieve the military government of a serious public relations problem: after all, the detention sites were concentration camps and conjured up exactly those images the phrase implies. Sensing that the regime's dilemma was an opportunity to win the freedom — and perhaps save the lives — of a great many detainees, FASIC's legal staff availed itself of the law to secure safe-conduct documents for prisoners.

FASIC's work, which was supported by the United Nations High Commissioner on Refugees, thus complemented that of the Vicariate of Solidarity. The two organizations' priorities were inverse, however. The Vicariate's contributions in the broad area of social work, as in its medical assistance program, were substantial, but the Catholic Church office gave priority to legal action before the courts. FASIC went to the defense of political prisoners as well, but its humanitarian work was not centered on legal defense per se. Indeed, the legal approach taken by the Vicariate had certain drawbacks. FASIC's work, essentially, had to do with refugees, and refugees are best taken to refuge by not confronting those from whom they are fleeing. Thus, in one chronicler's apt phrase, FASIC's struggle was purposefully silent.[41]

What most distinguished FASIC's silent struggle was psychological treatment for the severely traumatized victims of the repression. The program was initiated in 1977. Within seven years, the foundation's team of psychologists had attended to more than 4000 Chileans and was pioneering diagnostic and treatment techniques for victims of torture, for those who had suffered the death or disappearance of a loved one, and eventually for returning exiles. Psychologists like Elizabeth Lira (who eventually left FASIC to continue this pioneering work with the Latin American Institute for Mental Health and Human Rights, ILAS) were able to document the profound psychological harm caused by the sustained and deliberately created climate of fear. Through their clinical work Lira and her colleagues reached a conclusion that places state terrorism in its proper perspective: "the fear and paralysis that result from experiencing repression," they observed, "can be described as a political reality with personal consequences."[42]

After 1986 FASIC also began to produce its own trimestral bulletin, as well as a series of publications designed to put returning exiles back in touch with the reality of the country from which they had fled or been expelled. FASIC continues to operate from its small complex of buildings several blocks from the Moneda palace.

The religious community's response to the emergency was not the only one. Families were directly affected by the repression, and they began to organize under the protective gaze of the Catholic Church. Many Chileans had been sentenced to death by war councils; their survivors formed themselves into the Association of Families of Those Executed for Political Reasons. The loved ones of the disappeared formed the Association of Families of the Detained-Disappeared. The involvement of the families was understandable, but it was also revolutionary. Because the majority of political prisoners, disappeared, and executed were men, their survivors were most often mothers, grandmothers, and spouses.[43] Their protests in front of public buildings caught the carabineros off guard and ill-prepared: the police found it difficult to spray women bearing placards with water cannons to prevent them from demanding to know "¿Donde estan?"

The struggle of the Association of the Families of the Detained-Disappeared has continued after Chile's transition to democracy in 1990. Thousands of Chileans were disappeared by the security forces, and their remains have yet to be discovered in most cases. So the association, led by Sola Sierra, has been relentless in its demands that the truth about the fate and whereabouts of the disappeared be fully disclosed. The report of the presidential truth commission, published in 1991, did not satisfy the association's members, whose need to recover the truth is personal rather than political.

The leaders of Chile's centrist political parties were stunned by the widespread arrests, torture, and execution of Chileans. While leftists bore the brunt of the repression, their counterparts in the Christian Democratic and Radical parties had to confront the fact that the coup some of their leaders had welcomed had brought a nightmare. Many gave their services to the ad hoc committees that later became the Committee for Peace and the Vicariate for Solidarity. But at the end of 1978 a number of distinguished lawyers decided that it was necessary to form an independent, secular organization, the Chilean Human Rights Commission. Pinochet had completed his fifth year, and there was no end in sight to the regime. To the contrary, after the United Nations passed a resolution in December 1977 condemning human rights violations in Chile, Pinochet convoked a plebiscite on his continued rule. After winning it, the dictator announced an amnesty of human rights violations and ousted an outspoken critic from the junta. But Pinochet also attempted to mollify his critics. He closed the Directorate of National Intelligence, reduced the state of siege to a state of emergency, and permitted Jaime Castillo to return from exile after two years. Castillo returned and promptly formed the Chilean Human Rights Commission. Joining Castillo on the executive secretariat of the commission were some of Chile's most prominent constitutional scholars, including Máximo Pacheco, who would eventually become a judge on the Inter-American Court on Human Rights, and Andrés Aylwin, brother of the future president.

By the time democratic elections were permitted in December 1989, the Chilean Human Rights Commission had some 3500 members and nearly 200 offices throughout the country. Its Legal, Study, and Education Departments were preparing monthly and annual bulletins on the human rights situation, as well as a host of pamphlets and monographs on a range of human rights issues. The Chilean Human Rights Commission enjoys a stature surpassed only by the Vicariate of Solidarity. The archbishop's decision to close the Catholic Church's human rights office makes the commission all the more important. The commission is, in effect, the human rights ombudsman in democratic Chile.[44]

Three lesser known but indomitable organizations are the Commission for the Rights of the People (CODEPU), formed in 1980, the National Commission Against Torture, and the Sebastian Acevedo Movement Against Torture, formed in 1982 and 1983 respectively. The appearance of all three signaled the revival of civil society after nearly a decade of inactivity necessitated by state terrorism. The revival of civil society, in turn, marked the beginning of a concerted campaign to restore democracy in Chile. CODEPU was formed in reaction to the imposition of Pinochet's "Constitution of Liberty" in 1980. Its members fully understood that the political and legal order codified by the document did not augur well for democracy. In particular, the notion of an authoritarian democracy cleansed of the vices that once plagued Chile was repugnant to CODEPU's founders, who represented the very political tendencies the constitution attempted to ban. Among those serving on the executive council of the new commission was Fabiola Letelier, sister of Orlando Letelier, a person considered radical by the military government, but perhaps too prominent to assassinate. Although CODEPU operates a legal defense program, its most important activities are in the area of promotion and human rights education, especially in rural areas and among poor shanty-town dwellers.[45] This effort to empower the poor smacked of the leftist agitation the regime wanted to get rid of in Chile; thus CODEPU's activities were as much political resistance as human rights activism. After the democratic transition CODEPU made an issue of the many political prisoners languishing in prison for crimes allegedly committed during the dictatorship. It was a delicate matter for the democratic government, as was that of the disappeared. Pinochet had promulgated a sweeping amnesty in 1978, but a 1984 anti-terrorism law provided for severe sanctions for those engaged in resistance activities in the final decade of Pinochet's rule. CODEPU demanded pardon for them, since justice for former officials was out of reach. The spectacle of the *presos políticos* would bedevil the Aylwin government during its first two years in office, especially after prisoners in Santiago's central jail staged two long hunger strikes. CODEPU and other human rights nongovernmental organizations (NGOs) made certain that the issue of the *presos políticos* did not disappear.

The National Commission Against Torture came into existence in 1982, amid a renewed wave of complaints about torture and at a moment when national days of protest were about to become frequent occurrences. The commission's president, Dr. Pedro Castillo Yáñez, a physician, had offered medical assistance to torture victims from the beginning of the dictatorship and suffered the professional consequences. Because of his activities, in 1975 he was dismissed from his position at the University of Chile, where he chaired its Department of Surgery. Three years after he helped form the National Commission, Castillo was sentenced to a brief period of internal exile, or "relegation" as Chilean authorities termed it.[46] Under Castillo's direction the National Commission Against Torture undertook a comprehensive study of the dozens of torture techniques employed in Chile, and its booklet, *Así se tortura en Chile*, documents and categorizes the many forms of physical and mental abuse inflicted by agents of the dictatorship.[47] With this information the Commission Against Torture engaged in public campaigns to expose and denounce the practice. Moreover, Pedro Castillo and like-minded colleagues set out to take over leadership positions on the national council of the Chilean Medical Association in order to tighten and enforce the association's code of ethics. The participation of physicians in torture was an especially egregious lapse of professional responsibility, and the National Commission Against Torture wanted to see sanctions applied to offending medical practitioners.

The kindred Movement Against Torture was forming even before Sebastian Acevedo, a father from Concepción, immolated himself on the steps of the Catholic cathedral there in 1983. He was protesting the abduction of his two children and official denials of knowledge of their whereabouts. Incommunicado detention, everyone knew, meant torture, and the father was tormented by the idea to the point of desperation. (Both children were subsequently released.) The desperate act so dramatized the sentiments of the members of the new movement that it adopted the name of Sebastian Acevedo.

Protesting the practice of torture was the principal objective of the Sebastian Acevedo Movement Against Torture. And it was a genuine movement: its members were determined not to erect an elaborate organizational structure with an executive council, departments and sections, and the rest. The Vicariate for Solidarity was doing its important work, the Chilean Human Rights Commission was now functioning, CODEPU and the National Commission Against Torture had recently appeared on the scene: there was no reason to reinvent the wheel. The Sebastian Acevedo Movement Against Torture would make its mark in another way.

The Sebastian Acevedo Movement turned protest into a powerful art form. Members of the Movement would converge unexpectedly in a public place or in front of a known detention center, like the notorious one at 1470 Borgoño Street in Santiago, to denounce torture. They would unfurl banners, sing songs, chant choruses, and sometimes perform one-act plays of street theater, fully cognizant that carabineros armed with truncheons would descend on them to break up the protests and arrest the protesters. But that was the genius of the art form. When startled Chileans going about their daily business witnessed carabineros beating peaceful protesters, perhaps the unknowing and unbelieving public would begin to believe that "in Chile there is torture."[48] The Movement found an ally in Judge René García Villegas, one of the few magistrates who dared investigate charges of torture within his jurisdiction. The Movement awarded García its human rights award in 1989. García accepted the award and was forced from the bench for inappropriate participation in political activity—on the very eve of the democratic transition.

The regime was confronted with a serious challenge in the human rights movement, especially insofar as the Movement enjoyed the protection of the Catholic Church. Unlike security forces in Central America, Pinochet's secret police, mindful of the prestige of the church, did not murder human rights defenders. Instead, the regime was forced to attempt to discredit human rights organizations and to harass and deport human rights defenders. José Zalaquett, a cofounder of the Committee for Peace and one of the country's leading human rights lawyers, was forced into exile in 1975. This was the time of the omnipotent DINA, whose decimation of the MIR was now complete and whose attack on the Communist party just underway. The regime had no need for human rights defenders. Zalaquett fought back the best way he knew. In exile Zalaquett became chair of the International Executive Committee of Amnesty International. Later he would be named to the presidential commission created to produce an official report of the violations committed in Chile.

Jaime Castillo and Eugenio Velasco were abducted by the DINA in August 1976, driven to the airport, and placed on a plane for exile. They had had the audacity to sign their names to a carefully documented letter denouncing human rights abuses before the Organization of American States, which conducted its regular session in Santiago that year. Castillo was permitted to reenter Chile in April 1978, shortly after Pinochet won his plebiscite denouncing United Nations interference in Chile's affairs. It was then that Castillo formed the Chilean Human Rights Commission. (He was exiled again in August 1982, one week after U.S. Ambassador to the United Nations Jeane Kirkpatrick refused to meet with him.)[49] Like Zalaquett, Castillo would later be named to the presidential commission formed to investigate the abuses committed under Pinochet.

Hernán Montealegre, an attorney for the Committee for Peace, defended political prisoners until 1976. Among those he defended, against overwhelming odds, were a number of MIRistas, standing trial before a hastily convened war council in Temuco. By 1976 the authorities had had enough of his activism and imprisoned him for six months, during which time he was tortured.[50] Eventually Montealegre became associated with the Academy of Christian Humanism, which the Catholic Church established, in part, to provide an outlet for academicians dismissed from their academic posts by the military government. Montealegre moved on to the Inter-American Institute for Human Rights, where he could work in the safety of San José, Costa Rica. There he produced a massive volume on the very concept of national security that guided the Southern Cone military regimes, and resulted in so many grave human rights violations. Those regimes, he correctly observed, attempted to justify their security measures by claiming threats to the security of the state. But, he stressed, "by its direct effects, the violation of human rights attacks the security of one of the constituent elements of the state, that is, its inhabitants."[51] The point was lost on the regimes he was denouncing.

The staff of CODEPU suffered the most serious harassment, undoubtedly because of the leftist orientation of the organization. The secret police raided CODEPU's office several times, destroying files, breaking office equipment and furniture, and physically abusing the staff. But these tactics failed to intimidate CODEPU's members. The organization's principled commitment to human rights and a return to democracy would not be broken.

This dynamic human rights movement would be Pinochet's principal adversary for the duration of his authoritarian rule. A synergy developed between Chilean NGOs and international human rights groups and humanitarian organizations such as the International Committee of the Red Cross, Amnesty International, the International Commission of Jurists, and Americas Watch (now Human Rights Watch/Americas). These international human rights organizations came to depend on accurate and timely information from Chilean NGOs to prepare their influential reports, just as the Chilean NGOs counted on these prominent international organizations, working in a nonthreatening environment, to report the truth to the international community. Through their diligence these NGOs activated almost dormant inter-governmental organizations, the Inter-American Human Rights Commission of the Organization of American States and the U.N. Human Rights Commission. Information generated by the NGOs, and conveyed to the OAS and UN, led to a number of critical and even condemnatory resolutions passed by these official bodies.

The effectiveness of these nonbinding resolutions can probably never be ascertained, but they should not be undervalued. At certain junctures they appeared to have no effect whatsoever on the conduct of the regime's security forces. However, the dissolution of the DINA in August 1977 was arguably the result of the intense pressure from the international community. What is more certain is that the direct humanitarian action saved countless lives, and the human rights activism established an irrefutable record of the regime's crimes. At the same time, the concerted efforts of the human rights NGOs and the UN and OAS Human Rights Commissions was precedent-setting. The Chilean dictatorship and its counterparts in the Southern Cone, ironically, activated the dormant system of protections with implications that extend beyond Chile's tragic human rights calamity.

Chapter 4
A War of Extermination

It wasn't war, it was extermination.

— Sola Sierra, President,
Association of Families of the Detained-Disappeared

The MIR Disappears

Only a few months before the coup a brash Miguel Enríquez issued a warning on which he could not make good:

The levels of activity, organization, consciousness and readiness to fight that the working class have achieved are immense. The working class is today a constituted army, determined to fight for its interests and to resist the onslaught of the reactionaries. The working class and the people from the factories and the country estates, the neighborhood commands and the peasant councils, have already served notice to their political leaders that the struggle has left the aisles and the parliament and that they will not permit reversals or concessions. It is here and now that those in the vanguard, the leaders and the parties will be submitted to the test of fire.[1]

In fact, the army of the working class was virtually nonexistent, and it did not stand up well to the test of fire. The MIR's most militant organizations, the Revolutionary Workers Front (MIR-FTR) and the Movement of Revolutionary Shanty-Town Dwellers (MIR-MPR), were barely able to sustain symbolic acts of resistance on September 11; the Revolutionary Campesino Movement (MIR-MCR) suffered savage losses in the Valdivia and Osorno; and General Arellano's delegation had executed scores of MIRistas during its deadly rampage in the north in October. "Our response was not what had been expected," the hunted national leadership admitted in an assessment of the strategic situation circulated in December, but "our assessment is that we did everything that the objective conditions permitted." There were any number of reasons for the inability to put up effective resistance, including the absence of a unified command, Allende's decision to remain in the Moneda instead of removing himself to one of the contested industrial areas, the difficulty of transporting and distributing arms, and even the weariness of the militant workers who had watched as the socialist president made concession after concession to his enemies. The workers' lack of experience in combat was a major factor on the eleventh, but the members of the political commission were determined to emphasize the positive. "At the same time, that being so, today we can count on an appreciable contingent of 'veterans' who will be fundamental in the future."[2]

This was misplaced optimism, because the future would be bleak. Enríquez, the MIR secretary general, would produce several more manifestos, but this was about all the MIR could manage: its war on the military government was mostly a war of words. The MIR suffered appalling casualties in the aftermath of the coup, without inflicting any on the military. Eighty-seven MIR militants were known to have been killed by the end of December 1973, a period of three and a half months. The situation deteriorated after that. The MIR would suffer a total of 235 confirmed deaths by August 1977. Virtually the entire political commission, and much of the central committee, were disappeared. Then the foot soldiers of its supposed central force were sought out and killed. Few MIRistas were killed in firefights, fewer still in firefights initiated by MIRistas. The vast majority of them were abducted, taken to one of a series of detention sites, tortured, murdered, and disappeared.

Military intelligence had been preoccupied with the MIR, and moved decisively against it after the coup. The young radicals who joined the Movement had boasted of stockpiling arms and training combatants, and the military regime had every reason to be concerned about the formation of an irregular army.[3] As army chief of staff, Pinochet had in January 1972 ordered a review of the military's internal security plan, and then ordered that the plan be revamped to counter the threat of the MIR.[4] Now that the military had seized power, the MIR became an even more menacing adversary, at least in theory. For one thing, the MIR became the most credible force on the left. The shrill and provocative rhetoric of the ultra-left Movement threatened to undermine Allende's program, and it strayed from the canons of orthodox Marxism. But the coup d'état vindicated the MIR, whose original declaration of principles denounced the notion of a peaceful route to power. The moment to take up arms had come, and only the MIR was in a position, ideologically if not militarily, to lead the fight. (As the siege of the Moneda reached its climax, Allende is reported to have told his daughter Beatriz to pass a message on to Miguel Enríquez to the effect that, if there was to be a workers' revolution in Chile, the MIR secretary general would have to lead it.)[5] The MIR went underground rather than into exile, and began making overtures to the armed formations of the Socialist and Communist parties, and even the Christian Democrats, for an anti-fascist front directed by the MIR. Having failed to stave off the coup, the left now had to prevent the consolidation, in its jargon, of the "gorilla dictatorship."

The MIR's years of scheming also gave the military regime a pretext for its state of siege and its dirty war. If the MIR's boasts and the military's intelligence estimates were valid, hundreds of weapons caches were hidden and thousands of hardened cadres were hiding in Chile. And the MIR's compartmentalized structure and system of safe-houses meant that defeating it would not be easy. Pinochet found the existence of the MIR to be the most convincing argument for an entirely new intelligence service with unrestricted operational capabilities. The MIR and the DINA, in effect, existed in a destructive symbiosis. As the junta completed the initial phase of the war against Marxism, roughly in December, it defined a new strategic objective: the destruction of the political commission and central committee of the clandestine MIR. Once that mission was accomplished, killing off the MIR's rank and file militants would be relatively easy.

Believing that the mantle of Allende had been passed on to the MIR, the movement's political commission made the fateful decision to remain in the country to organize resistance from within. This despite the fact that five of the "ten most wanted" in Chile were senior MIRistas: Miguel Enríquez, Bautista Van Schowen, and Andrés Pascal Allende of the political commission, and Alejandro Villalobos Díaz and Víctor Toro, both directors of the MIR-MPR.[6] As a practical matter, the decision meant that these men had to remain in close contact to assess the situation and work out a resistance strategy. The leaders of the MIR were living dangerously.

Even before the DINA became fully operational, the air force's intelligence service, SIFA, was relentlessly pursuing these revolutionaries. It was air force general Gustavo Leigh who had declared war on Marxism, and it was his officers who would score the first victories against the MIR. Leigh had his own reasons to be concerned about the MIR: there was substantial evidence that the MIR had made contact with senior air force officers, possibly as part of a scheme to infiltrate the service. Now Leigh was out to eliminate the threat. The task fell to Edgar Ceballos Jones, chief of the "reaction teams" set up within SIFA's operations section. Ceballos proved to be a cunning adversary of the MIR and inflicted the first of a series of blows on the revolutionary Movement. Then he attempted to negotiate a truce with it.

Miguel Enríquez and Juan Bautista Van Schowen had been friends for a decade, since their days together at the University of Concepción. As the principal theoreticians of the revolutionary left they were close collaborators. Now their collaboration put them at grave risk. In the weeks since the coup they and other members of the political commission were hard at work drafting a lengthy communiqué, "The Tactic of the MIR at the Present Moment," disseminated in December. This would be the last time Enríquez and Van Schowen would collaborate. On December 13 they met for the last time. After a lengthy working session, Van Schowen left, en route to a safe-house. What happened next is unclear. Van Schowen and another man, Patricio Munita Castillo, made their way to the Capuchin church in Santiago in search of asylum. Intelligence agents followed them there. In the early morning hours the agents surprised and overpowered the men.

The abduction of Bautista Van Schowen was a serious blow to the MIR and the beginning of the rivalry between the SIFA and Manuel Contreras's DINA. It appears that personnel from both agencies participated in the operation, but the DINA took custody of the MIR leader, to the great consternation of the SIFA.[7] Bautista Van Schowen's trial by ordeal then began.

What ultimately became of Juan Bautista Van Schowen is a mystery. Munita was executed almost immediately; his body was discovered the following day and secretly interred in Lot 29 of the General Cemetery. Bautista Van Schowen disappeared, but the military authorities handled his disappearance badly. As late as August 1974 both the press and the interior ministry reported that he had been apprehended on December 13, that he was in custody at an undisclosed location, and that formal charges against him were pending. This was an incredible blunder. If the authorities had the MIR leader in custody, they would have to present him at some time. But the DINA never intended someone as dangerous as Bautista Van Schowen ever to see the light of day. The military government had to retract the statement. The interior ministry later announced that the police had arrested Bautista Van Schowen's brother, not the senior MIRista. As to Juan Bautista Van Schowen, the new information was that the physician-turned-subversive had actually managed to escape to Cuba on February 2.[8]

In its first report on the human rights situation in Chile, Amnesty International claimed to have evidence that the thirty-one-year-old physician was shuttled between different clandestine interrogation centers and subjected to severe torture. He was last seen in critical condition in a military hospital in the capital sometime in February.[9] That would be the pattern thereafter. Senior MIRistas were held and tortured, and almost never killed immediately unless they died resisting capture. Keeping prisoners alive as long as they were useful (and no longer) made good sense. Chilean intelligence was not about to commit the same clumsy error their Bolivian counterparts had committed in 1967 when they executed Che Guevara. As to the mystery of what became of Bautista Van Schowen, the military government's prevarication may have contained an element of truth: February 2, the date Bautista Van Schowen is alleged to have escaped to Cuba, could well be the date of his death.

The loss of Van Schowen was as much personal as tactical for Enríquez, but the MIR secretary general persevered. The operational concept that had been worked out by the political commission in December revolved around a Movement of Popular Resistance. The MIR's task became to organize resistance committees to set the movement in motion. Enríquez communicated secretly with the leadership of the parties of the deposed Popular Unity and even the Christian Democrats, inviting them to coordinate resistance activities as part of a Political Front of Resistance.[10] The idea was preposterous under the circumstances. The harsh reality was that the intelligence services were arresting, interrogating, and disappearing MIRistas at such an expeditious rate that the MIR could not long survive, much less function.

Meanwhile, air force intelligence intensified its search. By June 1974, just as the rival DINA was preparing for full-scale operations, the SIFA had three senior leaders, Roberto Moreno, Arturo Villavela, and Víctor Toro, and at least five other members of the central committee, in custody at the Air War Academy (AGA). These were crushing blows, as Enríquez acknowledged in a lengthy document prepared by the political commission for distribution to all MIR cells through the central committee.[11] But the ever confident Enríquez attempted to salvage a hopeless situation by instructing MIRistas to adopt measures to correct unconscionable lapses of security. Enríquez found himself discounting rumors about collaborators and explaining to the command structure that the air force was subjecting the MIR to a clever psychological operation to disrupt it and sow dissension in the ranks.

By Enríquez's own account the imprisoned MIRistas were victims of their own carelessness. Roberto Moreno, a member of the political commission, was arrested on the night of March 27. His arrest led in turn to the arrest two days later of Arturo Villavela, a member of the central committee. The men were to have exchanged safe-houses.[12] But they had failed to follow security procedures, and their failures (which included leaving written notations containing information about other cadres) enabled the SIFA to arrest five other members of the central committee. The security of three other members of the central committee was compromised, but they managed to elude capture for the time being. That was not the worst of it. The air force then proceeded to capture Víctor Toro in an independent operation in mid-April. Toro had held his position on the MIR's central committee for some time and was the director of the MIR-MPR in the central region which included Santiago. He was one of Chile's most wanted subversives. The army had raided several factories in search of him in the days following the coup, but he had remained at large. Even a distinguished leader such as Víctor Toro, Enríquez wrote the other members of the central committee, lacked the necessary experience to put up with the enormous rigors of clandestine life. It was shocking to the leadership of the revolutionary organization that the most basic security measures were being ignored at all levels. The simplest precautions — posting visible warning signals in safe-houses, frequent changes of rendezvous points, destruction of written materials, and the like — were being ignored. As a result MIRistas were walking into traps.

In the wake of this wave of arrests, Enríquez gave strict instructions for new security measures and outlined sanctions in case of noncompliance. Regional directors were forbidden to travel to Santiago, so information had to be conveyed through intermediaries. There was to be no horizontal contact among the MIR's organizations and regional directorates. No two national directors were to circulate together unnecessarily (perhaps it had been necessary for Enríquez and Van Schowen to meet to draft the December document, but that sort of contact was among "the most flagrant errors committed in the cases of the most recent arrests"). Members of the political commission and central committee were to surround themselves with the most experienced cadres for security, even if that deprived middle and base level cells of effective operatives. And Enríquez was beginning to rethink his position on exile. In April he sent his brother Edgardo out of the country for safety. Edgardo was not safe, however.

The arrests in March put the MIR under strain. Lines of communication between regional commands and MIR organizations were severely disrupted. Rumors were beginning to circulate that collaborators were imperiling the entire organization. Enríquez gave assurances that the reports coming to the political commission indicated that Van Schowen (who was now presumed dead), Moreno, Villavela, and Toro had shown tremendous courage and had not divulged damaging information. The pattern of arrests indicated carelessness, not betrayal. One collaborator, Osvaldo Romo, had been identified, but his was a special case. The most immediate problem was that less experienced and hardened cadres were breaking under torture. The rapid growth of the MIR in the three years of the Popular Unity experiment was coming back to haunt the movement. The political commission had discovered that the inexperienced MIRistas were the "exposed flank" of the movement, and that the intelligence services were attacking it. Enríquez had to remind MIRistas in his encyclical that they had to look inside themselves: if they doubted their commitment or courage in the face of torture and death, they should separate themselves from their comrades, with no sense of shame.

There was another matter. Enríquez detected that the air force was engaging in a clever psychological operation to demoralize the MIR. Reports filtering back to the political commission indicated that the SIFA was trying to soften, rather than break, MIRistas. Prisoners held in the basements of the AGA were not always mistreated; airmen gave them cigarettes and other luxuries, permitted contact with loved ones, and generally tried to convince them that not all members of the armed forces were gorillas. In one case, Enríquez reported, the air force captors gave condolences for the torture and death of Bautista Van Schowen and promised that such a thing would not happen again (notably, this is the only indication the political commission had that Van Schowen was dead). The MIR's official line was clear: no one should be misled by the ploy. It was senseless to make subtle distinctions between the SIFA and the DINA, just as it was senseless for the junta to draw fine distinctions among the MIR, the Communists, and the Socialists. There was no mistaking enemies. This would not be the last time Enríquez would have to judge the air force's sincerity.

The assessment of the political commission as of late May 1974 was that the setbacks of March and April were serious but not insuperable. Instructions had been sent down the line; now it was a matter of taking precautions, and reconstituting damaged cells of the clandestine organization. Enríquez ordered MIR activities to be curtailed for a full month, beginning on June 20, when it was expected the new instructions could be printed and circulated. The secretary general ordered, in his words, a temporary "pause along the road of the MIR's 'Long March' " — an inspiring allusion to Mao and the ultimately victorious People's Liberation Army. Every MIRista was instructed to study the document, reflect on it, and implement the new security measures. The very future of the MIR, Enríquez stressed, depended on this exercise.

The MIR never had the opportunity to pause on the road to implement the measures, however. The organization suffered another wave of arrests between late May and mid-June. Eight middle-level militants were swept up, taken to a house at 38 Londres Street, and disappeared. A new, more destructive force was at work: Londres 38, a spacious two-story house formerly belonging to the Socialist party in downtown Santiago, was a DINA facility.[13] These arrests would lead to the apex of the MIR's structure, and to Enríquez himself. In successive waves, each prompted by information obtained under torture, DINA abducted 220 MIRistas, possibly more. More than sixty of them would disappear from Londres 38, known to those confined to it as the "House of Bells" or the "House of Terror."[14]

The destruction of the MIR was entrusted to DINA's Caupolicán group, and its action teams: Vampire, Tucan, Eagle, and Hawk I and II. These five-to eight-man teams conducted surveillance, patrolled the streets, abducted MIRistas, tortured them, and disposed of the bodies. Caupolicán distinguished itself in this dirty war, and Hawk teams I and II distinguished themselves as especially effective within Cuapolicán. The junta could not openly commend the men for their service, but Pinochet could promote them. Cuapolicán's commander, known only as "Max," eventually became commander of the DINA's Metropolitan Brigade. Max was Marcelo Moren Brito, one of the men who accompanied General Arellano on his deadly helicopter tour in October 1973. His replacement as Cuapolicán commander was Captain Miguel Krassnoff Marchenko, who would earn a reputation for cruelty.[15]

The Hawk teams had an advantage: they had a collaborator, Osvaldo Romo Mena. Enríquez was aware of Romo's defection, and reported it to the MIR's central committee in his June communication. Known unflatteringly as the Paunch Belly (el Guatón), Romo had been a militant of the small Popular Socialist Union attached to Allende's Popular Unity coalition. As a shanty-town organizer, he could identify MIRistas.[16] Enríquez calculated that Romo had delivered three, possibly five MIRistas in the first week of May. He also gained a reputation for cruelty as a torturer, and in a number of known cases he tortured his victims to death. Even Manuel Contreras would admit Romo was a very effective collaborator.[17]

Romo's victims included Alfonso Chanfreau, a philosophy student and member of the MIR-FER; Lumi Videla, a member of the MIR central committee; and Sergio Pérez, Videla's husband and a member of the MIR's political commission. All fell victim at the height of the DINA's initial assault, which began in July 1974 and ended in December. A wave of arrests of inexperienced MIR intermediaries swept up by Cuapolicán led to more and more intelligence coups. In order to get at the MIR's leadership, the DINA required solid, timely intelligence. Romo, Krassnoff Marchenko, and the other interrogators had a pressing need to learn four things: the real identities of MIR cadres and directors known to intelligence officers only by their noms de guerre, the addresses of safe-houses, the sites of rendezvous points, and the location of weapons caches. Information about all four could be obtained by breaking the intermediaries under torture. These literally were, as Enríquez noted, the weak links in the organization.

The MIR had been hit in March and April, then again in June. The DINA's offensive accelerated and gained irresistible momentum in July. In the second week of July, the DINA abducted and disappeared Máximo Gueda, who occupied the number two position in the MIR's information department for the all-important Santiago, or central, region.[18] At the end of the month Cuapolicán seized Alfonso Chanfreau, a political director in the MIR-FPR student organization. Gueda and Chanfreau were among the most important prisoners captured by Cuapolicán to date. The Hawk team leader knew that they possessed information useful to him, and he knew Chanfreau personally. Chanfreau admitted to being a MIR militant, but no more. Paunch Belly Romo knew him to be a director charged with political indoctrination who was privy to more sensitive information than a lowly militant. The Hawk team operatives had arrested Chanfreau in the presence of his wife Erika Henning, who was nursing their young daughter. Romo had no qualms about threatening to torture the woman in Chanfreau's presence, and ordered Henning arrested and brought to Londres 38 the following day. It is impossible to ascertain whether the twenty-five-year-old Chanfreau betrayed his comrades' trust to protect the mother of his child; he was subsequently disappeared. Henning was later released and is now one of the many witnesses to Romo's cruelty.

Torture broke many leftists, however. The success of the DINA's operations virtually depended on it. Six days after the abduction of Chanfreau, DINA agents abducted Maria Angélica Andreoli, secretary to the MIR's political commission, and then proceeded to the house of her friend, Muriel Dockendorff, to seize her. Dockendorff had already been arrested and interrogated by air force intelligence, but was released. The SIFA had determined that Muriel Dockendorff was not important enough to detain any longer and certainly not dangerous enough to kill. The DINA had its own agenda and criteria. Both Maria Angélica Andreoli and Muriel Dockendorff were given up by a single informant, a MIR militant known to her former comrades as Flaca Alejandra (*flaca* means thin, but also weak, especially weak of character). Flaca Alejandra broke under torture and gave up the names of several important intermediaries, like Andreoli and Dockendorff, and she identified Lumi Videla, a member of the central committee.[19] Cuapolicán picked up Lumi Videla on a Santiago street on September 21. Flaca Alejandra had noticed her from a DINA vehicle in which she was traveling with Romo from the site of a DINA operation. Videla's arrest was a breakthrough and another chance for Romo to make his reputation as an effective collaborator.

The abduction of Lumi Videla, "la negra Luisa," precipitated the collapse of the MIR's political commission and the death of Miguel Enríquez. Videla was not only a member of the central committee, she was the wife of Sergio Pérez, a member of the political commission. Videla was not taken to Londres 38. By this time another interrogation site on José Domingos Cañas Street had been put into operation. The sheer scale of DINA's operations against the MIR and the rate of arrests had made the two-story house on Londres Street obsolete. And there was another inconvenience. The Inter-American Commission for Human Rights was due to arrive in Chile in the final week of July. Londres 38 had come to the attention of human rights defenders and it was on their list of places to inspect. Amnesty International, which had visited Chile in November 1973 and continued to scrutinize the human rights situation in the country, had heard testimony from some of those who had survived detention and torture there. Survivors had dubbed it the "House of Bells" because they could hear bells of a nearby church calling parishioners to mass.[20]

Romo personally tortured Lumi Videla at José Domingos Cañas to obtain the shreds of crucial intelligence the Hawk team needed to complete its mission. Even when disoriented by torture, militants like Videla could discern from the interrogator's questions what was already known and therefore pointless to deny. And they knew enough to stall for time by divulging pieces of useless information. Videla disclosed the location of her safehouse, but the information should not have been useful. Her husband, Sergio Pérez, was an experienced cadre who had risen to the top of the MIR. The security measures decreed by Miguel Enríquez after the wave of arrests back in March and April called for Pérez to abandon the safe-house when Lumi Videla did not return at a prearranged hour. Pérez took the precaution, but inexplicably returned to the residence the next day. Pérez was accompanied by Humberto Sotomayor, also a member of the central committee and the man who had commanded the MIRistas in President Allende's detachment of bodyguards. It was an extraordinarily risky—and costly—decision. Here were two senior MIRistas returning to a place that was almost certainly compromised. In fact, the Hawk team had set a trap for Pérez. Pérez and Sotomayor circled the block a number of times before Pérez decided it was safe to enter. Armed, Pérez ventured into the dark house and was shot and wounded the moment he entered the door. Sotomayor managed to escape and inform Enríquez. This would not be Soto-mayor's last brush with death.

Osvaldo Romo now had both Lumi Videla and Sergio Pérez in incom-municado detention. This was an intelligence windfall. Both were tortured to death. Pérez died of internal hemorrhaging caused by the beatings. His wife's ordeal lasted another month — Lumi Videla died on November 3. The DINA had a final indignity in mind for the young radical, and a message for the Italian government, which continued to grant asylum to Chileans with a well-founded fear of persecution. DINA agents brought the battered body of Lumi Videla from José Domingos Cañas on the fourth and hurled it over the garden wall and into the compound of the Italian embassy. The Chilean press did not question the government's account of the incident: Lumi Videla died during an orgy in the garden of the Italian embassy.[21]

Two weeks after Lumi Videla and Sergio Pérez fell into DINA's hands, Cuapolicán found and killed Miguel Enríquez. With the MIR secretary gen-eral were Carmen Castillo Velasco, who was pregnant by Enríquez, José Bor-das, chief of MIR's military operations, and Humberto Sotomayor, a mem-ber of the political commission.[22] Cuapolicán sentries had observed the men traveling in a car and tracked them to a house on Santa Fe Street. They called in other agents to surround the perimeter. But Enríquez, Bordas, and Sotomayor opened fire on them from the windows. In the two hours of fighting that ensued, Castillo was lightly wounded and taken into custody. Bordas and Sotomayor escaped unharmed through adjacent houses. Enrí-quez was killed in a hail of automatic weapon fire.

The death of Miguel Enríquez on October 4, 1974 marked the end of the initial phase of the DINA's campaign against the MIR's leadership structure. But the mission was not complete. José Bordas, Humberto Sotomayor, Nel-son Gutiérrez, Andrés Pascal Allende, and Alejandro Villalobos — all dan-gerous adversaries — were still at large. Edgardo Enríquez was out of the country, raising money and conspiring with his counterparts in Latin Amer-ica. And there were hundreds of rank and file MIRistas to be apprehended and eliminated. The campaign to annihilate the MIR's so-called Central Force, beginning with the arrest of its director, José Bordas, was launched almost immediately and would continue throughout the following year. Hundreds of MIRistas would be swept up, taken to still other detention centers like the Sexy Venda and the once elegant Villa Grimaldi estate in the Barrio Alto of Santiago, interrogated under torture, and either released or disappeared. The senior leaders did not escape either.

The air force, not the DINA, mounted the operation that killed José Bor-das exactly two months after he narrowly escaped the house on Santa Fe street. Bordas was betrayed by "Barba" (the Beard) Schneider, a MIRista "turned" by his air force interrogators. Schneider informed SIFA of Bor-das's plan to attack the United Nations Conference on Trade and Develop-ment (UNCTAD) building in Santiago. With renovations of the charred Moneda still proceeding, the junta needed a seat of government. The UNCTAD building suited its purposes, and the military government moved in. If Bordas's operation worked as planned, a team of MIRistas would fire rocket propelled grenades through the upper-story windows, killing the members of the junta meeting there. But commander Ceballos, head of SIFA's operations against the MIR, moved against Bordas first. Bordas, like Enríquez, refused to be taken. After a high-speed car chase in Santiago, Bordas was killed by a burst of automatic weapon fire as he fired his pistol at the air force troops pursuing him.[23]

Less than two months later, in the third week of January, the security forces eliminated another senior MIR leader, when the DINA routed a MIR cell in Valparaíso. Nine lost their lives. Among them was Alejandro Villalobos, the MIR-MPR leader who had been posted on the "ten most wanted" list along with Bautista Van Schowen, Enríquez, Pascal Allende, and Toro. He walked into an ambush set in his house, much like the one that resulted in the capture of Sergio Pérez. He was immediately shot and fatally wounded. The rest were disappeared.

Leadership of the tattered MIR now fell to the troika of Dagoberto Pérez, Nelson Gutiérrez, and Andrés Pascal Allende. Edgardo Enríquez was abroad and Humberto Sotomayor had fled to the Italian embassy with his wife the day after Miguel Enriquez was cut down. But the MIR was utterly demoralized. On February 19, 1975, as this destructive campaign was in full motion, four members of the MIR went on television from the DINA's interrogation center called Villa Grimaldi, where they had been held since their arrest sometime the previous November. For the junta, this was a dramatic propaganda event. The four men admitted that the MIR had been completely vanquished, politically and militarily. This was a far cry from the late Miguel Enríquez's last major communiqué in which he acknowledged "blows" and attempted to glean the appropriate lessons from the setbacks. The MIRistas repeated their remarks in a press conference arranged to forestall the criticism that the men spoke under extreme duress. For its part, the tattered MIR leadership responded by condemning the men to death for treason, but never had the chance to kill them. The DINA released the four men in September and rearrested and murdered two of them three months later.[24]

The campaign against the MIR slowed considerably after the death of Bordas in December and the destruction of the MIR's cell in Valparaíso the following month. The MIR was being bled of its militants, and its leaders were increasingly isolated. The final confrontation came in the second week of October 1975. One year and one week after the death of Miguel Enríquez, DINA agents arrested a MIR intermediary in a routine operation. The DINA found documentation on him that led them to what they believed was an isolated MIR-MCR cell just outside the capital. In fact the information led them to the hiding place of the MIR's most senior leaders, Dagoberto Pérez Vargas, Nelson Gutiérrez, and Andrés Pascal Allende. On October 16, 1975 carabineros and DINA operatives from Santiago converged on the farm. They immediately came under intense fire. Two carabineros were gravely wounded. Four hours of fierce fighting ensued.

The MIRistas were encircled, but most managed to fight their way out. Dagoberto Pérez was slain in the act of setting off a diversionary explosion, and in the smoke and confusion Gutiérrez and Pascal Allende escaped. With them were two women, Ann Marie Beausire, Pascal Allende's companion, and Maria Elena Bachman. Their situation was dire. Gutiérrez had suffered a serious wound in the leg and was in immediate need of medical attention, and they were on the run. The Carabineros and the DINA launched a massive manhunt that led them to Valparaíso and then back to the capital.[25] The ensuing events had all the qualities of a morality play.

The armed fugitives made their way to a convent belonging to the Holy Cross order in the capital, where they sought and were granted temporary refuge. High church officials, including the auxiliary bishop of Santiago, and Fathers Fernando Salas and Cristián Precht of the Committee for Peace, were informed of the unfolding drama. They had a decision to make, and the situation could hardly have been more complicated. The MIR had entangled the Catholic Church and the Committee for Peace, and it had put innocents in mortal danger. Pinochet had been dreaming of his chance to be rid of the Committee for Peace ever since May, when one of the committee's supposedly confidential internal memoranda on the repression was published in a Mexican newspaper. But there was a humanitarian concern, and the instinct for mercy prevailed. Church officials decided to assist the MIRistas because, as Father Salas later explained, there was every reason to believe that the MIRistas would have been disappeared if they had been surrendered to authorities. The decision taken, the church launched its own clandestine operation.

The most urgent matter was Gutiérrez's wound. Father Salas contacted Sheila Cassidy, an English physician preparing to take her vows as a nun, and asked for her help. Cassidy examined Gutiérrez and determined that his wounds required treatment in a more secure location. Meanwhile Pascal Allende, Beausire, and Bachman departed for a separate hiding place, but they remained in contact with Gutiérrez through church officials. As a condition for further assistance, the priests demanded that Gutiérrez surrender his arms, and then secretly disposed of them on a Santiago street. (Pinochet would hint in his memoir that the priests actually left the weapons in a place where other fugitive MIRistas could recover them.) Only then was Gutiérrez transported to the residence of Columban priests, where Cassidy treated the wounded MIRista for a full week. Eventually all were taken to safety. Pascal Allende and the women were granted asylum in the embassy of a Central American country; Gutiérrez was granted asylum by the Papal nuncio.

This was not the end of the affair. A wrathful Contreras ordered his agents to arrest and interrogate Sheila Cassidy, and on November 1, a week after the incident, DINA agents burst into the residence of the Columban fathers, killing a domestic employee in the process. The church officials who agreed to assist the revolutionaries had wanted to avoid violence, and had insisted that the MIRistas surrender their arms. Now the MIRistas were safe but a woman with no connection to the MIR was dead. The following day Ann Marie Beausire's brother Guillermo was arrested in Argentina as he stepped off a flight from Santiago. He was disappeared.[26]

Pinochet had the incident he had been awaiting. "All these facts," the general stated in his memoir in his characteristically cumbersome style, "evinced a decided collaboration between an important sector of the clergy, characterized by its left-leaning positions, with the marxist, insurrectional group MIR."[27] Several North American priests had actively participated in the affair, two from the Order of the Holy Cross, another from Maryknoll, the latter already famed for its belief in an affinity between the gospel and social justice as defined by Marxists. This was intolerable. Pinochet had no recourse but to write Cardinal Raúl Silva.

Pinochet did not explicitly mention the participation of priests working with the Committee for Peace in the October affair, or the content of an internal committee report on the human rights situation in Chile that had been published by a Mexican newspaper in May. But Cardinal Silva certainly understood that these events prompted the courteous but direct letter from the de facto president of Chile. Pinochet admitted to being profoundly concerned about, in his words, the international campaign "to create the false impression that there existed differences between the Apostolic Roman Catholic Church and the government of Chile." Pinochet was careful not to accuse the church or the committee. The problem was that "Marxists-Leninists avail themselves of the Committee as a means to create problems that affect the tranquility and the necessary calm, the maintenance of which is my principal duty as a ruler." "To avoid greater evils," wrote Pinochet coming to the point, "it would be a positive step, therefore, to dissolve the Committee."[28]

Cardinal Silva responded with a potent combination of candidness and subtlety. "The information that I possess," wrote the cardinal, "provides the basis, as far as I am concerned, for an overall judgement of the activities of the Committee that is very different from the one summarized in your remarks." Indeed, the Committee for Peace "has been carrying out, in the midst of very difficult circumstances, a task of assistance clearly deeply rooted in the gospel and within the confines of legislation in force." If others were using the work of the committee for their own ends, he commented, "that is a risk inherent in every act of goodness." That said, the cardinal would accede to Pinochet's request, although Silva forewarned Pinochet that the text of the general's letter would have to be shared with the heads of the other denominations involved in the committee, meaning that "its tone cannot remain private." Cardinal Silva, speaking truth to power, ended on a subtle but powerful note: "The sacrifice that this decision implies permits us to hope that, in a time not too far off, full authority will be restored to civil jurisdiction in matters now the object of the Committee's action, with the consequent recreation of a climate of social peace in the country, and an extraordinarily positive image abroad." The cardinal had been careful, but he did not avoid the imputation of blame. The matters now the object of the committee's action, of course, pertained to the human rights of Chileans—although the phrase does not appear in the letter—and if there was an international campaign against Chile Pinochet bore no small responsibility for it.

The MIR had been effectively driven from Chile. Miguel Enríquez, Juan Bautista Van Schowen, Sergio Pérez, Lumi Videla, José Bordas, Alejandro Villalobos, and Dagoberto Pérez Vargas were dead. Nelson Gutiérrez, Andrés Pascal Allende, and Edgardo Enríquez were in exile but not safe. In April 1976 Edgardo Enríquez was abducted by Argentinean police in Buenos Aires, where he had traveled to attend a meeting of an ill-fated Latin American Revolutionary Coordinating Committee. Argentinean security was already cooperating with Chile, at the initiative of Contreras.[29] The United Nations High Commission for Refugees ascertained that Edgardo Enríquez was taken to the Argentinean navy's Naval Mechanics School, a site where some of the most serious abuses committed during Argentina's "Dirty War" are known to have occurred.[30] He was probably then turned over to the DINA and taken to the DINA's Villa Grimaldi facility. He was disappeared.

The MIR had disappeared. Miguel Enríquez had been brash in the weeks before the coup, and defiant after the military intervention. The MIR, unlike the Socialists and Communists, would not desert the workers, he proclaimed. But, in fact, Miguel Enríquez had been offered the opportunity to retreat.

Three months before his death Enríquez was contacted by Edgar Ceballos, the man commanding SIFA operations against the MIR. The SIFA had the MIR on the defensive: Toro, Moreno, and Villavela were in custody in the AGA, and the MIR secretary general had to concern himself with infiltrators, psychological operations, and the most basic security measures. About the same time the DINA's bloody campaign was just beginning to amass victims. Enríquez had even reconsidered his decision about exile and had sent the principal leaders of the revolutionary movement out of the country, beginning with his brother Edgardo. Miguel himself was scheduled to depart in December.[31]

It was at this critical juncture, the first week of July 1974, that Ceballos made an overture to the MIR, which the MIR made public on the anniversary of the coup.[32] The SIFA offered the embattled revolutionary movement a truce. The SIFA would suspend its operations against the MIR if the political commission would agree to disarm, to halt its "political work" within the ranks of the air force, and to leave the country. Secret talks were proposed, with the expectation that once the SIFA and the political commission of the MIR had agreed in principle, formal negotiations with the junta would proceed. It was not a call for unconditional surrender. The junta (the SIFA confidently asserted) would guarantee safe passage, release imprisoned MIRistas, and even permit some approved members of the MIR to continue functioning in Chile, with the proviso that the most dangerous members, the senior leaders, and the "technical and military cadres" would go into exile and that they would not engage in political opposition activities for two or three years. There were drawbacks, however. The SIFA made it clear that it would not end its pursuit of the MIR until these terms were met, and it certainly had no influence over other agencies, undoubtedly an allusion to the DINA. The air force did offer guarantees to MIR negotiators, however, suggesting the participation of church officials.

The MIR waited until August, when the situation had deteriorated still further, to respond. Even at this point Enríquez demanded a good will gesture: the SIFA was to permit third parties to visit Moreno and Toro in the AGA to see that they had not suffered the fate of his friend Bautista Van Schowen. The SIFA was amenable. On August 10 Laura Allende, the sister of the late president and mother of MIR leader Andrés Pascal Allende, visited the Air War Academy with Catholic Bishop Carlos Camus on behalf of the MIR. The basic content of the SIFA's initial communication was confirmed, and the visitors were able to meet with two imprisoned MIRistas.[33] But, on the strong advice of the remaining members of the political commission, including the imprisoned Toro, the air force's proposal was publicly rejected. The MIR boldly proclaimed that it would not go into exile.

The SIFA's opening to the MIR is as intriguing as the MIR's public rejection is understandable. To Enríquez's way of thinking, nothing could have been more odious than a public admission of defeat, and Enríquez did not sense defeat. A week after Laura Allende and Bishop Camus visited the MIR's hapless prisoners in the AGA, Enríquez gave an interview to *El Rebelde*, the MIR publication formerly edited by Bautista Van Schowen, urging revolutionaries everywhere to convert "hatred and indignation into an organization of resistance." "The coming year," he announced, "promises to be a year of active resistance and combat, including armed propaganda and armed struggle against the gorilla dictatorship."[34] At any rate, the SIFA's overture had all the appearances of a ruse, a clever psychological operation aimed at dividing the leadership between idealists determined to make a last ditch stand, and realists who considered exile to be the better part of valor. The political commission's June letter to the central committee already indicated that Enríquez deeply distrusted the air force. Nelson Gutiérrez, one of the few senior leaders to survive the repression, later told interviewers that the political commission viewed the overture in the broader context of Ceballos's multifaceted strategy, which combined arrests, executions, and infiltration.[35] But even if the overture had been genuine, and even if General Leigh could have prevailed over Contreras in a policy debate within the military government—both highly questionable—there were reasons to shun the arrangement on principle. In a sense the decision was substantially the same as the one Allende had made exactly two years before, a symbolic death in the Moneda or opposition in exile. The MIR chose to make a stand, and disappeared.

The Night and Fog

Early in World War II, German Field Marshal Wilhelm Keitel, the Wehrmacht's chief of staff, signed the Night and Fog Order. The order was premised on a conclusion reached by Hitler's Secret State Police, the Gestapo, an agency concerned with intimidation as a professional matter: "intimidation can only be achieved either by capital punishment, or through measures by which the relatives of the prisoners or the population cannot learn of the fate of the criminals." Henceforth, by order of the general staff, German soldiers made it a practice to arrest suspected members of the French resistance in the middle of the night, and to disappear them. As Hitler quipped, they simply vanished into night and fog.[36] Now, decades later, the Chilean army—which modeled itself after the Prussian tradition even to the point of wearing the grey tunics of the Wehrmacht—adopted the practice. In the early months of the new order, the military sought to intimidate through capital punishment after hastily convened and grossly unfair war tribunals. In 1974, however, it opted to disappear Chileans into the night and fog to intimidate the families of the detained and the wider population. The International Military Tribunal at Nuremberg sentenced Keitel to death for the Night and Fog Order.[37] The Chilean generals would escape punishment for their part in the disappearance of thousands of Chileans because of an amnesty decreed in 1978.

Disappearance, as a tactic, had proven effective against the MIR, and beginning in mid-1975 the intelligence agencies were ready to employ it against the members of the political commissions and central committees of the Socialist and Communist parties. The leaders of Chile's two main Marxist parties did not distinguish themselves by their valor on September 11: army general Augusto Pinochet and MIR secretary general Miguel Enríquez had agreed on that much. Both heaped scorn on Carlos Altamirano and Luis Corvalán and their comrades. These men "who had incited the workers in those three years," commented Pinochet, "were the first to hide, to flee and to seek refuge in some embassy."[38] In a communiqué Enríquez revealed that on September 11 he had sent a senior MIR leader to met with his Socialist and Communist counterparts to coordinate resistance activities. He was rebuffed. The Communists were waiting to see whether the military junta was planning to close the congress before it decided on a course of action. Enríquez coldly accused them of desertion.

With the senior Socialist and Communist leaders in exile, important party functions became the responsibility of younger, mid-level cadres and directors. Many of them went underground immediately and worked secretly to reorganize the parties, both now illegal. Because the DINA was intent on destroying the MIR throughout 1974 and much of 1975, the Socialist and Communist parties enjoyed a temporary reprieve, and the relatively low intensity of the repression may have also lured socialist and communists into a false sense of security. Roughly 25 socialists and 22 communists were killed in all 1974, as opposed to some 150 MIRistas.[39] The priorities of the intelligence services were clear.

But beginning in the early months of 1975 the DINA set out to decapitate the so-called Internal Front of the Socialist party. The methods developed in the assault on the MIR were now honed: capturing and eliminating the Socialist leaders was mainly a matter of tracking intermediaries to members of the political commission and central committee. The Socialists were easier to apprehend. The DINA killed 35 Socialist militants and leaders in 1975, beginning with the New Year's Eve arrest of two young socialists, one a member of the central committee. Another central committee member was abducted in the first week of March. But the DINA scored its major coup against the party of Allende in the span of a few weeks in June and July 1975, when it apprehended the leading members of the party's political commission, Ricardo Lagos, Exequiel Ponce, and Carlos Lorca, and their intermediaries.[40]

The Moscow-line Communist party, the least revolutionary member of Allende's Popular Unity coalition, was targeted next. Communists were killed in the frenetic first weeks of the new order, but the party was temporarily spared in the waves of repression that followed. However, its fidelity to Moscow made the party especially loathsome to the junta. The campaign to rid Chile of this menace once and for all began toward the end of 1975 and culminated a year later. The Communist party of Chile lost more than 90 cadres, including senior leaders, in that period. The arrests came in surges: five were swept up between late November and the end of December 1975, six more in April 1976. May was disastrous for the party. Ten members of the central committee were captured and killed; five of the ten were arrested in the same house in an operation the DINA characterized as a rat-trap. Víctor Díaz, who as undersecretary of the party was the most senior Communist remaining in the country, was among those who fell into DINA hands in May. Sixteen ranking Communists were killed sometime after arrest in July, fourteen more in August. The year ended with another crushing blow; thirteen members of the central committee of the Communist party were arrested and disappeared in December.[41] Manuel Contreras's DINA was not responsible for the disappearances of all these communists, however; a third of the victims were claimed by a rogue agency set up by the air force's representative on the junta, General Gustavo Leigh.

DINA's Purén group was given the task of eliminating the hated Communists.[42] From Colonel Contreras's perspective, the war against subversion should have been the exclusive mission of his Directorate for National Intelligence. He lobbied tirelessly for an executive order from Pinochet that would grant him that authority. But the air force was especially eager to leave its mark in the destruction of the Communist party as well.

The Air Force Intelligence Service, SIFA, was restructured at the end of 1974. The SIFA now became DIFA, the Air Force Intelligence Directorate, under a new commander, General Enrique Ruiz Bunguer, and its headquarters were moved from the Air War Academy to a new location in Santiago. (Ruiz's predecessor had recently been killed in an air crash, sparking rumors that the DINA might have been behind the death; for their part, DINA officers took seriously rumors that air force intelligence operatives may have been conspiring to assassinate them.)[43] The intelligence departments of the other branches underwent a similar metamorphosis, and they began to coordinate activities as part of an informal "intelligence community" functioning within the National Defense General Staff, all working out of the same building. The DINA remained apart and aloof from the new arrangement.[44] Contreras wanted special prerogatives, one of which was to have anti-subversive operations all to himself. Contreras prevailed. In September 1975, just before the deadly confrontation with the surviving members of the MIR political commission at Malloco, and as the campaign against the Socialists was heating up, Pinochet issued a directive assigning the power to arrest political opponents to the DINA and to the DINA alone.[45]

But General Leigh, the man who had declared the mission to extirpate Marxism from Chile on the night of the coup d'état, was not prepared to suspend anti-subversive operations. Sometime late in 1975, the air force formed the Joint Command and began its own clandestine operations against the Communist party. Militants of the now disbanded neo-fascist Patria y Libertad organization participated actively, among them Roberto Fuentes Morrison, known by the innocuous sounding code-name "Wally." Fuentes Morrison was given the rank of squadron commander in the air force reserve, and assumed command of the reaction teams. (The reaction teams were formerly commanded by Edgar Ceballos, but Ceballos had made a favorable impression on his superiors in the campaign against the MIR, and had been dispatched to Israel to attend intelligence courses.) Wally was terribly effective, as effective as his infamous counterpart in the DINA's Cuapolicán group Miguel Krassnoff Marchenko. In fact it was Roberto Fuentes Morrison who fired the volley of shots that killed MIR leader José Bordas in December 1974. Early in 1976 Wally's recruits from the intelligence directorates of the army, navy, and Carabineros began conducting joint operations. So throughout 1976 the embattled Communist party had to contend with the Joint Command and the DINA.[46]

Both the DINA and the Joint Command disappeared their victims. A "disappearance" consists of a sequence of illegal acts shrouded in official denial: abduction, interrogation under torture, murder, concealment. Disappearance does not end with the murder and disposal of a body: a disappearance has an enduring and destructive legacy.[47]

Sometime in the third week of June 1975, DINA agents caught up with Ricardo Lagos, a member of the political commission of the Socialist party, and Michelle Peña, his contact person, in the apartment where they were hiding. The details of the abduction of these socialist militants are scant: the very fact that they were underground made knowledge of what became of them difficult to come by and actually facilitated their disappearance.

A few days later, around dawn on June 24, acting under the cover of the curfew, a DINA team traveling in three cars arrived at an apartment building in search of other high-ranking socialists who had also been underground. The owner of the building opened the door, and the agents burst inside. They immediately apprehended Exequiel Ponce and Mireya Rodríguez and began a search for documents, large sums of cash, and other evidence of clandestine party activity. Ponce was a member of the central committee of the Socialist party; Rodríguez was his intermediary.

In the afternoon of the same day a much larger contingent of DINA personnel, transported in as many as twelve vehicles, surrounded a laundromat in another part of Santiago. Inside they found and arrested Carlos Lorca, a member of the Socialist political commission, and Modesta Carolina Wiff, the owner of the business who also happened to be Lorca's intermediary. The laundromat was a convenient cover for a rendezvous point, but the DINA had discovered it. These operations effectively debilitated the internal front of the Socialist party, frustrating the concerted efforts of these and other militants to reorganize and revive a party still racked by the initial repression after the coup d'état.[48]

On August 10, 1975 Marta Ugarte's sister arrived at her apartment just in time to see Marta placed in the back seat of an unmarked car belonging to Investigations, Chile's plainclothes detectives. Ugarte, a member of the central committee of the Communist party, was between two men dressed in civilian clothes. Her face was obscured by dark glasses, and Marta's sister had the impression that she was blindfolded as well, because Marta appeared not to see her from only a few feet away. Marta Ugarte had been hiding ever since the coup; now she was in custody and about to disappear. One month after her abduction in front of her apartment, her body, stuffed in a sack tied at her throat, washed up on shore at a beach resort.[49] An autopsy revealed extensive injuries: all her ribs had been fractured, her legs were nearly severed from her body, and there were other unmistakable signs of torture. The press circulated the official version of the probable cause of Marta Ugarte's death. The story concocted in the death of MIRista Lumi Videla was rehashed: from all appearances she was killed by a sexual maniac, her lover, or perhaps even her husband.

At the end of March 1976 the Joint Command arrested José Weibel, the secretary general of the Communist Youth, in a carefully orchestrated operation. His brother Ricardo had been arrested the previous November and killed with a group of other Communists sometime after the new year. José Weibel had been alerted to the possibility of arrest and was fleeing with his wife and two sons when the air force unit moved in to abduct him on board a bus. His abductors had been following his movements from the moment he left his home early on the morning of March 29, and were in constant radio contact with the head of air force intelligence. They needed a diversion. As the bus stopped to let on new passengers, a woman aboard the bus began screaming that Weibel had stolen her purse. Agents suddenly boarded the vehicle and carried Weibel away, leaving his traumatized wife and sons behind.[50]

Sometime around 2 a.m. on May 12, 1976, at least six DINA agents converged on a house in the comfortable Las Condes section of Santiago. The owner of the house heard the commotion outside his home and drew back the curtains to see what was happening. A man dressed in civilian clothes ordered him to open the door. Armed men entered rapidly and canvassed the bedrooms. Inside were the owner, his wife and three daughters, and a pensioner who was renting a room. The intelligence agents confined the owner and his family to a single bedroom at gun point while they apprehended the pensioner, who identified himself as José Santos Garrido. The officer in charge already knew the man's true identity. Agents hurled the man to the floor, bound him at the wrists, and began kicking and punching him. They had located Víctor Díaz, undersecretary of the Communist party, the highest ranking member of the now illegal organization in Chile.[51]

The police arrived at the home and workshop of Juan Becerra, a leather artisan, on the last day of April 1976 to deliver the tragic news that his sister-in-law had been involved in a fatal automobile accident. Becerra was asked to identify the woman's body. It was a cruel ploy. His sister-in-law was not dead; she was being held by the DINA and interrogated about a member of the central committee of the Communist party. Now Becerra was in the custody of the DINA, too. The agents took Becerra to Villa Grimaldi and beat him until he admitted to knowing Mario Zamorano. The Communist party was about to be dealt a crushing blow. The DINA brought Becerra and his sister-in-law back to his home on Conferencia Street and held them against their will, while the DINA agents patiently awaited the arrival over the next few days of no fewer than five members of the central committee. The DINA had converted the small leather goods shop at the house on Conferencia Street, in its phrase, into a rat-trap.[52]

Carlos Contreras, secretary general of the Communist Youth Movement, was apprehended by the Joint Command on November 2, 1976. But Contreras kept his wits and attempted to trick his abductors. His interrogators demanded that he lead them to a rendezvous with his intermediary the following day. Contreras complied and led a team of agents to a bus stop on a Santiago street. Suddenly Contreras broke free of his captors and hurled himself beneath the wheels of a passing bus. With one of his legs crushed, Contreras screamed out his name and address and pleaded for someone to intervene. Witnesses were surprised that the men who came to his rescue threw him in the trunk of a car and carried him off.[53]

On December 15 Waldo Pizarro and Juan Ortiz were abducted by members of the Joint Command dressed in civilian clothes on a crowded thoroughfare near Plaza Engaña. This was another compromised rendezvous. Both were Communists and members of their party's central committee. The two were among the thirteen members of the central committee disappeared in December 1976. Their abductors violently overpowered the men, forced hoods over their heads, and pushed them into the backs of separate vehicles. One of the men attempted to shout something but was silenced by a blow to the head with the butt of a rifle, according to witnesses who viewed the incident from a bakery across the street. The wife of Waldo Pizarro saw the blackened bloodstain on the road the following day. She has since become an indefatigable champion of the disappeared in Chile.[54]

These were abductions, not arrests, for two reasons: they were not pursuant to warrants, and the purpose of the abductions was never to deliver the prisoner to the justice system under guarantees of due process for judgment of legal guilt or innocence. The courts, in fact, rarely intervened at any point in the sequence of events that began with abduction. Magistrates routinely ruled against habeas corpus petitions and other legal remedies permitted under Chilean law. Judicial investigations by civilian courts, when initiated at all, almost always ended soon after they began. Six witnesses signed an affidavit detailing the arrest of Carlos Lorca and Carolina Wiff. Their families went to the courts, but the civilian magistrate assigned to the case refused to pursue it, declaring himself incompetent to hear a case involving the security forces. The military government adamantly denied that the two had ever been taken into custody and simply ignored the inquiries the Inter-American Commission for Human Rights made on their behalf, prompting the IACHR "to regard as proven" the allegations about abduction and disappearance of the young socialists.[55] This case is typical.

The steady flow of denunciations about arrests and disappearances sometimes forced the DINA to fabricate stories about what might have become of a person alleged to be in the custody of one of the shadowy security services. The military falsified travel documents for Waldo Pizarro and contends he traveled to Argentina shortly before his alleged abduction in December 1976. The effort to deceive in the case of socialist Ricardo Lagos and more than one hundred other disappeared persons was overly ambitious. In an operation dubbed "Colombo," the DINA circulated a story in Brazilian and Argentinean newspapers alleging that some 119 Chileans who were supposedly disappeared had in fact been killed in internecine fighting in Argentina or in skirmishes with Argentinean forces. The falsehood was easily exposed: the Argentinean newspaper that first ran the story was proved to be a front, and the edition in which the story appeared was the first and only edition ever printed. The episode prompted calls from the Vicariate of Solidarity for the appointment of a special judge to investigate the matter. The petition was denied. The Chilean Supreme Court of Justice found that the petition signed by Cristián Precht, the vicar, contained enough factual inconsistencies to render it inadmissible. "The request made by Mr. Cristián Precht," read the court's ruling, "is hereby declared inadmissible, as are the other petitions formulated to this same effect by countless other individuals who claim to be relatives of alleged missing persons."[56]

Abducted prisoners were taken to one of a number of secret detention centers, where they were held incommunicado and interrogated under torture. Those abducted by the Joint Command were taken to a specially outfitted hanger at the Colina air base, to "Nido 18" and "Nido 20" (Nido 18 had been the safe-house of MIRista Humberto Sotomayor), or to a secret location known as "the Firm," a property in central Santiago where the Communist newspaper *Clarín* had been published before the coup. The DINA's victims were taken to several locations and often shuffled between them. Witnesses and survivors could place most of the victims named above at Villa Grimaldi.

Villa Grimaldi was a once elegant estate in the Reina section of the capital. It was an ideal site for the DINA's purposes. The spacious villa was surrounded by a high red adobe wall and had ample grounds. Colonel Contreras did not deny that Villa Grimaldi, which served as the headquarters of the Metropolitan Brigade and was known as the Terranova Barracks, was an interrogation center. But he did deny that prisoners were actually held and tortured there. In fact, by mid-1974 Villa Grimaldi was the DINA's most important detention/interrogation/torture site. Prisoners have vivid recollections of the small cubicles where they were confined, and the villa's ornamental "tower" that doubled as solitary confinement for especially difficult prisoners and as torture chamber. Prisoners entered the tower through a small door and had to stoop to enter. A wooden staircase led to a trap door and a water tank that sat atop the tower. DINA outfitted the tower with perhaps ten small cells, each barely wide enough to contain a single human being. The conditions of confinement were themselves degrading.

The abuse and interrogation of prisoners began at the moment of abduction. Even as they were en route to the secret detention facility (usually on the floor in the back of a car), agents kicked and beat their prisoners and shouted insults, threats, and questions at them. The methodical interrogation under torture began in earnest inside the isolated detention center.

At Villa Grimaldi the torturers-interrogators worked in teams, composed along the lines of a platoon with an officer, sergeant, and conscripts. Military discipline was strict in the sense that "due obedience" to officers was demanded even when illegal orders were issued. But uniforms were not worn, and the officers and men attached to the reaction or assault and interrogation teams grew their hair long, sometimes wore beards, and donned blue jeans. Each team was assigned a specific group of prisoners for the duration of their captivity. That allowed the teams to work the prisoners, in order to probe their weaknesses and to learn their secrets. It also carried the risk that captors might empathize with the captives, something that happened to Andrés Valenzuela, the man who exposed the Joint Command.

Torturers were imaginative, methodical, and cruel. But not all were maniacal anti-communist zealots like Osvaldo Romo. Survivors sometimes came away with the impression that their torturers found the sessions tedious — something that deepened rather than diminished the cruelty. Torturers invented or adapted countless methods to inflict suffering and break human beings, physically and psychologically. An internal document of the National Commission Against Torture, citing the Vicariate of Solidarity and the Chilean Human Rights Commission as sources, outlined seventeen separate categories of known torture techniques.[57] But interrogators seemed to have had a preference for a set of physical torments designed to elicit information, but also to punish victims for their political leanings.

Beatings were common and sometimes caused hemorrhaging and death. Often interrogators administered violent blows to both ears with cupped hands to rupture the eardrum (the Teléfono or Telephone). The blows caused instant imbalance and disorientation, making the prisoner fall down. Electricity proved to be terribly painful and disorienting, and interrogators commonly shocked or electrocuted political prisoners. In one variant interrogators shocked — or stung — their victims with an electric prod applied to the most sensitive parts of the body (the Picana, or Prod). In the other variation torturers strapped prisoners to metal bedframes and sent electric currents surging through them, causing the agonizing sensation of electrocution of the entire body, violent seizures, and, afterward, unbearable thirst (the Parilla or Grill). The threat of death by asphyxiation produced unnerving effects. Interrogators repeatedly submersed their prisoners' heads in barrels of water, usually mixed with urine and excrement, until the prisoner could no longer endure the fear of death (Submarino or Submarine). One especially inventive and traumatizing technique involved hanging prisoners by their limbs (Pau de Arará or Parrot's Perch). Prisoners were bound at the wrists and ankles, and the wrists and ankles were tied together behind the victim' back. Prisoners were then hoisted on a wooden pole with the weight of the body tearing at the shoulders, wrists, knees, and ankles with the slightest movement of the body. It was an absolutely vulnerable position, and victims of the perch were often beaten and shocked while at the mercy of their interrogators.

The combination of techniques was almost limitless. Even those prisoners with tremendous capacity and courage to endure physical pain and fear of death sometimes had to cope with mental anguish. The threat to torture a loved one, especially a child, often proved intolerable. Interrogators learned that just the taperecorded sounds of torture, supposedly of loved ones, could elicit information when all else failed. And, obviously, prisoners lived with the endless sounds of human suffering while in captivity; torturers at Villa Grimaldi and the other sites worked in shifts.

"I was taken from my cell blindfolded, with my hands handcuffed behind my back," one survivor told a fact finder from the Inter-American Commission on Human Rights.[58]

As you go down from the cells in this place, there are three or four steps to go down and then another four or five that must be climbed to get to the second floor where the interrogation room was located. They began breaking the prisoner by giving him as he went down the stairs blindfolded and handcuffed, a cuff on the ears with the open palms. . . . This caused the prisoner to lose his balance and go tumbling down the stairs. He was then led to the second floor, and there they began a treatment with blows to the stomach with each question. They didn't care what the reply was; regardless of the reply, the blow in the stomach was immediately given. This was repeated until you fell to the floor several times. You were then led to another room and forced to disrobe. But under the pretext that the prisoner was moving too slowly, his clothing was torn from him in shreds. After each prisoner was naked the treatment with blows then continued. Each person who passed by—and I understand this happened to everybody—stomped on the prisoner's bare feet with the heels of their boots . . . and then, while naked they proceeded to apply electric shock. . . .

In my own case, I can only tell you that it was really brutal. Because at times they applied shock—as several of you have heard—on the penis, testicles, in the anus, in the mouth, in the nostrils, and on the temples, simultaneously. I recall clearly that I staggered all around the place, through all the rooms, because I was really terrible. And then they prevent the prisoner from drinking. According to what I have been told, drinking and applying electricity produces shock.

"I was totally undressed," said another survivor describing the Parrot's Perch, "and they put plastic cloths on each knee, on each wrist, and on each elbow."

Then they made me squat down. . . . So, seated like this, you put your hands here, tied, and then they put a pole here. Then they raise you and hang you on two sorts of racks, so that if you breathe a little, just by breathing, you tend to move; this produces an imbalance, and causes the body to swing. When that happens, because one is resisting putting all of his weight on his wrists (and that is the reason for the plastic cloths, to avoid leaving marks) this produces a phenomenon that the doctor later— because after they torture you the doctor immediately sees you to see that you're in good condition to be able to continue receiving the tortures—said that it produces what they explained to me as ecchymosis. . . . All of this takes place while you are hanging there, and of course the electric shocks.[59]

Marisa Matamala, a physician and staunch supporter of the Popular Unity's initiatives in health care and education, also survived Villa Grimaldi. She was confined to one of Villa Grimaldi's small wooden boxes with Nubia Becker, who also survived.[60]

"Villa Grimaldi was a terrible place," said Becker, "a place that really meant horror, day and night you could hear the screams of the tortured, which is a very unique cry." Both women were arrested in a middle-class neighborhood in Santiago, taken to Villa Grimaldi, and tortured. "Naked, helpless, I was subjected to tortures, like the grill," Matamala recalled. "They would apply electric shocks to the most sensitive parts of your body. They would run an electric prod on your body, your mouth was gagged so your screams couldn't be heard, they played deafening music to drown out the screams." Matamala remembers vividly that they tortured her to the sounds of the beautiful and haunting melody of the Concierto de Aranjeuz.

"One of the things that violated women most," Nubia Becker explained, "was the brutality against them. . . . They looked for the breasts to hit you, or the vagina to put an electrode: they looked for the most sensitive and prurient parts of your body, it was done specifically to torment you. . . . For them it was routine. Afterward they'd continue talking or eating. They'd talk about the music they were playing or about soccer. They'd keep up the most absurd conversation while they were hurting a defenseless human being."

If the inaction of Chile's judges sealed the plight of the country's political prisoners, the actions of many of its physicians prolonged or concealed their misery. Some physicians, like the one mentioned in the account given to the IACHR fact finder, were present at torture sessions and revived victims so that they would remain lucid enough to provide information. Doctors sworn to do no harm sometimes ordered an end to the sessions until the prisoner-patient could sustain more trauma without undue risk of (immediate) death. Most medical professionals did not condone the practice, but many abetted it by treating victims brought to military installations without denouncing the torture. Physicians and nurses who happened to be on call when intelligence officers brought prisoners in for emergency treatment were intimidated into filing false or misleading clinical reports. Forensic pathologists for their part often covered up evidence of torture by filing false postmortem results. Some physicians did expose torture, like that of the widely-publicized case of Yuri Guerrero, but not until the dictatorship's second decade.[61]

Interrogation under torture compelled prisoners to make agonizing decisions. Some chose suicide to escape the torment. Others chose to collaborate. The story of the destruction of the Chilean left is replete with the tragic personal dilemmas of Chileans who betrayed loyalties just to survive. Flaca

Alejandra, the young woman who gave up a number of MIRistas, is one example. Barba Schneider, the man who compromised MIR leader José Bordas, is another. Miguel Estay, known as the Fanta, and Carol Flores also collaborated. It is believed that Estay gave information that led to the arrest of as many as eighty-four communists, including the thirteen disappeared in December 1976.[62] But collaboration did not guarantee survival. Carol Flores, a communist who had collaborated with the air force for nearly two years, was killed in the ravine at the Maipo River in June 1976 along with his handler, Guillermo Bratti.[63]

Many of the disappeared were subsequently released. They had been abducted and interrogated under torture, but their lives were spared and they "reappeared." However, hundreds of prisoners were murdered when their interrogators were finished torturing them, and remain disappeared. In many instances, virtually nothing is known about the circumstances of the death of abducted persons. The disappearance of Waldo Pizarro and Juan Ortiz, two of the thirteen communist leaders abducted in mid-December 1976, stands out. There is not so much as a witness-sighting that could place these men in a known detention facility, much less an account of where, when, or how they were murdered.[64]

Andrés Valenzuela's confessions to the Vicariate of Solidarity provided detailed information about the fate of a few victims of the Joint Command and the methods used to dispose of the bodies. Especially compelling is his account of the murder and disposal of a group of prisoners that included Miguel Rodríguez Gallardo and Ricardo Weibel. Rodríguez Gallardo had been in the custody of the air force since October 1975. Ricardo Weibel, whose brother José would later fall victim, was arrested in October, released, and rearrested on November 7. Valenzuela observed both men boarding a truck with a group of other prisoners, and admitted that he had helped load pickaxes, shovels, and containers of gasoline onto the truck. The repentant airman told the story with tremendous emotion. Rodríguez Gallardo shook his hand and thanked him for small acts of kindness during his captivity, like giving him cigarettes, Valenzuela told interviewers. "I began to cry when they tied him up, I was sure that they would kill him." When the truck returned a few hours later, the gasoline containers were empty, the pickaxe and shovels were covered with dirt, and the prisoners were missing.[65]

The bodies of some victims were disposed of at sea. Valenzuela also gave a second hand account of an air force operation in which victims were thrown into the Pacific Ocean from helicopters. The victims were drugged before the flight, then slit open at the belly just before being cast from the helicopter to prevent the bodies from floating to the surface. Valenzuela had heard the story from Luis Palma Ramírez, "Fifo," another former member of Fatherland and Liberty recruited by the Joint Command.[66] Perhaps most of the disappeared were buried at clandestine sites. More than one hundred of the regime's first victims were secretly interred at the General Cemetery in the Chilean capital, and their discovery the year after the country's transition to democracy would cause outrage. In all these cases, the search for their bodies and the effort to learn how they were killed has become an unending ordeal for the families.

A disappearance does not end with the murder of the victim and the concealment of his or her body. A disappearance has a destructive legacy; it is a continuing crime. For this reason, the relatives of the disappeared, who are themselves victims, have led the fight to have disappearance declared a crime against humanity. The International Military Tribunal at Nuremburg, which sat in judgment of the Nazis, defined crimes against humanity, but did not list disappearance among them. Nonetheless, the condemnation of Wilheim Keitel for the Night and Fog Order provides the historical precedent. Disappearance rises to the level of a crime against humanity because it is deliberately intended to cause interminable suffering and torment to the loved ones of the disappeared. This legacy of uncertainty, anguish, and guilt is as much a part of the phenomenon of disappearance as the abduction, interrogation under torture, and murder of the victim. It is the sequel of concealment and official denial.

Chilean psychologists specializing in the enduring and destructive legacy of disappearance have documented the effects of coming to the realization that a loved one is in fact dead. Some of those who courageously choose to confront the horrible reality in order to get on with their lives suddenly find themselves overwhelmed by guilt. In the absence of incontrovertible proof that a loved one is dead, the survivor becomes culpable in the murder simply by acknowledging the unavoidable truth. The perverse psychological reaction is very much part of a disappearance. Disappearance implicates the innocent in the crime.[67] The loved ones of the disappeared live with that reality.

"It wasn't a war," Sola Sierra protests, referring to the dictatorship's justifications, "it was extermination." Her husband Waldo Pizzaro was disappeared in December 1976, in the Case of the Thirteen. "From the very day of the coup they began looking for him," she remembered, "but we did not hide, we did not leave the country together as a family because we always told ourselves we do not have anything to fear. Believing in an ideology, belonging to a party, being Catholic, being Protestant — that is not a crime anywhere in the world. But in Chile, during the military regime, yes, it was a crime, and they arrested him on December 15, 1976."

Sola Sierra was never informed of Waldo Pizarro's arrest, of course. Pizarro simply never arrived home on the evening of the fifteenth. But there was talk of an abduction at the Plaza Engaña, and Sierra went there herself carrying her husband's photograph. Witnesses recognized him and described how the rapid operation unfolded, and how one of the men was struck in the head with a rifle, no one knows who for certain because hoods had been forced over their heads. "The blood was still there as evidence of the brutal way they acted, I saw the blood myself, the black stain from the day before."

Fear, frustration, and guilt are all part of the frantic search that begins with the first news of the abduction. Family members are painfully aware of the authorities' hostility toward them. "People were afraid that if they spoke, if they said anything, they could be arrested and become one more disappeared person. . . . In those first moments it was such a brutal situation that, for example, there were people who did not say who the missing person was when they came to the courts to file a habeas corpus petition. In my own case, my husband was a mining engineer, and I could have gone to the courts and said only that my husband was a mining engineer and that's all. But I know that they did not take my husband because he was a mining engineer: they took him because he was a member of the Communist party. That is what I did, that is what I stated in the complaint. So, when I arrived at the Vicariate [of Solidarity] after I presented the habeas corpus petition stating that my husband was a member of the central committee of the Communist party, other family members said 'you just killed your husband because you denounced him.' "

The president of the largest victims' association is convinced that this emotional legacy of a disappearance is not incidental, it is intentional. "They wanted to crush the families," she said, adding that "but they did not anticipate that we were going to organize ourselves and denounce the practice." The personal and societal consequences are tremendous. "I am always thinking, they must have tortured him, yes they killed him, he died. But you just never know." At one time or another Sola and her companions in the association have found themselves behaving strangely. "You are out on the street and suddenly you see someone who resembles him and you begin following close behind." Family members leave clothes laid out for the person thinking they will eventually find him, and of course they have a place set at the table at Christmas time. "It is really terrible in our homes because you just cannot take the absence for granted."

Disappearance causes financial and legal problems, and leaves spouses and children in a macabre legal limbo. But attempting to resolve them by taking the legal steps necessary to have a loved one declared presumed dead can be devastating. Sola Sierra has observed the physical and emotional deterioration of some of the association's own members. "When they have had to petition for a declaration of presumed death, it provokes physical distress so that most of these people are ill. They have not been able to recover because they feel as if, because they are the ones that filed the death certificate, they actually killed the person. They feel responsible because of the fact that they have had to assume that he is dead and to declare him presumed dead."

"In your case, personally, did there come a moment when you decided he must be dead?"

"Yes. No. Look, I cannot bring myself to think . . ." Sola Sierra had to pause in order compose herself. "I know that he is dead. I know that rationally . . ."

"I apologize for the question."

No. No, it is all right. One rationally thinks that no one could be hidden for eighteen years as a prisoner or anything else. And, the tortures that one knows from other prisoners that people were subjected to, whether they were in the hands of the DINA, the CNI or the Joint Command, no human being could resist that. All of this makes one suppose, rationally, that they are dead. But emotionally, as long as one does not have to confront that reality as something that is one hundred percent certain, no one can just assume it to be true. That is so frequently the case that there are people who, for example, when mortal remains were recently found in Pisagua or Colima, immediately begin to think that, possibly, here is the person whom they have been looking for for so many years, and that he really could be dead. And when the body is identified, and it isn't the body of that person, it comes as a relief. "Ah, it wasn't him." So, it is a tremendous situation, because one knows that he is dead, but it cannot be assumed with one hundred percent certainty. Look, I cannot tell you with complete certainty that I am a widow. I cannot tell you that. My husband is "disappeared" that's all.[68]

The men behind the disappearances in Chile — Manuel Contreras, Gustavo Leigh, Miguel Krassnoff Marchenko, Osvaldo Romo, Roberto Fuentes Morrison, and above all Augusto Pinochet — have yet to acknowledge the disappearances, much less explain the reason for the policy. But it is a fair inference that these men intended to punish the families as much as to conceal the crimes. The legacy of the policy to disappear political opponents was not incidental. The rationale behind the Night and Fog Order had not lost its cogency in the half century since Keitel signed his name to it. In the campaign against Chilean Marxists, as in the campaign against the French partisans, intimidation was a political objective.

Chapter 5
The Court of World Opinion

> The dark history of secret police, developed in the shadow of the total-
> itarian states of the present century, cannot continue without leading
> humanity to a new primitivism.
> — Chilean attorneys' letter addressed to the
> General Assembly of the OAS

Making the System Work

In one of history's small ironies, the decision to create the Inter-American
Commission on Human Rights was made in Santiago, Chile in 1959. Thereafter the historical relationship between Chile and the IACHR seemed almost fated. In 1972 the Commission returned to Chile to hold its twenty-
seventh annual meeting in Viña del Mar on the invitation of beleaguered
President Salvador Allende. Less than two years later, in July 1974, the
IACHR would again convene its annual session in Chile; the thirty-third
meeting of the region's inter-governmental human rights organization
would coincide with its fact-finding mission to Pinochet's Chile. In June
1976 the OAS would hold the sixth regular session of its General Assembly
and adopt a resolution on the IACHR's second report on the situation of
human rights in Chile, in the midst of a concerted campaign by the Chilean
security forces to decapitate the Socialist and Communist parties. Chile
became a preoccupation of the IACHR for good reason.

By 1985 the IACHR had reported on the human rights situation in Chile
six times: it produced special reports in 1974, 1976, 1977, and 1985, and
included sections on Chile in its regular annual reports in 1979 and 1980.
The Commission would make determinations in numerous individual cases
denounced before the Commission. Moreover, the General Assembly of the
OAS would adopt three resolutions specifically concerning Chile in con-
secutive years between 1975 and 1977, and would mention Chile in another
resolution passed in 1980.[1]

The resolution creating the IACHR, adopted during the fifth meeting of
the OAS's Consultation of Foreign Ministers in Santiago in 1959, reflected
the intention to create a truly effective regional system of human rights

supervision. The OAS had adopted the American Declaration on the Rights and Duties of Man in Bogotá in 1948, as one of its very first acts, even before the more renowned UN Universal Declaration on Human Rights was elaborated in San Francisco. Now, eleven years later, the foreign ministers gathered in the Chilean capital declared their collective belief in the pressing need for the rights codified in the American declaration to be protected by a juridical system. For that purpose, the foreign ministers resolved to create the IACHR, and instructed the Inter-American Commission of Jurists to begin drafting a convention containing provisions for an Inter-American Court for Human Rights. The Council of the OAS drafted and approved IACHR's statute in 1960 and significantly revised it in 1965, thereby expanding its functions. Five years later, the very year Salvador Allende was elected to the Chilean presidency, the IACHR became a principal organ of the OAS when the amendments of the organization's charter went into force. This complicated series of juridical and institutional developments was complete on the eve of what would prove to be a human rights catastrophe in Latin America's so-called "National Security States."

For the system to work, however, synergy between the IACHR and nongovernmental human rights organizations, and among the NGOs themselves, would be crucial. No human rights organization, per se, existed in Chile on September 11, 1973, but that soon changed. The ferocity of the repression prompted the creation of the Committee for Peace, and eventually led to the creation of the Vicariate of Solidarity, the Chilean Human Rights Commission, and other NGOs and victims' associations. Moreover, two renowned and influential NGOs, Amnesty International (AI) and the International Commission of Jurists (ICJ), reacted immediately. AI and the ICJ, and eventually other international NGOs, became the indispensable partners of the Chilean organizations, and activated the IACHR and the United Nations Human Rights Commission.

The military government did not make it easy for them. The military government could not completely stem the flow of information, but it could intimidate and disappear witnesses, deny human rights defenders and even judicial authorities access to detention and interrogation sites, and run massive propaganda campaigns to discredit all those inside and outside Chile who would denounce violations. Human rights organizations had to negotiate entry into Chile. Amnesty International and the ICJ managed to send delegations in late 1973 and early 1974, respectively, but they did not have unlimited access to witnesses or detention centers or the cooperation of crucial ministries and agencies. The IACHR conducted an on-the-spot investigation in 1974, but Pinochet denied the UN Special Rapporteur entry until 1978, a full four years after he was appointed. Moreover, the military government's diplomats could manipulate the procedures of the OAS and United Nations to thwart efforts to investigate abuses and officially condemn them. And, of course, Pinochet could simply ignore the clamor of human rights organizations, dismissing the reports about massive and systematic human rights violations as part of an international campaign launched by Moscow. Most pertinently, Pinochet had endorsed a dirty war against Marxism, and nothing appeared to dissuade him from permitting Manuel Contreras to conduct it. There was only the court of world opinion to consider, and Pinochet's disdain for any verdict it might render soon became apparent.

International reaction to the human rights violations resulting from the coup was immediate. Amnesty International and the International Commission urged OAS intervention in a matter of days. The Inter-American human rights system was about to have its first real test. The task fell to IACHR. Prompted by the numerous unconfirmed reports about serious abuses from AI and the ICJ, both reliable sources, the commission chairman, Justino Jiménez, cabled the Chilean foreign minister, Rear-Admiral Ismael Huerta, on September 17. The IACHR was deeply concerned about reports of mass arrests, summary executions, and the military government's (lack of) respect for the "traditional right of political asylum granted to all political refugees in Latin American countries."[2] Huerta, however, did not respond. The IACHR communicated with the foreign ministry a second time on the twentieth to express concern about new information that the military government might "apply imminent and severe repressive measures" to its enemies. There was still no response from the de facto Chilean government. On the twenty-sixth the commission changed its approach and requested permission to send the commission's secretary general, Luis Reque, to observe first-hand the situation in Chile. Only then did the foreign ministry reply.[3] Admiral Huerta responded the very same day the request for an on-site visit was conveyed, and gave solemn assurances that "the Chilean government will continue faithfully to fulfill its obligations derived from Inter-American agreements concerning respect for human rights." But, notably, he made no reference to the request for a visit. The authority to grant such a request was clearly above the rear admiral's rank. The next day, Olegario Russi, Chile's acting representative to the OAS, paid Luis Reque a visit in Washington, ostensibly to reiterate his government's reassurances about human rights in Chile. Negotiations surrounding Reque's proposed visit were clearly underway. A week later, on October 5, Russi wrote Reque to inform him coldly that his government "has no objection to your coming to the country, if the commission deems it appropriate."

Luis Reque visited Chile between October 12 and 17, 1973. His first official meetings were with Gonzalo Prieto, the minister of justice, and General Oscar Bonilla, the minister of interior — the two men who should have been most knowledgeable about the human rights situation in the country. The justice minister dutifully explained that, under the simultaneous states of siege and war decreed by the junta, the courts had virtually no jurisdiction in Chile. This would be the same discouraging conclusion reported by members of Chile's high court on countless occasions in the years to come. The encounter with General Bonilla was more intriguing.

Reque's concise report of the meeting with Bonilla only adds to the mystery concerning how much Chile's new interior minister — and other senior military officers — knew about the repression in the first months of the regime. Reque came away with some interesting strands of information, and some personal impressions about the general. The Chilean armed forces had been compelled to intervene "much to his regret," Bonilla told Luis Reque. As to how many were detained, Bonilla stressed that thousands were released after interrogation, and revealed that 35 interrogation teams were operating at detention sites, making sure that the innocent went free (he appears not to have mentioned the summary executions these teams committed). But what is noteworthy is the information about the number of trained intelligence teams already active. The general quoted other figures: 13,000 foreigners were in the country without proper papers, but the military government had already granted 1300 safe conduct passes. Then Bonilla gave a rundown of military casualties suffered to date: nearly 250 casualties, including 40 killed by sniper fire. These figures, it turns out, were incorrect.

The intriguing question relates to Bonilla's knowledge about, and attitude toward, the repression. In death General Bonilla, who was killed in a helicopter crash at the beginning of 1975, came to be considered a moderate man who might have prevented much bloodshed. Carlos Camus, the bishop of Linares who was active in the Committee for Peace and later the Vicariate for Solidarity, has only kind words for Bonilla.[4] Military insiders reported that he opposed Manuel Contreras, and was the only man who possibly could have stopped him. Some Christian Democratic politicians who supported the coup believed Bonilla's off-the-record assurances that the period of military rule would be brief.[5] Moreover, around the time of Reque's visit, Bonilla was making arrangements to have the Bar Association of Antofagasta defend prisoners who were to be brought before war councils by General Arellano. Instead, those prisoners were summarily executed by members of General Arellano's delegation. This suggests that the officers who proposed the iron fist kept other officers, including some very senior officers, in the dark. The head of the ICJ delegation that visited Chile in April 1974 would come away with the same impression about the power of some officers to override the orders of others, including those more senior.

The visit of the IACHR's general secretary provided some painful lessons about the attitude of the Pinochet regime. Permission to travel to Chile would have to be negotiated; thus the work of the IACHR (and especially the UN Special Rapporteur on Chile) would become complicated by the diplomacy of the Cold War, and charges of selective investigation of human rights violators. More dramatically, the attention of human rights monitors would not deter the military government from murdering its enemies.

As Luis Reque made arrangements to travel to Chile, General Arellano, carrying special orders from Pinochet, embarked on the infamous helicopter tour dispensing drumhead justice. Reque arrived in Santiago on October 12 for his five-day inspection visit. He had not yet left the country when Arellano's men went on their bloody rampage in the north. In 72 hours 68 Chileans were murdered, beginning with the executions of 28 leftists in La Serena and Copiapó on October 16 and 17, as Reque concluded his stay.

Reque could not have learned of these crimes even in their immediate aftermath, of course. But he had heard and seen enough to conclude that a formal visit of the IACHR was urgently needed. At the IACHR meeting in Colombia on October 24, Reque told the commissioners that "the Commission should consider the possibility of establishing a subcommission to visit the territory of Chile." General Bonilla, he added, assured him that "there would be no objection." The IACHR was just beginning to exercise its oversight responsibilities, and Reque may have wanted to see it be more assertive. An in loco investigation of Chile, he reported, "would be of major importance, not only to examine on the spot the events mentioned in this report and others, but also to study the full status of human rights."[6]

The commission did not endorse his recommendation regarding an IACHR visit until the following April and did not conduct its inspection until some months later. Instead, the IACHR traded letters with Ismael Huerta, the minister of foreign affairs, in an effort to clarify cases brought to its attention. This would provide another lesson about human rights in Pinochet's Chile. The procedures established to monitor compliance with human rights norms have built-in safeguards to protect the sovereignty of offending states. Pinochet's ministers made the most of them.

The IACHR's original statute permitted it to receive and act on individual petitions, and it began to receive them within months of the September coup.[7] But that same statute also outlined a set of procedures that proved time-consuming and enabled Chile to delay, though not block, the publication of a critical report. Case 1790 is paradigmatic.

On November 9, 1973 the IACHR received a communication denouncing "the arrest, torture and presumed death" of Dr. Enrique París Roa.[8] The denunciation had been brought by María Eugenia Horwitz Vásquez, París's wife. París was one of two dozen individuals who surrendered outside the burning Moneda palace. París was taken with others to Peldhue, the Tacna regiment's headquarters, sometime around 6 p.m., according to eyewitnesses. There, officers separated out Allende advisors and members of his detachment of bodyguards. París, a member of the Communist party and one of Allende's personal physicians, was among a number of Communist or Socialist party leaders who subsequently disappeared. Nothing is known of him after September 17.

París's wife immediately turned to the justice system on September 29 and filed a detailed affidavit with the First Chamber of the Santiago Court of

Appeals. The affidavit contained the names of eyewitnesses, but noted that "mentioned only are those witnesses not subject to further danger should they be called upon to provide information in this case." On October 1 the Investigations Police reported that it had no arrest record for París. Two weeks later the commander of the Tacna regiment went still farther, reporting that "this individual is not being held by order of the military courts in this jurisdiction and having made a number of inquiries, it has not been established that this individual had been detained by any order from administrative authorities."[9] The response that no administrative authority had ordered París's detention and that he was not (or no longer) being held in the jurisdiction was probably true in its specific assertions. But it concealed the more sinister reality.

The failure of the courts to turn up evidence of París's fate and whereabouts meant that domestic remedies had been effectively exhausted. The IACHR's involvement then became possible, but the process would prove lengthy. The communication informing the commission of the case was dated November 9. Exactly two months later the IACHR requested that the military government provide it with information making it possible to determine whether París's rights were violated. In the interim, the seven-member Commission, which included a Chilean jurist, Manuel Bianchi, had to determine the admissibility of the case. Three months after the IACHR made its inquiries, Chile's envoy to the OAS gave word that it could not develop any information about the case of Mr. París "who seems to have disappeared." Investigations by competent Chilean authorities, the envoy assured, were continuing and it promised to report the results of those investigations as soon as it obtained them. The Chilean government was stalling for time.

On April 12 Chile's OAS delegation reported that it still had not been able to develop useful information. Meeting in its thirty-second session, the commission decided to delay further consideration of the case until the Chilean government provided additional information as promised. About the same time, April 18, 1974, the IACHR officially requested that the military government consent to an in loco investigation by the commission. (At that very moment, a delegation from the International Commission of Jurists was already in Chile.) So the commission's decision to postpone consideration of the case, consistent with the IACHR's mandate to arrive at a friendly settlement, was both opportune and diplomatic.

Two weeks before the IACHR delegation arrived in Santiago in late July, the Chilean government followed up its April letter to the commission with an official note. Essentially, nothing had changed. The Chilean government reported that "investigations to establish the facts concerning Mr. París are still continuing," and then requested a delay of 90 days as provided for by paragraph two of Article 51 of the IACHR's rules of procedure. This was a second delay. The IACHR delegation interviewed París's wife and other relevant witnesses when it toured Chile between July 22 and August 2. But the IACHR took no further action. When the commission met again for its thirty-fourth session in October, it decided yet again to postpone its decision on the merits of the case. At this stage, the Chilean government might have provided information, and avoided the publication of a resolution presuming the truth of the charge. But of course somewhere in the Chilean government someone knew what had become of Enrique París and fully understood that providing accurate information would be more damaging than providing none at all.

By the time the IACHR convened its thirty-fifth session the following May, Chile had been afforded more than the normal 180 days and allowed a 90-day extension. This was the limit of the commission's patience. The commission prepared a resolution drafted by commissioner Robert Woodward, an American. "The Government of Chile," said the document, "had failed to provide further information on the case," thus "the Commission feels that the situation denounced is adequately proven."[10] The Commission voted to approve the report on May 29, and resolved to "presume confirmation of the allegations," and to "urge the Government of Chile to continue its investigations as to the fate of Dr. París Roa, assigning responsibility to those who have violated his basic rights."[11] A few days later, too late to block the resolution, the Chilean government cabled the IACHR to inform it that it had made "every possible effort to clarify the situation, but obtained negative results." The commission simply had to understand, said the cable, that "on September 11 and the days following, a real state of war existed, where a number of people died, possibly including Mr. París. Nevertheless, neither his arrest nor his death is on record in any service." No military service had recorded an arrest and death in Case 1790. The IACHR had put the facts on the record, but the matter had consumed a full 18 months, and what must have seemed an eternity to Enrique París's wife. The IACHR's statute was revised, for the second time, in 1979, giving the commission the power to employ emergency measures that might have enabled it to save Enrique París. But, in practice, the military regime's determination to act lawlessly effectively nullified international human rights law. The military regime's power over life and death exceeded anything the IACHR could marshal.

The difficulties in obtaining information about human rights violations from a government bent on committing them made in loco inspections critically important. For their part, AI and ICJ also wanted to observe first-hand a situation that information coming to them indicated was extremely serious. Amnesty International was the first to gain entry.

Two weeks after the IACHR secretary general Luis Reque visited Santiago, an Amnesty International delegation arrived to make its own assessment. The International Committee of the Red Cross was already present, drawing up lists of detainees in the Chile and National Stadiums, and quietly attempting to assist them. Amnesty International had worked out the mission's diplomatic-sounding terms of reference with the foreign ministry, but its real mission, the head of the delegation was told, was to try to put an end to the killing and to protect those in detention regardless of nationality.[12] Frank Newman, then vice chairman of the International Institute of Human Rights in Strasbourg, France, led the three-person team. His testimony before the U.S. House Foreign Relations Committee in the first week of December would be the first of many congressional hearings on what was taking place in the Southern Cone country, and the degree of U.S. responsibility for it.[13]

The AI delegation met with the interior and justice ministers, deputies of the foreign ministry, and legal advisors to the defense ministry. It also met with the chief justice of the Supreme Court, and an unnamed former justice minister—almost certainly Jaime Castillo, an advocate who would factor prominently in the human rights struggle in the coming years. The most interesting meeting, said Newman, was with the executive board of the Chilean Bar Association. Interesting, but unsatisfactory.

Testifying some weeks later, Newman explained to the members of Congress that the legal situation in Chile was in many ways unprecedented, because international human rights law was still very much in its infancy. The International Covenant on Civil and Political Rights was only opened for ratification in 1966 (and would not come into force until 1976). Still, Chile was among the few nations that had ratified all three of the most important human rights treaties by 1973, and it had ratified the Geneva Conventions of 1949. So its conduct toward Chileans could be held to those standards, and in that respect serve as a test case. Committee members, however, wanted to know certain details. How many executed, how many prisoners, what was the U.S. role, and what could Congress do in response?

The numbers, he reported, were uncertain, a fact that invited speculation. Citing the Chilean defense minister's statistics, he told chairman Dante Fascell that at the time of the delegation's visit there were some 550 prisoners charged with various crimes under Chilean law, and another 1000 prisoners the authorities anticipated would be detained for as long as a year without charge. This figure was for the Santiago area alone: comparable figures were given for the situation in the rest of the country. There were more ominous numbers. The International Committee of the Red Cross issued an estimate of 15,000 detentions from the day of the coup until October, just before the AI delegation's visit, said Newman. The ministry of defense openly reported that 95 persons had been killed as of the end of October, as a "result of combat or executions." But, he warned, there was no information as to how many were killed, as he said, "by warfare, death sentences after trial or summary execution."

The delegation's principal task was to end the killing. Newman came away with the impression that the killing had slowed somewhat. But, he noted, "it is certainly difficult to speculate. As far as I could tell, the Ministry of Defense was trying to stop most of the killings. I don't think there is any question that there is less torture." Newman's comments invite inferences about the mood at the Ministry of Defense, where the AI delegation met with "legal advisors." It may very well be that Newman's impressions were given by General Oscar Bonilla, the minister of interior, with whom the delegation had met.

Newman, it turns out, was terribly wrong about the trend of repression, but his mistaken perceptions are understandable. The chaotic first weeks of the new order, with its mass roundups and summary executions, were drawing to a close. But what no one yet realized was that the repression was to take on a new, more selective, form, in the not too distant future.

The plight of refugees, especially foreign refugees, was on the mind of the representatives just as it had been a primary concern of AI. Americans Charles Horman and Frank Terruggi had been arrested and executed in the National Stadium only days after the coup. This tale, depicted first in Thomas Hauser's controversial book and later the Costa-Gavras film, both entitled *Missing*, implicated American officials in the coup. Newman confessed that the situation posed difficult legal problems, and noted that AI and the United Nations High Commissioner for Refugees viewed the matter differently. An immediate objective of the delegation, in conjunction with the effort of the Committee for Peace, the Red Cross, and the UNHCR, was to work out an agreement with foreign, interior, and defense ministries aimed at protecting refugees. The problem was that there were many foreigners in Chile who did not exactly match the UNHCR definition of refugee. These were foreigners "attracted by the Allende government who are not refugees . . . like a lot of Americans who thought it was a great experience, who for one reason or another are in trouble." The dire situation of Chileans attempting to flee certain persecution and death was a separate matter altogether. The root of the problem was the junta's myths about foreign agents. The Interior Ministry was reporting that up to 13,000 foreigners were in Chile. Chile's UN ambassador was claiming that as many as 3,000 of them were in Chile as armed mercenaries prepared to stage an uprising. "A number were killed," Newman told the committee, "thousands were jailed and things looked pretty rough" before the UNHCR pressured the junta.

Foreign embassies were providing refuge and asylum, but this angered the military government. In fact, the junta had just declared the Swedish ambassador, Harald Edelstam, persona non grata and expelled him. Questions were posed about the American embassy, and a different picture emerged. Representative Donald Fraser then alluded to a disconcerting story Newman had heard while in Santiago, and invited him to repeat it. It concerned American Charles Horman. A journalist, who Newman described as "first-rate," related to him that he had been in the U.S. embassy when the Hormans arrived seeking help, only to be turned away. Horman was killed the following day. More troubling, the reporter said, knowledgeable persons knew enough not to make their way to the U.S. embassy, because it could only imperil them. It became "very clear," Newman told the panel, "that the American Embassy was not one of the embassies participating in this humanitarian effort."[14]

The AI delegation had also met with the executive council of the Chilean Bar Association. The meeting evidently did not go well, judging from a letter Newman later sent to the association's president, Alejandro Bascuñán.[15] The AI delegation was astonished to learn, Newman wrote, that it was the consensus of the lawyers on the association's executive board that they did not need a transcript of a televised speech of the interior minister, Oscar Bonilla, in which he specified citizens' rights during searches and seizures. The delegates were also surprised by the board's "seeming lack of concern regarding the need for a public listing of detainees' names." The Committee for Peace had briefed the delegation on the difficulties of identifying prisoners and their place of detention. A list would help immensely. The bar association's lack of concern was a serious matter, the letter stated, because "if lawyers care not, who will be able to expose errors such as mistaken identity and over-zealous prosecuting?"

Amnesty International acted quickly on the report of its delegation. On New Year's Eve 1973, Martin Ennals, then AI's secretary general, wrote General Pinochet that the delegation was "appalled by many summary executions which continued even while the Amnesty International delegation was in Chile." His letter also expressed concern about the number of prisoners shot allegedly while attempting escape, and noted that upon its return the delegation convinced AI's International Executive Commission that "torture has taken place on a large scale." Among AI's other concerns were the right of defendants to counsel, preventive detention, and retroactive enforcement of law. The expulsion of the Swedish ambassador also raised concerns: "Following the recent expulsion of the Swedish Ambassador from Santiago, it would be highly desirable for the Chilean Government to renew its assurance to respect the right of asylum." Then AI's broader understanding of the concept of a refugee in contrast to that of the UNHCR surfaced. "Governmental obligations," Amnesty International's secretary general explained to the Chilean army general, "extend to the many foreigners who, under classical definitions, may technically not be 'refugees' but nonetheless are not protected by modern human rights law."[16]

General Pinochet may have believed it was below his station to comment, but the chief justice of the Chilean Supreme Court of Justice believed himself honor bound to respond publicly. His response was harsh, but it missed the point. Opening the 1974 session of the high court, Chief Justice Enrique Urrutia gave a speech deploring the AI report, remarkably for its lack of candor. As to the delegation's concerns about the violation of human rights alleged to be taking place in the country, Urrutía said, "these concerns were unfounded as they [the AI representatives] had easily been able to see for themselves during their stay in Chile." The chief justice had told the delegation as much, and he was irked that his assurance was nowhere mentioned in the AI report. Whatever allies the international human rights organizations would find in Chile, few were to be found on the high court. It was not a coincidence that Amnesty International's first comprehensive report on the human rights situation in Chile, published on the first anniversary of the coup, carried on its cover a photograph of a smiling, even jocular, Judge Urrutia walking amiably with the members of the junta who had called on the members of the court as one of the junta's first official acts.

The International Commission of Jurists did not gain entry into Chile until April 1974. The situation had changed dramatically by then, but the ICJ delegation's experience was essentially the same as Amnesty International's. The ICJ delegation, dispatched at the behest of the World Council of Churches, was led by the organization's secretary general, Niall MacDermot. It visited Chile April 19–29, 1974.[17] During that time, it met with Cardinal Silva, members of the Supreme Court, the Bar Association, and representatives of the Committee for Peace. It was a critical moment, even if the three-person delegation did not entirely sense why.

For one thing, midway through the delegation's visit, Chile's Catholic bishops issued a statement entitled "Reconciliation in Chile," at the guidance of Cardinal Silva. It was the same theme that Cardinal Silva had been raising from the day of the coup, but now it had an added urgency. In March, the junta published its "Declaration of Principles," in which it indicated that the military government would remain in power indefinitely, because, in its view, "it was absolutely imperative to change the mentality of Chileans."[18] The bishops praised the document's "Christian tenor," and went on to note that "despite certain inadequacies in stating the Christian ideal for social and political life, it offers a basis for guiding civic and social life in this emergency situation."[19] But the bishops were profoundly concerned about what was occurring in Chile during the emergency: worried about the climate of insecurity and fear, about the social aspects of the economic situation, and about the restructuring and reorientation of the educational system. The bishops' most pressing concern, however, was the ineffectiveness of the courts of law when it came to personal security and arbitrary or prolonged detention.

We are worried, finally, in some cases, by the lack of effective juridical care for personal security, which shows up in arbitrary or excessively prolonged detentions in which neither those held nor their relatives know of the concrete charges that prompt them; by the interrogations with physical or moral pressures; by the restrictions on access to legal defense; by unequal sentences for identical causes from place to place; by restrictions on the normal use of the right of appeal.[20]

The leaders of the Roman Catholic Church in Chile carefully selected the euphemism, but the denunciation of torture conveyed by the phrase "interrogations with physical and moral pressure," was unambiguous.

The ICJ visit also came at a time when one of the international human rights movement's main concerns, the fate of foreigners, had all but been assuaged. Based on appearances, the delegation could report that arrests had peaked and were diminishing. The delegation could thus hope, in the words of one of its members, that its mission ("to encourage and hasten as near as may be to Chilean normalcy regarding the arrest, detention, treatment, trial and sentencing of a large number of human beings") might be successful.[21] What the commission did not know was that the Directorate for National Intelligence, the DINA, had been formed secretly at the end of the previous year — the decree-law announcing its existence would not be contrived for another two months. The delegation, however, did receive an inkling of its existence and its methods.

One of the delegates, American Covey Oliver, had ample experience in Latin America, having served as U.S. Ambassador to Colombia and as Assistant Secretary of State for Inter-American Affairs. Testifying before the same congressional committees that had heard the testimony of the AI representative, Oliver gave Congress a first hand account. He had abiding impressions as to how deeply Chilean society had been traumatized over the previous three years and most of all by the coup. He and the other delegates were already aware that the security forces were operating in a different, more cruel manner. And he had some practical advice about dealing with the junta. "It would be," Oliver testified, "counterproductive as to the cause of human rights in Chile to tell the Chileans that they don't know what they are talking about, that there is nothing to fear, or that they are just finding excuses for cruel revenge on now helpless former political opponents. It seemed better to induce the relevant power groups in Chile to see that whatever be the threat situation, it can be managed at less social cost (in human rights terms) and with the saving of what Chile is now paying in serious damage to its reputation abroad." Oliver, a former diplomat turned human rights defender, had an instinct for the politics of human rights. Better to induce the relevant power groups in Chile, he counseled, to recalculate the costs of repression relative to the threat as they saw it. There is no disputing the wisdom of the comment, but as a practical matter it was almost impossible to determine the identity of the relevant power groups, and to assess their relative power, at any given moment in a dynamic and indeterminate situation.

Oliver's overall impression was that the human rights situation he witnessed was "unsatisfactory but remediable."[22] In fact, the situation was about to worsen, and the ICJ delegation saw early signs of that. The DINA had been turned loose against those now helpless former political opponents. The delegation did not know that to be a fact, but recognized that something different was occurring. The new prisoners, he reported ominously, were in a different situation. These people "are being picked up in the dead of night in unmarked jeeps by intelligence officers," and subjected to systematic torture. "A big question," he confided, "is where the intelligence services are at this point and whether they might constitute a state within a military state, as it were." The fear was not groundless. "We have some indication that the intelligence services can override ministers, even ministers in uniform." Whether or not this was a reference to General Bonilla and officers like him, an important reality was beginning to take shape. The relevant power groups, it was already becoming apparent, could not be induced to view the costs of repression as excessive in terms of the damage done to Chile's reputation abroad. Not until mid-1977 did General Pinochet begin to recalculate cost and benefit.

The ICJ report and public comments by its secretary general angered the Chilean government and the president of the Supreme Court. Yet again, the reaction of the chief justice of the Supreme Court, Enrique Urrutia, was defensive, even exasperated. The ICJ was critical of the chief justice of the Chilean Supreme Court for the court's failure to intervene to end the repression. Urrutía felt aggrieved. "Some lawyers have criticized decisions by one of the Panels of this Court," he acknowledged, "that military commissions in times of war are by their nature not within the supervision that is entrusted to this court." The bases for that opinion said the judge, were "clear and fundamental," and as chief justice of the Supreme Court he concurred with it. The continuing criticisms, which focused on the subtle distinctions between the varying states of emergency declared by the junta, were misguided. "This viewpoint overlooks the fact that whatever the actual situation as to internal war is, the said state of war has been legalized, and our legal system does not make any distinctions as to the state of war which the courts have the jurisdiction to find and apply."[23] Urrutia's defensive response made no reference to the central contention of the ICJ report—that, although the Chilean military had declared the country to be in a state of war, its actions were in violation of the Geneva Conventions of 1949.

Controversy did not end there. Niall MacDermot, who had taken over the position of secretary general of the ICJ from Sean MacBride in 1970, had made public statements to the effect that the Chilean military had plans to establish reeducation camps for Chilean children. The charge caused outrage, and led to the resignation of an ICJ member, former Chilean Supreme Court judge Osvaldo Illanes Benítez.[24] Illanes, who had helped with the arrangements for the mission, resigned after MacDermot and the Chilean embassy began to exchange public letters. For its part, the Chilean embassy in the United States assailed the ICJ's findings and MacDermot's allegations through a series of newspaper ads and op-ed pieces in the *New York Times* and the *Washington Post*. Undaunted, MacDermot issued several press releases and a confidential correspondence documenting his allegation. In what was already a familiar refrain, reports critical of Chile's human rights abuses were dismissed as lies emanating from Moscow. "We rejoice over the present communiqué of the International Commission of Jurists," said an ad placed in the *Washington Post* in November 1974, "since it demonstrates the latter's relationship with the Soviet Union and its allies in pursuance of identical objectives."[25] There was something ironic about the charge in this instance. In 1967 it was revealed that the Central Intelligence Agency had been instrumental in creating the ICJ and secretly funded it through a series of fronts. Covert funding was subsequently ended.[26] Despite the circumstances of its origin, the ICJ had earned the reputation as an independent, balanced human rights organization. But if it had been the instrument of any interest it certainly was not part of the international communist campaign to malign the military government of Chile.

The amount of solid evidence of human rights abuses uncovered by these nongovernmental organizations in their in loco visits is quite remarkable. Estimates of the number of dead and detained were faulty and subject to change, but that is understandable. General Bonilla's interior ministry did not have accurate or timely information, and the general himself might not have had full knowledge that Pinochet had approved of a war of extermination. Indeed, Manuel Contreras had not yet briefed his superiors on his plan for the DINA when Luis Reque visited Chile on behalf of the IACHR or when Amnesty International came to the country.[27] But solid, detailed information about (many) detention centers, the prevalence of torture, and the abdication of the courts and legal profession was obtained and published. The independent existence of the DINA was not made public until some months after the ICJ conducted its investigation, but its delegates sensed that a new, more destructive force was at work. Covey Oliver even had the insight to compare Contreras's DINA to a state within the military state. The court of world opinion may have had its deficiencies, such as the inability to remand the defendants into custody, but lack of incriminating evidence was not one of them.

Even while the mission of the International Commission of Jurists was still in Santiago, the Inter-American Commission on Human Rights decided that a full-scale investigation was in order. Luis Reque, the IACHR's general secretary, had reached that conclusion back in October, when he recommended that a subcommission be created to visit Chile. By April 1974 the relationship between the IACHR and the military government had become so tense that the commissioners decided that a visit of the entire IACHR was warranted. On April 18, 1974 the IACHR made the formal request, noting that "while some denunciations on individual cases might be clarified through an exchange of notes with the Government of Chile, no decision on the general situation, that is to say, on the repeated denunciation that serious and massive violations of human rights occurred in Chile, could be adopted without resorting to the procedure of examination in loco of the situation."[28] Now the Pinochet government would have to decide whether to tolerate yet another intrusion into its affairs. The military government would stall. The commission's president, Justino Jiménez, would have to resort to a press release to gain the military government's cooperation, notwithstanding General Bonilla's confident assurances, made back in October, that there would be no objection to such a visit.

The formal request for a visit was transmitted to Chilean authorities in a letter dated April 18, 1974. It was not well received by the Chilean government, despite the fact that the IACHR intended to convey "the broadest and most absolute recognition of the incontrovertible right of the Government of Chile to grant or deny the consent requested of it."[29] The Chilean government was more in the mood to deny than to grant consent. First, however, it would play for time.

Patricio Carvajal, the defense minister, responded to the IACHR's letter in his capacity as acting minister of foreign affairs, as Huerta was out of the country at the time of the request, accompanying Pinochet on a visit to Peru. Carvajal's response came a full month after the request had been made. "A concrete response," Carvajal wrote, would have to await their return, but Carvajal felt confident enough to add that the June 1 date for the visit, suggested by the IACHR in its initial request was, in any event, "premature."

The IACHR wasted no time in answering this note via a cable sent the following day. The commission's president expressed "regret" that the Chilean government believed a June visit would be premature, and then reiterated the request more forcefully:

COMMISSION IN EXERCISE OF ITS IRREVOCABLE MANDATE TO WATCH OVER OBSERVANCE OF HUMAN RIGHTS, AND IN VIEW OF THE SERIOUSNESS AND URGENCY OF THE ACTS DENOUNCED, HOLDS TO ITS FIRM INTENTION TO VISIT CHILE AS SOON AS POSSIBLE TO STUDY *IN LOCO* DENUNCIATIONS WHICH ALLEGE VIOLATIONS OF HUMAN RIGHTS.[30]

Six days later the commission intensified the pressure by bringing the matter to the attention of the press. "There was great interest in the press to know the status of these actions," the head of the commission explained, so the purpose of the press release was simply to ensure that "any information published on this matter would be true and objective."[31] The move was effective, but the military government would be forever mindful of the power of the press. When Niall MacDermot, secretary general of the International commission of Jurists, went public with accusations some months later, the regime launched a newspaper ad campaign attacking him. Public relations would become a fixation for Pinochet, even if his ministers often handled things badly.

When Ismael Huerta returned from his trip abroad with General Pinochet, he fired off a letter to the president of the commission. The admiral who had become a diplomat by dint of a coup d'état felt compelled to express his "surprise" over the content of the cable sent to Carvajal in his absence. He did not mention the press release. The directness of the cable, which reiterated the commission's "firm intention to visit Chile as soon as possible," seems to have conveyed the point, because the foreign minister repeated it in his letter. Huerta was perturbed that the head of the region's human rights organization seemed to have forgotten that "the prior consent of the Chilean government is required," before a visit could be made. The president of the commission had not forgotten, of course — he merely wanted the foreign minister of Chile to remember the IACHR's "irrevocable mandate to watch over [the] observance of human rights," and the Chilean government's obligation to abide by the Geneva Conventions of 1949. Huerta (who would be replaced before the IACHR arrived) was forced to relent: "I have no objection to granting the consent of my government."[32]

The IACHR finally conducted its investigation between July 22 and August 2, 1974. It had negotiated access to Chile a second time, counting the executive secretary's visit in October 1973. The pattern, evident during Luis Reque's visit, was repeated: some prisoners were transferred, but the repression did not cease. The presence of the full commission in Chile complicated matters, but the complications were not insurmountable.

The IACHR's authority as an organ of the OAS gave it access to information and sites that the Amnesty International and the International Commission of Jurists delegations to Chile, in November 1973 and April 1974 respectively, simply could not obtain. The ICJ delegation, for example, had met with Cardinal Silva, representatives of the Committee for Peace, the Bar Association, and the Supreme Court. The IACHR mission, however, succeeded in visiting jails and other detention sites, interviewed hundreds of Chileans from all walks of life, examined judicial files, observed war councils, and traveled widely in the country.

The junta was not oblivious to the significance of the visit, or to the potentially damaging consequences of its report. But it was not so intimidated by the presence of the commissioners that it would discontinue what, at least for the hardliners, was its mission — to extirpate Marxism from the Chilean body politic. The DINA was in the midst of an intense campaign to capture Miguel Enríquez, the head of the hunted MIR, and dozens of militants were abducted, tortured, murdered, and disappeared in the process. The high profile prisoners, the senior officials in Allende's Popular Unity government, were transferred on the eve of the IACHR's visit. The treatment of these men was scandalous to the diplomatic community. So, in anticipation of the IACHR's visit, the military government transferred these prisoners from the barren Dawson Island to a new internment camp constructed at Ritoque, not far from the Pacific coast resorts of Valparaíso and Viña del Mar. The commissioners would visit the men there, and would hear some bold testimony about their treatment.

Other prisoners were being moved as well. The property located at 38 Londres Street had been the main interrogation-torture center of the DINA. The prisoners taken there in the DINA's fierce campaign to destroy the Movement of the Revolutionary Left were far less prominent than the men who had been sent to Dawson Island, but they were far more dangerous in the eyes of their interrogators. These were the armed revolutionaries, not the bombastic bureaucrats of the Popular Unity. If the commission had any testimony about Londres 38, an important operation would be compromised, and a terrible truth would be revealed.

The solution was to evacuate Londres 38, and to move the prisoners to another facility located on José Domingos Cañas Street.[33] The campaign against the radicals would not subside, even temporarily. The DINA was closing in on the Movement's leader, Miguel Enríquez (in October 1974, it caught up with him and killed him). The juxtaposition of circumstances is revealing. Edgardo Enríquez, Allende's minister of education, had been moved from Dawson to Ritoque to placate foreigners; meanwhile, militants in the Movement headed by Miguel Enríquez, Edgardo Enríquez's son, were taken to a more secure and secret location on José Domingos Cañas Street to be tortured and disappeared beyond the prying gaze of the IACHR.

After an initial round of interviews with the ministers, and an audience with Cardinal Silva, the IACHR set out to conduct its investigation.

The high-ranking officials of the deposed Popular Unity government recently transferred from remote Dawson Island to the comparative comfort of the camp at Ritoque were of special concern to the commissioners. The brutality of their treatment symbolized the intensity of the soldiers' contempt and vengefulness. Some men, like former Allende defense minister José Tohá, died as a result of the harsh climate and difficult conditions on Dawson. If this group of prisoners was transferred, it was not because the military was concerned about their condition. So, if these men were treated so inhumanely before the IACHR arrived, what was the plight of the rank and file supporters of the leftist parties, people who did not enjoy the protection of notoriety and personal contacts made at cocktail parties and official receptions?

The commission made it a point to visit these prominent former officials, and heard some harrowing testimony. These men were highly educated professional politicians. They could describe the maltreatment they and others received, and provide details relevant to the case of missing or dead colleagues, like Enrique París. They even provided the names of at least some torturers. Some prisoners requested anonymity, but Luis Corvalán defiantly spoke out.

"This is Luis Corvalán speaking," he began, and then entered on a careful discussion of the regime's abuses. "The present government stated several weeks ago in a public declaration," he observed, "that there are no tortures, and if there had been any, they are foreign to the government's way of thinking and acting and would therefore be the responsibility of isolated officials. That is not true. The responsibility for the tortures falls to the government, and, first of all, to General Pinochet, because there is an entire apparatus set up." Corvalán concluded his denunciation by addressing the

Chilean member of the IACHR delegation to underscore the point that, whatever the shortcomings of the Allende government (Corvalán was even willing to concede that the Socialist president had "used loopholes in the law"), the "current government is absolutely arbitrary, absolutely illegal, absolutely unconstitutional." Pinochet's government, he said plainly, "has liquidated the rule of law that existed in this country. And Mr. Bianchi, who is a Chilean, knows perfectly well that there has never been in the history of Chile a dictatorship as brutal as that which our people unfortunately have and now suffer."

An unnamed prisoner delved into the politics of human rights. "I appreciate, Mr. Chairman, the openness with which you have indicated the Commission's authority, because I want to tell you in all frankness that there are undoubtedly few of us who thought the OAS has the necessary structure to be able to attain full observance of human rights in all member countries." The commission had some very real limitations, he went on, "we understand all of those limitations perfectly, and we have exchanged opinions among ourselves, even with respect to the ultimate meaning that your report might have, because we understand perfectly well the political way this material will be discussed, if it is ever discussed, someday in the Assembly of the Organization of American States."[34] It was an apt comment. The highly charged theme of human rights was bound to be politicized in a forum like the OAS General Assembly, and even more so in the United Nations Human Rights Commission, the Economic and Social Council and, above all, the UN General Assembly.

What was to be the first of several reports was approved by the commission on October 24, 1974, exactly one year after Luis Reque's visit. The politics of the situation were carefully skirted. "This report does not seek to make comparisons," it began.

It is the result of objective examination, in a particular political-social situation, of one single topic, which is, whether human rights are actually observed and protected. It is not for the Commission to decide whether the present political regime is more or less desirable than the previous regime. Only the citizens of Chile, acting freely, can validly pass judgement on that.[35]

The normative standards to which Chile was to be held was another matter. The commission could cite the authority of several sources. One was the American Declaration on the Rights and Duties of Man of 1948; another was the American Convention on Human Rights, also known as the Pact of San José. The Pact, drafted and opened for signature in 1969, was not yet in force. But Chile was one of 12 states that had already adhered to the convention, and the commission could note that "ratification is well underway." Finally, the commission had the authoritative norms of the Geneva Conventions of 1949, especially article 3, common to the four conventions.

The commission was quite insistent about the applicability of the Geneva

Conventions, especially in meetings with General Bonilla, recently made minister of defense. The relevance of the laws of war, however, would be a controversial matter long after the Pinochet regime had ceded power to civilians, a transition that was still some sixteen years in the future. The military had declared a state of war, and was applying wartime provisions to civilians. Yet the commission took issue with the junta's claims; "a normal observer would not have imagined that he was in a country in a 'state of war'."[36] This same conclusion would be reached after the transition by the presidential commission of inquiry. Human rights defenders were reluctant to concede to the soldiers that Chile was in a state of war. Nevertheless, the military government's assertion to the contrary, although made to justify its violent repression, made the regime subject to the conventions.

The commission could conclude that it had "collected information, which, after rational analysis, it feels is sufficient to assert that, under the regime instituted in Chile beginning September 11, 1973, extremely serious violations of human rights occurred."[37] The whole panoply of human rights was being violated, according to the commission. The right to life was not adequately protected, despite the fact that soldiers had stopped summary executions on the pretense of applying the "law of flight," an expedient that had served General Arellano's delegation well the previous October, while executive secretary Reque was in Chile. The pattern of disappearances, however, was not yet visible to the commission. Nor could the commission determine with absolute certainty whether torture was being practiced as a matter of policy. There was no doubt that the practice was widespread; the testimony of scores of victims convinced the commissioners of that. The exact methods were beginning to be catalogued. "The use of electric shock, the threat of harm to close relatives, sexual attacks, covering persons with a hood, blindfolding the person for weeks, etc., are reasonably proven facts." But, it could not assert that "a 'policy of torture' was practiced." What was certain was that "no effective 'policy against torture' had been carried out."[38] Nevertheless the IACHR confirmed that torture was being inflicted in a number of locations, and the commission specified them. Londres 38 appeared on the list, José Domingos Cañas Street did not.

The General Assembly of the OAS acted on the IACHR report during its sixth plenary session in May 1975, by adopting another resolution.[39] (Notably, it was at this same time, mid-May, that the Mexican daily *Excelsior* printed leaked excerpts from an internal memorandum of the Committee for Peace. The episode proved useful to Pinochet, who wanted to be rid of the committee.) The resolution called on Chile to "give the most careful attention to the suggestions and recommendations of the Inter-American Commission on Human Rights." It also called on the IACHR to submit a second report during the next session of the General Assembly. The next session of the supreme organ of the OAS, it turns out, would take place in the Chilean capital.

The OAS in Santiago

In a masterful stroke of diplomatic maneuvering, the Chilean representative to the OAS succeeded in bringing the OAS General Assembly to Santiago to hold its sixth regular session in June 1976. This was an excellent opportunity to improve the regime's tarnished public image. There had already been some gains. In May U.S. Treasury Secretary William Simon visited Chile and made positive remarks about improvements in the human rights situation. When Secretary of State Henry Kissinger attended the OAS meeting in the Chilean capital the following month, he made similar comments. Kissinger had been the implacable enemy of Allende. He could be the protective ally of Pinochet.

But the OAS regular session would be marked by two dramatic events. Making the most of the opportunity, a group of six prominent attorneys would address a public letter to the OAS denouncing human rights abuses. The open letter touched off a fire storm of controversy, and would lead to the abduction and exile of two of the jurists. That was not all. While foreign representatives of the American republics were in town, a desperate group of Chileans would attempt to storm foreign embassies seeking refuge, thinking that the glare of publicity would deter the regime from causing them harm. They were mistaken. In what was already a pattern, the security forces would not back off from their campaign to kill off their enemies while foreign dignitaries were present in the country. In fact, they turned on a new victim, the central committee of the Communist party.

By the time the OAS convened its General Assembly, the IACHR had produced its second report on the human rights situation in the country. It now fell on the foreign ministers to consider the report and draft the appropriate resolution. To influence the deliberations, and shed more light on the reality behind the diplomatic niceties, six distinguished lawyers from the Christian Democratic and Radical parties took the risky decision to address a letter to the foreign ministers assembled in the Chilean capital.[40]

It was a trenchant document prepared by men who, by their own accounts, had opposed the Allende government. "Because of our professional experience," they wrote, "we are in a position to offer such a testimony, not because of any personal grievance, but because we know the law, appear before the Tribunals, have contact with political and administrative authorities, collaborate in social and legal assistance programs of the churches, and above all because we are in contact on a daily basis with a great number of concrete experiences relating to this matter." They knew the human rights situation very well and understood their obligation to denounce it, even though they anticipated that "they would receive attacks, insults and threats from sectors of the press and even from government officials."

The authors' legal and constitutional analysis of the state of siege in effect now for nearly three years was impeccable, as was the point by point refutation of the junta's arguments on the issue of human rights. As learned jurists and experienced attorneys, they could advise the OAS delegates that the state of siege and now the state of emergency, supposedly temporary measures, had been transformed into a permanent regime that led to repression and abuse of power. And they could attest that the DINA was entirely above the law. "No one doubts," they conceded, "that a nation's internal security demands an intelligence service, given the complexity of contemporary problems. But neither does any one doubt that the dark history of secret police, developed in the shadow of the totalitarian states of the present century, cannot continue without leading humanity to a new primitivism." Chile had arrived at that point. There is "an impressive amount of testimony and every sort of proof" that torture was practiced in Chile and that Chileans simply disappeared after arrest by the DINA.

Lately, arrests are being made in a simple procedure by which armed men dressed in civilian clothes arrest citizens in their home or on the streets without leaving any trace. There is no evidence of their actions. The Minister of Interior does not know the facts. The DINA denies them. But, a whole group of persons have disappeared from their home after these armed men arrived there to arrest them. The security services have not found that these kidnappings are carried out by any group of extremist subversives, and everything is covered by an a priori explanation: that these acts are premeditated to influence the mood of the foreign ministers assembled in Santiago.

As members of the Bar, the authors were profoundly dismayed by the attitude of the courts and the legal profession. During the Allende years, they recalled, the courts acted with complete independence from the executive. Judges were not reluctant to defend the rights of citizens, especially property rights, and they even "participated in public polemics with the president." "We supported that attitude," they boasted, "but today nothing of the kind is happening."

Habeas Corpus is null and void in our country of an exemplary democratic tradition. The Supreme Court voluntarily abandoned, contrary to its own history and the relevant legal norms, its right to issue complaint appeals [*recursos de queja*] against abominable sentences of Military Tribunals, particularly during the first years of the military government. The lower courts, sometimes because of a lack of interest or fear, other times because of the extra-judicial situations created by the Secret Security Service, have not gone farther than the reluctant indictment for homicide, kidnapping, rape etc. Frequently, the only possible attitude for the judges and other court officials, is purely and simply to declare themselves incompetent. Even the regime's journalists appear to enjoy the right to insult and slander citizens. Nothing and no one stops them. Only a few judges have retained their honor, and as a consequence have suffered the hostility of the unconditional supporters of the regime.

As to the regime's arguments about human rights in general, the six authors were unconvinced. These men had heard and could counter all the arguments representatives of the Pinochet government could propound. The letter to the OAS ministers contained a succinct, point-counterpoint refutation that neatly summarizes the problem of human rights.

In comparison with the human rights record of the Allende government the situation was not so bad: not true, the authors of the letter had practiced law during the Allende years and were capable of making comparative judgments. Other governments lack the moral authority to denounce violations in Chile because they commit them as well: spurious, because another government's failures do not excuse the crimes of Chile's military government. Criticism of the human rights situation in Chile constituted a violation of the principle of non-intervention: false, because international organizations are mandated to promote human rights and can fulfill their mandate without undue interference in Chile's internal affairs. The critical human rights reports are based on information gathered outside the country: irrelevant, because there is no other way to obtain evidence, especially since the Chilean government refuses to permit the United Nations Human Rights Commission to conduct an in loco inspection. The charges leveled against Chile have no validity: untenable in light of the incontrovertible evidence contained in the reports produced to date.

It was a incisive analysis that could only earn the authors the scorn of the regime's "unconditional supporters." The attack was not long in coming. The regime's principal theoretician, Jaime Guzmán, led the assault. The authors fought back as best they could, given the regime's control of the media. What ensued was a semi-public debate that gave Chileans the rare chance to see two of the country's most formidable legal minds arguing about the meaning of patriotism, human rights, and even the Judeo-Christian values underpinning the law. In years past this might have made for a lively, academic debate organized by the law schools of either the Catholic University or the University of Chile. But now the issues were deadly serious.

Guzmán was professor of constitutional law at the prestigious Catholic University and had been one of the directors of Jorge Alessandri's 1970 presidential campaign. Not only was he one of the regime's unconditional supporters, he was its leading proponent. It was Jaime Guzmán who had drafted the 1974 Declaration of Principles, and it was Guzmán who had convinced Pinochet of the wisdom of pursuing neo-liberal economic reforms. Now Guzmán was an influential member of the commission created by Pinochet to draft a new constitution. When the document was unveiled in 1980, most observers recognized Guzmán's mark. Understandably, Guzmán enjoyed ready access to the media.

Four days after the letter had reached the OAS delegates, Guzmán took to the air waves to vent his anger and present the regime's view of things. The constitutional scholar attempted to cast the polemic in abstract terms of the problematic of human rights in the modern world. But Guzmán was incensed and his short television address rapidly turned to ad hominem attacks on the authors and Christian Democratic leaders, including former president Frei. "The theme of human rights is a problem of free, modern States," he began, warming to the topic. The crux of the problem is that many modern states "are subject to ideological aggression by international communism," and to "terrorism which threatens innocent victims and often sows chaos." Therein lies the challenge, because "it is necessary to guarantee the rights of all the persons within a community, especially the right of the vast majority that wants to live in peace and that the government has the obligation to protect." Guzmán was disturbed that Castillo and the other authors would "try to sling mud at the fatherland, and join in the foreign conspiracy," at the very moment the OAS was meeting in the country. The authors, Guzmán asserted, had insulted the president, the government, the Supreme Court, the Bar Association — indeed virtually everyone who practiced law.

Guzmán admitted that he knew some of the signatories personally, and felt sorry for them, "sorry that political meanness, that passion, could bring them to such an extreme of blindness that would make them become involved in such a tremendously anti-patriotic act." But sorrow was not the only justified emotion: Chileans should feel defrauded and betrayed by these "petty men" whom they had once entrusted with political authority. By petty men Guzmán had in mind once respected figures "like don Eduardo Frei who," Guzmán noted, "refused to assist the Council of State just a short time ago."

Jaime Guzmán's desultory remarks were not worthy of the man, as Jaime Castillo would duly note in his attempted rebuttal. The notion that a government's obligation to protect its citizens somehow justified the lawless conduct of the security forces was deeply flawed. It was hypocrisy coming from a man who later told interviewers that Manuel Contreras, the man entrusted with protecting innocent Chileans from the onslaughts of international communism, was an amoral individual.[41] The notion of a concerted propaganda attack on Chile was routinely worked into every public pronouncement of regime spokesmen, but the accusation that the authors of the OAS letter were somehow party to a conspiracy to demean the Chilean government was ludicrous. The attack on Frei, the symbol of the Christian Democratic party, was spiteful. Jaime Castillo had been one of the authors of the 1970 statute of constitutional guarantees intended to constrain Allende (the military government constantly cited the Christian Democratic party's accusation that Allende had violated the accord to justify the coup) and was a vociferous critic of Marxist philosophy, having authored tracts on the subject. Eduardo Frei, of course, had anchored the right wing of the Christian Democratic party, and his tacit support of military intervention provided powerful impetus for it. But Frei was a decent man with deeply rooted democratic convictions, and he repeatedly embarrassed the de facto government. He had refused to shake the hands of the junta members when he appeared with them and other former presidents the week after the coup, and he had published a book critical of the human rights violations of the regime just the year before. Now, Frei had refused to participate in the Council of State, an essentially powerless advisory body set up by Pinochet to give the appearance of consultation.

Frei's refusal detracted from the regime's legitimacy. Guzmán and other figures from the once moribund Chilean right were resentful of the Christian Democrats and looking to permanently replace them as the custodians of Chile's political future. The Christian Democrats may have believed that they would be the political beneficiaries of military intervention, but Guzmán and the others who now enjoyed privileged access to Pinochet were claiming their rightful place as the true victors of September 11. It was Guzmán who displayed the pettiness and political meanness that he had attributed to Castillo and other Christian Democrats.

Jaime Castillo, responding on behalf of the other five authors of the letter, immediately countered the allegations of disloyalty. Castillo had been dean of the equally prestigious School of Law of the University of Chile and former justice minister under Eduardo Frei. But Castillo did not enjoy access to the official media outlets. The day after Guzmán's tempestuous address, Castillo sent a letter to the manager of the television station that broadcast Guzmán's editorial, a letter subsequently read over Radio Chilena (he was not granted television air time). Castillo immediately drew attention to Guzmán's demeanor on television, and then moved on to his spurious argument that by criticizing the country's government, the authors were somehow attacking the fatherland itself.

His style did not correspond at all to his usual serenity, intelligence and clarity as demonstrated on other television programs. This change is explicable. Before he was in truth: he used to defend democratic rights. Now he is in error: he attacks those who defend them.

Here was the former dean of a prestigious law school lecturing a professor of the nearest competitor. "What Mr. Guzmán is forgetting," Castillo wrote, "is the Christian notion of the person, and what he is emphasizing is the totalitarian notion of society," because in the latter, only adherents to the regime are granted rights. Castillo too was pained: that Guzmán had sunk to the level of "immoral and unscrupulous newspaper editors." "Mr. Guzmán is entering the same waters as persons of a far lower intellect than his. He claims that we want to sling mud at the fatherland, and that the document accuses Chile. By that he is saying that a country's government is confused with the country itself."

Castillo took solace in the fact that he and his coauthors found themselves in admirable company. "There is no defender of the dignity of man that has not received this attack. Solzhenitsyn is criticized with exactly this argument," he observed, alluding to the Russian dissident who had written the acclaimed *Gulag Archipelago*. (It was a timely allusion, since Chilean Communist party chief Luis Corvalán, held without charge by the military authorities, would be exchanged for Soviet dissident Victor Bukovsky a few months later.) Then the former justice minister laid down a challenge to his counterpart who enjoyed uncensored access to the mass media. "Mr. Guzmán hardly refers to the content of our letter. He knows perfectly well that the public at large does not know it. The public receives a broadside of epitaphs but it lacks the capacity to judge for itself. Stalin did not argue with his enemies — he stood them in front of a firing squad." Over the next week or so Castillo and his colleagues found themselves writing judiciously crafted letters in response to newspaper columns printed by those "immoral and unscrupulous" editors of the pro-regime papers. Some of these responses were published, but most were not.

Other legal professionals could not remain impassive, although it took considerably more courage to back the six dissidents than the regime. Thus the episode was important for what it revealed about the legal profession in a country ruled by a repressive regime. On June 17, one hundred and fourteen law students of the University of Chile, where Castillo had formerly been dean, sent an unsigned letter abroad for publication. Their profound concern for fundamental rights motivated them to manifest their adherence to the letter originally sent to the OAS, they stated. They were inspired to write, albeit anonymously, by the example shown by these prominent figures, "as jurists and good men." Their letter was countered by pro-regime lawyers in a letter dated June 20 and circulated abroad by the junta. One hundred and seventy-six practicing attorneys characterized the letter sent by Castillo and his colleagues to the OAS as "false and unacceptable." The very next day twenty-one of their colleagues wrote in support of Castillo and the others, decrying the "defamation campaign against them." They had studied the document and found it to be "serious, objective and true." Among the signatories of this letter were future members of the Chilean Human Rights Commission, headed by Castillo, after he returned from two years of exile.

The legal profession was struggling with its conscience. Two weeks after the controversy exploded, attorney and author Claudio Orrego Vicuña addressed a poignant open letter to Jaime Guzmán. He asked the regime's leading theoretician to search his conscience and answer the same three soul-searching questions that he had asked himself:

Could you swear with your hand upon the Lord's Bible that you are convinced that in Chile there have not been hundreds of dead, disappeared, and tortured by the security services? Could you swear with your hand upon the Lord's Bible that the DINA is a secret service that acts within the parameters of the constitution and the existing laws, or even within those of the legal provisions set by the government? Could you swear with your hand upon the Lord's Bible that it is a lie that the majority of the Supreme Court and the lower courts have not accepted even a single writ of habeas corpus, and have left the citizenry defenseless before the abuse of power?

Orrego reached his own conclusion, "I cannot now swear to that, and I am convinced that you cannot either." Neither the pro-regime papers nor Guzmán published the letter.

General Pinochet could afford to let the semi-public debate continue for the duration of the OAS session. The sparring of the lawyers gave the impression that freedom of expression was alive and well in Chile — something Pinochet's representative before the OAS duly noted in his comments before the regional organization — and the regime controlled most media outlets for the debate. But Pinochet could not let the debate probe too deeply, or continue indefinitely. After all, to paraphrase Castillo's cogent response to Guzmán, the signatories of the letter were in truth, their detractors in error. On June 20, the junta issued a public edict forbidding further public discussion of the OAS letter, as well as the abortive attempt of a group of Chileans to enter the Bulgarian embassy for the purpose of receiving asylum. But that was not the end of it.

A month and a half after the controversy died down, and the OAS had departed from the Chilean capital, Jaime Castillo and Eugenio Velasco were abducted, rushed to the international airport, and expelled from the country. At the time of their arrest, both men were characteristically pressing the human rights issue. Eugenio Velasco was on his way to his office carrying the text of an appeal that he planned to file with the courts when DINA agents nabbed him. Velasco had been working on the document with another of the authors of the OAS letter. The prolific Castillo was drafting yet another manifesto, this one about the rights and duties of lawyers, when agents burst into his home. He later told investigative journalists that his first sensation was one of incredulity. He demanded that the men identify themselves and state the charge against him. But the DINA agents had not come to debate the law. The men yanked him from the sofa, snatched his thick eye glasses, and pushed him toward the stairs. Outside they handcuffed him, forced him into the back of a car, threw a jacket over his head, and threatened to kill him. He remembers the sensation of nearly suffocating. The agents who had abducted Velasco were already waiting at the airport when the car carrying Castillo arrived. Both men were hurried into the terminal, boarded on a plane, and sent into exile.[42]

The incident at the Bulgarian embassy was the other dramatic event of the OAS session in Chile. On June 15, a number of Chileans rushed to the embassy seeking asylum, but were arrested. This was an unexpected opportunity for the regime to cast itself in a favorable light. Almost all were released in Santiago's principal downtown park as the alerted media watched. But two young men, both MIRistas, were secretly held. The regime had had a stroke of good luck. Pinochet could release most of the arrested to the flash of cameras. The DINA, after a routine check of its files, could eliminate two MIRistas who had somehow survived the assault on the MIR completed at the end of the previous year. Neither would be heard from again.[43]

Forty-eight hours later, on June 17, the supreme organ of the OAS adopted a resolution on the IACHR's second report. The public remarks of William Simon and Henry Kissinger seemed partially borne out by the report which concluded that "there has been a quantitative reduction in the infringement of certain fundamental human rights."[44] The language contained in the report, and adopted by the OAS resolution, was vaguely reminiscent of the observations of Covey Oliver, the member of the International Commission of Jurists delegation that had visited Santiago in late April 1974. The situation was "unsatisfactory but remediable," he had told members of the House Foreign Relations Committee. Foreign observers, it seemed, were continuously caught off guard. Signs that the repression might be diminishing were observed and noted, but the possibility that, in fact, it was secretly being intensified was hardly imagined. The truth was that, beginning in April, the security forces had begun disappearing Communist party leaders. The campaign would continue through the end of the year. The IACHR's third report would contain evidence of what had occurred on the very eve of the sixth regular session of the OAS General Assembly.

Chapter 6
A War of Resistance

> "What other images have you been unable to forget?"
> "When they sprayed benzene all over my body."
> "Did you think that they were going to burn you?"
> "No, never."
> — Journalist's interview with Carmen Gloria Quintana

A Critical Juncture

By the time Pinochet and his most fervent supporters celebrated the fourth anniversary of the coup d'état in 1977, the transformation of Chile was well underway. The security forces had all but eliminated the most dangerous elements of the left; neo-liberal economists had redefined the country's role in the international economic order; and a small group of constitutional scholars, led by Jaime Guzmán, had sketched the contours of a new order. Pinochet would defiantly preside over the new order for another decade, despite misgivings from within and criticisms from abroad. Events over the next three years made it all possible. Chile was at a critical juncture.

Many Chileans who had secretly desired military intervention four years before had anticipated a brief period of military rule. Those who had openly militated for a coup made no secret of their desire that the armed forces would make a revolution. For them General Pinochet was an almost messianic figure, and their support for his indefinite rule, buttressed by a new constitutional order, was unconditional. In fact, the junta began to search for a formula for continued rule early on. The junta created a commission to draft a new constitution only one month after seizing power.

The first formal attempt to enunciate a set of principles to define the new regime came in March 1974 with the publication of the Declaration of Principles of the Chilean Government. Jaime Guzmán was its principal author and would become a leading figure in the dictatorship, but not before he had a philosophical conversion. The declaration was important mainly because, it signaled that the junta would "take upon itself the historic mission of giving Chile new governmental institutions."[1] But Pinochet ultimately did not embrace the corporatist vision of society it contained. The junta crafted another statement, the National Objectives of the Chilean Government, at the very end of 1975, a document that a leading Christian Democrat aptly described as "based on the concept of national security, conditioned by economic liberalism."[2] The ideas contained in these documents reflected the interests of quite different constituencies, and Pinochet was the one man who could decide which of them would prevail—the victors of September 11 were now squabbling over the spoils.

The first of the two main groups vying for influence were gremialistas and neo-fascist nationalists, who were guided by a neo-corporatist ideology and who advocated a civic-military movement resembling what Franco had established in Spain. Pinochet was initially amenable to the idea.[3] A second group consisted of neo-liberal economists, the now famous "Chicago boys." Although not entirely antagonistic to the gremialists, they argued successfully against the state protection of economic sectors implied by their views. Jaime Guzmán was a prominent figure in this connection. Guzmán had been enamored with gremialist thought, but his thinking changed after he read the works of Friedrich von Hayek and North American Michael Novak. Having been converted, Guzmán was determined to guide Pinochet away from a corporatist vision of Chilean society to a neo-liberal one.[4] He succeeded. In March 1975 Milton Friedman made the first of a series of visits to Chile to counsel the junta. Friedman, who would be awarded the Nobel Prize for economics the following year, advised the junta to apply "shock treatment" to the Chilean economy to bring inflation under control and to reactivate an economy in deep recession. The following month, advocates of the neo-liberal policies outlined by Friedman assumed control over the ministries of the economy and finance and the Central Bank.[5]

Pinochet's endorsement of neo-liberalism settled one controversy. But Chile's political situation, although stable, was unsustainable. While the junta was searching for direction, the security forces were amassing victims and compiling a condemnable human rights record. Human rights organizations in Chile and abroad actively pressed for an end to repression. Moreover, pressure would build over the next few years for the announcement of a timetable for a return to democracy. Pinochet moved on all these fronts beginning in mid-1977. By 1980 he had successfully imposed a new constitution fitted to his specifications, and was preparing to rule Chile for another sixteen years.

Pinochet gave one of the most important speeches of his dictatorship on the evening of July 9, 1977. The Chacarillas speech, as it has come to be known, announced a drawn-out transition to what would he preferred to call a "protected," or even an "authoritarian" democracy. "September 11 signified not only the overthrow of an illegitimate and failed government," said the dictator, "rather that event represented the end of a spent political, institutional regime, and the consequent imperative to construct a new one."[6] He denounced those who "intended to make us kneel with threats or pressures, internal or external" — an allusion to the United Nations Human Rights Commission. Such threats and pressures "are even less acceptable when the supposed defense of human rights is invoked as a cause."[7] Having prefaced his announcement, Pinochet informed Chileans what the new institutionality would look like.

The imperative to construct a new order drove Pinochet and the architects of that new order to the conclusion that Chile really needed a new form of democracy, "one that would be authoritarian, protected, integrative, technified, and of authentic social participation." These desiderata were restated in a letter to the commission established to draft a new constitution, and formed the basis of the constitution Pinochet would later impose. Two of the provisos, that the new democracy be authoritarian and protected, were especially alarming to many constitutional scholars and, of course, to politicians. Pinochet elaborated. "A democracy is authoritarian," he told the supportive audience, "when it possesses strong and vigorous authority in order to defend citizens from demagoguery and violence, and is capable of ensuring the rule of a legal order that guarantees individual rights."

But, Pinochet told his listeners, the task was an immense one, and the process of instituting such an order had to be gradual. He envisioned three phases, without setting out a timeframe. The constitution, revealed some two years later, laid out an incremental, controlled transition lasting as few as nine and as many as eighteen years for the process to unfold. What was certain, from Pinochet's perspective, was that the armed forces and Carabineros would reserve the constitutional role of protecting the new order and defending the national security. And, he warned, even the gradual realization of this plan would be possible only if "the country continues to show positive signs" that have permitted the regime to come this far.[8]

A few weeks later, on August 6, Pinochet dissolved the DINA and replaced it with the National Center for Information, or CNI. The announcement came on the eve of a visit to Chile of the U.S. assistant secretary of state for Latin American affairs, Terence Todman.[9] General Pinochet announced that "progress in our domestic situation recently enabled the Government to do away with the Department of National Intelligence" (sic). The DINA, he said, was "a body set up to come to grips with the toughest phase of subversive action and, while some mistakes were difficult to avoid in such a stubborn task, it has to be remembered that it contributed in no small manner to the peace and tranquility of the entire population."[10] The DINA was replaced because it was opportune to replace it. By mid-1977, the regime had abducted, murdered, and "disappeared" about as many of its enemies as was feasible. During its four years of existence, the DINA and the other intelligence services had managed to decimate the Movement of the Revolutionary Left, had crippled the internal front of the Socialist party, and had decapitated the central committee of the Communist party. The dissolution of the DINA did not mean the end of state terrorism — because the regime was inherently repressive — but it did coincide with a sharp fall-off in the number of disappearances.

Manuel Contreras, who had headed the DINA from its inception, was briefly kept on to run the CNI, but he too was gone within a month. Taking over the CNI would be retired General Mena, who had opposed the creation of the DINA to begin with, and who was named ambassador to Panama after he exposed DINA spying on the army. But Mena's reign was relatively short. After operatives of the newly formed Manuel Rodríguez Patriotic Front assassinated an air force intelligence officer, calls went out for a tougher approach. Pinochet chose another man of confidence, General Humberto Gordon, to direct the new agency.

The DINA had been closed, but international human rights organizations were still reacting to its crimes. In the second week of December 1977, the UN General Assembly passed by a wide margin a resolution accusing Chile of serious human rights violations.[11] "Notwithstanding recent developments, mainly due to the continuous efforts of the Chilean people and the international community," said the resolution, the General Assembly reiterated "its profound indignation that the Chilean people continue to be subject to constant and flagrant violations of human rights and fundamental freedoms." The General Assembly had approved identical language now three years running. The General Assembly then demanded "that the Chilean authorities put an immediate end to practices of inadmissible secret arrests and subsequent disappearance of persons," and it deplored the failure of the Chilean authorities to comply with their own repeated assurances to allow the Ad Hoc Working Group on the Situation of Human Rights in Chile to visit the country. Pinochet responded deftly to the resolution by convoking a plebiscite on January 4, 1978, the year the Catholic cardinal declared the "Year of Human Rights." It was an act of utter defiance that constituted a turning point for the regime.

The plebiscite served two purposes: it deflected criticism of the human rights violations, and it enhanced Pinochet's standing vis-à-vis the other junta members. The choice given Chileans was stark.

In the face of international aggression unleashed against the government of the fatherland, I support President Pinochet in his defense of the dignity of Chile, and I reaffirm the legitimate right of the republic to conduct the process of institutionalization in a manner befitting its sovereignty.[12]

Pinochet won the plebiscite with 75 percent of the vote, but the voting was conducted without the most minimal procedural guarantees. After the victory, the dictator could afford to be magnanimous. In the span of a few weeks in March and April 1978, Pinochet made several policy decisions intended to soften the image of his regime. Only then, in July, did Pinochet finally grant the United Nations Ad Hoc Working Group access for its long-awaited in loco inspection. In March, Pinochet reduced the state of siege to a state of emergency. In April he lifted the dusk-to-dawn curfew that had been imposed since the coup, and permitted Jaime Castillo to return from exile. Castillo had been expelled in August 1976, together with Eugenio Velasco, after he denounced the human rights violations of the regime in a letter addressed to the OAS. This was the sort of gesture that many were hoping for, but it was only a gesture. For his part, Castillo promptly founded the Chilean Human Rights Commission, and pressed ahead with his important human rights advocacy, an activity that would prompt his second exile in August 1981.

The most consequential measure, however, was the promulgation of a general amnesty. The amnesty would cover, in retrospect, the worst years of the repression. Pinochet said that he considered it "an ethical imperative" to decree the amnesty; he saw it as a means of "leaving behind hatreds" and promoting "national reunification." Anyone who had committed a criminal act between September 11, 1973 and March 10, 1978 was granted amnesty. The general amnesty extended to those who were accomplices, or engaged in cover-ups of such crimes. In theory, anyone convicted by a military tribunal also benefited.[13] Only those already implicated in the murder of Orlando Letelier and Ronnie Moffitt were excluded from the amnesty. Pressure from Washington, which Pinochet referred to in his memoirs, accounted for that exception. That too, in retrospect, would be consequential, because the masterminds of the murder would be tried, convicted, and imprisoned almost two decades after the crime.

The amnesty generated controversy for some obvious reasons. An amnesty was small comfort to the families of those convicted by war councils, because many of those convicted were convicted for acts that were not crimes when they were committed, and many of the war tribunals were fraudulent to begin with. To grant amnesty to persons wrongly convicted, or convicted without due process of law, compounded the initial injustice. Another reason for controversy was the manner in which the courts interpreted the amnesty law. The position adopted by the courts was that the law served not only to block criminal prosecution and punishment, but to block further investigation of human rights violations as well. Chilean legal scholars continue to debate the point, but a significant number of them hold the traditional view that the chief executive has the prerogative to grant amnesty only after a court of law has determined an accused's degree of guilt. Not surprisingly, the military courts observed that even investigations intended to clarify the truth without the threat of criminal sanction, would "render illusory the objectives of social peace and tranquility."[14]

Chilean legal scholars contend, moreover, that whatever the merits of granting amnesties, amnesties are not permissible in cases of crimes against humanity. The issue is a charged one, and places opponents to the amnesty law in the awkward position of arguing for the applicability of the laws of

armed conflict despite their deeply held conviction that Chile had never really been in a state of war. Human rights advocates contend that the war was invented, but that so long as the armed forces claim to have engaged in one with seditious forces, they should be held to international standards.

The January plebiscite marked Pinochet's definitive break with other members of the junta, especially with air force General Gustavo Leigh. The announcement of the plebiscite infuriated the air force commander, who believed that Pinochet had exceeded his authority and resented the fact that "in this case, as in other, previous cases, we the members of the Junta, have been presented with a fait accompli." So angry was Leigh that he addressed a letter to Pinochet, a letter that found its way into the February 1978 report of the UN Human Rights Commission, the very entity that had provoked Pinochet to call for the plebiscite in the first place.[15] Leigh's letter reveals that Pinochet's decision was precipitous, and taken without consultation. Late on the afternoon of December 20 Pinochet informally alerted Leigh, and presumably the other members of the junta, of the decision, and called a formal meeting of the junta for the following morning. The dictator publicly announced the plebiscite at nine o'clock that same night. Leigh spent two hours trying to dissuade Pinochet, but to no avail. On the twenty-third he addressed the letter to Pinochet.

The letter could not have framed the issues in a more dramatic tone. "The Air Force rejects the announcement of the plebiscite," Leigh began, then reminded Pinochet of the nature of the authority of the military government. "It is not a government of four people, but rather a Government of four institutions. Power, therefore, does not lie in any one of us, but, rather, in the Government Junta."

"You nevertheless called for a plebiscite, even though you were aware of the opposition of two members of the Junta," Leigh charged, coming to the principal indictment of the dictator, "thus, you have breached the Statute of the Government Junta and placed yourself outside it. The consequences of this action are therefore your sole responsibility." Leigh ended by pointing out the irony of the plebiscite. "It is contradictory that you, who have denounced interference by the United Nations in the affairs of the Chilean Government, would base your calling of a plebiscite on a resolution adopted by that international body."

Leigh challenged Pinochet again in mid-May by proposing that the transition to civilian rule be accomplished in five years, this at a time when Pinochet was intent on staying in power until almost the end of the century.[16] Leigh also moved to rescind Pinochet's right to vote on the junta, reasoning that since Pinochet was chief executive, his legislative role should be eliminated to preserve a separation of powers. Pinochet reacted by ousting Leigh from the junta. Pinochet convinced the other members of the junta, whose support he needed, that Leigh had leaked sensitive information to the media. A June interview with an Italian newspaper sealed Leigh's fate. Leigh, who refused to step down from the junta and resign from the armed forces, found army paratroopers posted at the door to his office in the defense ministry when he reported for duty on July 24, 1978. It so happened that the members of the UN Ad Hoc Working Group on Chile were in Santiago at the time, repeating a pattern: Pinochet did not shy from dramatic moves while human rights observers were in the country. Pinochet had no legal authority to force Leigh from the junta, because the decree creating it provided for the replacement of one of its members only on the grounds of physical and mental incapacitation. Pinochet and the two other members simply declared that Leigh was mentally incapacitated.[17] Pinochet could now move ahead with his plans for a new constitution.

As the end of this eventful year approached, the Catholic Church drew attention to the human rights problem yet again — first by issuing a declaration on the disappeared, and then by convening a three-day symposium on human rights. But an appalling discovery of a mass grave did far more than any pronouncement or symposium to place the problem of the disappeared in its proper perspective.

On November 9, the Permanent Committee of the Episcopal Conference, the conference of the country's Catholic bishops, felt compelled to address the issue of the disappeared. The junta had absolved itself of legal responsibility for the disappearance of Chileans, but had not resolved the agonizing problem of those who simply vanished after being taken away by the security forces. There was a connection with the amnesty law in the sense that the amnesty might have provided the legal impetus to efforts to discover the fate and whereabouts of the disappeared — if the courts had determined that the amnesty could not be applied until the facts of individual cases were clarified. An amnesty could have prompted soldiers to divulge information without fear of prosecution, but the military closed ranks on the issue. The bishops declared:

> At various times, we have approached the responsible persons in government regarding the problem of disappeared persons. Responses have thus far been unsatisfactory. The persons referred to as detained-disappeared, who now number several hundred according to data presented to the government, ought to, with few exceptions, be classified as detained by the security forces of the government. . . . We have done everything that depended on us to establish the truth regarding this grave problem. We have handed over to the authorities all the information we have, both that given by relatives and that procured through legal procedures. We have also indicated significant avenues for a government investigation. Unfortunately we have come to the conclusion that the government will not pursue a thorough investigation of what has occurred, one that would establish the truth of each case and the corresponding responsibilities.[18]

Less than two weeks later Cardinal Silva convened a three-day symposium on the theme of "The Dignity of Humanity: People's Rights and Obligations in Today's World." The list of those in attendance symbolized the concern for the grave human rights situation in Latin America's Southern Cone. Two of Latin America's most prominent clerics conceived the idea of the symposium to dramatize the end of the Year of Human Rights proclaimed in January. Cardinal Silva, archbishop of Santiago and the undaunted founder of the Committee for Peace and the Vicariate for Solidarity, was one. The other was Silva's counterpart Cardinal Paulo Evaristo Arns, archbishop of São Paulo. Among those attending the event were Martin Ennals and Niall MacDermot, secretaries general of Amnesty International and the International Commission of Jurists respectively, and Theo van Boven, director of the then UN Human Rights Division. All had clashed with Pinochet previously; indeed, only five months earlier van Boven had led the long-delayed UN fact-finding mission to Santiago.

The cardinals had reason to make the dignity of humanity the subject of a high-profile event. The Chilean dictatorship was now in its fifth year and appeared to have consolidated itself; the Brazilian military regime was now fourteen years in power. The Brazilian coup of 1964 had begun a trend, but it did not end with Chile's 1973 putsch. Uruguayan democracy had gradually succumbed to a military regime in a process that culminated about the time of Pinochet's coup, and Argentina, which had a brief flirtation with military rule in the mid-1960s, was now in the first year of its so-called Process of National Reorganization — and, of course, its "dirty war."

The final communiqué of the conclave was careful not to specify countries or name names, but there was no need to state the obvious. Thirty years after the unanimous adoption of the Universal Declaration of Human Rights, it began,

in many member states of the United Nations there are systematic and direct violations of the fundamental rights of the people. Many governments have imposed systems which denigrate the person and these governments often seek to justify various forms of institutional violence and torture for reasons of State. Many countries are governed by regimes whose policies and methods divide their citizens into friends and enemies, victors and vanquished, and impose a war mentality in which the logic of eliminating one's adversaries prevails. . . . Secret security and intelligence services operate in this kind of regime with all embracing powers beyond all legal controls, giving rise to the worst excesses against the physical integrity and safety of persons, as well as to generalized terror.[19]

These observations captured perfectly the awful reality of the final convulsions of the Cold War in Latin America. The communiqué concluded with an appeal for "all believers to unite in a common effort of prayer and action in order to seek truth and justice with courage based on faith." It added hopefully, "we ask the governments of all nations to exercise their power on behalf of human rights."

General Pinochet was characteristically disgusted by the public event, considering it to be nothing less than the culmination of the "pro-Marxist-Leninist intervention of the Catholic Church in politics on the continent."

The event, which ended with a reception at the Vicariate of Solidarity, occurred, said Pinochet, "at precisely the moment when the fatherland needed sustained spiritual and pastoral support."[20] It seems not to have occurred to the general that the bishops had come to Santiago for that very reason.

Five days after the closure of the symposium and the release of its communiqué, representatives of the Vicariate of Solidarity responded to an anonymous tip about a mass grave; there is no way of telling if the bishops' exhortation had moved someone to reveal the truth. Cristián Precht, the Vicar of Solidarity, led a group of church officials that traveled from Santiago to Lonquén and discovered the remains of fifteen persons sealed in an abandoned lime kiln. An atrocity that had occurred five years earlier, on October 7, 1973, had come back to haunt the conscience of Chile. On that day, fifteen campesinos were abducted by carabineros on Maipo Island, taken to the remote site, murdered, and placed in the kiln. As with the experience of many other Chilean families, efforts to locate the men proved futile. Nor did the courts provide assistance, even after the case was revived.

The gruesome discovery prompted the reopening of the case, but the amnesty Pinochet had decreed prohibited a judicial remedy. Judge Adolfo Bañados was assigned the case, and established the fraudulence of the carabineros' account of events. But Chilean judges must adhere to the letter of the law, so Bañados disqualified himself once the evidence had been gathered. The case was properly in the jurisdiction of military courts. A military court, citing the 1978 amnesty law, closed the books on the episode. Tenacious human rights defenders would make similar discoveries for years to come, well after the democratic transition, forcing the desire to look to the future into direct conflict with the imperative to recover the truth about the past. General Pinochet, who does not mention Lonquén in his memoir, seems to be one of the few principals whose conscience was not disturbed by the discovery.

Pinochet's grasp on power, already firm, was uncontested after the ouster of Leigh in July. But the regime over which he presided lacked the institutional basis for permanence. If the military's pronunciamento was a revolution, a new constitutional order would be needed to codify it. Pinochet issued the call. In fact, the junta had created a commission, headed by jurist Enrique Ortúzar, to draft a new constitution only a month after the coup in 1973. The Ortúzar Commission had already labored quietly for nearly four years when Pinochet announced the Chacarillas plan in July 1977. In October 1978 the study commission submitted its preliminary draft to the Council of State, an advisory body composed of former presidents that the junta had created to give the appearance of civil participation in the political process. Jorge Alessandri, as president of the council, reviewed and modified the draft produced by the study commission. On June 1, 1980 the Council of State presented Pinochet with a draft constitution.

Alessandri, however, was alarmed and made significant changes to the draft presented by the Ortúzar Commission. This was an ironic twist because Jaime Guzmán, the principal author of the draft document, had supported Alessandri's presidential candidacy in the historic 1970 race. At the center of contention were the timing of the return to full democracy and the permanent guardianship of the military after the transition. In the Chacarillas speech Pinochet had outlined a lengthy three-phase process. Transitory articles of the new constitution would set the actual timetable. The Council of State wanted to see presidential elections and an elected congress as early as 1985, but Pinochet had a very different idea. The general made his own changes and on August 10 announced that a new constitution had been drafted. He then scheduled a plebiscite, the second of the dictatorship, for September 11, the anniversary of the coup.

When Alessandri saw the changes Pinochet had insisted on, he resigned from the Council of State, pleading ill health. He later admitted that he had resigned in protest.[21] Three members of the original study commission resigned as well, and joined the "Group of Twenty-Four," prominent jurists who opposed and campaigned against the final version. Opponents had no realistic chance to block ratification in the month that remained before the plebiscite. The constitution was ratified with 67 percent of the votes, but the plebiscite was conducted without proper procedural guarantees. It went into effect in 1981. Thereafter opponents would attempt first to annul it, then to radically amend it.[22]

Alessandri, the members of the Group of Twenty-Four, and others had opposed the new constitution for a number of reasons. The former president, in particular, opposed putting off the transition, and favored elections as early as 1985. Pinochet, however, wanted the transitory articles of the new constitution to permit him to remain president for 16 years, until 1997. Pinochet offered one concession, an eight-year term to be followed by a plebiscite on his continued rule through 1997. That provision proved to be the means by which the opposition eventually removed Pinochet from power. By voting to approve the constitution along with its transitory articles Chileans would be voting for Pinochet. The same article reduced the status of the junta itself. Because Pinochet would become constitutional president, he would be replaced on the junta by another army officer. Several men, all close to Pinochet, would serve in that capacity.

Constitutional scholars expressed serious objections to many features of Pinochet's (and Jaime Guzmán's) "Constitution of Liberty," including restricted civil and political rights, sweeping emergency powers, a weakened congress vis-à-vis an excessively strong president, appointed senators, special prerogatives for the armed forces, and barriers against amendment. Some provisions were especially egregious. The junta's desire to extirpate Marxism from Chile was codified in article 8, which declared unconstitutional and illicit groups advocating any doctrine that is totalitarian, is based on class struggle, promotes violence, or even "does harm to the family." Luis Maira, who as a Christian Democrat had helped draft the 1970 Statute of Constitutional Guarantees signed by Allende, commented that the provisions of constitutional article 8, if read carefully and taken seriously, would have outlawed the very regime that framed it.[23] Article 93 insulated senior military commanders from dismissal. Article 95 established a National Security Council authorized to rebuke the president if he did not heed its warnings about threats to national security. Constitutional scholars agreed that the language of article 95 could provide the military with legal justification for a coup d'état—something the high command, which had struggled so hard to justify the 1973 coup, deeply coveted. In an interview years later General Pinochet attempted to dismiss concerns about the nefarious NSC. "If there had been a National Security Council in 1973," he said, "probably nothing would have happened."

"There probably would have been a bloodless coup?"

"Most likely."[24]

No knowledgeable person could take comfort in such a disingenuous comment. The coup had been relatively bloodless—the bloodshed came afterward.

By Reason or by Force

When Augusto Pinochet Ugarte donned the presidential sash on March 11, 1981, Chile was experiencing an economic expansion that surprised even some of the Chicago Boys. The ceremony in the restored Moneda palace marked the end of the military government and the beginning of constitutional government, in Pinochet's parlance. To his many opponents, nothing much had changed: Chile was still governed by a hybrid personal dictatorship and military regime.

But Chile was almost immediately beset by an economic crisis that threatened political upheaval. Somewhat ironically, the policies of the Reagan administration, which had come to office in January of the same year, initiated the crisis. A slow-down of international lending threw Chile, and most of Latin America, into deep recession. By the end of the next year, Chile's international reserves had been seriously depleted, the central bank was experiencing dramatic balance of payments difficulties, and Chile suffered a substantial 14 percent decline of its gross domestic product. Several major banks became insolvent, and the stock market crashed.[25] The regime, which was quite literally banking on the success of the economic model to resolve its legitimacy problems, soon found itself confronting resistance on separate fronts.

The regime was confronted with two simultaneous but distinguishable challenges, strikes and street protests, and terrorist violence. Both were intended to bring Pinochet down, and the chant "va a caer" ("he's going to fall") echoed in Santiago streets. But these challenges had different protagonists, and the differences between them were too great to overcome. The labor leaders and politicians who coordinated the strikes and street protests believed social mobilization was justified and could be effective, but armed struggle never figured in their ethical code. The advocates of armed rebellion misread the mood of the country and the meaning of the street protests, believing that selective acts of terrorism could spark a massive popular insurrection. The opposite was true. The violence actually diminished the enthusiasm for the street protests, and in the end, neither social mobilization or terrorism led to Pinochet's fall. True to form, the Pinochet regime responded to both challenges by ratcheting up the repression.

On May 11, 1983 the Copper Workers Union called for a general strike to protest the harsh effects of the economic downturn and the regime's economic policies in general. After a decade of severe repression, Chileans were prepared to take to the streets. The strike was the first of some fourteen National Days of Protest staged between May 1983 and 1986.[26] The reaction of the police and armed forces was predictably harsh: all the protests were violently put down, almost always with lethal force. The first protest, on May 11, resulted in two deaths; six more Chileans were killed in the protests on June 14 and July 12.

Sensing that the regime was vulnerable after the third protest in July, Gabriel Valdés, recently chosen president of the Christian Democratic party, announced the creation of the Democratic Alliance.[27] The announcement came on August 5, a week before the next scheduled protest. The Christian Democratic party finally ended its long sojourn in the political wilderness and went into the opposition in earnest. The party had been disbanded by a junta decree in 1977 but defiantly continued to operate. The Democratic Alliance, although ultimately unsuccessful, brought together the centrist parties, including the Radical party and the moderate, "renovated" faction of the Socialist party. That achievement was remarkable in and of itself.

That same month, August, Archbishop Francisco Fresno, who had replaced the venerable Raúl Silva Henríquez, called on the government to negotiate with the Democratic Alliance. It was a dramatic moment: exactly a decade earlier, Cardinal Silva had called on President Allende to open negotiations with the leadership of the Christian Democratic party. Pinochet appeared to be receptive, and named Sergio Onofre Jarpa, president of the now suspended National Party, interior minister and instructed him to initiate discussions. But the gesture did not mean that General Pinochet was averse to resorting to violence to control the situation. The dialogue, such as it was, was not destined to produce a political settlement.

In anticipation of the fourth National Day of Protest Pinochet imposed a 6 p.m. curfew for August 11 and deployed some 18,000 army troops in and around the capital. This massive show of force exceeded even the deployment of troops on the day of the coup. The general was not one to make idle threats. Twenty-five protesters were killed during the protest on August 11 and 12, 1983.[28] Nine more were killed in the marches on September 8, just prior to the anniversary of the coup, and four more in a protest staged in October. The pattern would continue over the next three years, until enthusiasm for the protest movement dissipated in mid-1986: eleven dead in March 1984; eight in September; nine in October; three in August 1985; four in November; ten more in December; and eight in one of the last protests in July 1986. Among the dead was Rodrigo Rojas, a Chilean with U.S. residence. He and Carmen Gloria Quintana were victims of one of the more horrifying episodes of the repression.

Pinochet, recalling the early years of his iron rule, explained the reasons for harsh measures applied to those who would "challenge the legal norms in force." "As a husband and father," he wrote in his memoir, "I have been moved by this reality many times, because I comprehend the pain that it causes in some homes. Believe me, in terms of my personal sensibility, it would be easier to relent, and to not punish. But if I were to do that, I would be betraying my responsibility as ruler."[29] Accordingly, in November 1984, Pinochet saw fit to call on the sweeping emergency powers granted him by the 1980 constitution and declare a state of siege (which had been downgraded to state of emergency in March 1978). Amnesty International, Americas Watch, and the Lawyers Committee for Human Rights, as well as the Chilean human rights organizations, began to report on new patterns of repression: excessive use of force to put down the demonstrations, massive shanty-town raids to prevent the radicalization of the poor, and violent intimidation of labor leaders, student activists, and human rights defenders and priests working among the shanty-town poor.

Amnesty International's account of the raid on the Raul Silva Henríquez shanty-town was reminiscent of the massive, combined military operations staged in the first days after the coup. During a raid on November 10 on the shanty-town named for the Catholic cardinal, army troops rounded up thousands and took them to the San Bernardo Military School, a site that had been used as a detention camp after the coup. Most prisoners were later released, but some 153 were "relegated" — banished to internal exile — at an undisclosed camp. Americas Watch and the Lawyers Committee for Human Rights reported that La Victoria shanty-town was raided three times by January 1985.[30] Even the 1984 U.S. Department of State annual country report tracked the alarming increase in repression: "Using these extraordinary powers, the Government conducted several mass sweeps of poorer neighborhoods involving the detention of over 8,000 persons, sent 421 persons, mainly alleged petty criminals, to a remote detention camp without trial and internally exiled another 257 persons without charges or trial."[31] The Americas Watch/Lawyers Committee for Human Rights report issued in early 1985 cited higher figures. "Tens of thousands" were swept up in the shanty-town raids in the first two months of the state of siege, 7,000 were detained in a raid near Pudahuel in the vicinity of Santiago.[32] Again, the detained were herded into a local stadium, dozens of them were harshly interrogated, electric shock was employed.

The massive shanty-town raids and brutal crowd-control tactics were not the only reasons for grave concern: the intelligence services, the CNI, and the Carabinero intelligence unit known as DICOMCAR began to abduct human rights and community activists, and torture, rape, and threaten them with death. More ominously, in 1984 government-sponsored vigilante groups began to appear.

Human rights defenders had begun to oppose the repression of dictatorship years before the political opposition appeared. The Vicariate of Solidarity was the rock on which the Chilean human rights movement was built. But by 1984, six years after Jaime Castillo returned from exile and helped found it, the Chilean Human Rights Commission had become a force as well. As of 1980 the Commission on the Rights of the People (CODEPU) was also active. The Vicariate, the Chilean Human Rights Commission, and CODEPU were all prepared to counter the repression unleashed to control the peaceful protests. That made their members potential victims.

In December 1984 CNI agents raided the regional headquarters of the Chilean Human Rights Commission in the northern cities of Arica and Iquique, arresting eleven members and the two regional presidents in the process. They had been active in the defense of political prisoners confined to the Pisagua camp. The human rights defenders were themselves "relegated," under the authority of the emergency measures in effect, but pressure from the now savvy human rights movement led to the release of most of them in a matter of weeks. The Chilean Human Rights Commission's offices in Santiago, Concepción, Antofagasta, and Rancagua were also searched by CNI agents soon after the declaration of the state of siege. Apparently, these raids were intended to dissuade the Commission's attorneys from defending those swept up during the National Days of Protests planned for the November 27 and 28.[33] Attorneys working with the Vicariate of Solidarity were threatened the following March, in the context of one of the most brutal crimes committed during this entire period. Gustavo Villalobos, Héctor Salazar, and Hernán Quezada all received threats in the mail. One was a crude sketch depicting a decapitated stick-figure; that same month one of their colleagues, an archivist for the Vicariate, was found nearly decapitated in a field with two other men.[34]

Priests working among the shanty-town poor were also harassed. A group of men dressed in civilian clothes assaulted a shanty-town priest in Concepción in May. The following month a Belgian priest working in the La Legua shanty-town, a scene of combined search and destroy operations during the coup, was repeatedly threatened with death. One of his parishioners was abducted and on two separate occassions cut with a knife. The same form of intimidation was used in the Puente Alto shanty-town; at least three parishioners were abducted and beaten. One of the victims was cut on the throat, another was branded with a cross by a searing hot pipe. Threatening slogans were painted on the walls of the churches, "death to the red priests," capturing the tenor of the threats.[35]

The Commission on the Rights of the People suffered more violent and humiliating treatment. CODEPU was considered the most leftist of the human rights organizations by a regime that believed human rights activism to be essentially a leftist vocation and an international conspiracy. After all, one of the directors of CODEPU, Fabiola Letelier, was the sister of Orlando Letelier, the man the DINA had assassinated in Washington. The Santiago offices of CODEPU were raided on March 7 and again on March 22, 1985. During the second raid on the offices, CNI agents destroyed furniture and typewriters, scattered files, and harmed and sexually humiliated the activists working there. The raiders had concocted a unique indignity for the twenty CODEPU members they found in the offices. They forced them to strip and lie on the floor, then agents sprayed their nude bodies with bright orange spray-paint.[36] Sexual humiliation became a tactic to intimidate human rights defenders thereafter. Four weeks after the Santiago raid, a CODEPU activist from Valparaíso was abducted and raped. Her assailants, who identified themselves as belonging to ACHA, Chilean Anti-Communist Action, sprayed her body with red paint after they sexually assaulted her. In June 1985 an ACHA team raped a student at the University of Concepción as she left a human rights seminar.[37] That same month a group of men abducted Mirta Navarrete as part of a concerted campaign to intimidate a special prosecutor assigned to a controversial case. The woman's husband was a court reporter working with the specially appointed judge who was investigating a suspicious case of a young man alleged to have committed suicide; his body bore the signs of torture. Navarette was forced into a van and threatened; at one point one of her assailants brandished a knife and carved a cross in her left breast. Exactly one month later she was abducted again; this time a cross was cut in her forehead.[38]

The ACHA, a previously unknown organization, was becoming a threat to Chileans who did not simply acquiesce to the regime. The emergence of a right-wing paramilitary organization was ominous; others, like the September 11 Command and the Avengers of Martyrs Command, followed. Chile was beginning to resemble El Salvador, where privately financed death squads employing off-duty members of the security forces were killing suspected subversives with complete impunity. But the connection between ACHA and the Chilean security forces was actually much more direct. ACHA was a front: the presidential commission of inquiry established that ACHA was in fact a CNI operation.[39]

The CNI was heavily involved in the wave of intimidation and repression, but the Corps of Carabineros also took part. In fact, one of the most brutal and shocking crimes of this phase of the repression was committed by agents assigned to the Carabinero intelligence unit, the Directorate for Information and Communication, DICOMCAR. In what was almost certainly a revival of old inter-agency rivalry, the CNI presented judicial investigators with evidence of DICOMCAR's involvement in the crime.

The wave of street protests and terrorism put the Carabineros on the defensive and at risk. It fell to the crowd control units of the Carabineros to put down the protests, making them the most visible symbol of the repression. At the same time, carabineros became easy targets of opportunity for the remnants of the MIR, and later the Manuel Rodríguez Patriotic Front, who were stepping up their campaigns of bank heists, bombings, and assassinations. The final months of 1984 were particularly bad for the police. On November 2, a bus carrying carabineros was attacked with a grenade during Chile's national cycling championship; four carabineros were killed. Two days later a Carabinero station in Cisterna was attacked by urban commandos armed with automatic weapons; two more carabineros were killed in that incident. A month later another carabinero was killed in a similar attack.[40] Then DICOMCAR went on the offensive.

In January 1985 command of DICOMCAR changed hands. The new commander, Colonel Luís Fontaine, was determined to avenge these deaths by striking back at the Communist party independently of the CNI. History was repeating itself. Carabinero intelligence, DICOMCAR, would undertake to do what air force intelligence, DIFA, had done in 1975 when Gustavo Leigh set up the Joint Command. In fact, many of the old hands from the air force anti-subversive command were called on to renew the assault on the hated Communists. History repeated itself in another way: the violence practiced by the commanders of both the Joint Command and DICOMCAR would in time visit them.

The sequence of events that led to the execution of three communist leaders in March 1985 and the resignation of Carabinero director general and junta member César Mendoza five months later, began in early 1984 with a phone call from Roberto Fuentes Morrison, "Wally," to Miguel Estay Reyna, "Fanta," both of Comando Conjunto fame.[41] Fuentes, former commander of the Joint Command, approached Estay, his most effective collaborator, to offer him an assignment with DICOMCAR. Estay, an ex-communist turned first informant and then intelligence officer in 1975, readily accepted the challenge. His new task was examine the raw daily intelligence on the activities of the Communist party and help smash it, again.

A month after Raúl Fontaine assumed command of DICOMCAR, the intelligence unit developed leads about the possible involvement of the Chilean Association of Teachers (AGECh), in coordinating street protests, and more seriously, in printing clandestine Communist party materials. The interrogation of a Communist party member arrested during a February demonstration yielded names of active communists, including Santiago Nattino, Manuel Guerrero, and José Manuel Parada. An operation to destroy the printing shop and capture these men went into motion — and then went quickly out of control.

On March 28 DICOMCAR agents raided the headquarters of AGECh, where, as suspected, they discovered the print shop and Communist party documents being prepared for circulation. They arrested a dozen AGECh members, but released them the following day. Also on the 28th, almost unnoticed, DICOMCAR agents abducted Santiago Nattino in front of his home. Early the next morning, March 29, DICOMCAR agents took up positions around a private school that DICOMCAR believed secretly generated revenues for Communist party activities. The agents were looking for Guerrero and Parada, who had eluded arrest in the AGECh operation the day before.

Why Parada and Guerrero were selected for abduction and death seems to be connected with the activities of the old Joint Command. Nattino was targeted for other reasons. Santiago Nattino was an ailing artist, known for his graphic designs and cartoons; his abduction was probably connected with DICOMCAR's intention to destroy the propaganda machinery of the party. The other victims were more formidable adversaries. DICOMCAR had concluded that Parada and Guerrero were counter-intelligence agents of the Communist party. Parada, an archivist with the Vicariate of Solidarity, was known to be tracking the activities of the various security agencies, especially the now defunct Joint Command. Pinochet endorses the view, in one of the few passages where he directly addresses human rights violations, that "the intelligence apparatus of the PC . . . worked below the respectable mantle of the Catholic Church."[42] It is true that Parada had detailed knowledge of the inner workings and the activities of the Joint Command. Parada was so knowledgeable that journalist Monica Gonzalez turned to him to verify some of the revelations made by Andrés Valenzuela, the repentant Joint Command functionary, in her August 1984 interviews with him. Indeed, he was one of the first to review the manuscript of *Los Secretos del comando conjunto*, a book that exposed the activities of the secret air force agency.[43]

Miguel Estay, Fanta, was pivotal to the operation. His role was to identify the men, whom he knew from his days as a Communist militant, and alert the other agents when they arrived for work. But the abduction of Guerrero and Parada went badly. As agents rushed from the cars to apprehend them, other professors came to their defense. Shots were fired, and one professor was seriously wounded. The daylight abduction of two professors in front of a private school caused the rapid mobilization of the AGECh and, more importantly, the Vicariate of Solidarity. Confessing his involvement in the abduction years later before the judge assigned to the case, Miguel Estay admitted that in the confusion after the shooting, the agents' mood turned grim. Nattino, Guerrero, and Parada were transported to DICOMCAR headquarters on Calle Dieciocho, the very same location from which the

Joint Command had operated.[44] The order to execute the men came down almost immediately. The mood of the agents turned even more grim.

That same night, Estay and five other DICOMCAR agents took Nattino, Guerrero, and Parada to a remote location near the old international airport under the cover of the curfew. Nattino and Parada were locked in the trunk of one car, and Guerrero was bound in the rear seat. Estay and two senior officers traveled in a second car. They had had the entire day to plan the murders. The death squad selected a deserted stretch of road near the old airport to execute the men. Estay seized on the idea to slash their throats, fearing that gunshots would be heard and compromise the mission. The manner of death contributed to the outrage of the murders, and the word *degollados* now epitomizes this phase of the repression.

The three men were taken one at a time down an embankment and out to a field and forced to kneel, Guerrero first, then Nattino, then Parada. Each victim had a different executioner, who slashed a man's throat, carefully removed the handcuffs from his wrists, then returned to the car to pass the crescent-shaped knife, or *corvo*, to the next executioner. Parada, the last to die, was by now aware of what was happening and had to be carried out to the field. His murder was in some ways the most horrible. Claudio Salazar, the man who murdered him, could not bring himself to slash Parada's throat and thrust the blade of the corvo into his abdomen instead, making Parada cry out horribly. The agents recalled the agonized scream.

At noon the following day, as colleagues and human rights defenders frantically searched for Guerrero and Parada, the Carabineros issued the first tentative report of the discovery of three bodies beside the road leading to the airport. The announcement that three bodies had been discovered caused confusion, because there were three victims, not two. The abduction of Nattino on the twenty-eighth had not been connected with the abduction of Guerrero and Parada on the twenty-ninth. Families, friends, and human rights activists established a sort of vigil outside the coroner's office awaiting word on the positive identification of the victims. Then came the official announcement of the identities of the three men, and the cause of death, exsanguination.

The execution of three communists in 1985 caused a public outcry that would lead to the resignation of a member of the junta. The disappearance of the entire central committee of the Communist party a decade before generated nothing of the kind. Chile was a changed nation. Even the media sympathetic to the regime printed stories reporting that senior government officials condemned and repudiated the crimes. Calls for the appointment of a judge to investigate the case were quickly answered. Judge José Cánovas Robles took up the case with characteristic vigor, and was able to determine the extent to which DICOMCAR agents were involved. Astonishingly, it was a CNI investigative report that provided Cánovas with the crucial evidence of DICOMCAR complicity. The motive that prompted the primary Chilean intelligence agency, the CNI, to investigate the murders and to turn evidence implicating another intelligence agency—institutional rivalries, genuine repulsion at the crimes, or whatever—remains one of the intriguing mysteries of the times.

On August 2, César Mendoza Duran resigned as director general of the Carabineros, and also from the junta. The man who had effected the barracks coup on September 11, while the titular head of the Carabineros stood by Allende in the Moneda, was now forced to return to obscurity. Mendoza offered no convincing public explanation. He told journalists that he was leaving on a whim. He gave Pinochet a more direct answer, telling him, "this is going to cause us more problems than any other thing." Mendoza was officially cleared of any direct involvement in the crime. But years later, as a lengthy legal proceeding dragged on, Pinochet was still unwilling to concede that DICOMCAR was involved. Pinochet jousted with reporters:

Pinochet: "Do you believe that [Mendoza] was involved?"

Reporters: "No, but a group of carabineros, from DICOMCAR, yes."

Pinochet: "I don't know. I cannot tell you yes or no."

Pinochet added this comment in his memoir: "not even now, as the case continues to be investigated by the civilian courts, can I add anything, because I do not know anything more."[45] By the time this comment appeared in print, the involvement of carabineros was a matter of public record. The lengthy judicial investigation in the case is a story in its own right. But whereas justice was slow and uncertain, vengeance was swift and sure.

In June 1989 Roberto Fuentes Morrison, the former Joint Command commander who put Miguel Estay Reyna to work with DICOMCAR, was assassinated by members of the Manuel Rodríguez Patriotic Front. Eleven months later, in May 1990, just as the presidential Commission on Truth and Reconciliation began its investigation, unknown assailants ambushed and assassinated Raúl Fontaine, the man who had commanded DICOMCAR and ordered the murders of Nattino, Guerrero, and Parada.

The triple throat-slashing, or *degollados* case, shocked the public and briefly animated the opposition. But it was not the last or the most horrible. A year later, under very different circumstances, the security forces again outraged the public and international opinion with their proclivity to do harm to Chileans.

By mid-1986 the opposition was struggling to maintain the momentum of strikes and street protests. A wave of terrorist violence that ran parallel to the National Days of Protest made moderates uneasy. Some of the leaders of the movement, particularly the Christian Democrats, were becoming convinced of the futility of the strategy of political mobilization. Yet the National General Strike called for July 2–3 came remarkably close to achieving a shutdown of the economy. The discontented middle class actually outnumbered the more militant shanty-town poor in the July protest, reversing a trend evident since the earliest protests more than three years before. But the strike generated a final spasm of regime violence. Eight were killed during the two days scheduled for the protest. All were young people, the youngest just thirteen, the oldest twenty-six. Most were killed by indiscriminate fire. Rodrigo Rojas's death was unique.

In the pre-dawn hours of the second day of the strike, a military patrol came upon a group of young protesters building a bonfire in the road. It was a common street tactic that kept soldiers busy and at bay. But the soldiers managed to get their hands on Rojas and a young woman, Carmen Gloria Quintana, aged nineteen and eighteen respectively. Either to make an example of the two, or to vent their hatred and frustration, the soldiers doused them with benzene, set them ablaze, and left them to die in a ditch beside a deserted road. Both lost consciousness after the flames were extinguished, but Rojas struggled to survive. He arose and revived Carmen Gloria, and the two of them walked half dead until they reached construction workers who called the police for help. Rojas perished four days later after an agonizing ordeal. He had suffered severe burns over 60 percent of his body. A burn specialist with the Shriners Burn Institute in Boston was flown to Chile to treat the two young victims at the behest of Senator Edward Kennedy, but arrived only hours after Rojas had died as a result of renal failure. Three weeks later the specialist testified before a subcommittee of the U.S. House of Representatives. When asked whether he had seen evidence that Rojas had been beaten before being set aflame, Dr. Constable responded metaphorically: "if you paint a canvas black, you can't really tell whether it had been a Monet or Titian before you painted it."[46]

Carmen Gloria survived but was horribly maimed. "What do you remember, what did you see in the face of the soldiers?" a journalist from the newsmagazine *Analisis* asked Carmen Gloria a year after the incident.[47] "There was hate, rage," she recollected, "I realized that the dictatorship had filled the soldiers' heads with the idea that the people who struggle for freedom are their enemies."

"What other images have you been unable to forget?"

"When they sprayed benzene all over my body."

"Did you think that they were going to burn you?"

"No, never!"

The pain must have been excruciating. "I sincerely pleaded with the *pacos* [policeman] that found us to put a bullet in me to end the suffering," she admitted. Then Carmen Gloria Quintana mused about the possibility of ever marrying after suffering so grotesque an injury, "I don't know if I will marry some day or if I will be able to have children. I don't want to think about it."

The onset of terrorist violence actually preceded the street protests, but the National Days of Protest provided impetus to armed rebellion. The left had never eschewed armed struggle, and the popular discontent manifested by the protests led some leftist leaders to believe that Pinochet could be toppled. The MIR, once the most savagely hunted adversary of the regime, never abandoned hope. Its leadership had been decimated in the first three years of the dictatorship, but senior leaders managed to survive the onslaught. The most influential figures of the historic nucleus of the Movement were Andrés Pascal Allende and Nelson Gutiérrez, survivors of the botched operation at Malloco in 1975, and Arturo Villavela, whom the air force had held captive at the Air War Academy before sending him into exile in 1977. Hernán Aguiló, the director of the MIR-FTR in the Popular Unity days, had remained in the country and was in charge of keeping the MIR together body and soul. The men vied for leadership of the renascent MIR. Exile had its advantages: MIRistas could intensify their guerrilla training in Cuba, East Germany, and elsewhere. But the MIR would eventually have to make its presence felt in Chile. And so, while Pinochet was jousting with the United Nations and maneuvering to oust Leigh from the junta, the MIR was preparing to stage a dramatic "Operation Return."[48]

Andrés Pascal Allende, the secretary general, was the first major figure to temporarily reenter Chile, making the clandestine passage across the Peruvian border in February 1978. By August he was residing in Chile on a permanent basis.[49] The dangerous business of renewing contacts and reviving a mortally wounded movement proceeded cautiously. By September, Pascal and Villavela (who initially remained in Cuba to coordinate the infiltration of the cadre) were overseeing the return of most of the MIR's senior leadership. Villavela had overall responsibility for military operations. By the middle of the following year, about the same time that the Sandinistas were on the verge of victory against Somoza in Nicaragua, the MIR was ready to become active. But the intelligence services were ready for it.

The MIR's leadership had decided to create rural guerrilla "focos," in addition to the reorganization of the Central Force to carry out "armed propaganda" in the capital. The operational concept had been advanced by Che Guevara, now dead more than a decade, and Régis Debray. The idea was to establish a guerrilla cell of a handful of lightly armed guerrillas who would mount heroic actions, like the ambush of an army outpost, to acquire weapons and to make their presence known. Their courageous acts of symbolic resistance, so the theory went, would gain them the admiration of the local population and begin to win them over to the idea that a courageous few could bring a seemingly invincible enemy to its knees. It was a recruitment technique as much as anything else. As young men and women made their way into the mountains, the initial foco would bifurcate; the same would happen to the new cell, and on and on, until the focos were replicating and a revolutionary vanguard was springing into existence.

That was the theory. The MIR formed its first foco, consisting of only thirty guerrillas, in a remote Andean region of Neltume to take advantage of the isolated mountain passes leading to Argentina. This was the same part of Chile, around Valdivia, Osorno, where the air force had routed the MIR in 1973. That should have been an omen. The idea was doomed from the beginning, and not just because Che's concept was operationally flawed. In fact, Chilean intelligence had been informed of the operational and logistical details of Operation Return by a senior Cuban intelligence officer attached to the America Department, tasked by Fidel Castro to foster revolution on the continent.[50]

The operation was commanded by Enrique Reyes Manríquez, who had received his military training in the Chilean air force. Reyes had fought with the Sandinistas in the insurrection against Somoza. After the Sandinista National Liberation Front succeeded in bringing the Nicaraguan dictator down, Reyes became one of the many foreign nationals who stayed on to help organize, train, and indoctrinate the Sandinista Popular Army. Now he was back in Chile, but he would not have the chance to celebrate the fall of another right-wing dictator.

The army moved against the foco in Neltume in June 1981, in a massive operation spearheaded by the elite corps of Black Berets. For the first time since the coup, regular troops went into action against an armed and potentially dangerous enemy. Operation Machete was intended to rout the MIR guerrilla fighters, and ultimately to thwart the division of the embryonic guerrilla cells. But first they had to locate a series of underground bunkers housing the guerrillas and storing their weapons and supplies. Intelligence had detected the existence of the network, but not the precise locations of the concealed encampments. Operation Machete, involving some 2,000 troops, got underway on June 6. The special forces troops discovered the first underground hideout on the twenty-fifth, and four more by the end of the first week of July. The first armed engagement came three days after the discovery of the first bunker, but there were no casualties despite an intense fire-fight. It took some time to find the MIR's main encampment, but when the Black Berets came across it the MIR was caught off guard. The guerrillas managed at least to escape into the thick surrounding forests. But the withdrawal was disorderly and the fighters were forced to abandon substantial quantities of medical supplies, food, and ammunition. The army set ambushes for the exhausted guerrillas. Seven MIRistas were killed in the third week of September, just after the armed forces' celebration of their 1973 triumph.[51] The foco strategy had been defeated, but fewer than a third of the guerrillas had been killed. The CNI launched another search and destroy operation in the south late in August 1984, concentrating on the areas around Concepción, Valdivia, and Los Angeles. Seven more MIRistas were killed in those operations.[52]

In the capital, Operation Return involved the reconstruction of the MIR's Central Force (an undertaking thwarted by the death of José Bordas, the MIR's military chief, in late 1974), and the formation of Popular Resistance

Committees to engage in a Popular Anti-Fascist War. More concretely, the MIR was preparing for a campaign of bank robberies, bombings, and assassinations of intelligence officers. The MIR found itself in a nearly impossible situation: the MIR had barely survived, and if it were to have any credibility it had to make its presence felt; but the very acts of "armed propaganda" that announced its "return" would only prompt the intelligence services to move against it with the same ruthless determination as before. That, in fact, is what transpired.

The campaign of robberies, bombings, and assassinations began slowly and then increased dramatically. Official accounts and media reportage — which often amounted to the same thing — reported a dramatic escalation of the terrorist violence, from 15 incidents in 1977 to 212 in 1981.[53] The terrorist bombings killed carabineros riding in buses or trying to defuse them; too often innocent bystanders were killed by blasts. A booby-trapped bomb planted by MIR urban guerrillas near CNI headquarters exploded, killing an army lieutenant detailed to the CNI's bomb disposal unit in April 1979. A year later a ten-year-old boy was curious about a package dangling from a tree near a Carabinero post and had the misfortune to grab and detonate a bomb. A month later a bomb exploded in the building housing the provincial government offices in Valparaíso, killing two day-laborers ironically employed in the military government's work program. Military vehicles were special targets. A bomb placed beneath a bus carrying special forces troops was detonated by remote control in March 1984, wounding several and killing a corporal. Four carabineros being transported aboard a bus to provide security for Chile's national cycling championship were killed when the bus was attacked with a bomb. A bomb destroyed another Carabinero special forces bus in February 1986, killing one and injuring sixteen. A year and a half later, two more carabineros died in an identical attack.

Then there were the assassinations. In July 1980, just as Chileans prepared to vote on Pinochet's constitution of liberty, a MIR assassination squad ambushed the director of the army's intelligence school on a Santiago street. It was a classic and carefully coordinated ambush. Two MIRistas, traveling in a light pick-up truck, pulled alongside the car carrying Lieutenant Colonel Roger Vergara and blasted it with automatic weapons. Vergara was riddled with bullets and died en route to the hospital; his driver was gravely wounded but survived.[54]

The repercussions were understandably great and swift. Cries went up for the removal of Ordlanier Mena, the retired general and long-time opponent of Manual Contreras, who had taken over the CNI. Nine days after Vergara's murder, Pinochet replaced Mena with General Humberto Gordon, a man of confidence. The move presaged a tougher approach, as Gordon immediately set up an Anti-Subversive Command composed of homicide detectives, Carabinero intelligence operatives, and the Metropolitan Brigade of the CNI itself. It went into action almost immediately. In the third week of July, men claiming to belong to a previously unknown Avengers of Martyrs Command (COVEMA) abducted nearly a dozen suspected leftist sympathizers. In fact the men of COVEMA were agents assigned to the Anti-Subversive Command.[55] The agents interrogated their captives under torture to obtain information about the Vergara assassination. One MIRista died as a result of his injuries, but the others were released within a matter of weeks.

A year after Vergara's ambush and murder, unknown assailants gunned down Carlos Tapia, who had retired from the CNI. Four months later, in November, a MIR squad fired on a passing patrol car in a Santiago suburb, killing three carabineros. The men were on patrol near the house of General Santiago Sinclair, Pinochet's chief of staff, and the squad was probably moving into position to assassinate Sinclair. Coming so soon after the debacle in Neltume, the assassination of such a well-placed individual would have been a rare victory. The MIR struck again in August 1983, just as the protest movement was getting started, killing Major General Carol Urzúa and two of his bodyguards. The response to the assassination of Urzúa was considerably more harsh than the response to the Vergara assassination, because the regime was ratcheting up the repression to deal with the protest movement, as well as escalating terrorist violence. A wave of reprisal killings followed, and they impacted the MIR tremendously.

On September 7 CNI agents captured and summarily executed Hugo Ratier and another man. Ratier had led the squad that murdered Urzúa; in fact, he was one of the two men who had fired the volleys that had killed Roger Vergara in 1980. The same day, in another part of the capital, the CNI killed two more MIRistas, including Arturo Villavela, the senior MIR leader who had survived detention exactly a decade before.[56] A member of the central committee, Villavela was then in charge of MIR's military operations. Villavela's loss, coming at this juncture and in the wake of the disaster in Neltume, was irremediable. The overall toll was disastrous. Some forty MIRistas lost their lives between 1978 when Operation Return was set in motion and 1984 when, for all intents and purposes, the MIR was superseded by the Manuel Rodríguez Patriotic Front.

The gestation of the FPMR was as long as its paternity was complex. The front can trace its lineage to the Communist Youth, to Cuba, and to Nicaragua. The Communist party that had once denounced the ultra-leftist adventurism of the MIR had been radicalized in the years since the coup and had reoriented its strategy accordingly. In a break with its historic line, the party began to emphasize military and paramilitary action. The central committee had acknowledged in 1977 that the lack of military capabilities with which to defend Allende's coalition government had contributed to its overthrow.[57] Thereafter, it began to reconstruct its clandestine cells in Chile, and to prepare for armed struggle to drive Pinochet from power.

The victory of the Sandinista National Liberation Front in Nicaragua in July 1979 encouraged the radicals. The following year the Communist party advocated a new strategy, "Mass Popular Rebellion," and took steps to translate its new policy into action. The protest movement in Chile, particularly in the shanty-towns, reinforced the conviction about the possibility of insurrection. The Manuel Rodríguez Patriotic Front or FPMR was formed at the end of 1983 to lead it. The front was closely linked to the armed formations of the Communist party of Chile, but was formally separate from it.[58]

Recruitment of the men and women who became combatants of the FPMR began as early as 1974, from the ranks of the Communist Youth. For some years the Chilean situation seemed hopeless, or at least less hopeful than the situations in Nicaragua and El Salvador. Scores of Chileans fought in the civil wars in those Central American countries and gained invaluable combat experience in the process. Their acknowledged leader was known as "Benjamín" in Nicaragua and "Comandante Rodrigo" back in Chile. His true identity was Raúl Pellegrin, a twenty-eight-year-old engineer by training, son of lifelong Communist militants. Pellegrin and his compatriots also received guerrilla training in Cuba and in the other countries on the guerrilla circuit. So, when the FPMR began infiltrating militants into Chile sometime after 1980, it was deploying the officer corps of a future popular insurrection.

The unorthodox relationship between the FPMR and the Communist party proved unworkable, and deceived no one. Nominally the FPMR was a separate entity, but it was supposed to adhere to the political line of the Party. The entire enterprise was beset by confused lines of command and inevitable controversies and jealousies. Middle-level Communist directors were cool and even hostile to the infiltrated Rodriguistas, who initially had no contact with anyone for obvious security reasons. Moreover, the caliber of the Rodriguista officers exceeded by far the level of preparedness existent in Chile. Thus, despite the immense logistical effort that went into the successful infiltration of guerrillas into the national territory, the expertise of this hardened and experienced corps of resistance fighters was squandered. And, of course, neither Chilean intelligence nor the U.S. Central Intelligence Agency had any doubts about the connection between the front and the Communist party.

The FPMR announced its existence on December 14, 1983, and went into action almost immediately, kidnapping the assistant editor of *La Nación* less than a week later, according to Chilean military intelligence.[59] The journalist was released unharmed on Christmas Day. A wave of bombings, robberies, and armed take-overs occurred in the first quarter of 1984, and at least five of the incidents were the work of the FPMR. On two occasions, in January and March, commandos occupied radio stations and broadcast propaganda. The first fatality attributed to the front came in June, when commandos stormed a train in Linares, to demonstrate their prowess and to announce their presence with authority. On July 19, 1985 (the sixth anniversary of the Sandinista revolution in Nicaragua), the FPMR detonated a car bomb outside the U.S. consulate in Santiago, killing a bystander. In 1986, the front began its campaign of assassinations, and in September of that year, the FPMR only just failed to assassinate Pinochet himself.

In April 1986 FPMR assassins killed a leader of the Independent Democratic Union, UDI, the party of Jaime Guzmán, the regime's ideologue. The UDI had become a hated symbol of the regime, as the most fundamental supporter of Chile's new institutional framework and the free market miracle the neo-liberal economic reforms had supposedly made possible. In March 1989, an assassination team nearly assassinated Gustavo Leigh, the man who had first announced the crusade to extirpate Marxism from Chile, and who oversaw the Joint Command to see to it that the Communist party of Chile was dealt a crushing blow. Chile's first democratic elections since March 1973 were only months away, but fortunately the wounding of Leigh did not dissipate the momentum toward democratization. Less than three months later, in June 1989, the front was more successful. Gunmen ambushed and killed Roberto Fuentes Morrison, the pivotal man in the Joint Command. In May 1990, gunmen assassinated Raúl Fontaine, the director of DICOMCAR, the Carabinero intelligence unit guilty of the March 1985 murder of Santiago Nattino, José Manuel Parada, and Manuel Guerrero. Then, in April 1991, the FPMR assassinated Jaime Guzmán himself, as he left the Catholic University after teaching constitutional law class. By now Patricio Aylwin was in office and the restoration of Chilean democracy was well underway, even if the "protected democracy" Guzmán had been instrumental in instituting was anathema to democrats. The assassination punished a hated symbol of the regime, but it had a harmful effect on the recovery of the truth about the human rights violations of the dictatorship. The murder led to the cancellation of a nationwide tour of Aylwin cabinet officials and members of the National Commission on Truth and Reconciliation. Suddenly the truth seemed to be dangerous and destabilizing.

The failed attempt on Pinochet's life was by far and away the most dramatic and consequential: dramatic because of its audacity; consequential, despite the failure, because of its effect on the course of the protest movement. The elimination of the dictator, the supreme hardliner and the center of gravity of the regime, might have precipitated the collapse of the military government, much as the death by natural causes of Francisco Franco had in Spain a decade before. Instead, the act frightened the moderate opposition, which to that point had pegged its hopes on the street protests, into accepting Pinochet's terms regarding the transition. And it isolated the Communist party, which could not convincingly dissociate itself from the violent Manuel Rodríguez Patriotic Front. The most direct consequence of the front's violence was that the security forces reacted to it by decimating the ranks of the FPMR.

At the end of the first week of September 1986, Pinochet's motorcade drove down to Santiago from Melocotón, his mountain residence, and into an ambush from which the dictator only narrowly escaped. The attempt on Pinochet's life was an elaborate, carefully coordinated, and well executed operation dubbed "Operation XX Century."[60] The FPMR's operational planning of the complex mission was meticulous. Pellegrin, who had overall command of the operation, assigned teams separate tasks, each critical to the mission: to acquire safe-houses and vehicles, to provide logistical support, to assemble an inventory of weapons, to train the commandos, and to work out the tactics of the assault. Pellegrin even had the foresight to assemble a medical team consisting of four physicians and two paramedics to treat wounded combatants.

Operation XX Century involved a classic ambush, and the commandos who participated had recent examples to study. Anastasio Somoza, the anachronistic Nicaraguan dictator so many Rodríguistas had helped to topple, was killed when his limousine was attacked by a Sandinista hit team in Asunción, Paraguay in 1981; Admiral Carrero Blanco, the hardest of the hardliners in the "Bunker" of the ailing Francisco Franco, was killed by ETA guerrillas in 1973. General Pinochet, a man trained in military science and the operational arts, admitted that the assault team had achieved all three factors for a successful engagement: superior fire power, surprise, and favorable terrain.

The site of the ambush could not have been more favorable, and only a gigantic security lapse could explain how a large commando team could have been positioned along an isolated mountain route Pinochet routinely traveled. On weekends Pinochet customarily retired to his mountain residence, Melocotón, and returned to the capital Sunday evenings. The comfortable isolation of the mansion may have contributed to his security, but the predictable drive to and from Melocotón gave the general's enemies foreknowledge of his exact whereabouts twice a week. Inexplicably, Pinochet did not travel by helicopter. More inexplicably, his motorcade was lightly guarded.

On the evening of the seventh, the eve of the triumphal celebrations of the September 11, 1973 pronunciamento, Pinochet departed for Santiago. Riding with him in his Mercedes Benz limousine were his naval attaché and his nine-year-old grandson. Two carabineros mounted on motorcycles led the five-car motorcade. Pinochet's limousine was second in the procession, positioned between the lead car carrying a four-member Carabinero security team and another carrying a four-member security detachment from the army. Behind that car was another Mercedes, similar to the presidential car, along as a decoy. The decoy limousine was followed by another car of army security personnel, acting as the rearguard of the entourage. Altogether, Pinochet was protected by only fifteen bodyguards, not counting the two Carabinero motorcycle outriders: four carabineros in the lead car, four army officers in the car following the presidential limousine, three soldiers in the decoy car, and four more in the final car. They were lightly armed with Israeli-made Uzis and Galils and a few hand grenades.

Their attackers were well positioned and adequately armed, and they were undetected. Indeed, the presence of FPMR commandos had gone undetected for some time. As many as fifteen of them, posing as seminarians in a nearby seminary, were living near the site of the ambush and were able to familiarize themselves with the terrain and escape routes. The FPMR had also acquired a strategically located safe-house overlooking the mountain highway on which the motorcade would travel. The assault teams were alerted to the approach of Pinochet and his bodyguards from that house, setting Operation XX Century in motion. The site of the ambush itself was ideal, a mountain overlook, El Mirador, on a narrow highway flanked on one side by a retaining wall and a precipice falling off into a canyon, the Cajón de Maipo, and by a steep side of the mountain on the other. Snipers armed with M-16 assault rifles and armor-penetrating LOW rockets were strung out along the ambush site, dug in on the side of the mountain wall.

When the presidential motorcade reached the stretch of highway selected for the ambush, it encountered a Peugeot station wagon pulling a recreational trailer and blocking the road. Three commandos jumped out and opened fire on the lead car, killing one carabinero and seriously wounding the others. The entire presidential motorcade then came under a furious and lethal barrage of automatic weapon and rocket fire from the commandos positioned along the now blocked route. The use of the decoy limousine made no difference: all five vehicles were hit by small arms fire and rockets. In fact, Pinochet's car came under the most intense fire; the commandos had guessed right and aimed accurately. Three rockets actually hit Pinochet's Mercedes, but none exploded. This bit of luck was enough to enable Pinochet's skillful driver to reverse course and race back to Melocotón. An assault team had taken up position behind the motorcade after it had passed in order to seal off the escape route, but it could not accomplish what the larger contingent of commandos had failed to accomplish up the road. Pinochet was extraordinarily lucky, but five of his bodyguards were killed in the ambush. The car immediately behind his was completely destroyed in the attack, killing the four soldiers riding in it.

The army and the Carabinero units assigned to provide security to the dictator were guilty of a serious security lapse, but the affair did not end there. The commandos, some twenty-five in all, managed to escape with only two light casualties. All managed to make it back to Santiago, and eventually to Argentina, where Raúl Pellegrin and César Bunster, the man most directly involved in planning the operation, gave a clandestine press conference.

Pinochet also commented on the action of the FPMR and came perilously close to acknowledging that his attackers had mounted an impressive operation. The commandos had brought superior fire power to bear on an enemy caught by surprise on ideal terrain, the general admitted. This was, after all a military-style operation, not a bank robbery or indiscriminate terrorist bombing. Ambush is perhaps the most common tactic of irregular warfare; setting and avoiding them is a skill every foot soldier and field commander, every guerrilla and guerrilla comandante must master in order to win and survive. Nowhere in Pinochet's memoirs, not even in *The Decisive Day*, does the general describe combat in such vivid detail as in recounting the ambush. The general who claimed to be at war for the duration of his rule saw action just this one time.

But Pinochet denounced this as terrorism, and in so doing drew a false contrast between his attackers and his subordinates. The attack revealed "the abysmal difference between a soldier trained in conventional war, respectful of the wounded and the vanquished, and those predators of irregular war, who assassinate the wounded and finish off the injured and immobilized." The shooting of carabineros posted at an intersection through which the motorcade had passed, claimed the general using the language of the Geneva Conventions, "was not justified by military necessity." The attackers, he said, "almost seem not to be human beings."

The irony was palpable. Only ten weeks before, carabineros under General Pinochet's overall command as commander-in-chief had doused Rodrigo Rojas and Carmen Gloria Quintana with benzene, set them aflame, and left them to die an agonizing death or live with disfiguring scars. Nowhere in his memoirs does General Pinochet mention that atrocity, nor does he attempt to explain how the tactics of the men under his command — abduction, torture, murder, disappearance — had been justified by military necessity.

The security forces' reaction to the attack on Pinochet was as deadly as the attack itself. The secret police swept up four men, two communists and two MIRistas, in four separate operations between 2 a.m. on September 8 and 3 a.m. the following morning. The bodies of all four men were later recovered.[61] "Divine justice," said Pinochet, "made its presence felt." Retribution did not end there. Almost a year after the failed attempt on the dictator, the CNI conducted a series of raids that resulted in the death of some thirteen persons who either belonged to the FPMR or were unfortunate enough to be caught in the cross-fire.

Ignacio Valenzuela, a founding member of the front who had participated in its first armed actions, was the first to fall. In the early morning hours of June 15, CNI agents shot him to death on the street without attempting to arrest or subdue him, according to witnesses. Valenzuela became the first victim of the Corpus Christi massacre carried out over a span of twenty-four hours as part of the security agency's Operation Albania.[62] Later that evening, Patricio Acosto was executed on the street with a single shot to the head. Then in the morning hours of the sixteenth the CNI moved against FPMR militants in separate actions; two were killed in a residence used as a guerrilla training school, a third was shot to death trying to escape in the midst of a CNI raid, seven more were killed in a similar raid just before dawn. The CNI was not concerned in the least with abducting and interrogating these militants, whom they had identified and located after painstaking intelligence work.[63]

In July 1986, even before the assassination attempt on Pinochet, the Chilean intelligence service discovered a major arms cache in the northern fishing village of Vallenar. The discovery seriously weakened the front, which had been stockpiling the weapons for some time. The FPMR would be able to carry out assassinations even after the democratic transition, but it was more of a nuisance to be eliminated than a force to be reckoned with. The inevitable death of the front's leader, Comandante Rodrigo, was the confirmation of that. At the end of October 1988, the bodies of Raúl Pellegrin and Cecilia Magni, Pellegrin's comrade-in-arms and lover, were found in the shallows of the Tinguiririca River. A week before, a now hopelessly isolated group of guerrillas led by Pellegrin had staged an attack in a remote military outpost in Los Queñes, some hundred kilometers southeast of the capital. They managed to kill one carabinero, but troops stalked them and soon caught up with them. Pinochet comments that Pellegrin and Magni drowned while attempting to cross the river and to escape encirclement. But an autopsy revealed that they had been beaten and shocked with electricity before they were drowned.[64] Here was the senior guerrilla commander who had trained in Cuba and fought in Central America; he must have been more valuable alive than dead. But his captors did not hesitate to mete out "divine justice." Fourteen years before, the intelligence services placed a premium on capturing and interrogating the MIR's Miguel Rodríguez and Juan Bautista Van Schowen; Rodríguez, of course, died resisting capture, but Van Schowen's ordeal lasted weeks and perhaps months. In comparison, Pellegrin's death seemed undignified for a guerrilla comandante. Perhaps that was the thinking of his killers.

The war of resistance of the MIR and the FPMR was futile at best. None of these sporadic actions, bombings, ambushes of carabineros, or even the assassinations of high profile figures could topple the regime. What is worse, the actions fortified regime hardliners and frightened the nonviolent opponents of the regime into accepting the regime's terms regarding the transition. The failed assassination attempt on Pinochet was the turning point, although ironically it was the one action that could have influenced future events. Killing an intelligence officer whose hands were stained with the blood of fallen comrades would do nothing to shake the regime at its foundations. The elimination of Pinochet, however, would alter the regime profoundly, as no one in or around the military government had acquired the stature or the mystique of the Generalissimo. There are parallels between Operation XX Century and the assassination of Spanish Admiral Luis Carrero Blanco by Basque separatist guerrillas in 1973, the year Pinochet came to power. Eliminating him changed the internal political dynamic and opened the way for an *apertura* rather than the unaltered continuation of Franco's rule.

But the democratic transition in Chile would not be the result of the death of the Chilean caudillo, or of the protest movement, or of pressure from abroad. The failed attempt on Pinochet's life only convinced the moderate opposition — which now included the party of Allende — of the need to find a peaceful way to democracy.

Chapter 7
The Peaceful Way to Democracy

> It was something never seen before: the vanquished were asking uncon-
> ditional surrender from the victors, from those who held power. The
> Armed Forces of Chile were not a defeated militia in rout, completely
> the contrary.
>
> — General Augusto Pinochet

Pinochet, the United States, and the United Nations

The simmering three-year crisis between 1983 and 1986 had economic
causes, but it was paramountly political. The crisis became an opportunity to
challenge the regime at its core and to initiate in Chile a process of democratization that was already culminating in the other countries of the Southern Cone. Consequently, the crisis became a test of the regime's institutional resilience, a test that centered on the timing and circumstances of the
transition as set down in the 1980 constitution. Pinochet felt pressures from
three sources, the United States, the United Nations, and his domestic opposition. Pinochet succeeded in resisting each of them.

Richard Nixon and Henry Kissinger were determined to remove Allende
from power once the Chilean congress had done the unimaginable by voting to confirm the Socialist president-elect. Indeed, successive administrations dating back to 1958 had been desperate to prevent his election; the
possible election of an avowed Marxist had been a truly bipartisan preoccupation. The covert operations to funnel monies to the Christian Democrats in 1964 constituted intervention in Chile's domestic affairs as much as
the CIA's quiet encouragement to militant officers to oust Allende. Congressional hearings after the September 1973 coup disclosed some embar-
rassing revelations about these matters, and the Church Committee hearings led to much consternation in Washington and some inconsequential
legislation aimed at curbing future abuses.

The ouster of Salvador Allende was an unambiguous foreign policy victory of the national security, foreign policy, and intelligence establishments,
despite any embarrassment the revelations of covert action might have
caused. The human rights record of the regime prevented the United States

from having a completely amicable relationship with the Pinochet regime, however. Congressional Democrats, in particular, saw to it that the Chilean government was punished. As regards U.S. policy, there were several matters, each with a different degree of importance as time passed. In the immediate aftermath of the military intervention, the questions raised related to the degree of U.S. participation in the coup and the nonparticipation of the American embassy in the humanitarian effort to protect the lives of refugees. Later the issue became what the United States could do to bring pressure to bear on the dictatorship to improve its human rights record and to hasten the return of democracy. This question was relevant to both U.S. bilateral dealings and its multilateral diplomacy.

The Nixon and Ford administrations took no action to punish the junta for human rights violations. Indeed, to the consternation of congressional liberals, they circumvented Congress's efforts to curtail economic and military assistance to Chile. And the Republican administrations generally supported multilateral development assistance to Pinochet's Chile. Funds from these sources probably off set reductions in bilateral aid. Within months of the coup, while the armed forces were still in the first phase of repression, the Nixon administration arranged for $52 million in commodity credits to be made available to the new military government.[1] As 1974 opened, Chile had already agreed to pay compensation for North American firms affected by Allende's economic measures, the United States and Chile had reached a bilateral agreement with respect to Chilean debts, the Paris Club was finalizing the details of a plan to reschedule debt payments, and Export-Import Bank credit had again been extended to Chile.[2]

Efforts by Congressional Democrats to block or reduce aid levels to Chile to punish the junta for its human rights practices met with resistance from the executive branch and its supporters in Congress. Senators Kennedy of Massachusetts and Harkin of Iowa, and Representative Fraser of Minnesota, were among the most vocal opponents of the new Chilean regime. They had two avenues, to reduce economic aid substantially, and to eliminate military aid altogether. For his part, in December 1973 Kennedy added language to section 35 of the Foreign Assistance Act that would have forced the president to request that the Chilean government respect human rights, as well as to support the humanitarian efforts of the United Nations and human rights investigations of the Inter-American Commission for Human Rights (the latter two efforts were already underway).[3] Kennedy did not prevail, however, and the final bill only urged the president to request that the Chilean government respect human rights. But the message was sent that Congress would be activist. The compliance of the executive branch was another matter.

Harry Shlaudeman, who in 1974 was the deputy chief of mission at the Santiago embassy, was among the first called before congressional committees to state administration policy. Revelations about covert funding to op-

ponents of Allende were already coming to the fore, and the career diplomat's appearance before the combined subcommittees on Inter-American
Affairs and International Organizations and Movements on June 12, 1974,
promised to be tense. Shlaudeman was scheduled to appear on the second
of three days of hearings. His testimony got off to a bad start.

Representative Fraser, who was presiding over the hearings that Wednes-
day afternoon, had just invited Shlaudeman to read his prepared statement
when Representative Michael Harrington of Massachusetts rose with a point
of order: "Would a motion be in order to ask that the testimony presented to
us this afternoon be sworn to by the witness?" After some informal discussion he made his point more forcefully: "Is there objection to having the
veracity of [witness'] statements determined?"[4] The distrust between liberal
members of Congress and administration and State Department officials
was palpable, and Harrington was especially perturbed by the turn of events
in Chile. Harrington had visited Santiago in October 1973, and was scornful
of the officers who had overthrown Allende. Upon his return he pressed for
hearings to determine the extent of U.S. complicity, of which he was convinced. Nathaniel Davis, ambassador to Chile at the time, had arranged
interviews for the congressman from New England, but the congressman
was unimpressed. Harrington met with reporters before his return to the
United States, Davis recounted, and "expressed regret that his only opportunity to talk with U.S. ambassador to Chile Nathaniel Davis, was in the
presence of three or four Chilean generals." "The generals were three of
the four members of the Chilean Junta," Davis later wrote with evident
satisfaction.[5] The other members of the committee, however, saw no need to
make Shlaudeman swear to the veracity of his statements. After Shlaudeman's reference to "the commitment, strongly affirmed by the Secretary [of
State, Henry Kissinger] to the hemispheric principle of non-intervention,"
some committee members perhaps began to rethink the wisdom of taking
the witness at his word.

"Despite pressures to the contrary," Shlaudeman said, reading from his
prepared statement, "the U.S. Government adhered to a policy of non-
intervention in Chile's internal affairs during the Allende period." As to
efforts to persuade the military government to halt human rights violations,
Shlaudeman insisted that "for those efforts to be effective they must show an
awareness not only of the abstract principles to whose universal realization
we are dedicated but also of the practical conditions under which they must
be promoted." A misinformed Shlaudeman then made an assertion contra-
dicted by every human rights organization that monitored the situation in
Chile. "The Chilean authorities have acknowledged instances of mistreatment of detainees; they have declared that such abuses are not sanctioned,
and that the persons responsible for them are being tried and punished."[6]

Representatives, in particular Fraser, Dante Fascell, chairman of the
House subcommittee on Inter-American Affairs, and above all Harrington,

were not in a receptive mood. "Have you, the Ambassador, or someone specifically discussed with the Chilean Government the actions and feelings of the U.S. Congress on the subject [of human rights]?" Fascell asked. They had, Shlaudeman assured. "I can say quite confidently that they are indeed aware of the concern of the Congress in these matters and the relationship between these matters and the aid." Fascell rephrased the question in a manner that encapsulates the human rights dimension of U.S. policy. Shlaudeman's response reflected the evasiveness of the White House and Department of State.

Mr. Fascell. . . . . It is important to for us to know whether the moral persuasion of the United States is being used, whether there is an adequate reaction to it and whether there is a point in time at which you could begin "normal" relationships with that government in terms of consideration of either economic or military assistance. Has the [State] Department given consideration to the fact and do they take the position that the representations by the United States and other interested organizations have had some impact on the human rights issue in Chile?

Mr. Shlaudeman. I would say, and this is very strongly my own view and I think it is certainly shared in the Department and in our Embassy in Santiago, that the Chilean Government is responsive to responsible international human rights opinion on a number of subjects and in a number of areas. I think to me in any case it has been impressive the number of people who have gone to Chile and have been admitted and in many cases assisted by the Chilean Government in their investigations which in some cases at least did not turn out to be all that friendly. I think it shows a sense of responsibility which I think is most commendable.[7]

But when it came to the specifics of the aid requests, the amounts, and the need for it, exchanges became heated. Shlaudeman, for example, told Ohio Representative Charles Whalen, Jr. that the State Department had not yet made a formal finding as to whether section 32 of the 1973 Foreign Assistance Act, which addressed the problem of internment and imprisonment for political purposes, was even applicable to Chile. The uncertainty, Shlaudeman explained, was that the declaration of the state of siege permitted the Chilean military authorities to hold Chilean citizens "in preventative detention" without charge.[8] He assured Whalen that State Department attorneys were studying the language of section 32. This was the kind of casuistry practiced by the Chilean Supreme Court and the Chilean Bar Association. According to this reasoning, the provisions of section 32 would not apply in any country whose de facto rulers had been foresighted enough to declare legal the arbitrary detention of political opponents.

The moral persuasion of the United States, of course, did not amount to much unless backed by the credible threat of an aid cutoff from the executive branch. In fact, the Nixon White House worked to undermine the intent of Congress. Many members of Congress were keenly aware that the Nixon administration, taking advantage of ambiguity in the language of the law, had managed to off set the spending limits by extending other forms of assistance to Chile. The mood of the Ninety-Third Congress was confrontational. Soon after the first anniversary of the coup, more than one hundred members of Congress addressed a letter to Henry Kissinger, the secretary of state, on the matter of the administration's support for oppressive regimes. "It may not be realistic," they wrote to the most unapologetic proponent of Realpolitik, "to expect strict observance of political, civil and other human rights by [oppressive governments] while their political systems are still evolving. Nevertheless, even within such countries, the observance of certain fundamental human rights is practicable, including freedom from torture, arbitrary arrest and detention and arbitrary curtailment of existing political rights." They raised the specter of a political backlash. "Unless U.S. foreign aid policies—especially military assistance policies—more accurately reflect the traditional commitment of the American people to promote human rights, we will find it increasingly difficult to justify foreign aid to our constituents."[9] But Kissinger's cynicism on the matter was legendary. The House committees holding hearings on the human rights situation in Chile made it a point to include in the public record a *New York Times* article written by Seymour Hersh, an acerbic critic of Kissinger, which alleged that the secretary of state rebuked U.S. Ambassador to Chile, David Popper, for raising human rights issues with the junta. Kissinger scrawled "Tell Popper to cut out the Political Science lectures" in the margin of a cable reporting Popper's conversations with General Bonilla, the Minister of Defense.[10]

According to Schoultz, who has undertaken the most careful study of the aid packages, "the implementation of the 1974 and 1975 limitations on aid to Chile will probably stand for some time as the classic example of executive branch contempt for congressional directives on foreign aid."[11] Arguably, this classic example stood for only a decade: the Reagan administration's circumvention of congressional prohibitions of funding for the Nicaraguan insurgents, the Contras, certainly surpassed anything the Nixon-Ford administrations concocted with respect to Chile. Congress had more success with military aid. In 1974 Congress managed to restrict military assistance to Chile to less than $1 million of International Military Education and Training program funds. Two years later much more stringent restrictions were enacted, and by 1977 a ban on military assistance and sales went into effect.[12]

The Nixon-Ford administrations were protective of the military regime in multilateral diplomacy, as well. Secretary of State Kissinger instructed his subordinates to vote against multilateral development assistance only once, in June 1976, the same month he traveled to Santiago to attend the Sixth Regular Session of the OAS. American diplomats consistently abstained on United Nations votes critical of Chile, beginning with the Economic and Social Council's first resolution (passed 41–0 with two abstentions, the United States and Chile) in early 1974. When the Third Committee of the UN General Assembly considered a mildly worded resolution expressing "its deepest concern that constant flagrant violations of human rights and fundamental freedoms continue to be reported," Tapley Bennett, Jr., the U.S. representative on the committee, rose in defense of Chile. "To a degree substantially greater than that which other governments faced with similar reported violations have been able to match, the Government of Chile has taken note of concerns expressed by friendly governments and in recent months has taken actions responsive to those concerns."[13] Then Bennett launched into an attack on the "double standard on human rights and democracy." "Some of the [resolution's] cosponsors have denounced reported violations of human rights in Chile in the strongest terms while many of these same rights do not exist in their own countries." The U.S. position, therefore, was clear: "my government, along with all free peoples, will support genuine and objective efforts to secure full enjoyment of basic human rights in Chile, or in any country. However, we cannot support a resolution so lacking in essential balance and fairness."[14] But not even Secretary Kissinger could completely ignore human rights violations in Chile, perhaps because of the "traditional commitment of the American people to human rights" about which concerned members of Congress had attempted to remind him. The following June, when Kissinger traveled to Santiago, he delivered a fairly blunt statement about human rights, in which he noted that "the condition of human rights . . . has impaired our relationship with Chile and will continue to do so."[15] Kissinger could not have foreseen that the issue of human rights in Chile would quite literally explode in Washington, D.C.

Only weeks after Kissinger's visit to Santiago, a bomb exploded beneath the car of Orlando Letelier on Embassy Row in Washington, killing the former Allende foreign minister and Ronnie Moffitt, an American citizen. It was a terrifying and bloody spectacle. Letelier, whose legs were blown off above the knee, had to be hoisted from the demolished Chevrolet through the hole that had been blasted through the floorboards directly beneath his seat. He bled to death in a matter of minutes. Moffitt, who was seated beside Letelier, also bled to death. A single piece of shrapnel had pierced an artery. She died on the curb, coughing up blood, while her dazed husband and frantic bystanders looked on.[16]

Jimmy Carter took the oath of office the following January. President Carter's fundamental emphasis on human rights was likely to complicate relations with Santiago, but an act of terrorism in the United States promised to disrupt them. If any of the five administrations demonstrated that it could exact concessions from Pinochet, however, it was the Carter administration.

The Carter administration had some advantages, apart from its express commitment to human rights. Pressure was mounting on the Chilean government, and even the xenophobic Pinochet could not entirely ignore the international community, although, as with the United Nations, he attempted to make the most of the inevitable confrontations. There were a series of meetings that would give the administration the opportunity to send clear signals and attempt quiet diplomacy. The Seventh Regular Session of the OAS was scheduled to be convened on the island of Grenada in June. Among other items on the agenda, the delegates would be considering the third report on the human rights situation in Chile, released in mid-February 1977. It would be a repetition of the events the year before, when the OAS met in Santiago, only this time the dictatorship's violations committed in the prelude to that previous meeting would be exposed.[17] Carter's secretary of state, Cyrus Vance, would avail himself of the opportunity to meet and discuss the situation with his Chilean counterpart, Admiral Patricio Carvajal. Carter administration officials wisely made it a point to meet with former Chilean president, Christian Democrat Eduardo Frei, and even with socialist leader Clodomiro Almeyda, in May. The White House was reaching out to the Chilean opposition, and some response from Santiago was required.

Moreover, Latin American leaders were scheduled to arrive in Washington in September for the signing of the Panama Canal treaties. Pinochet wanted very much to be invited to attend: if Carter did not extent the invitation, Pinochet would be classed with Fidel Castro, who was left off the list of invited dignitaries. It turns out that Manuel Contreras wanted high-ranking personnel of the DINA, including himself, to accompany the dictator.[18] But at this very moment U.S. prosecutors were piecing together evidence implicating the DINA in the Letelier assassination. Indictments and a diplomatically delicate extradition request for Contreras and DINA operation's chief Pedro Espinoza would soon follow.[19] It was at this juncture, July–August 1977, that Pinochet announced the Chacarillas plan and dissolved the DINA. If any U.S. administration had succeeded in gaining concessions from the Chilean dictatorship, it was the much maligned Carter administration.

By the time Augusto Pinochet staged the 1980 plebiscite on the new constitution, Jimmy Carter's presidency was very much in trouble. The fall of the Shah of Iran in February 1979, followed by the hostage crisis; the victory of leftist Sandinistas in Nicaragua in July; and the Soviet invasion of Afghanistan in December—all seemed to validate charges that criticism of friendly dictators merely opened the way for hostile ones to come to power. Ronald Reagan's resounding victory in the presidential election in the fall of 1980 was in some measure a result of such perceptions. Ronald Reagan and Augusto Pinochet would now cross paths. They would serve the next eight years as presidents of their respective countries, and both men would narrowly survive assassination attempts.

Ronald Reagan admired Pinochet, according to advisors in charge of Latin American affairs. "Pinochet saved Chile from communism," the president reportedly commented when the Chilean dictator's name came up in a White House briefing, "we should have him here on a State visit."[20] During his first term, Ronald Reagan was surrounded by advisors who shared that view. Jeane Kirkpatrick, whom Reagan appointed permanent representative to the United Nations, extolled right-wing autocrats. Kirkpatrick had written a highly influential piece lambasting the Carter administration entitled "Dictatorships and Double Standards." The article virtually became a synopsis of the Reagan policy in the Americas, at least during the Republican president's first term in office. Kirkpatrick's one idea was that right-wing dictators were less likely to endanger U.S. interests and far more susceptible to gradual change. The article was written after the fall of Anastasio Somoza in Nicaragua, but Pinochet could easily fit Kirkpatrick's benign image of right-wing despots. Kirkpatrick's theorizing about geopolitics and her insensitivity towards human rights had real-life consequences in Chile. Kirkpatrick refused to meet personally with Jaime Castillo, director of the Chilean Human Rights Commission, during a visit to Chile in August 1981. Two days after her visit ended, Castillo was arrested and sent into exile for a second time.[21]

Despite his admiration for Pinochet, Reagan never invited him to Washington. The only occasion he traveled to the capital was to attend the Panama Canal Treaty signing ceremonies, and the dictator made it a point to have photographs of a leisurely stroll with Jimmy Carter placed in his memoir. But the Reagan administration invited high-level Chilean officials, including junta member Fernando Matthei, to visit. The Defense Department restarted the joint U.S.-Chilean naval exercise, Operation UNITAS. And conservatives in Congress, led by the arch-conservative Senator Jesse Helms of North Carolina, managed to lift the ban on military assistance and sales to Chile.[22]

But well before Reagan stood for reelection in 1984, Pinochet would face an unanticipated crisis indirectly brought on by Reagan's economic polices and the Latin American debt crisis they produced. Beginning in 1983, a series of National Days of Protest staged by a renascent civil society shook Chile. Pinochet reacted violently and in 1984 reimposed the state of siege. Reagan administration officials, although highly supportive of the Pinochet regime's economic reforms, were deeply concerned about the turn of events in the country, especially the emergence of the Manuel Rodríguez Patriotic Front. The fall of Anastasio Somoza in Nicaragua had become a cautionary tale for U.S. foreign policy, national security, and intelligence establishments. Many believed that Carter had lost Nicaragua to the radical Sandinista Front for National Liberation by failing to support the moderate opposition to the obstinate dictator when they enjoyed the political initiative. The Central Intelligence Agency was aware that guerrillas of Chile's Manuel Rodríguez Patriotic Front had been combat tested in Nicaragua, that they were receiving arms from Cuba, and that history could repeat itself thousands of miles to the south. Support for the moderate opposition, and careful cajoling of Pinochet and the bunker, became administration policy.

Salvador Allende had been immensely popular at the United Nations. He had given one of his most eloquent speeches to the General Assembly at the end of 1972, denouncing an invisible blockade erected by the United States to destabilize his government. It was an allegation that resonated among many of the developing nations comprising the UN General Assembly and the Non-Aligned Movement to which Allende had attached Chile. General Pinochet would have to contend with Allende's almost mythical stature in the United Nations, which he considered to be a nest of Marxist vipers. He rejected its condemnations of human rights violations committed by agents of the military regime, and accused it of selective prosecution, a charge not entirely without validity. In Pinochet's view, Marxist states and their fellow-travelers were bent on persecuting his government for having saved Chile from Marxism.

The UN Human Rights Commission reacted strongly to the coup d'état and became intensely concerned with the situation in Chile. In March 1974, the commission invited Salvador Allende's widow to address it. Then the commission decided to make the human rights situation in Chile a separate agenda item, and to subject the Chilean government to the glare of public, as opposed to confidential, proceedings. These actions infuriated Pinochet, but they invigorated the United Nations human rights organs.

The UN bodies concerned with human rights had became more active during the previous decade, with apartheid and racism being the main catalysts. The adoption of two resolutions in particular dynamized the UN: Economic and Social Council Resolutions 1235 and 1503.[23] Resolution 1235, adopted in June 1967, authorized the UN Human Rights Commission and the Sub-Commission on Prevention of Discrimination and Protection of Minorities to "examine information relevant to gross violations of human rights and fundamental freedoms" and "to make a thorough study of situations which reveal a consistent pattern of violations of human rights." It was relevant because it entailed UN scrutiny of the human rights situations in countries other than South Africa and what was formerly Rhodesia, and because it permitted the United Nations to examine individual communications, albeit for the purpose of discerning "a consistent pattern." Resolution 1503, adopted in 1971, established a cumbersome confidential procedure that was intended to elicit the cooperation of offending states. The UN Centre for Human Rights was charged with sifting through communications alleging human rights violations and reporting them to a special Working Group of the Sub-Commission on Prevention of Discrimination and Protection of Minorities. Meeting in closed session for two weeks in June each year, the Working Group examines the communications directed to it and the replies of governments alleged to have committed violations to determine whether the cases brought to its attention warrant action by the Sub-Commission. After that, a Working Group of the Human Rights Commission meets to consider the information, before the case is taken up by the entire commission. The entire process is confidential, and petitioners do not themselves know whether their communication had prompted action. In fact, the only time a "black listed" country is identified is when it is dropped from the list. These were the lengthy procedures in place on the day the Chilean armed forces overthrew the government of Salvador Allende. But, to the great displeasure of the Chilean government, the 1503 procedure was not employed in the Chilean case.

The Chilean case was thus precedent-setting, and extremely controversial. It was precedent-setting, because the Chilean case was the first examined by the Human Rights Commission that did not involve racially motivated violations of human rights, as authorized by Resolution 1235; controversial, because the confidential procedure outlined in Resolution 1503 was ignored in favor of public scrutiny of the conduct of the military government. Instead of the closed-door examination of the evidence of human rights violations, the UN Human Rights Commission made Chile a separate item on its agenda, meaning that session time was set aside to denounce Chile publicly, making Chile one of the damned trinity along with South Africa and Israel.[24] It was entirely permissible but nevertheless controversial for the commission to avoid the confidential 1503 procedure. Not only was the option of placing Chile on the 1503 black list not chosen, the same bloc of countries that voted to publicly castigate Chile prevented similar treatment of Doctor Idi Amin's bloody regime in Uganda.[25] That was not the end of it. In 1974, the General Assembly endorsed a commission recommendation to establish an Ad Hoc Working Group on Chile.[26] In 1978, the Human Rights Commission went so far as to create a special trust fund for victims of torture in Chile.[27] The following year, after the Chilean government finally permitted an on site visit by members of the Ad Hoc Working Group, the United Nations created a Special Rapporteur on the human rights situation in Chile. Much to the chagrin of the Pinochet government, Chile remained a separate item on the Human Rights Commission's agenda, and the Special Rapporteur's mandate was renewed each year until 1990, the year Pinochet formally ceded power.

"What had the greatest effect on our national dignity," General Pinochet wrote some years later, "was the naming and the visit of the Ad Hoc Group on human rights."[28] Comparing Chile to David and its enemies to Goliath, Pinochet complained, "We were a permanent target of Marxist attacks in international organizations." But Pinochet acknowledged that the majority of his advisors were in favor of a visit by the Ad Hoc Working Group. Pinochet reluctantly agreed to permit the visit, and then reneged at the last moment. Pinochet remembers "meditating a few days" on the request to visit Chile, before announcing to the nation that he had taken a "transcendental decision" to cancel it, fully cognizant that it would "bring violent and acid reactions, not only from the Marxist world, but also from the world of their sympathizers." The UN Working Group would not visit Chile until July 1978.

The already strained relations with the UN Human Rights Commission and the Ad Hoc Working Group deteriorated further after the abrupt cancellation of the inspection visit. A steady stream of critical resolutions came in ensuing years, and virtually every UN body concerned with human rights made its indignation known. When the United Nations in December 1975 passed one of many resolutions accusing Chile of serious human rights violations, including torture, Pinochet took to the airwaves to denounce the action. "The UN has the mission to promote human rights," he said in a televised speech, "but no one has as yet given it the authority, in fulfillment of that mission, to censure arbitrarily, violating the principles of non-intervention, self-determination, and the juridical equality of states." He concluded with a categorical repudiation of the United Nations' criticism of his government: "The United Nations resolution against Chile is not only completely lacking moral authority, it has no juridical value whatsoever, and is contrary to the law."

The general had his own musings about human rights and fundamental freedoms, and did not believe that an international body that counted the likes of the Soviet Union, Cambodia, and Cuba as member states, had much to say about the matter. "Human rights are universal and inviolable," he acknowledged, "but are not unrestricted nor of equal hierarchy."

Among natural rights there exist some that are more fundamental and important than others. Normally, the exercise of all rights can be enjoyed simultaneously. But when the social body becomes ill, that becomes impossible. This is just the sign of political abnormality which demands the rule of a juridical regime of exception. In such a regime, the exercise of some rights is limited to a great degree or even suspended, in order to guarantee the vigilance of the most important rights.[29]

The general was correct in the sense that, in regimes of exception, the exercise of some rights may be limited and even suspended. But the most egregious practices institutionalized by the regime over which he presided — torture, extrajudicial executions, "disappearances," application of ex post facto laws, denial of legal remedies — constituted impermissible derogations from international legal norms. This judgment was sophistry, as far as General Pinochet was concerned: he was far more concerned in curing the social ill that plagued the Chilean body politic.

The UN General Assembly resolution passed overwhelmingly in December 1977 marked the culmination of the first phase of tense relations between the Chilean government and the international body. Pinochet, eager to consolidate his personal power as much as to deflect international condemnation, convoked a plebiscite in response to the resolution. Pinochet the career soldier appreciated the potency of nationalist sentiment, while Pinochet the shrewd dictator understood how to turn adversity to his political advantage. After winning the plebiscite he could not lose in January 1978, some opening to the United Nations seemed a wise move. In February, the Ad Hoc Working Group submitted its third report on the human rights violations in Chile to the Economic and Social Council, the principal UN body charged with protecting and promoting human rights. Its conclusions were familiar. The Working Group noted that some political prisoners had been released, that the rate of arrests was down somewhat, and that fewer denunciations of torture were being made. But the overall situation remained bleak: "there remain critical areas where violations of human rights and fundamental freedoms, in some cases open and systematic, continue to exist." Chileans continue to disappear, it noted, and it observed an ominous new trend, the banishment of political leaders, including now Christian Democrats, whose party had been banned in 1977. The Working Group called on the government to prosecute those responsible for serious violations, especially torture, "to deter future violations," and renewed its incessant call for an on site inspection.[30]

This time those who had counseled Pinochet in 1975 to permit the abruptly canceled visit of the UN investigators prevailed. The repeated calls for an in loco visit, reinforced by United States insistence that the government permit one, convinced them that Chile would ultimately benefit from the gesture. The propaganda value for the regime was potentially great, because the inspection was unprecedented and no Soviet bloc country was being pressed to grant the commission entry. Negotiations between representatives of the military government and Theo van Boven, director of the UN Human Rights Centre, began the following month, March, in New York.[31]

In July Pinochet finally relented and permitted the Ad Hoc Group to make its long-delayed visit. Only three members of the group, Abdoulaye Dieye from Senegal, Mariam Kamara from Sierra Leone, and Felix Ermacora from Austria, participated in the mission. Ghulam Allana, the Pakistani head of the Working Group, remained behind at the vehement insistence of the Chilean government. Theo van Boven, director of the then UN Human Rights Division, accompanied the team with a number of very capable assistants.[32] The Ad Hoc Working Group arrived well prepared to conduct the precedent-setting mission. Its rules of procedure, drafted in 1970, represented the standard for such fact-finding missions.[33] The group had interviewed scores of witnesses over the three years it had been working on the Chilean case, and van Boven had met secretly with representatives of the Vicariate of Solidarity in France prior to departure for Chile.[34] The most dramatic moment of the visit came when the inspectors visited the infamous Villa Grimaldi torture center operated by the now disbanded DINA. The Villa Grimaldi was once the headquarters of the DINA's all-powerful Metropolitan Brigade and its anti-subversive action teams. General Orlandier Mena, the man in charge of Chile's new intelligence agency, the CNI, accompanied the UN inspectors. So did Rodrigo Muñoz and Hector Zamorano, Chileans who had been detained and tortured in Villa Grimaldi's "Tower." The team was able to confirm the men's harrowing testimony about the place, which they could describe right down to the blue ceramic tiles covering the walls in a room where they had been tortured.[35] A picture of Zamorano with the blue tiles serving as the backdrop was subsequently published in a popular Santiago daily, and Ad Hoc Working Group gave the remarkable story considerable coverage in the appendices of its October 1978 report.

The final report of the Ad Hoc Working Group was not what some in the Chilean government might have expected, given Pinochet's magnanimity in permitting the visit. Pinochet's comments for posterity about the 1978 visit were more acerbic than those about the abrupt cancellation of the planned visit three years before.[36] His estimation of the advisors who had convinced him to permit the visit, against his better judgment, come across with remarkable clarity. "The pressure to permit the famous commission to come from numerous collaborators and persons close to me continued," he admitted. "At that moment my arguments—that these gentleman were functionaries of an organization infiltrated by Marxism, that they were servants of the Communists, and that its report was going to cause us more harm than good—were worth nothing. Many times people are blinded by their ideas."

Pinochet, unlike his advisors, was not under the illusion that by permitting the visit he was buying the good will of the commission. "The report is going to be negative" he recalls telling his advisors. "Now, as I have said, they will believe them much more abroad because they have visited the country. Marxists are very skillful and experts in deceit." As to the visit to Villa Grimaldi, the dictator is remarkably terse and unexpansive. "They also met with the director of the CNI [General Mena] and were authorized to visit Villa Grimaldi—about which a thousand tales have been spun." Pinochet made no effort to unravel the tales or to comment on the photographs appearing in the paper. The commission's conclusions and recommendations did not move the dictator at all. "There are other countries that have systematically violated human rights, but that are not affected by this arbitrary measure, because they are ideologically Marxist-Leninist or from the Club of Democracy." One wonders if General Pinochet misspoke when he admitted that there are *other* countries that systematically violate human rights.

Pinochet's indignation at the report prompted him to cease cooperating with the UN Human Rights Commission altogether: for the next several years Chilean representatives did not even attend the annual meetings of the UN Human Rights Commission in Geneva to plead Chile's case before the "servants of the Communists." The response of the United Nations to this latest and most comprehensive report was to establish a Special Rapporteur to replace the Ad Hoc Group. General Pinochet now had a new diplomatic battle to wage: to make sure that the Rapporteur was sympathetic to Chile. Some observers believe that Pinochet eventually succeeded in that.

End Game

As important as signals from Washington and UN resolutions were, the missing element was a united opposition with a coherent and realistic strategy. The disparate forces working to bring Pinochet down had been their own worst enemies. The centrist Christian Democrats were wary of the many factions of the left, especially the Communist party. And all opposition forces misjudged the potency of the protest movement and the resilience of the regime. It would take more than three years for party leaders and protest organizers to overcome their suspicions and converge on a common course of action to remove Pinochet: the peaceful way to democracy.

Gabriel Valdés, the newly chosen president of the Christian Democrats, and Cardinal Fresno acted first. In July 1983, soon after the third National Protest and on the eve of the fourth, Valdés announced the formation of the Democratic Alliance (AD). Joining the Christian Democrats in the AD were the tiny Republican party on the right, the Radical and Social Democratic parties in the center, and the Socialist party and Popular Socialist Union on the left.[37] The Democratic Alliance was destined for oblivion, but its partners had good reason to believe otherwise. The August protest was brutally put down with more than two dozen dead, and Pinochet seemed vulnerable. The dictator had a proclivity to react violently, but he was also clever enough to open a dialogue to play for time. In the third week of August, the general named Sergio Onofre Jarpa minister of interior and dispatched him to speak with the members of the alliance. Archbishop Fresno offered his good offices to the interlocutors. The dialogue, such as it was, broke down six weeks later without producing anything that resembled a political settlement aimed at ending a decade of dictatorship.

The left could not leave the field to the Christian Democrats, so in September the Communist party, the MIR and the radical Almeyda faction of the Socialist party formed the Democratic Popular Movement, or MDP, an attempt at unification that had even less chance than the AD to amount to anything. In fact, the Constitutional Tribunal quickly applied the new constitution's article 8 provision banning Marxist-Leninist parties, groups, or movements, and declared the MDP unconstitutional and illegal. That did not matter, of course, since the groups in the MDP were committed to the violent overthrow of the regime anyway.

These two blocs differed sharply over both the efficacy and the legitimacy of armed struggle, but both the AD and MDP were set on the immediate departure of Pinochet, free elections, and a constituent assembly to draft a new constitution. "Democracy Now" became the slogan of both opposition camps, and the mounting protest movement led them to believe that that democracy would return much sooner than later. They were mistaken. Genaro Arriagada, a leading Christian Democrat, later explained the reason for the failure of the AD. "In actuality, this program was not realistic because it did not take into account Pinochet's power," Arriagada wrote. "The notion that Pinochet could be forced to resign, like most all-or-nothing strategies, immobilized its supporters and cost them time and credibility."[38]

The next attempt at uniting the opposition under a common banner came in late July 1985. In mid-March, Chile had been shaken by the brutal murder of three communists; the triple throat-slashing reinvigorated efforts to bring democracy back to Chile. So, with the encouragement of Cardinal Fresno, the opposition reached the National Accord for the Transition to Full Democracy.[39] The position of the opposition had softened somewhat. The accord called for congressional elections by popular vote, direct election of the president, and a set of constitutional reforms. But it did not insist on Pinochet's resignation, a transitional government, or the abrogation of the 1980 constitution. Nonetheless, it was destined to go nowhere. Pinochet was committed to his timetable and his terms. When the archbishop broached the subject of the National Accord with the dictator, Pinochet abruptly cut him off, "it would be better if we just turned the page."[40]

That was effectively the end of the National Accord as a basis for a negotiated transition. But the accord was important for other reasons. The acceptance of the 1980 constitution was one. The accord's attention to the demands of justice, national reconciliation, and due process was another. "It is imperative," the document read, "that the demands of justice be attended to in a manner congruent with the spirit of national reconciliation. For this reason, those trials that might be granted for the violation of human rights will require the responsible accusation of a specific crime, formulated with grounds. The recognition of those crimes will belong exclusively to the existing courts, thus assuring due process, free from humiliation, vengeance and *ad hoc* collective trials." Whatever agreement might be reached with the government regarding constitutional reforms and direct election of public officials, the document stated plainly the principle that "effective protection of human rights will be a preferential concern in the duties of public authorities."[41]

It was a timely pronouncement, even if democracy was a long way off in Chile. Trials of high-ranking military officers resulting in the conviction and imprisonment of junta members responsible for Argentina's "dirty war" began that same year. A democratic transition, followed by justice, was on everyone's mind. The human rights position of the drafters of the accord reflected values that would eventually guide the democratic government of Chile. Both the commitment to meet the demands of justice in a spirit of national reconciliation and the absolute respect for the jurisdiction of existing courts of law and due process would be incorporated into the mandate for the presidential truth commission created after the transition. But it was a transition on Pinochet's terms, and due process and the rule of law could not be made retroactive to a regime that operated outside its bounds. There would be few trials in existing courts, and the armed forces' preoccupation with humiliation and vengeance would thwart even effective investigation in many cases.

The National Accord came to naught as the basis for a negotiated transition. None of these pressures dissuaded the Chilean dictator from pursuing his chosen course of action: Pinochet saw no reason to surrender battlefield gains to a defeated adversary. "The vanquished were asking unconditional surrender from the victors, from those who held power," said Pinochet, recalling the early demands for his immediate resignation with incredulity; "the Armed Forces of Chile were not a defeated militia in rout, completely the contrary."[42] It was not until late 1986, after military intelligence had discovered a large hidden cache of arms and the FPMR had nearly assassinated Pinochet, that the democratic opposition crystallized around the risky option to defeat Pinochet in a plebiscite.

In the meantime, the United Nations and the United States remained engaged. At the end of 1984, Rajscomer Lallah, a jurist from Mauritius, stepped down as UN Special Rapporteur for Chile. Pinochet sensed an opportunity to ease the pressure on his government. Lallah's resignation created an opportunity to appoint a Rapporteur who could at least gain a measure of cooperation from the Pinochet government. The man selected was Fernando Volio Jiménez. Volio had served on the Human Rights Commission in the early 1960s, was a Latin American, and was known for his anti-communism. If any one could be trusted to be at least fair, if not sympathetic, to the regime, it was this Costa Rican jurist. Negotiations surrounding his appointment had been intensive, with the United States heavily favoring his candidacy. He accepted the appointment in January. Soon after he was selected by the Human Rights Commission, Chilean representatives began to negotiate with him as well. His first report to the General Assembly prompted one human rights organization to suggest that Volio was eager to placate Pinochet.

Pinochet responded to Volio's appointment by instructing Chilean officials to make unofficial contacts with him. Volio had been selected to take up the cause of human rights in Chile at a dramatic moment: the campaign of national protests was entering its second year, the conscience of the country had been shaken by the triple throat slashing in March, and in July the Roman Catholic archbishop facilitated the National Accord among moderate opposition forces. Pinochet may have sensed that, if skillfully managed, a rapprochement with the new Special Rapporteur could result in a tolerable report on the human rights situation in Chile. For his part, Volio reported that he had "always been aware of the importance of securing the cooperation of Chilean authorities."[43] Contacts between Volio and Chilean representatives began in May and continued through August, just before Volio's first report to the UN General Assembly. The new Special Rapporteur was either so impressed by the contacts or so pleased at his apparent ability to restore relations between the UN and the Pinochet government that his first report is dominated by accounts of the developing dialogue with Chilean emissaries.

Volio was visited in Geneva by senior representatives of Chile's missions to the UN offices in Geneva and New York. Later, in San José, Volio was twice visited by Chilean representatives. The first was Chile's Ambassador to Costa Rica, who clearly went to break the ice with the Costa Rican working for the United Nations. Subsequently, Volio was visited by a higher-ranking delegation consisting of representatives of the foreign ministry and the Office of the President. The dialogue in the Costa Rican capital went on for three days, although the Chileans insisted that they were meeting in a personal capacity since their government still refused to recognize the Special Rapporteur.[44] But that soon changed. In mid-July, the Chilean envoys visited Volio in Montevideo, Uruguay, where he was again conducting interviews. This time they informed Volio that the Chilean government had agreed to cooperate with the Special Rapporteur and that henceforth all contacts could be considered official. Volio, reporting the contacts in his first "preliminary" report, welcomed the full normalization of relations as "constructive."[45]

If Pinochet had instructed his emissaries to restore relations with the Special Rapporteur in order to soften the next UN report on Chile, the maneuver seems to have succeed. Volio's report, issued in September, was remarkable for the consternation it caused, not with Pinochet, but with human rights organizations. Volio's report began well enough, noting that "the Special Rapporteur is deeply concerned at the human rights situation in Chile," and that the various "individuals and organizations which have made . . . accusations have to their credit a record of serious and responsible commitment in the field of the protection of human rights." But the format and especially the tenor of the Volio report made critics of some of those serious and responsible organizations, none of which are named in the report itself. The timing of the report, coming at a moment when the democratic opposition was searching for as much international support as possible, might have given added impetus to the momentum for democratization. The Volio report addressed that issue, but it is replete with concessions to the point of view of the Chilean envoys with whom Volio met. One concession was to accept at face value the regime's claim that terrorism was impeding democratization.

Terrorism is, without doubt, one of the factors which most influence the situation afflicting Chile, from a human rights standpoint, and is also clearly a formidable adversary of the creation of a climate propitious to the restoration of representative democracy in Chile . . . It is an inescapable obligation of every civilized country to combat terrorism, a malignant growth which threatens the existence of society. In Chile, there is an urgent need for all sectors of the community, in particular political and government circles, to tackle terrorism if genuine progress is to be made in the field of human rights, of which terrorism is a determined and ruthless adversary.[46]

The activities of the FPMR were serious and lethal, and the parties to the National Accord, the "political circles" to which Volio was evidently referring, were seeking to isolate the radical left as much as to achieve a democratic transition. Indeed, the two objectives were mutually reinforcing. But the commentary on terrorism, which probably reflected Volio's political inclinations as much as a desire to demonstrate that General Pinochet's gesture would not go unrewarded, reads like something Pinochet might have said to justify the harsh measures that began long before the FPMR even existed. Notably, there is no mention in the Volio report of the fact that Pinochet was opposed to even the moderate proposal contained in the National Accord. Terrorism was an aggravating factor, but Pinochet was the one obstacle to a transition that really mattered.

Americas Watch, which was by now publishing regular reports on the human rights situation in Chile in close collaboration with Jaime Castillo's Chilean Human Rights Commission, found itself in the awkward position of criticizing the report of the Special Rapporteur. Suddenly, the synergy between Chilean and international human rights NGOs and the UN Special Rapporteur, so crucial to the effective protection and promotion of human rights, was dissipated. "The weakness of the current report as an instrument for verifying the condition of human rights in Chile," Americas Watch noted in a critique published in November, "is of grave concern to Americas Watch, as it is to human rights organizations in Chile with which previous Rapporteurs have made extensive and productive relations."[47] It was as if Americas Watch was denouncing the sort of evasive reports offending governments often make as States Party to the various human rights conventions. The Americas Watch comment on the Volio report is scathing:

This report differs substantially in method and content from those of previous Rapporteurs on Chile. While Prof. Volio notes that conditions in Chile constitute a serious violation of human rights, he presents this information in a manner so informal and so circumscribed as to make the report's omissions more glaring . . . The current report offers not a single substantive quotation from a written source documenting human rights violations by the government of Chile. Although his account of his investigation . . . contains numerous references to receiving written documentation prepared by Chilean human rights organizations, Prof. Volio neither cites these documents nor describes their specific contents, thus implicitly judging them to be of doubtful relevance and reliability.[48]

Compounding the problem, said Americas Watch, Volio described witnesses as "petitioners" rather than "witnesses," further diminishing the credibility of their accounts, and, what is worse, did not provide the kind of formal and secure setting to interviews characteristic of previous Rapporteurs. All this stood in dramatic contrast to the credence apparently given to the Chilean delegation's version of events. The fact that the Volio report concluded with "observations" or "comments" rather than firm conclusions is also singled out for criticism. But Americas Watch had reached some conclusions of its own: "Prof. Volio's interpretation of his mandate is inadequate to address the Chilean situation effectively or to inform the General Assembly and Commission on Human Rights as requested. He has consciously broken continuity with previous Rapporteurs on Chile."[49] The criticism may not have been entirely fair, but for the first time, Pinochet was not entirely displeased by the report of a UN body on the situation of human rights in the country which he had now ruled for twelve years.

The actions of a resolute United States were likely to be more consequential. The Reagan administration and the Congress took a keen interest in political developments in Chile at this critical moment, albeit for different reasons. By mid-1986, the tensions caused by the escalating repression forced the Reagan administration to decide on a course of action to bring Chile into line with the trend of democratization in Latin America's Southern Cone. Brazil, Argentina, and Uruguay had already made the difficult transition to democracy. Only Chile and Paraguay resisted the trend. Paraguay's perennial dictator, Alfredo Stroessner, who had outlasted even Fidel Castro, Cuba's guerrilla caudillo, would eventually be removed in a palace coup. Pinochet, however, had every intention to remain in power.

The Chilean opposition was demanding the immediate resignation of the dictator and the installation of a government of national reconciliation, but Pinochet was in no mood to make unnecessary concessions. The Reagan administration did not endorse the idea of "Democracy Now," but neither would it tolerate any reversals in the scripted transition. Personnel changes signalled the end of any internal debate about the appropriate policy of the United States. James Theberge, the unabashedly pro-Pinochet Ambassador to Santiago, was replaced by Harry Barnes in 1985. Then assistant secretary of state for Inter-American affairs Langhorn Motely, another Pinochet sympathizer, was replaced by Elliot Abrams, who had previously served as assistant secretary of state for human rights and humanitarian affairs.[50]

Multilateral Development Bank loan requests from Chile were pending, and the Reagan administration, now headed by a new team, had to make a crucial decision. The House of Representatives scheduled hearings and summoned Elliot Abrams, assistant secretary of state for Inter-American affairs as of May, to testify before representatives who had introduced a bill to block multilateral financial aid. The hearings before the House Subcommittee on International Institutions and Finance came in the wake of the immolation of Rodrigo Rojas and Carmen Quintana. To dramatize the horrible crime, the subcommittee heard testimony of the Massachussets burn specialist who had examined the two horribly disfigured Chileans. Rojas had just died of renal failure and other complications caused by the burns.

Representative Bereuter, a Republican from Nebraska and a cosponsor of the bill to block aid, made his feelings known before the witnesses spoke. He framed the issues cogently:

While most of Latin America has turned toward democracy, movement in Chile seems to be in the opposite direction, toward greater repression. The Chilean constitution provides for the election by plebiscite in 1989 of a new President. The sole candidate for that election is to be named by the Junta. It increasingly appears to be the case that General Pinochet intends to be that candidate. Many Chileans and certainly most outside observers had hoped and expected that Pinochet would step down and that a candidate acceptable to most of the Chilean people would be elected as the transitional President. Now it appears possible that General Pinochet may cling to power through the end of the century. . . . I ask my colleagues to join me in defining where the United States stands with regard to human rights and democracy, if you prefer, in the hemisphere. Our position in Nicaragua and Cuba is a matter of clear record. It is time to make our opposition to the Southern Cone's rightist dictatorships be just as clear.[51]

The representatives then heard testimony from Peter Hakim, staff director of the prestigious Inter-American Dialogue and former Ford Foundation official with ample experience in Latin America. Hakim went directly to the point: multilateral bank loans had become crucial to the health of the Chilean economy ever since the 1982 debt crisis (the precipitating factor in the current political crisis) prompted private banks to curtail lending. Hakim estimated that commercial lending had declined from about $3.3 billion in 1981 to about $750 million in 1985; multilateral lending had increased from only $13 million to $1.1 billion over the same period. Blocking multilateral development aid would bring tremendous pressure on Chile, given its heavy reliance on it, and send a clear message to Pinochet to quicken the pace of reforms and dissuade him from maneuvering to become the sole candidate in the upcoming plebiscite.

Elliot Abrams, who had just come from his post as assistant secretary of state for human rights and humanitarian affairs, was the next to testify. In his prepared statement, Abrams made it clear that it was the administration's view that "we have in fact very limited real influence. We have few carrots and few sticks available." But the prevailing situation in Chile placed the United States in an awkward position. "Further delay in taking concrete steps to give the Chilean people confidence that their nation is headed for democracy and to restore full civil liberties," Abrams said, stating the administration position, "can only benefit enemies of democracy on the extreme left and right." To be sure, Abrams was more concerned with the extreme left than the extreme right. Then, typically, Abrams asked Congress to refrain from taking any action that might reduce the president's room for maneuver, and suggested that, with final decisions on the loans not due until October, a decisive answer about a negative vote by the United States at such an early date would eliminate any incentive Pinochet might have to make desired concessions in the coming weeks and months.

Questioning the assistant secretary of state, Representative Esteben Torres of California was blunt about the administration's request for congressional restraint in light of its record on loans to Chile. "It seems that if the administration refuses to announce its voting position ahead of time, then what you said earlier in your answer to the chairman is that you are asking us to trust you. Frankly, Mr. Abrams, the Reagan administration has been voting in favor of loans to Chile since 1981 despite repeated Congressional protests and a persistent record in Chile of human rights abuses. I think that the time for trusting is kind of over."[52] In fact, the Reagan administration had been actively encouraging an orderly transition in Chile, both to avoid a second Nicaragua and to capitalize on the free market miracle the Chicago Boys had wrought. Elliot Abrams expressed it best, acknowledging in his prepared remarks that Chile's economic policies provided a strong basis for voting in favor of most loans to Chile, "if considered in isolation from human rights concerns . . . The economic management team of the Government of Chile has a solid free market orientation and is considered by the IFI's to be skilled." Notably, Abrams conceded that "torture takes place by the security forces in Chile," adding that "if the government were intent on stopping it, they could stop it."[53] The notion of voting against loans to such a regime on principle alone never seems to have occurred to Abrams. If the United States did vote against (or abstain on votes concerning) such loans, it was because it was impolitic to do otherwise at a moment when the Reagan administration was involved in the Central American imbroglio and later the Iran-Contra scandal.

On August 6, only days after Abrams testified, Chilean military intelligence discovered a vast arsenal of arms in separate locations in the arid north. The caches included more than a thousand U.S.-made M-16 assault rifles from the Vietnam War era and U.S.- and Soviet-manufactured rocket-propelled grenade launchers. American intelligence produced satellite photos of Cuban fishing trawlers off the coast, and it was quickly determined that the weapons had been offloaded from the Cuban vessels and brought ashore by small craft.[54] Exactly one month later, the FPMR mounted its failed attempt on Pinochet's life. Had the dictator been killed by one of the rockets that struck his limousine, the trajectory of Chile's transition might have been very different and the role of the armed left in it more prominent. But the incidents succeeded only in isolating the Communist party and the Manuel Rodríguez Patriotic Front. Ironically, the specter of the armed left prompted the moderate opposition to join forces and agree to abide by Pinochet's terms for an orderly transition.

Throughout 1987 the moderate opposition continued to meet to reach agreement on a common strategy. The announcement of a united front, the Concertación de Partidos para el NO, came on February 2, 1988. The Concertación was an alliance of some sixteen parties, excluding the Communists and the breakaway Socialists. It was both the product of discussions dating back to the formation of the Democratic Alliance in 1983 and the predecessor of the Concertación de Partidos para la Democracia, the coalition that would govern Chile after Pinochet's defeat. But there were no guarantees that the new alliance would be any more successful than the Democratic Alliance or the National Accord. What was different was that the Concertación was formed to defeat Pinochet in the plebiscite to be announced later that year: it was an agreement to work toward the NO option on the ballot.

The moderate opposition had finally reached agreement on a common strategy. But two critical matters remained to be settled. The regime had yet to announce its sole candidate. The air force and navy representatives on the junta were remarkably open about their conviction that a civilian candidate should stand in place of Pinochet. Pinochet's most ardent supporters were found in the army and in Jaime Guzmán's recently formed Independent Democratic Union, UDI. This raised the possibility of a schism in the armed forces. Moreover, an early announcement of Pinochet's candidacy could actually help the Command for the NO to generate needed votes. A civilian candidate would be less likely to lead undecided voters to vote NO. The ideal tactic for Pinochet, then, was to withhold the announcement of the regime candidate for as long as possible. The courts, however, ruled that the candidate had to be named no later than August 1, 1988. Pinochet, characteristically, overcame internal opposition to his ambitions, and after being designated the regime candidate on the date set by the courts, fixed the date of the plebiscite for October 5. The second undecided matter could not be resolved until the plebiscite was held and the votes were counted. There were really two uncertainties: could the opposition win, and would the regime respect its victory?

The opposition mounted a concerted effort that entailed civic education and voter registration, as well as traditional campaigning. A Committee for Free Elections sprang into existence, along with a Command for the NO set up by the Concertación. Much of the voter registration and civic education activities were conducted by an entirely new entity, the Crusade for Civic Participation, or Civic Crusade. As with the human rights NGOs with which they were allied, the Command for the NO, the Committee for Free Elections, and the Civic Crusade would need moral and material support from abroad. It came. Ronald Reagan, concerned about his international image as an unrepentant supporter of right-wing autocrats—in part the legacy of former UN Ambassador Jeane Kirkpatrick's flawed argument about dictatorships and double standards—had launched Project Democracy in June 1982.[55] Congress responded by creating the National Endowment for Democracy. The National Endowment for Democracy, a privately incorporated entity established by an act of Congress in 1983, directed $1.6 million into the process, all of it going to the opposition.[56] Pinochet denounced the assistance provided by the NED and the active role played by Ambassador Harry Barnes, whom he called "Dirty Harry" after the rogue detective portrayed by Clint Eastwood in Hollywood films. "The shameless yanqui interventionism, which presages the final stage of its imperialism," he would write, sounding like Sandinista Daniel Ortega or even Salvador Allende, "produced on a weekly basis news articles in Chile at the time of the plebiscite. And in most of them appeared the ineffable facade of Mr. Barnes. . . . The visible face of imperialism in Chile, in 1988, was that of this ambassador the daily *La Nación* called 'Dirty Harry'."[57] The Reagan administration's desire to see a transition that would put moderate, pro-market Christian Democrats in office was by now unambiguous. But Pinochet saw a conspiracy of much greater dimension, a conspiracy that included the United States through the NED, the leftist currents in the Roman Catholic Church through the Civic Crusade, and the Committee for Free Elections. He dubbed it "Operation Sleight of Hand."[58]

For its part, the regime's campaign was, in the words of two experienced observers, "conducted like a military operation."[59] The campaign for the Yes resorted to time-tested themes and images: the shortages, violence, and near chaos of the Popular Unity days, the patriotic service of Pinochet, the success of economic reforms. Pinochet's supporters believed they had good reason to be as optimistic as they had been eight years earlier, when Chileans approved the constitution by plebiscite. But the country had changed dramatically in eight years, and the fear of the past could not overwhelm the desire for positive and meaningful change.

The mood in the country on the day of the plebiscite was understandably tense. Early voting tallies, released by the regime and broadcast by pro-regime media outlets, put Pinochet ahead. But the Command for the NO, which benefited from the technical expertise of North American poll watchers, had a sophisticated operation in place. The Command's parallel count revealed the opposite trend. Very early on, by late morning, the information coming to the Command for the NO indicated a convincing margin of victory. But the regime continued to release disinformation, until it ceased releasing information altogether. Tension mounted. By midnight, even Sergio Onofre Jarpa, once Pinochet's interior minister, was threatening to disclose the truth of the victory of the NO in the face of the silence of official sources of information. Appearing on television with Patricio Aylwin, Jarpa conceded that the opposition forces had won. The NO had prevailed against what might have seemed insurmountable odds. The first uncertainty (could the opposition win?) was settled. The second (would the regime respect the outcome?) was now on everyone's mind.

Inside the Moneda, Pinochet fumed and briefly flirted with the idea of ignoring the electoral results. Apparently, the official disinformation about the true vote count was meant to coincide with right-wing plots to foment violent protests, which, in turn, would prompt the military to intervene and perhaps annul the election. And there was acrimony in the presidential palace. Pinochet denounced his advisors, demanded emergency powers, and then impetuously threatened to resign when the other members of the junta counseled against the maneuver. Air force commander and junta member Fernando Matthei was the most vocal, according to his account.

Matthei, who had replaced Leigh after Pinochet had succeeded in ousting him in July 1978, simply announced to reporters that the NO had won, adding, "we are calm."[60]

Fifteen years earlier, on the evening of September 11, Pinochet and the other members of the just-formed junta came forward to justify their actions and declare their intentions. Of the original four, only Pinochet and navy admiral Merino remained. But now Merino opposed Pinochet's desperate bid to contrive some pretext to retain power, and the dictator relented. The triumphal atmosphere of September 1973 was replaced by tension and sarcasm. Pinochet, who during the National Days of Protests had proclaimed defiantly that the Chilean armed forces were not a routed militia, now had to concede defeat. Pinochet had been defeated, not by force, but by reason.

But Pinochet had lost a plebiscite, not his wits. The outcome of the plebiscite only guaranteed that the regime would have to call general elections sometime the following year. There was no guarantee that Pinochet would not run for the presidency again, or that he would be defeated if he chose to run. And the constitution granted the armed forces, the guardians of the old order, and Pinochet himself, considerable powers. Pinochet, for example, would remain in command of the armed forces until 1998, and would become a "designated senator" for life thereafter.

Pinochet was persuaded not to run in the elections, slated for December 1989, and the right selected Hernán Buchi, Pinochet's young and dashing finance minister, to carry on the neo-liberal free market economic revolution. The Concertación chose Patricio Aylwin, the very man who had led the Christian Democrats in the fateful negotiations with Salvador Allende on the eve of the coup. He was a perfectly acceptable successor.

In the meantime, the opposition set out to amend Pinochet's prized Constitution of Liberty. Having been unable simply to abrogate it, and having chosen to accept it as the framework for the strategy to defeat the dictatorship, the democratic opposition now had to eliminate the many authoritarian features of the 1980 charter. Negotiations began almost immediately, and eventually produced substantial modifications to Chile's basic law, as a result of another referendum held in July 1989, before the general elections. The democratic opposition had made a promising start, but the reforms did not cover many objectionable features that would constrain the future democratic government, as was intended by the document's drafters.

When in December 1989 Patricio Aylwin won the presidency at the head of the Concertación de los Partidos para la Democracia, the end of an unprecedented period of authoritarian rule came into view. But it faced formidable challenges. The regime had wasted no time in promulgating "binding laws" to confine and constrict the Aylwin government. Pinochet cleverly offered inducements to aging magistrates to retire, so as to enable him to appoint younger judges to replace them and guard the legal and constitutional order ordained by the regime from the bench. After all, justice was certain to be one of the most contentious issues after the transition.

Pinochet, who some seventeen years earlier had declared war on Chile's leftist enemies, ceded the presidency with a declaration of victory. His legacy was a "mission completed." But when journalists asked him about the more insidious aspects of military rule, Pinochet was characteristically disinterested and dispassionate. As to his views with respect to accusations of human rights violations, he offered Raquel Correa and Elizabeth Subercaseaux, two of the most prolific journalists of the period, his "formula for reconciliation." "Don't ask if the burning firewood is oak, walnut, pine or eucalyptus, just throw a bucket of water on the bonfire and 'the problem is finished.' It has to be forgotten!"[61] This was a new metaphor for the general, who was more accustomed to casting the discussion in terms of extirpating the evil or cutting out the cancer. The military regime had extinguished several thousand lives to put out the bonfire. But the man who succeeded him as president, and most sectors of the society over which he would govern, were not content simply to forget. The formula for reconciliation, if there was to be meaningful reconciliation, was to be truth.

Chapter 8
Recovering the Truth

> The moral conscience of the nation demands that the truth with respect
> to the disappearance of persons, horrendous crimes, and other grave
> violations of human rights be clarified.
>
> — President Patricio Aylwin

A Political Mandate

The inexorable reality of Chilean politics in 1990, given the trajectory of
that nation's democratic transition, was the latent antagonism between the
first democratic government in more than seventeen years and the armed
forces still firmly controlled by Augusto Pinochet. Pinochet had been repudiated, but he remained a formidable actor in Chilean politics and had
managed to place enormous constraints on the new government. "Everyone is aware of the fact that the previous government intended to remain in
power for eternity," President Patricio Aylwin Azócar told the audience
assembled in the National Stadium for what was tantamount to his inaugural address the day after taking the oath of office. "Our satisfaction this day
cannot prevent us from issuing a clear warning about the many limitations,
obstacles and forced steps which, in its zeal to remain in power, the regime
dominant until just yesterday left us." The posturing of the defeated officials
of the Pinochet regime, he said, merited nothing less than "moral condemnation." But Aylwin urged caution. "Should we, in order to avoid those
limitations, have exposed our people to the risk of renewed violence, suffering, loss of life?"[1]

Now, in order to make the democratic transition, Aylwin would have to
confront the legacy of the human rights violations committed by the Pinochet regime. First there was the question of the truth about the past. The
period of military rule was either a glorious period of national renewal
following the military's decisive effort to save Chile from Marxism-Leninism
or an unprecedented and unjustifiable breach of Chile's constitutional heri-
tage that produced a human rights calamity. Then there was the question of
justice. As transitional president, Aylwin had to safeguard himself from the

opposite — albeit unequal — dangers of ignoring the victims' clamor for the truth and a measure of justice and sparking the military's ire. The first would have been to render the transition meaningless, the second might have imperiled it.

The dilemma was a personal one for Patricio Aylwin. Almost two decades before, Aylwin had led the Christian Democrats in the confrontation with Allende's Popular Unity government. "I was a harsh opponent of his government," Aylwin acknowledged during the solemn public funeral ceremony for Salvador Allende in Santiago's General Cemetery in September 1990, seventeen years after the junta had ordered his body interred in a cemetery in Valparaíso, adding that, "if the same circumstances were to repeat themselves, I would again be a decided opponent." But political differences "never prevented him or me from entering into a dialogue in search of formulas for agreement in order to save the democracy."[2] Now, as the first democratically elected president since Allende, Aylwin would have to find a formula to achieve a measure of justice that would preserve the nascent democracy.

The democratic opposition had thought long and hard about such a formula, and its thinking evolved to conform to the inexorable reality of the transition. The National Agreement for the Full Transition to Democracy, elaborated in 1985, had articulated the principle that "the demands of justice be attended to in a manner congruent with the spirit of national reconciliation." The agreement called for prosecutions under the most rigorous guarantees of due process and impartiality.[3] The platform of the Concertación was just as committed to justice, but it had an added tone of realism. "The democratic government will put forth its best efforts in order to establish the truth in the cases of human rights violations that have occurred since September 1973. It will also procure the trial according to the existing criminal law of human rights violations that represent atrocious crimes against life, liberty, and personal integrity."[4] Of course, the reality was that prosecutions were not legally permissible in all but a few cases, because of the 1978 amnesty law, and were not politically possible in almost all cases, because of the power retained by the armed forces. Nevertheless, the Concertación was determined to conduct a full investigation and to establish criminal responsibility before the courts granted amnesty on the grounds that "the amnesty Decree-Law of 1978 . . . cannot become an impediment for the disclosure of the truth, the investigation of the facts, and the establishment of criminal responsibilities in cases of crimes against human rights."[5] The election of Patricio Aylwin presented a real opportunity to recover the truth about the past. But there were obvious constraints. In his inaugural address in the National Stadium, Aylwin articulated his policy as the names of the hundreds of disappeared flashed on the stadium scoreboard.

We have said—and today we solemnly reiterate—that the moral conscience of the nation demands that the truth with respect to the disappearance of persons, horrendous crimes and other grave violation of human rights that occurred during the dictatorship be clarified. We have also said—and today I repeat—that we ought to address this delicate matter by reconciling the virtue of justice with the virtue of prudence, and that when personal responsibility is established, the time for pardon will arrive.[6]

Now it fell to Aylwin to make good on his pledge. On April 24, 1990, only a month after assuming the presidency, Patricio Aylwin went on the air to announce his decision to create a National Commission on Truth and Reconciliation. Aylwin opted to create an official truth commission not unlike the one Aylwin's counterpart, Raúl Alfonsín, had created in Argentina some seven years earlier.[7] Aylwin, like Alfonsín, had to decide several delicate matters. "God can attest," Aylwin said later in an address to the Chilean Congress, "that in the decision about the [commission's] nature, character, functions and membership, I made an exhaustive effort to achieve the greatest consensus, I considered the most diverse opinions, I was not subject to any kind of pressures, and I decided what in my conscience I believe best for Chile."[8] Aylwin at least had the benefit of learning from the Argentine experience; but the circumstances in Argentina were more conducive to both truth and justice. Prosecutions were possible in Argentina, because of the military's debacle in the Falklands/Malvinas conflict. Aylwin created the truth commission to make an official accounting of the past for the most part in lieu of the possibilities of prosecution.

The human rights strategy chosen by President Patricio Aylwin—and which would be continued by his successor, fellow Christian Democrat Eduardo Frei—was basically consistent with the overall strategy that the Concertación had pursued from the moment of its formation in February, 1986. That strategy had been cautious, non-confrontational, and highly sensitive to political, legal and constitutional constraints. The political constraints related directly to the threat of the military, and the cautious, nonconfrontational posture of the Concertación was adopted so as not to imperil the democratic transition. Other perceived constraints related to the scope of the president's and the commission's legal and constitutional authority. The president and the members of the commission were careful to adhere to legal precepts and constitutional principles that predated Pinochet's 1980 constitution, not just to avoid conflict with the military, but to remain faithful to highly valued principles that the military regime had breached.

So, to extricate himself from his moral and political predicament vis-à-vis both the military and the families of the military's victims, Aylwin formed a presidential rather than parliamentary commission of inquiry, and he framed its mandate so as to avoid legal challenges, and to placate the military. Aylwin's mandated definition of a human rights violation had the effect of authenticating the military's claims that its members were victims on par with those murdered by the regime. Moreover, he withheld from the commission the power to subpoena witnesses and to divulge the names of the culpable, and he denied it sufficient time to fulfill its most compelling task, to identify the victims by name and to locate their mortal remains.

Aylwin selected distinguished jurist Raúl Rettig to chair the commission; therefore, the commission is commonly known as the Rettig Commission.[9] Rettig was an attorney affiliated with Chile's old Radical party. He had served as the president of the Chilean Bar Association before that body became, in the eyes of human rights activists, an apologist for the Pinochet regime. And he had been Salvador Allende's ambassador to Brazil. "Raúl Rettig," said one of the members of the commission he chaired, "is an authentic, traditional Chilean democrat in the tradition of the democratic left" from an epoch before "the Left" took on ominous connotations in Chile. The commission's members included two noted human rights activists, both of whom had been forced into exile by the regime. One was Jaime Castillo, a prominent Christian Democrat who had been justice minister under Christian Democrat president Eduardo Frei. Castillo, along with Patricio Aylwin, had been a member of the PDC Commission that drafted the so-called Statute of Guarantees signed by Allende in order to gain Christian Democrat support for his ratification as president in 1970. Castillo was exiled in 1976 after he and several colleagues addressed a letter denouncing human rights abuses in Chile to the General Assembly of the OAS meeting in Santiago. When he was allowed to return two years later, Castillo founded the Chilean Human Rights Commission. The dictatorship sent him into exile again in 1982.

The other human rights activist was José Zalaquett. As a young lawyer Zalaquett had directed the legal department charged with conducting the Popular Unity government's land expropriations. He then served as deputy provost for the Catholic University. After the coup, Zalaquett co-founded the Committee for Peace, the predecessor to the Vicariate of Solidarity. He was imprisoned for some months in 1975 and banished the following year. Zalaquett went on to chair the International Executive Committee of Amnesty International. Prior to being named to the commission, Zalaquett had written a seminal essay, published by the Aspen Institute, on the obligation of democratic governments to confront past violations.[10] After the release of the Rettig Report, Zalaquett became one of the commission's most vocal and quoted members. Zalaquett would later involve himself in controversy as the United Nations Commission on the Truth for El Salvador prepared to release its report and publicly name notorious human rights violators.

The commission also included figures associated with the center-right and the right. Laura Novoa, a respected private sector attorney, described herself as a "dissident" of the center-right and as a "peculiar" choice because she had not been affiliated with any political movement or human rights organization, although she had been involved in human rights cases at the "individual level." She would take on the challenge of drafting the sections of the report concerned with the reaction of Chilean society to the atrocities committed by the regime. Ricardo Martín Díaz, who had been a Supreme Court judge, was described by a colleague as a "typical, classic Chilean judge, a person who is very much a judge!" The military junta had considered appointing Martín its first justice minister on the recommendation of Supreme Court president Enrique Urrutia, but Martín could not be located in the confusion after the coup. Eager to maintain the appearance of legality, the junta named someone else out of a sense of urgency. That is ironic. In a speech, Zalaquett observed that Martín "wrote a seething criticism of military court proceedings, earning the anger of his former colleagues."[11] Gonzalo Vial Corea is an historian who once served as Pinochet's minister of education, and was serving as one of the nonelected "designated" senators appointed by General Pinochet when he was appointed to the commission. He may also have had a hand in the drafting of the commission's mandate.

The remaining members were generally considered political moderates or associated with President Aylwin. José Luis Cea is a highly noted professor of constitutional law. During the prolonged negotiations concerning the reform of Pinochet's constitution, Cea was part of the technical team assembled by the right-wing National Renovation party. He would later serve as a member of the council of the Corporation for Reparation and Reconciliation, set up by President Aylwin on the recommendation of the Commission on Truth and Reconciliation to continue the search for the "disappeared." Monica Jiménez, the only member besides Vial who is not an attorney, was involved in grass-roots voter mobilization through PARTICIPA, an NGO funded, in part, by the National Endowment for Democracy. Having worked so vigorously with PARTICIPA to defeat Pinochet in the 1988 plebiscite, Jiménez would now be included in a commission that would reveal the crimes of her electoral foe. The commission's executive secretary was Jorge Correa. Members of the commission are generous in their praise of Correa, attributing the success of the commission to his skillful management. Correa has written extensively about the Chilean judicial system. In a book chapter appearing in 1993, Correa attributed the human rights violations not to Pinochet's interference with the courts, but to a formalistic legal culture. This is substantially the same analysis, drafted by Martín, that appears in a report of the Rettig Commission.[12] Like José Luis Cea, Correa became a member of the council of the Corporation for Reparation and Reconciliation.

Aylwin, according to several accounts, some of them off the record, gave considerable thought to the mandate of the commission, and even consulted some of those he would later name to it. Gonzalo Vial was among those whose opinion was heeded. "Gonzalo Vial is a man who prides himself on being on the political right, but he is absolutely committed to human rights," said one of his colleagues on the commission on the condition of anonymity. "He laid down his conditions . . . so that the decree [that created the commission] would be sufficiently prudent and would not cause any problems." José Zalaquett apparently exercised the most influence. There is an unmistakable resemblance between the mandate the commission was eventually given and the guidelines developed by Zalaquett in his seminal article on the subject of confronting violations by former regimes. Zalaquett has acknowledged that Aylwin personally asked him for his views about the mandate. "I discussed plans for the commission with [President Aylwin] and the Minister of Justice," Zalaquett told Daan Bronkhorst of Amnesty International's Dutch Section. "My chief objection to the initial plan was that the names of the perpetrators would be stated in the final report."[13] The question of naming — or not naming — names would be among the most controversial matters for the commission.

The Rettig Commission was established by Supreme Decree 355. Its short preamble is an eloquent statement of the moral and social concerns of a nation that had endured seventeen years of dictatorship. "The moral conscience of the nation demands the truth," it read, because "only upon a foundation of truth [would] it be possible to meet the basic demands of justice and to create the necessary conditions for achieving true national reconciliation." Full disclosure was imperative and urgent, because "only knowledge of the truth will restore the dignity of the victims in the public mind," and because any delay in the "formation of a serious common awareness in this regard may potentially disrupt our life as a national community."

In view of these moral and social imperatives, Aylwin gave his commission four tasks: "to establish as complete a picture as possible [of] the most serious human rights violations committed in recent years," "to gather information that may make it possible to identify the victims by name and to determine their fate and whereabouts," "to recommend such measures of reparation and reinstatement as it regards as just," and "to recommend the legal and administrative measures which in its judgment should be adopted in order to prevent further grave human rights violations from being committed." The president instructed the commission to prepare a report based on the evidence it would gather "in accordance with the honest judgment and conscience of its members," and to forward any information relevant to criminal prosecutions to the appropriate courts of law.[14]

The overall purpose of the commission was "to clarify in a comprehensive manner the truth about the most serious human rights violations" committed during the dictatorship. But the very definition of what constituted a serious human rights violation was controversial, because it confused two distinct phenomena, human rights violations and political violence. The effect of this, if not the intent, was to make soldiers killed by the armed resistance out to be victims on par with those systematically murdered by the state. According to Article 1,

[Serious violations of human rights] are here understood as situations of those persons who disappeared after arrest, who were executed, or who were tortured to death, in which the moral responsibility of the state is compromised as a result of actions by its agents or persons in its service, as well as kidnappings and attempts on the life of persons committed by private citizens for political purposes.

This expansive concept of a "serious human rights violation" is inconsistent with both international human rights law and international humanitarian law, the normative bases for human rights investigations. At issue is the legal status of violence committed by private individuals or paramilitary organizations. Actions committed by private persons at the behest of the state, or with its acquiescence, can be considered human rights violations according to international human rights law. By contrast, kidnappings, assassinations, and other violent acts committed by paramilitary organizations are generally not considered human rights violations in the strict sense. When committed by private individuals they are generally considered common crimes; when committed by armed groups they may also be violations of international humanitarian law, the so-called laws of armed conflict as codified in the Geneva Conventions of 1949 and the 1977 Protocols to the Conventions. But the Rettig Commission did not firmly establish its conclusions about such actions on the basis of the laws of armed conflict. The commission's report does not explicitly mention the four Geneva Conventions of 1949, which encompass civil conflicts involving irregular forces. Moreover, the commission's report states, in several contexts, that the sort of armed conflict envisioned by Article 3, as such, did not exist in Chile. Finally, a substantial number of the cases the commission classified as violations could not have been considered violations under the laws of armed conflict. Indeed, some cases are questionable by any standard.[15]

The members of the commission were aware of this conceptual problem, grappled with it in a section of the report entitled "Who is Guilty of Violating Human Rights?" and finally articulated a normative rationale for the inclusion of cases of violence committed by private individuals for political reasons. Central to the commission's reasoning was "the idea that there are certain values of humane behavior that not only the state but all political actors must respect has become enshrined in the public conscience."[16] It is this broader normative standard that permitted the commission to report on terrorist acts because "such a practice [terrorism] is incompatible with the value of human life as embodied in the modern conception of human rights."[17] According to the commission, whatever justification armed groups like the Revolutionary Movement of the Left (MIR) or the Manuel Rodríguez Patriotic Front (FPMR) might have offered for their armed resistance, the commission could not ignore the fact that the line had been crossed into terrorism. The commission thus formulated a normative rationale for what was unmistakably Aylwin's politically expedient gesture of good will to the military and the Carabineros. This inventive definition of a "serious violation of human rights" made it possible for the commission to observe in its report that "The institutions in which these men served honor their memory," and to express the hope that "our whole society will remember them among the victims of a painful situation that we must not repeat."[18] Aylwin's gesture to placate the military was futile, however. The Chilean armed forces were not favorably impressed by it; they opposed the formation of a truth commission, effectively impeded its investigation, and violently attacked the commission's report.

Ironically, this expansive definition also permitted the commission to consider as victims members of the very armed groups with which the military claimed to be at war, even in cases where they were killed in fire-fights or committed suicide to avoid arrest and torture. The connection with the laws of armed conflict is again tenuous: the Geneva Conventions and the protocols to them condition the use of lethal force by government forces against rebel groups, but they certainly do not prohibit it. The Rettig Commission, guided by this definition, included some extraordinary cases in the report. Among them were cases of individuals who "took their own life in a situation of armed conflict from which they had little hope of escape," or were killed "using weapons of self-defense" attempting to resist arrest because they could "reasonably fear that their fate would be torture or death."[19] The commission openly recognized that these are not "serious violations of human rights" in the usual sense of the term.

To avoid legal challenges and to placate the military, Aylwin placed three debilitating limitations on the commission: he denied it the power to subpoena witnesses, he enjoined it from naming the culpable, and he limited the duration of its existence to less than one year. Each restriction had a sound constitutional or political rationale, and each would have a demonstrable impact on the commission's ability to discover the truth. The president might have ventured to endow the commission with greater powers in order to force the Supreme Court to determine whether he had exceeded his authority. The court might have ruled in his favor, but that is unlikely. Even if the court had issued a favorable ruling, the ruling might have angered the military and precipitated a serious crisis.

According to Raúl Rettig, the reasons the commission he chaired was not given subpoena power and could not name the culpable were "legal and practical, at the same time." Sitting in his office directly across Santiago's Plaza de Armas from the Catholic cathedral that was once the site of the Vicariate of Solidarity, Rettig reflected on the work of the commission. "The president of the republic wanted to avoid that the decree would be struck down as illegal because it granted powers that are properly those of courts of law."[20] Three years after the release of the report, Rettig reacted to the frustration of those who wanted a broader investigation and a more damning report with frustration of his own. "The government is reproached because we did not say that this or that officer was responsible for a specific act. But we could not do that because the decree prohibited us from doing it, and because if the decree had granted those powers it is very likely that the Comptroller's Office would have sent it back or that the Constitutional Court would have rejected it." Aylwin's concern that these bodies would frustrate the search for the truth was well founded, because both bodies were manned by Pinochet loyalists. Aylwin and his advisors demonstrated considerable shrewdness when they framed the mandate. "None of those things happened," Rettig asserted with growing intensity, "the Comptroller declared the decree legal, and no one was able to bring the matter before the Constitutional Court." What, then, about a parliamentary commission possessing subpoena powers derived from the legislative branch's constitutional authority? Argentine president Raúl Alfonsín had had to grapple with this same issue almost a decade earlier when he created the National Commission on the Disappeared at the end of 1983. Like Aylwin, he opted for a presidential commission, and was severely criticized by some human rights organizations that had demanded a parliamentary investigation. Rettig, an elder jurist who had taught many Chilean judges over the years, believes it would have made no difference in Chile. Rettig is convinced that either the Comptroller's Office or the Constitutional Court would have invalidated any decree establishing a parliamentary commission with such powers, for the same reasons that they would have blocked a presidential commission possessing them.

The question of naming — or not naming — the guilty was even more controversial than the lack of subpoena power. Article 2 of Aylwin's decree stated that "in no case is the Commission to assume jurisdictional functions proper to the courts or to interfere in cases already before the courts," and that as a consequence "it will not have the power to take a position on whether particular individuals are legally responsible." In chapter 1 of its report, the commission paraphrases this article in a manner that sounds even more restrictive: "the Commission was expressly prohibited from making pronouncements on whether and to what extent particular persons might be responsible for the events it investigated." It went on to note that this restriction was "in accordance with a solid and well-established principle in the area of human rights." This restriction had tremendous implications for a complete rendering of the truth, and consequently touched off a debate among the commissioners, and especially among their young staff members, as how best to comply with this enjoinder. In fact, not all members of the commission interpreted that clause to expressly forbid the commission from naming names.

Asked if he would have personally preferred to have been able to name the culpable, Raúl Rettig responded without a moment's hesitation. "No, because to conclude the Report by indicating that such and such a person is culpable would be to declare him guilty and only courts of law have that power." Rettig did not believe that the restriction made much difference in terms of the historic importance of the report. To the contrary, because the commission adhered to the letter of the law, the legitimacy of the report was enhanced. "We had to work with what was given us, and I think that was correct. Look, if there was any doubt, if any one believed such things never occurred, our Report established the magnitude of what happened, and after three years no one has been able to accuse us of having lied in the report."

Jaime Castillo concurred with much of what Rettig said, but there were differences of emphasis. From Castillo one is quickly made to understand how, in the midst of a negotiated transition, the line between the legal and the political is blurred. The Chilean Human Rights Commission, which Castillo founded and still directs, works out of cramped quarters in a two-story building located across from the Santa Lucia monument a few blocks from the Moneda palace, the Plaza de Armas, and Rettig's law offices. There, in the commission's conference room on the second floor, Castillo explained why a presidential commission was preferable to a congressional one, then turned to the question of naming the culpable. A congressional commission would have had to represent the entire political spectrum, Castillo explained. President Aylwin, in fact, gave some attention to the commission's representativeness when he selected commission members, but did not unnecessarily entangle himself or the commission in the intricacies of Chilean party politics. Because of the disproportionate presence of right-wing deputies as a result of Chile's biased electoral rules and Pinochet's designated senators, President Aylwin's governing coalition did not possess the necessary clout in the Chilean congress to be able to control the investigation of a parliamentary commission. Together, the designated senators and the right-wing deputies would probably have inhibited any investigation or at least have forced a congressional commission to issue an innocuous, negotiated, report.

Castillo shared the chairman's views about naming the culpable, but would have preferred to disclose more, rather than less, information. And he connected the inability to name the culpable to the lack of subpoena power. He understood where the border line was: "to say that, at three o'clock in the afternoon, this or that officer shot someone in the back" is to level an accusation against that officer. But, he added, "I supported the idea that all the facts be mentioned in such a way that any investigation would have been easier. For example, we might have stated that, at a particular time, this or that officer was commander of this or that regiment, and although we would not have said that he committed a crime, well yes, at the time that it is supposed that they committed certain acts, who was the commander of the regiment?"

"The reason that this approach was not adopted was a political or legal one?"

"Legal, because most of us were lawyers." "I myself," he said, then paused to gather his thoughts, "I myself do not think it was possible to give names, because that was to make an accusation, and it was very difficult to obtain proof, let's say absolute proof, without having all the power necessary to subpoena people. That is a tribunal, and at the time all that was done, it was politically too complicated for the government. I think that not having named an investigative commission that would have substituted for the courts to have been a logical measure of political rationality."

It is difficult to argue the point. Castillo had shown tremendous audacity and unwavering conviction when he directed an open letter to the diplomats attending the OAS regular session in Santiago in 1976. Castillo's denunciation of Pinochet's secret police and his comparison of the Pinochet regime with a totalitarian state led to his expulsion from Chile. Now Castillo would be vindicated by the truth, but the truth required "a logical measure of political rationality." President Aylwin had made essentially the same point in the National Stadium the day after taking the oath of office, when he spoke of "reconciling the virtue of justice with the virtue of prudence."

Laura Novoa, who was named to the commission because of her affiliation with Chile's center-right, was surprisingly candid on the question of naming names. Sitting in her husband's law office, Novoa was eager to criticize the regime that, admittedly, was partial to the private enterprise on which her practice was built. Photographs of Novoa standing beside President Aylwin as he accepted the Report of the National Commission on Truth and Reconciliation were proudly positioned on a bookshelf near the conference table. Notably, her recollections of the debate over whether names should have been disclosed differed from those of Rettig — they differed precisely because she recalls that there was debate. Rettig and to a lesser degree Castillo were convinced that Aylwin's decree, as written, categorically prohibited the identification of those found to have been implicated in acts investigated by the commission. But Novoa interpreted the mandate differently.

"We would have liked to give names because it did not appear to us really to interfere with the courts to do so. . . . But, obviously, there prevailed the more political spirit of the rest of the members of the commission who preferred, correctly to be sure, that we gain a place in the society, and that we not have the open opposition of the armed forces which had to resign themselves because, in reality, the commission came in with a great deal of restraint." Novoa recalled, moreover, that the young lawyers in particular were fervently in favor of naming names, and she found herself in agreement because, "giving names, in itself, could also be a sanction or at least force the courts to investigate, or even obligate them to conduct a better investigation." But, when pressed on the matter, Novoa was ambivalent.

"In retrospect, do you believe this was a failure of the report?"

"No, no I wouldn't say that it was. Well, one can interpret it subjectively. As I say, we probably would have had more problems doing our work if we had given names, and that is why I would not go so far as to say it was a failure. On the contrary, I tend to think that my opinion was a little imprudent under the circumstances prevailing in the country, because this transition has its stamp, and to this day every activity is stamped by it. There are things that cannot be done because behind everything is the threat, or the possibility, that there might be a violent reaction."

The position of José Zalaquett was particularly important. Zalaquett had articulated his views on these questions during a conference on State Crimes sponsored by the Aspen Institute in 1989, after Pinochet had been defeated in the historic plebiscite but before Patricio Aylwin had won office.[21] He has repeated them many times since. The mandate of the Rettig Commission bore a close resemblance to Zalaquett's argument. In his often cited article, Zalaquett developed a normative framework for a policy of confronting past abuses that was attentive to political constraints. Such constraints included, in his words, "political or military forces," and even the "general attitude of relevant sectors of the population." Zalaquett forcefully argued that any policy for dealing with past human rights violations must represent the will of the people, and must not violate international human rights law. The policy must be designed to achieve the dual objectives of the prevention of future abuses and the reparation of damage caused by those of the past. The complete truth, he asserted, must be made known and officially proclaimed.

This last phrase is important. For Zalaquett, the official proclamation of the complete truth meant that "the nature and extension of the violations committed should be disclosed, as well as how they were planned and executed, what is the fate of the victims, individually, who gave the orders and who carried them out." This included violations committed by the armed opposition. But there was an important caveat. Zalaquett advised that a special commission of inquiry not be permitted to disclose names: "if such a body does not have prosecutorial powers, and if it names names, then some individuals may actually be signaled as culprits without having had the benefit of a proper defense." Zalaquett insisted on this point when President Aylwin and his justice minister, Francisco Cumplido, consulted him about the mandate of the commission. "I argued this on legal grounds," Zalaquett said later. "No one branded in that fashion can defend himself. The President, who is a fine lawyer, agreed with that objection."[22]

All of the basic contours of the Rettig Commission's mandate are visible in Zalaquett's article. The Chilean transition was a negotiated one, much like the transition, analyzed in Zalaquett's article, that had taken place in Uruguay; the Rettig Commission was not given prosecutorial powers; it did not venture to name the culpable; and it incorporated the truth about the violence committed by the armed opposition in violation of certain normative standards. In the final analysis, the commission's mandate conformed to Zalaquett's central contention that human rights investigations should not undermine democratic transitions, and that outside observers should not second-guess a government's good faith: "Must a government attempt to carry out [an investigation] even at the cost of being overthrown by those whose responsibility is being investigated? Who is to judge when a government really lacks the power or required will or wisdom instead?"[23] Again, the concern to reconcile the virtue of truth and the virtue of prudence.

These commissioners rejected the propriety of naming names, because of constitutional issues, political concerns, and even because to do so would have clashed with a legal culture shared by most commissioners. But there were equally cogent reasons for printing the names of the "culprits," to use Zalaquett's term. Above all, it would be absurd and imprudent not to name them, especially in those cases when their identities were common knowledge. The most absurd example of withholding the name of individuals known to all is found in the commission's otherwise excellent overview section on the DINA, the notorious agency created in 1974 to systematize the repression. There the report mentions "an army officer who was later head of the DINA throughout its whole existence," and explains that the DINA "reported only to the president of the Junta and later the president of the republic."[24] The identities of these powerful men were obviously common knowledge. General Manuel Contreras, who directed the DINA until it was replaced by another agency in 1977, had even been convicted of a crime for his part in the Letelier assassination. And Augusto Pinochet made no secret of the fact that he was president of the junta and the republic. Indeed, one of the few instances that Pinochet's name is placed after the recurrent phrase "president of the republic" is in connection with an attempt on his life in 1986. In an official report that otherwise only names victims, Pinochet's name is printed despite the fact that Pinochet himself was not seriously wounded in the attack.

The Chilean National Commission on Truth and Reconciliation was only the second officially sanctioned truth commission in the Americas. Aylwin's presidential commission of inquiry had only the precedent of Alfonsín's Argentine National Commission on the Disappeared to guide it. But the precedent was not entirely relevant because of the differing trajectories of the Argentine and Chilean transitions to democracy. So the men and women upon whom Aylwin relied for counsel had to be guided by their instincts, and those instincts counseled fairness for the accused. The National Agreement on the Full Transition to Democracy, and virtually every pronouncement on the matter of justice, had promised to respect the most basic principles of the rule of law. But the most distinguished human rights defenders could disagree on the matter of naming names.

Only two years after the Chilean National Commission on Truth and Reconciliation issued its report, El Salvador undertook its own controversial exploration of the truth about the past. Salvadoran guerrillas had demanded the formation of a truth commission as one of the conditions for ending a twelve-year civil war, in the belief that an assiduous truth-telling would prove that government forces and death squads funded by the coffee oligarchy had terrorized the population with impunity for decades. Of course, in the process the guerrillas' own crimes would be revealed as well. Representatives of the Salvadoran government and the Farabundo Martí National Liberation Front agreed to a truth commission in one of the first in a series of accords brokered by the United Nations between 1990 and 1992, when the definitive settlement of the armed conflict was reached.[25] But the political environments in Chile and El Salvador could not have been more dissimilar. The Chilean opposition had agreed to a transition on Pinochet's terms; the Salvadoran guerrillas had negotiated a revolution. The mandates of the two truth commissions reflected the crucial difference. For one thing, UN Secretary General Boutros Boutros-Ghali, who had promoted the peace process in El Salvador as part of his ambitious agenda for peace, personally appointed three foreign dignitaries rather than Salvadoran nationals to the Commission on the Truth for El Salvador to preserve the commission's credibility. More importantly, the UN-appointed Commission on the Truth for El Salvador was explicitly charged with putting "an end to any indication of impunity on the part of the officers of the armed forces," a charge that led the commission to name names in its controversial report.[26]

Thomas Buergenthal, one of three commissioners appointed by Boutros-Ghali, had dramatically different views about identifying the culpable from those of his Chilean counterparts. "It never occurred to us that we wouldn't name names. When I read this mandate and it says 'the whole truth' it never occurred to me that the whole truth didn't mean that you identified the people you thought were responsible."[27] Buergenthal, a prolific scholar who like Raúl Rettig has trained a generation of attorneys as professor of law at George Washington University, believed that the principal duty was to respect Salvadoran citizens' demands for the truth rather than Salvadoran magistrates' claims to be the sole arbiter of it. "To us the notion of not naming names in that society would have been a complete sell-out, because it would have just perpetuated the impunity." Buergenthal, the first president of the Inter-American Court of Human Rights, was certainly mindful of the requirements of due process, but he saw no conflicts. "Unless you are told that there is some truth you can't tell, then the natural thing is to say everything you find, it being understood that you're not convicting them or making other judgments, but that this is what you find."

Judge Buergenthal was perplexed by the position adopted by the Chileans, and wondered aloud if the mandate of the Rettig Commission was framed to protect the Chilean military. "The Chilean situation is incomprehensible," he said repeatedly. This was not a theoretical matter up for debate. José Zalaquett's adamant opposition to the policy of naming the culpable compelled him to go public on the eve of the release of the report of the Commission on the Truth for El Salvador, *From Madness to Hope*. Buergenthal and the other commissioners were by then under tremendous pressure not to release names, once it became clear to both sides to the conflict that the commission had developed solid evidence and was determined to publish names. Buergenthal remembers that the military was putting "unimaginable pressure" on the commission when Zalaquett arrived in San Salvador to make his views known. "A member of the Chilean commission came to El Salvador to a conference that just preceded the release of our report and made a big fuss about the fact that we shouldn't name names." This was "a very distinguished human rights advocate who lent his name to this last minute effort" to prevent the release of names, Buergenthal said, before acknowledging that it was Zalaquett. "I tried to explain to him that we were dealing with a very different environment," different because the mandate of the Salvadoran truth commission was explicit about the need to breach the wall of impunity and because both the government and the guerrillas initially anticipated that names would be named. "He just didn't understand that."

Zalaquett was later quoted as saying that the members of the Salvador truth commission "concentrated more on the principles than on their practical application," but it may have been Zalaquett who was adhering too rigidly to principle. He told his interviewer that he had urged the members of the Commission on the Truth for El Salvador to pass the names of the accused officers on to the courts instead of naming them publicly. And he hinted that the publication of names had prompted the Salvadoran legislature to enact an amnesty law soon after the release of the Report of the Commission on the Truth for El Salvador. "My impression was that the commission's members didn't sufficiently realize what the consequences of their work might be."[28] The reality of the situation, however, was that the only way to breach the wall of impunity in El Salvador was to name names. Even if the Salvadoran legislature had not enacted the amnesty law, the Salvadoran courts, notorious for their complicity in the human rights violations, would not have carried out justice. It was for that very reason that the UN truth commission recommended that cases not be sent to the courts— as Zalaquett had urged—until the courts were purged of corrupt judges. So, the practical consequences of adhering to the principle that only courts of law can name names simply would have been, as Buergenthal observed, to perpetuate impunity. What was true in the case of El Salvador was also true of Chile. The 1978 amnesty law decreed by Pinochet obstructed justice and perpetuated impunity. Omitting the names of the culpable might have secured peaceful coexistence between the Rettig Commission and the Chilean high command, but the consequences of that omission were not altogether favorable for justice.

A Contentious Report

The Truth and Reconciliation Commission did not conduct an original investigation so much as it officially corroborated the evidence gathered by the human rights organizations that emerged in reaction to the state terrorism unleashed by the regime. This attests to the inestimable value of nongovernmental human rights organizations to the international protection and promotion of human rights. Because of the meticulous work of the Vicariate of Solidarity, the Chilean Human Rights Commission, the Foundation for Social Assistance of the Christian Churches, and the other human rights organizations, the Truth and Reconciliation Commission managed to produce a report, based on overwhelming if incomplete evidence, that must be construed as an indictment of Chile's military regime.

That is one part of the story of the Report of the National Commission on Truth and Reconciliation. The other is that the commission's investigative efforts to officially corroborate the information brought to it, or to develop new evidence, were deliberately impeded by the armed forces. The halting cooperation of the military, and its deplorable silence on the fate and whereabouts of the arrested-disappeared, combined to perpetuate the pattern of impunity through an official policy to cover-up evidence crucial to the work of the commission. None of this is surprising, given that Chile had just experienced a negotiated democratic transition that left the dictator as commander of the armed forces in a constitutional scheme of power substantially of his own design.

Aylwin did not intend for the commission to perform prosecutorial or judicial functions, and so limited its powers. But by denying the commission the power to subpoena witnesses and documents he made it difficult for the commission to perform even its more modest investigatory function. The commission was given the authority to gather evidence from voluntary witnesses, and to take measures to protect their identity. The commission also had the authority to request reports and documents from all governmental agencies and to gain access to any sites it deemed it necessary to visit. But the commission did not possess the legal authority to demand documents or access to important locations, much less to compel the testimony of unwilling witnesses. Consequently, the documents turned over by the military and police were selective.

The one advantage that the commission had, precisely because it did not possess prosecutorial or judicial powers, was that it did not have to adhere to requirements of due process or to strict standards of evidence. So the commission did not have to reveal the identities of witnesses to afford the accused the right to confront their accusers. This was indispensable because of the widespread perception that the military retained power to commit reprisals with impunity. Aylwin's instruction to the commission that it base its findings on the "honest judgment and conscience of its members" gave the commissioners greater latitude. Even so, they took care not to reach un-founded conclusions. If there were dubious judgments, the doubt derived more from the definition of a human rights violation than the commission's examination of the facts.

The commission was initially given six months to complete its work, then granted an additional three months. It worked from late April 1990 until February 1991, when it delivered its multiple-volume report to Aylwin. In that time, the commission compiled a massive archive of evidence, pro-cessed an impressive number of cases, and produced a trenchant report. But it could not complete its most important task: to identify all of the victims by name and to determine their fate and whereabouts.

The commission actually began its investigation in June 1990, after it had hired support staff and drawn up its internal by-laws. It engaged in a multi-plicity of tasks: it had to register cases, interview witnesses, cross-reference information gathered from government agencies, and contend with the armed forces and police. Then the commissioners had to reach judgments in the cases brought to it, transmit any new evidence to the courts, and draft a report—all before Chile completed a year of a negotiated transition to democracy.

Generating a list of victims was not difficult, but compiling a complete list posed problems. The Rettig Commission publicized notices in a number of domestic and foreign publications to alert families of its work. Witnesses could denounce violations during a ninety-day period beginning in June 1990, in the commission's office in the capital, in governmental agencies at the regional and provincial levels, and in embassies and consulates abroad. But it was the work of the more than a dozen human rights groups that had emerged in Chile over the previous seventeen years that provided the bulk of the information. The Vicariate of Solidarity, which had filed some 8,700 writs of habeas corpus between 1973 and 1988 alone, possessed the most ex-tensive archive of cases. It was not the only repository of relevant informa-tion. Jaime Castillo's Chilean Human Rights Commission had also worked up thousands of case files since the founding of the Commission in 1978. The Foundation for Social Assistance of the Christian Churches (FASIC), the Commission for the Rights of the People (CODEPU), the Sebastian Acevedo Movement against Torture, the Association of Family Members of the Arrested-Disappeared, the Group of Family Members of those Executed for Political Reasons—each had documented cases. Political parties, labor unions, even professional organizations had information about what had happened to their members. The MIR, the regime's principal initial target, also presented a list of victims.

When the Rettig Commission began examining individual cases in June 1990, some 3,400 alleged cases of human rights violations involving death had been registered. This figure alone gave a sense of the enormity of the human rights catastrophe. Thousands upon thousands of allegations of arbitrary detention, torture, and other abuses fell outside the commission's mandate to consider only the "most serious" violations. And hundreds of Chileans would come forward with new denunciations after the commission completed its work and submitted its report. Even so, the case load was enormous. But the Rettig Commission was determined to sift through all these cases by October in order to have time to draft what promised to be a contentious report.

The Rettig Commission was a relatively modest operation, given the gravity of its charge. There were eight commissioners, but Raúl Rettig acted as the commission's spokesperson and only rarely involved himself in individual cases. The commission hired 17 staff lawyers, each of whom was assigned a law student. Four social workers also worked with the commission. By force of habit the commission organized itself into separate "chambers" on the model of the Chilean judicial system. Each was assigned many as 200 cases.

The staff attorneys and legal assistants cross-referenced the information developed during the interviews with medical, forensic, and burial records, the civil and electoral registries, records of judicial investigations and war tribunals, military situation reports, and documentation from internal military disciplinary hearings. This examination of the documentary record yielded valuable information that belied the armed forces' claims that "disappeared" persons had actually fled the country or that they had never existed at all.

The interview process was the most dramatic phase of the commission's nine months of work. "I would say that was the hardest part of the work," said Laura Novoa, "because interviewing people, the families, receiving their testimony, that was cathartic." After seventeen years of terror, a fact-finding process had become cathartic. "If you were to ask me what was most important in that I would say that it was that people had the possibility of being heard in a dignified way, that people could enter places where there was the Chilean flag and where amiable people listened to them, let them sit down and just tell their story. I think that was very important for the families."

The witnesses told harrowing stories, and they left deep impressions on the commissioners and legal staff. Witnesses recounted how they watched as a disappeared person was arrested and provided details suggesting which branch of the military was implicated; detainees who were later released stated that they had seen persons at a detention site exhibiting the signs of torture, belying the armed forces' assertions that the person had ever been in their custody; family members told of witnessing their loved ones executed in their presence, or discovering bodies in the morgue after a frantic search. The commissioners even heard the extraordinary account of the mayor of Entre Lagos, who was arrested less than a week after the coup. She was taken to a bridge over the Pilmaiquén River together with four men; all were forced to kneel near the edge, then shot at close range. All five fell into the river, but she survived to tell her story. Her testimony led the commission to conclude that the men, whose bodies were swept away by the current, had been murdered.[29]

"What surprised us were the details, the refinement of the cruelty that there was sometimes," Raúl Rettig admitted. "One time I took part in the proceedings when a person, a woman, was telling how they killed her husband. The only thing that I remember wanting was that this poor lady would hurry up and get to the point and say that the poor man died. It was less tragic for her that she just come out and say it."

The sheer number of Chileans who came forward confirmed President Aylwin's assertion that Chilean society demanded the truth as a measure of justice. But the period opened for the registration of cases was arbitrarily limited to ninety days. Complicating matters was the fact that the commission conducted its work in the first months of a transition that left the armed forces in a strong position vis-à-vis the government. Laura Novoa's observation, that the transition had its "stamp and that every activity was stamped by it," was certainly not lost on the families of the victims. In fact, hundreds more Chileans would come forward over the next four years, so that, well after the Rettig Commission submitted its report, the commission's work would have to be carried on by another agency.

The armed forces and police possessed but concealed the most crucial information of all. The testimony of soldiers and police whose identities became known to the commission could have solved all the mysteries of what had happened and where the missing could be found. But such testimony was rare. The military's conspiracy of silence perpetuated its impunity, and the anguish of the families of the disappeared. Neither the amnesty law, nor the policy not to name names, induced soldiers to disclose the truth.

"We didn't have any difficulty with the air force or the navy, but the army and the Carabineros absolutely refused to cooperate," Rettig recounted. "The commander of the national police at the time of the investigation was initially disposed to cooperate, but, unfortunately, that cooperation was never manifested." The army replied to only two-thirds of the commission's requests for documents and other information, and it gave a number of excuses for not providing crucial information. The army asserted that much of the documentation was deliberately destroyed after the normal period for retaining information had lapsed, in accordance with its standard procedures and with the law. The army also claimed that records of its own war tribunals were destroyed when terrorists attacked an army repository in November 1989. In fact, the commission would eventually conclude that some of the war tribunal verdicts were falsified to cover extrajudicial executions. In other instances, the military simply ignored commission requests, and the commission was dissolved without ever having the opportunity to review information it deemed important. The security agencies denied access for information on the grounds that they were legally prohibited from divulging it.

The military could not withhold all information, and sometimes it served their ends to make information available. The armed forces were not reluctant to provide information in cases involving the death of soldiers. Aylwin had instructed the commission to decide whether soldiers had been victims, and the army high command understood the value of guiding the commission to the appropriate conclusion. However, some of the other documents the army handed over proved harmful. Commanders' situation reports indicated that the military quickly took control of the country, and that it was not at war with organized rebel forces. The military's justification for its repressive operations was challenged by those in charge of conducting them.

The other branches of the armed forces and the police were not entirely uncooperative. The Investigations Police and the International Police were cooperative. Both agencies possessed important documents that the staff lawyers needed to cross-check, such as the emigration record of someone thought to be disappeared, but neither of these police agencies was heavily implicated in the most serious abuses. The air force and the navy turned over records related to war tribunals; the navy provided only copies of the sentences that were handed down, but the air force granted permission to review all pertinent documents it retained.

Identifying individuals who may have participated in a crime was a nearly insuperable obstacle. The commission's investigation turned up partial evidence. It might learn a soldier's rank or unit, but not his name; or it might identify a unit involved in an operation but no more. None of the services were willing to release personnel rosters that might have enabled the commission to find individuals assigned to units known to have been involved in an operation for the purpose of eliciting testimony. The military claimed that their code of justice protected the confidentiality of personnel rosters. The commission countered that it sought specific names, not entire lists, but it still did not succeed in acquiring all it requested. The navy and air force provided the names of unit commanders in most cases, while the police sent only the names of unit commanders in retirement. The military leadership, of course, fully appreciated the consequences of divulging the identities of unit commanders. As Laura Novoa remarked in the context of the commission's internal debate over whether to give the names of unit commanders without accusing them of anything, "it is a very fine line between describing facts and imputing guilt, because, when the description is complete enough, it is a very small intellectual step of deduction to get to the casting of guilt."

The commission did manage to identify a number of individuals, but its efforts to obtain their testimony were generally frustrated, especially in the case of active-duty personnel. The commission requested interviews with 160 members of the armed forces and police. These men and officers had every reason to withhold evidence, even though guarantees of confidentiality applied equally to them as to the family members of victims. The commission was not permitted to name anyone publicly, and most were protected by the amnesty law. Reasons for refusing to be deposed in an interview or to respond to questions in writing varied according to the report: some disavowed any knowledge of an incident; others claimed to have nothing to add to testimony already given in judicial proceedings; others, aware of the voluntary nature of the solicited testimony, simply refused without comment. The balance of fear of self-incrimination and reprisal probably varied from case to case, but both had to be taken into account. Guillermo Bratti, who had been associated with the air force Joint Command, was killed in 1976 by fellow officers for passing information to another security service, the DINA. In October of the following year, Juan René Muñoz Alarcón, the mysterious hooded man depicted in the Costa-Gavras film *Missing* who singled out leftists for summary execution in the National Stadium in the first days after the coup, was found stabbed to death in the capital, shortly after he told his story to the Vicariate of Solidarity.[30] Andrés Valenzuela, the repentant member of the Joint Command whose confessions were published in 1991, lives in exile for fear of reprisal.

The men who sat at the pinnacle of power were far beyond the reach of the Rettig Commission. The commission could neither name nor interview them. Raúl Rettig may have been told as much in person in May 1990, when the army sent an envoy to meet with him.[31]

"Did you succeed in interviewing General Pinochet?"

"No, we never requested it."

"Why not?"

"No. [pause] That, of course, would not have been possible."

Rettig thought the question presumptuous. "Pardon my annoyance about this," he said, and then set the record straight. "The object of the Commission was to establish the general truth. When the dictatorship ended, many people said that these things are lies. Someone might have been killed in a fight, but all this about there having been persecution, a series of crimes and heartbreaking acts, none of that is true. But we established that it was true, and nobody has been able to refute it. . . . I am satisfied because we completed what was charged to us. Now, if the discussion is about something else, if it is about whether a parliamentary commission should have been named instead with the power to carry out some resolution, and even the with power to stand people before a firing squad, that is something else entirely. But that is not what we were charged with doing!"

But Raúl Rettig believes that the leadership of the army and Carabineros committed an error by not permitting their members to tell their version of events. "I believe they committed an error that was very prejudicial to them, because many of those who had been publicly imputed, who for personal reasons went before the Commission, frequently received, at least, what you Americans call a reasonable doubt." An example came quickly to his mind, but Rettig was careful not to name names. "Even one of the principal figures, a general who was accused of killing people on an aerial tour, whom no one would have considered, I don't want to say innocent, but well yes, there was some doubt regarding his responsibility, he went and confronted things." Rettig was undoubtedly talking about General Sergio Arellano Stark, whose helicopter tour of the north in October 1973 left some seventy-two victims. "I'm telling you, he left us with some doubts. So, it was an error [that the armed forces made]. They had every kind of guarantee."

The Chilean High Command could not prevent the Truth and Reconciliation Commission from developing damning evidence and from exposing the essential truth. But the military might have avoided leaving the impression that, by its very silence, it confessed corporate guilt. It might even have manipulated the story by implying by its cooperation that it was interested in cashiering rogue officers who committed isolated human rights violations on their own authority. In the best of worlds, the high command might have seized upon the historic opportunity to scrutinize its own conduct and to strengthen the military as an institution.

Laura Novoa remembers that, even though they could not speak with the senior commanders, their silence reinforced the members' conclusions. Direct evidence of complicity was difficult to come by, but unavoidable inferences were possible. "Look, we never got to the top leadership, if that means Pinochet. But, yes, we got as far as Manual Contreras and mainly the people of the DINA. I would say, there, that if you examine the death of General Prats, or the death of Letelier [there is evidence]." The assassinations of General Prats and his wife Sofia in 1974, and of former foreign minister Orlando Letelier and Ronnie Moffitt two years later, were among the most notorious carried out by the DINA. The outrage they caused, especially in Washington, ultimately led to the DINA's dissolution. The case of General Prats, whom Pinochet had replaced as commander of the armed forces only a month before the coup, is supremely sensitive. The murders were almost identical, but Michael Townley, who admits to planting the bomb that killed Letelier, adamantly protests his innocence in the Prats assassination. Journalists' insinuations about Pinochet's possible prior knowledge of the plot to assassinate a former superior officer still provoke Pinochet to anger. "Yes, it is a question that hasn't been opened, because we ourselves in the commission, when we determined that he was a victim within the [decree's] concept of a victim, we knew that we were going to have a horrible reaction from the armed forces," Novoa said. "But, they pretended to be ignorant of the whole thing and never responded, and it was then that we reached the conclusion that the death of Prats was sponsored by big names, by the military government of Pinochet without any doubt. I recall the personal impression that [when one reads the case material] one formed the conviction that the death of General Prats was really planned and developed by the top leadership."

One commissioner, who spoke on the condition of anonymity, made a dramatic assertion of Pinochet's personal knowledge of these crimes. Asked if the commission possessed evidence that Pinochet was in the room when the order was given to violate someone's human rights — evidence that would win a conviction in an American court of law — he answered in the affirmative.

"But I wouldn't call it a human rights violation."

"What was it then?"

"An act of international terrorism."

The commissioner was alluding to either the Prats or the Letelier assassinations or both.

The Rettig Commission began to meet in plenary session to draft its report in October. The commissioners had developed good working relations, but it remained to be seen whether such a diverse group could arrive at common conclusions about highly controversial cases. Aylwin's mandate to the commission complicated matters. The definition of what constituted a serious human rights violation, and the instruction to clarify the circumstances and antecedence of the calamity, only made the commission's obligation to reach a "moral conviction" more difficult. There were other pressures, although the extent to which commissioners felt them is uncertain. In December, while the commission was sifting through the case files, General Pinochet placed the Chilean armed forces on nationwide alert. The 1973 coup d'état had been hastily organized, as the orders to stage it were signed late on the night of September 9, 1973, a little more than 28 hours before army units deployed around the Moneda palace. Pinochet's stunt was meant to convey the simple but ominous message that the possibility of military intervention was now part of operational doctrine.

In the preceding months, the staff had worked up some thirty-five hundred cases, reduced files of evidence to case summaries, and attached recommendations. Couriers delivered the case files to the homes of commission members, who then read them well into the night.[32] The following morning, the entire commission assembled in its Santiago office to discuss the cases and to reach a "moral conviction" in each of them. In practically all cases, the conclusions stated in the report were arrived at by consensus, but there were an unspecified number of cases in which the conclusion that a person was a victim was made on the basis of a simple majority. The commission members voted on the content of the report page by page.

If there was doubt as to whether someone had been a victim of a human rights violation in the strict sense of the concept, it was generally because of the lack of evidence. The real areas of controversy and possible disagreement among members were four: death as a consequence of torture occurring sometime after the fact; the fate and whereabouts of the disappeared; deaths resulting from actions by private individuals for political reasons; and deaths resulting from the general situation of political confrontation, a category that included shootouts, suicides, and excessive use of force during protests.

The security forces and military tortured tens of thousands of Chileans. Some have criticized the commission's mandate because it did not permit the commission to examine and document individual cases, unless the victims died as a consequence. But there are numerous cases of Chileans being tortured to death. Such was the case of Lumi Videla, who died under torture in the José Domingo Cañas facility in Santiago in late September 1974. Her torturer was the infamous Osvaldo Romo Mena. In more than a few instances it appears that their torturers unintentionally caused the death of the victim or caused it sooner than they had hoped. The body of Jaime Ossa was taken to the Medical-Legal Institute after he died at the Villa Grimaldi. The commission in its summary of the facts of the case reported that "agents who were overwhelmed with nervousness were heard to say that he had died of a stroke after being given water."[33]

Death due to maltreatment presented a different problem, one that was exacerbated if the death occurred sometime after the abuse. The problem was less serious in the high-profile cases. José Tohá, Allende's interior minister, was taken to Dawson Island in the Strait of Magellan with other high-ranking UP officials. There his health deteriorated precipitously, and Tohá died on March 15, 1974 in a military hospital. Military officials claimed that Tohá took his own life. The Rettig Commission concluded that "even if José Tohá took his own life, he died as a result of human rights violations." The commission noted that all testimony indicated that he was malnourished and in extremely poor condition.[34] An even more intriguing case is that of General Alberto Bachelet. In March 1974 Bachelet died of cardiac arrest in a cell in the air force war academy, where he was being held with more than a dozen other air force officers on charges of conspiring with the MIR to infiltrate the service. Bachelet, according to both the official inquiry and independent sources, was severely mistreated, humiliated, and tortured.[35] Bachelet was a victim of the armed forces paranoia about leftist infiltration of the air force. The most serious accusation against him was that he was directly involved in the infamous Plan Z to decapitate the leadership of the armed forces in a leftist coup during Chile's independence day celebrations. But Plan Z was concocted by military intelligence after the coup as a pretext for the purges that followed. The commission determined that the mistreatment aggravated a preexisting heart condition, so his death constituted a violation of his right to life.

Determining the fate and whereabouts of the disappeared presented a unique and agonizing problem. The DINA "disappeared" Chileans in order to conceal guilt, but also to sow terror. Once the armed forces had defeated subversion and declared, in Pinochet's terms, "mission completed," the high command could have discreetly aided in the recovery of at least those victims interred in clandestine burial sites. Victims whose bodies were cast into the sea from helicopters or, like those murdered on the Pilmaiquén bridge, were swept downstream were beyond recovery. But the security forces could have discreetly provided definitive information. The amnesty law placed the guilty beyond prosecution, but the Geneva Conventions nonetheless required the high command to make a good faith effort to restore the dead to their families. The Chilean high command, however, was not acting in good faith.

In the case of the disappeared the commission had to rely on "the power and agreement of convincing circumstantial evidence . . . that a person had suffered a forced disappearance even though it did not have proof."[36] In the judgment of the commissioners, the disappeared are deceased. It was a reasonable conclusion, one that the commissioners could make with a degree of emotional detachment. Thousands of Chileans have had to form the same conclusions about their loved ones after a torturous psychological process of acceptance. Many Chileans have yet to permit themselves to believe that their loved ones are dead, so the anguish and torment caused by forced and involuntary disappearance persist.

No one that the Truth and Reconciliation Commission declared disappeared and deceased has ever reappeared in Chile. If the commission erred, it erred on the side of caution. The secretive ways of MIRistas and Rodriguistas complicated matters. After the military had taken power, Hugo Fernando Amaya, a MIRista, began to arrange secret visits with his family in Concepción. In July 1976 the visits suddenly stopped, and nothing has been learned of him since. The commission could not come to a conclusion about what happened and does not consider him a disappeared person. Alfonso Díaz was another MIRista who had gone underground after some of his friends were arrested. In June 1974 he confided to his family that he was under surveillance; his parents' home was searched twice that same month. He has not been seen since June 5, but the commission could not reach a conclusion that he was forcibly disappeared. Fernando González had been a member of President Allende's detachment of bodyguards. His family rarely saw him because of the nature of his work. In October 1973, as the repression intensified, he visited his family to announce that he would be going away indefinitely. He asked that they not try to locate him and said his good-byes. He has not been heard from since that time, but the commission could not declare him disappeared.[37]

Ruling out that a person voluntarily left the country could prove painstaking. The military still claims that this is what became of the "missing." Military intelligence sometimes tried to fabricate information that would lead the curious to conclude that a person had traveled abroad. The infamous Case of the Thirteen illustrates the point. At the end of 1976, the Air Force Joint Command intensified its assault on the Communist party. By the end of December, the party's central committee had been arrested and disappeared. Waldo Ulises Pizarro was among a group of seven central committee members arrested on December 15. The military attempted to cover the crimes by forging a false travel certificate that stated that Pizarro had left the country for Argentina. The Rettig Commission proved that to be false. Pizarro's wife, Sola Sierra, would later become the president of the largest organization representing the arrested-disappeared.

If there was a kind of case that could fall through the cracks, this was it. The pressure of an approaching deadline, the enormity of the case load, and the deliberate forgery of documents—all conspired against the members of the commission. "There was a case that Pepe [José Zalaquett] had pulled out and had succeeded in getting the commission to vote against it," Laura Novoa recalled. "The person had apparently been arrested, then had left the country in the month of November of a particular year, and that demonstrated that he was free." Here the commission was in possession of an official document stating that an individual had been arrested and released. In the absence of additional evidence, the commission could not declare the person a victim of an involuntary disappearance. But Novoa acted on instinct and pursued the case. "I took it upon myself to look into the case, and I realized that the crucial date wasn't November but February. The November date led to the case being thrown out. But it was February, not November, because the police report which was summarized said November as indicated by a two-letter abbreviation, and the others read it as November, but it was February. I showed it to Pepe and he said to me, 'my God Laura, what a shame we didn't realize that before, please forgive me,' and we put the name back on the list."

Aylwin's effort to placate the military by including the death of soldiers and carabineros within the scope of the commission's mandate offended the families of the victims of the regime. The unintended but unavoidable effect was that the publication of the name of a solider or carabinero in the report would appear to authenticate the dictatorship's claim that it had been at war. The commission's findings in such cases made a victim's survivors eligible for reparations. If there are any latent disagreements among the ideologically diverse commissioners, this category of victim would likely to bring it out. Notably, some of the more questionable conclusions reached by the commission had to do with this category of violations.

A third of the soldiers and police killed during the period studied by the commission were killed in the immediate aftermath of the coup. Thirty members of the armed forces and police were killed between September 11 and the end of 1973; twenty-four of them were killed in the metropolitan Santiago area. Among those are the four non-commissioned officers killed by sniper fire during the siege of the Moneda palace. Six carabineros were killed in an operation in the La Lengua shanty-town, three more were killed in the seizure of the Indumet factory—all on the day of the putsch.

Whether these cases could have been considered violations of the laws of armed conflict is debatable. There are a few cases in which it can be fairly said that the commission exceeded even the mandate to consider cases involving violations committed by private individuals. On the night of September 14, 1973, in the tense atmosphere of the first days of the military's repressive operations, an army corporal was shot to death on the Maipo bridge in Santiago by members of the Chilean Air Force who mistook him for an attacker. The army corporal is listed as a victim. The very next night another army corporal leading a squad of soldiers searching dormitories at the University of Chile was killed when a rifle accidently discharged. He too is listed as a victim of the situation of political violence, simply because he was on duty at the time. A week later, in Concepción, a solider shot and killed a detective assigned to the Investigations Police. The death of this detective, as a result of both mistaken identity and a propensity to shoot suspects on sight, was considered by the commission to be another consequence of the situation of political violence.[38] Statistically, these cases do not significantly inflate the figures of soldiers killed. But such cases do rankle those whose loved ones were tortured to death, shot, or simply disappeared by the comrades in arms of these unfortunate men.

Judgments as to who was a victim of the situation of political confrontation were equally likely to divide those members of the commission with differing perspectives. The commission had to consider cases of MIRistas or Rodrigistas killed in genuine firefights, a large number of ordinary Chileans killed during protests, and a few who even took their own lives rather than risk capture or to protest the regime. Fault lines could easily develop between those whose predilections led them to think differently about justifications for opposition to the regime and the need for law and order.

"There is the case of a MIRista," explained Jaime Castillo, "they've got surrounded, and they start shooting. Someone can say that this was an armed engagement, the MIRistas are armed, the soldiers know they are armed, and so they go there and there is an engagement. But I can say that the MIRista really didn't intended to engage the army militarily, he's trying to escape and to hide, and after they've got him corralled, he fires. So, you see, the same fact could be interpreted differently."

There are many such cases, although the majority of MIRistas were abducted and murdered. The most controversial cases of MIRistas involved the MIR's leadership. Miguel Enríquez was killed in a firefight with DINA agents in October 1974. The commission had to acknowledge that, although it could not regard the death of Miguel Enríquez as "a human rights violation in the strict sense, it could conclude that he lost his life as a result of the situation of political violence, since he died resisting arrest by an agency [the DINA] which he had grounds for believing would torture and kill him if he were arrested." The commission reached the same conclusion in the case of José Bordas, the chief of MIR's Military Commission. Bordas had survived the operation in which Enríquez was killed but was shot to death by agents of the air force intelligence in December of the same year. There should have been less controversy in the Bordas case, since witnesses suggest that Bordas was shot to death without warning. The commission mentions a shootout.[39]

The commission reserved a section of the second volume of its report to the 131 deaths due to the excessive use of force by police once the Days of National Protest began in 1983. Depending on the complex circumstances and the available evidence, the conclusion sometimes classified individuals to be victims of a human rights violation, and other times victims of political violence. This category of cases presented challenges, and could easily divide members of the commission predisposed to come down on different sides of the issue of the right to protest and the right to maintain law and order. There were hundreds of cases, some of them complicated by the fact that the victims had shouted insults, thrown stones, and even set barricade bonfires. The commission appreciated that the Carabineros, and to a lesser extent the army, were legitimately charged with maintaining order.

"Discrepancies with respect to the interpretation of the facts were possible," said Castillo, moving from the cases of political violence to excessive force. "For example, there was a demonstration, or a mobilization as they were called here, and someone is killed." Castillo did not want to indicate which, if any, of his colleagues on the commission were reluctant to declare protesters innocent victims. But Castillo, who had been abducted by government agents in 1976 and thrown into the back of a car, had personal experience of the disposition of soldiers and police. "I myself presupposed that those people who demonstrated did not set out to kill anybody, but to demonstrate. It was the pug-nosed soldiers or the DINA who went there to repress, they were the ones capable of killing. So for me, whenever there was a death, it was the fault of the DINA, not the guy from the barrio."

Ronald Wood's death in May 1986 appears to have become fixed in Laura Novoa's memory. Wood, a part-time student, joined a large group of students who staged a demonstration to coincide with the celebration of the International Parliamentary Assembly in a Santiago hotel. The students faced down an army patrol on the Loreto bridge. The soldiers advanced, firing shots in the air in an attempt to disperse the protesters. The students held their position on the bridge. Some witnesses observed private citizens firing shotguns at the students. Wood was struck and killed. Because of "credible testimony" that the student demonstration was peaceful, the commission concluded that the soldiers used excessive force and violated Woods' right to life.[40]

The incident came at a time when Laura Novoa, a conservative corporate lawyer, was asked to support a colleague's election to the Chilean Bar Association. But Novoa became dismayed at the right's refusal to condemn the violence, something she took to mean that the right condoned it. "I had to reject the request that I support a colleague's election to the Bar Association," she remembered. "They came to ask that I do it taking it for granted that I would be party to the idea. But that same day they [the army] had shot a university student to death right here on a nearby bridge, and I was feeling a sense of repulsion. I remember the look on one of my colleagues' face when I told him that I would not participate in the election as they wanted, because that would just be to support the military dictatorship, and I was not going to adhere to a position that would permit such horrible things to ever happen, because that could have been one of my sons at a given moment."

Whatever the predisposition of other members, all eventually discerned a pattern and signed the report. "Little by little," according to Castillo, "a consensus formed about the reality of the existence of the violations, and about the inclination, I would say, the destructive inclination of some members of the armed forces to just destroy all opposition to the regime without any regard for the law."

The commission reached the judgment that a number of persons who took their own lives were, under certain circumstances, victims of the situation of political confrontation. Nowhere is the commission's departure from the strict concept of a human rights violation more glaring. But, in a strange sense, the case of suicides also makes the rationale for an expansive understanding of human rights violation intelligible. What the suicides make clearer than any other category of victim is the pathological political climate of the era.

Death by suicide was an especially charged issue, because Salvador Allende had taken his own life rather than abandon the burning Moneda palace. The controversy over Allende's death raged for years, and the commission's findings, based on eyewitness testimony, dispelled the notion that he had been murdered by the soldiers who stormed the building. A 1993 television documentary, "The Eleventh — Twenty Years Later," settled the controversy even for true believers by airing graphic photographs of the president's body slumped on a sofa, and brain matter still sticking to the high ceiling above where it was driven by the force of the blast.

The Rettig Commission, however, refused to classify Allende as a victim, reasoning that his situation was unique. Only minutes before Allende took his own life, journalist and Allende loyalist Augusto Olivares had committed suicide in a bathroom in the basement of the palace. "This fascism is going to be terrible," he forewarned a few minutes before ending his life.[41] The commission concluded that he was a victim of the situation of political confrontation. But the commission would not pronounce judgment on the suicide of Salvador Allende. "The commission has not regarded it either possible or relevant to assess the death of President Allende . . . the historic circumstances of his death and the undeniable connotation of his final decision confer on his death a meaning that goes beyond the capabilities and responsibilities that this commission seeks to elucidate."[42]

The suicide of Colonel Gustavo Cantuarias, commander of the High Mountain Training School, has the appearance of the act of a man presented with an ultimatum. Those seeking to make sense of it find themselves making inferences about Pinochet himself. Pinochet had sent his wife and children to that installation, located a short helicopter flight from Argentina, on the eve of the coup for their protection. But Cantuarias had been close to General Prats, whom Pinochet replaced as commander-in-chief of the armed forces and later had assassinated. He had also served in the mining ministry under the Unidad Popular government. More than a few believe that Pinochet, who was the last armed forces commander to sign the coup declaration, was more of an opportunist than a staunch anticommunist. If the coup had gone amiss, Pinochet would have been able to rally the constitutionalist officers from a base commanded by one of their number. After the ouster of Allende, Cantuarias became a serious liability. Sometime after September 11 he was arrested and taken to the Military Academy in the capital. On October 3, he died there, ostensibly of a self-inflicted gunshot wound to the head. A number of Chilean journalists surmise that Cantuarias's death was in some way connected to Pinochet's double dealing and to General Arellano Stark's helicopter tour. The Rettig Commission reported that it "believes this was the suicide of a person who was being subjected to so much pressure by government agents that such a decision offered an avenue of escape."[43]

The suicide of Sebastian Acevedo was both a public spectacle and a passion play. On November 11, 1983 he walked to the steps of the Catholic cathedral in Concepción and drew a chalk line on the pavement. Two days earlier, armed civilians had abducted his two children; military and civil authorities refused to provide him with information about their condition and whereabouts. Carabineros standing nearby instantly realized that Acevedo intended to make a public demonstration, and moved to prevent it. What they did not know was that Acevedo, who warned the carabineros not to cross the line he had drawn, had doused himself with paraffin. As the carabineros approached to arrest him, Acevedo immolated himself.

In the commission's view, even though "strictly speaking his death cannot be classified as a human rights violation, he was a victim of political violence, since he made the decision that cost him his life as an extreme measure to save his children from consequences that were not clear but which certainly could have been extremely serious, or as a desperate way to protest what was tormenting him as a father."[44]

The tally of the National Commission for Truth and Reconciliation was grim, but it was not final. The Report identified by name 2,279 victims as it was instructed to define a victim, 2,115 of them victims of human rights violations in the traditional sense.[45]

Had there been more time to develop evidence or to review evidence already in its possession, the figure would certainly have been greater. The Rettig Commission left a backlog of 642 undecided cases. In case after case, additional information — and the time to obtain it — might have permitted the commission to arrive at "a moral conviction."

There is an aphorism in Spanish that warns "lo perfecto es el enemigo de lo bueno" — the perfect is the enemy of the good. President Aylwin charged the National Commission on Truth and Reconciliation with producing a definitive report, an official truth. But the magnitude and importance of that charge made it inevitable that in fulfilling it the commission would please no one and anger everyone. The commission could not publicly expose those responsible for what had happened; it could not even print the names of those, like Manuel Contreras, who had been convicted of their crimes; it had to consider military and police to be victims because of an expansive definition of a human rights violation that appeared to many to be Aylwin's concession to placate the military; it could not reach a conviction in all cases brought to its attention, and did not even consider a substantial number of cases that would subsequently come to light; and it could not discover the fate and whereabouts of thousands of victims and end the anguished uncertainty of the families. A leading critic would call these the "little secrets of the commission."

The publication of the Rettig Report was for many Chileans the end of the story. The military regime's human rights violations had been investigated and reported. Now there was the future to think about. President Aylwin, whose paramount concern was the democratic transition over which he was presiding, could now hope that this contentious issue had been settled. But it was not the end of the story. There were known cases still to be resolved, disappeared persons to be found, and there was the question of how Chilean society would react to the truth. Those are the sequels to the work of the National Commission on Truth and Reconciliation.

Chapter 9
The Politics of Human Rights

> The Report did not help us very much with respect to the clarification of
> the fate suffered by our family members, and to this day, we are in the
> same situation as before.
>
> — Sola Sierra, President,
> Association of the Families of the Detained-Disappeared

Reactions to the Report

As one of his first acts as president, Patricio Aylwin assigned the National
Commission on Truth and Reconciliation four tasks in order to satisfy a set
of moral and national imperatives. When the commission delivered its report to Aylwin in February 1991, it had substantially accomplished three of
those four tasks. The commission had established a reasonably complete
picture of the most serious human rights violations committed during the
years of the dictatorship; it had recommended a set of creative measures
aimed at just reparation; and it had likewise recommended sweeping constitutional, legal, and institutional reforms which, if adopted, could plausibly
be expected to prevent further grave human rights violations from being
committed. But, because it possessed limited powers and was given a short
life, the commission was simply incapable of completing the most compelling task of all, that of identifying all the victims by name and determining
their fate and whereabouts. Of course neither Aylwin nor the commission
had the power to achieve the transcendent goal of the commission: national
reconciliation.

Patricio Aylwin made the Rettig Report public during the first week of
March in a national television address. The president had reflected on the
report for just over a month. Aylwin decided to address the nation, he said,
in order share his personal reflections, and to announce the measures he
intended to take to implement the recommendations contained in the report.[1] Aylwin had tears in his eyes. Before going on the air, the president had
handed the report over to representatives of victims' organizations, including Sola Sierra's Association of the Families of the Detained-Disappeared.

The truth is essential, Aylwin reflected, "because deceit is the antechamber to violence, and it is incompatible with peace." The commission had clarified the truth, he asserted, and no one should deny it, especially the armed forces. Anticipating challenges to the objectivity of the commissioners, the president pointed out that some had been supporters of the regime, one had even been part of it. Nothing could justify the violations, he said, not even the claim that there existed an internal war against terrorism. "Nothing justifies the torture and execution of prisoners, or that their remains be made to disappear," he said, "even war has its laws."[2]

Then the president appealed for reconciliation and pardon. "All of us always desire greater justice," he said in a memorable and telling phrase, "to the extent it would be possible." He acknowledged that "pardon cannot be imposed by decree," but "dared, in his capacity as president, speaking on behalf of the entire nation, and in the name of the nation, to request pardon from the families of the victims."[3] As dramatic as this was, neither the armed forces nor representatives of the victims' families were favorably impressed. The army would later declare in its written responses to the report that "we have no reason to seek pardon." Sola Sierra, president of the Association of the Families of the Detained-Disappeared, angrily countered that "no one has asked us to pardon them, nor do we want them to ask us to pardon them." Even Jaime Castillo, President of the Chilean Human Rights Commission, and one of the members of the now discharged Commission on Truth and Reconciliation, found the often repeated phrase, truth and justice to the extent possible, worrisome. "Aylwin is correct when he says justice to the extent possible," said Castillo, "but it's a phrase that should not be spoken, because when it's said it reduces the momentum needed to accomplish things."

Paradoxically, the onus of accountability shifted away from the armed forces and onto the civilian president the moment Aylwin made the Report of the National Commission on Truth and Reconciliation public. Now that an official accounting of the truth had been rendered, the issue was no longer what the military had done, but what the democratic government would — or could — do in response. Unless he chose utterly to ignore the report of his own presidential commission, Aylwin now had to make progress in four critical areas: delivery of reparation to surviving victims; implementation of scores of recommendations for reform; completion of the commission's grim work of identifying the victims and finding the missing; and fulfillment of the demands of justice "to the extent possible."

The Aylwin government could offer symbolic and material reparations to the families of the victims as a measure of partial justice, but no one believed that these could repair the great harm that had been inflicted. Implementation of the dozens of recommendations made by the commission was sure to be a formidable challenge that would test Aylwin's political savvy. The Rettig Commission's recommendations encompassed constitutional, statutory, and institutional reforms that together were intended to prevent a repetition of the tragedy that Chile had endured. It was uncertain whether Aylwin possessed the power to push reforms through a legislature packed with Pinochet supporters.

There were nearly one thousand Chileans still unaccounted for when the Rettig Commission's time ran out. That figure would increase over the next two years. Some were known to have been executed, but their families never recovered their remains. Others were disappeared, and their fates remained shrouded in the military's continuing denials of knowledge and complicity. Accordingly, Aylwin announced that, after forwarding the report to the Supreme Court, he would urge the high court to investigate the cases forwarded to it by the commission, especially those involving the disappeared, regardless of the amnesty law of 1978. Aylwin pledged he would personally request the military service commander's collaboration in the search for the disappeared and the resolution of cases not resolved by the commission. But there was no reason to believe the armed forces would collaborate now, after having impeded the Truth and Reconciliation Commission's investigation.

The possibilities for justice were limited. The judicial system, if so inclined, could prosecute individuals, but only for violations committed after 1978, the year the military government granted itself an amnesty. The only exception to this sweeping pardon applied to those implicated in the Letelier-Moffitt assassination, because it had been carried out in Washington. Not surprisingly, soon after the formal transfer of power the armed forces began militating for an amnesty covering the entire period of military rule. Aylwin would propose a law to settle the matter, but it placated almost no one and angered nearly everyone.

Aylwin had formed the Truth and Reconciliation Commission in order to impart a "common awareness" of the truth, and issued a "fervent call" to all Chileans to accept it. There were plans to follow up the March publication of the report with a national tour of cabinet ministers and commission members to publicize it and to drive home its sad lessons. But only a very few trips were made. On April 1, less than a month after the report had been made public and only a few days after the military warned that the report would generate hatred, commandos of the Manuel Rodríguez Patriotic Front ambushed and assassinated Senator Jaime Guzmán, the Pinochet regime's principal theoretician, as he left the Catholic University where he taught constitutional law. The publicity campaign was abruptly canceled, and Aylwin's already cautious and conservative legislative strategy became even more cautious and conservative. Guzmán's assassination suddenly raised the specter that a campaign to publicize the Rettig Report would be more likely to occasion revenge-taking than soul-searching. And the military's claim that it had been engaged in a war against leftist terrorists seemed validated. Within a few months, the massive Rettig Report could be found in most bookstores, but public debates about its content were rare. In the meantime, the two institutions most responsible for what had transpired, the armed forces and the Supreme Court, responded publicly and harshly to this new, "official truth."

The Report of the National Commission for Truth and Reconciliation treated the Chilean Armed Forces with considerable circumspection.[4] The Rettig Commission "refrained from taking a stand on whether the use of force on September 11, 1973, and immediately thereafter was legitimate," acknowledged the armed forces had earned "the well-deserved respect of our citizens," and warned against using "the subject of human rights to denigrate these institutions." The warning was not only the commission's way of fostering national reconciliation. Raúl Rettig had been told almost at the onset of the investigation that the armed forces high command was concerned that any report would be used for propagandistic purposes.

As much as these introductory comments irked human rights activists and the families of the victims, the commission was unequivocal that military's actions on the day of the coup and for the following seventeen years were demonstrably illegal and unjustifiable. The evidence presented to the commission with respect to the illegal conduct of the military and police was overwhelming, though it may have taken some of the more conservative commissioners more time than others to arrive at that disturbing conclusion. Citing military commanders' own situation reports in some instances, the commission found that Chilean armed forces were not at war, and that "for the most part the events did not take place in the heat of an armed clash nor immediately thereafter," but "were assaults on people who were unarmed or imprisoned."[5]

The commission criticized the armed forces' doctrine of national security and military culture. The former made commanders of a mind that the country was clandestinely besieged by agents of international communism; the latter accounted for the ubiquity of torture, summary executions, and other abuses. Consequently, the commission would recommend that the doctrine of national security be revamped, and that human rights courses be incorporated into the armed forces training programs. The commission framed the issue in stark terms that revealed just how alien, in the commission's view, was the notion of human rights to the military mind: "each member of the armed forces and police must be clearly aware of being a person and that awareness must be extended. Each must feel that he or she has human rights and must respect those rights in others."[6]

The commanders of the armed services and police delivered their official responses at a special session of the National Security Council, and later published them as "The Responses of the Armed Forces and [Forces] of Order." The document was dated March 27, 1991. The special session of the National Security Council had a symbolic importance: Pinochet was making a gesture intended to intimidate. The provision for the NSC had been placed in the 1980 constitution to permit the armed forces and police to admonish the civilian government, and to provide "legal justification for a coup should the authorities that are admonished, including the President and the Congress, not heed the warnings of the National Security Council."[7]

No one expected the high command to accept passively the commission's findings or to accede to its recommendations. The armed forces' response was "very violent," Raúl Rettig acknowledged, but quickly added, "that was expected." It was expected because the army had sent an envoy to meet personally with Rettig sometime in May 1990, when the commission was still in the early stages of its work. According to the army's account, prepared after the publication of the Rettig Report, the army had sought the meeting to express the armed forces' concerns about an investigation. The army twice went public with those concerns, once on May 25 and again on June 13, 1990. In the second of these public declarations, the army expressed its concern that "an irresponsible treatment of the high purpose [of the commission to report the truth] might lead to the exacerbation of hatred."[8] So, even before the commission really began its work, the high command of the armed forces was on record opposing its efforts.

Pinochet was the only service commander left from the junta that took control of the nation in 1973. Admiral José Toribio Merino, who had been a militant opponent of Allende, was gone. His replacement as service chief, Admiral Jorge Martínez Bush, faithfully defended the navy's role in the seizure of power and adamantly denied wrongdoing, but his response lacked the personal rancor that characterized Pinochet's lengthy attempted rebuttal. The air force commander, General Gustavo Leigh, had been ousted from the junta two months short of the fourth anniversary of the coup. His successor, Fernando Mattei, was less troublesome to Pinochet than Leigh, but he was not a sycophantic officer by any means. Mattei had opposed Pinochet's candidacy in the 1988 plebiscite, and it was he who first admitted publicly that Pinochet had lost it. Mattei delivered the most terse and conciliatory response to the Report of the National Commission on Truth and Reconciliation and in the process made a veiled criticism of Pinochet's failed bid to remain in power. Carabinero Director General Rodolfo Stange assumed command of the national police force when César Mendoza was forced to resign in the aftermath of the murder of three communists in March 1985. The unit involved in the crime was disbanded, but Stange would not escape scandal. In March 1994, a civilian judge recommended that Stange be prosecuted for leading a cover-up in the decade-old case. Stange, who refused to resign over the affair, took an extended vacation while the controversy settled.[9]

The army's rejection of the findings and recommendations contained in the Report of the National Commission for Truth and Reconciliation could not have been more categorical. The other service branches, perhaps because they were now commanded by men who had not been part of the original junta, were less acrimonious, but none admitted guilt in the slightest degree. The response of the air force was the only one that sounded conciliatory.

"The army certainly sees no reason to seek pardon for having taken part in a patriotic labor," said the report Pinochet submitted to the National Security Council. "The Army of Chile declares solemnly that it will not accept being placed on the dock of the accused for having saved the freedom and sovereignty of the Fatherland."[10] If there is a single issue that perturbed the army high command, it was the Rettig Commission's alleged failure to appreciate that Chile had been at war and that the armed forces' resort to force was therefore legitimate. Salvador Allende's Popular Unity government had aided and abetted subversives in their efforts to create a parallel army, claimed Chile's oldest and largest armed service. It was only because the armed forces had launched a preemptive attack on September 11 that "the revolutionary civil war was averted in its larval phase."[11] "By its very nature," contested the army, "the legitimate use of force can affect the life and physical integrity of persons," but the cold hard fact of the matter is that "from the perspective of any armed force, when it confronts a situation of war, total victory is the only fitting objective." All of them echoed the often quoted doctrine of the U.S. Civil War victor and villain General William Tecumseh Sherman: "war is hell," and therefore anything is permissible.

War is never bloodless, and it always furnishes sorrows, hatreds, injustices and inhumanities. . . . It is not the soldiers who provoke war or who convince the people to employ arms. . . . Soldiers make war, and when they are victorious they face forgetfulness, if not incomprehension and censure. . . . The army has the conviction that during all these years it has not stopped for even a moment from serving Chile and it takes pride in the imperishable honor that springs from the fulfillment of an historic mission.[12]

"The Army, the Truth and Reconciliation," as the response of the army was entitled, never mentions the Geneva Conventions. The army's silence on that point raised an ominous prospect: in future wars against subversion as in the most recent one, the armed forces would recognize no limits on their conduct, much less apologize for their conduct afterward. If the Report of the National Commission for Truth and Reconciliation contained any lessons about the past that the military ought to heed in the future, they were not the ones most Chileans would have desired.

The navy dismissed the report with a brusque statement that "the 'truth' which the report proclaims is nothing more than a simple opinion which may be shared or rejected." After enumerating the many provocations of the Popular Unity government that compelled the armed forces to intervene, the navy's response carefully restated the argument, rejected by the Commission on Truth and Reconciliation, that a genuine state of war existed in Chile during the more than seventeen years of the dictatorship.

Most interesting was the navy's semantic tussle with a single word, "conviction." President Aylwin had ordered the commission to reach a "moral conviction" about the thousands of cases denounced before it. But a conviction, countered the navy, "presupposes that a judge or tribunal has eliminated every possible doubt and on pronouncing sentence proclaims the truth by declaring the existence or nonexistence of facts and the guilt or innocence of those who appear implicated."[13] So, by stating its "conviction" in the 2,279 cases listed in its report, the Commission on Truth and Reconciliation had overstepped its authority and had usurped the powers reserved for courts of law.

The Carabineros also opted to make a narrow legal point in their effort to dismiss the report. "Given the real impossibility of establishing an absolute truth in relation to the presumed violations of human rights in Chile between 1973 and 1990," Stange told the National Security Council, "we must understand that the work of the National Commission on Truth and Reconciliation was oriented to present a version of those events, and that, because it lacks any legal value, it in no way obliges its complete and total acceptance."[14] But the uniformed police concentrated more on the potential consequences of the many reforms proposed by the commission. The commission's recommendations, although designed to prevent another human rights catastrophe, would seriously impede legitimate police work. The Carabineros went so far as to accuse the commission of attempting to foster an "anti-police culture."

Fernando Mattei delivered a terse, five-paragraph response on behalf of the air force. It was also the most conciliatory. "We lament today, as we have always lamented, all loss of human life," he began. The air force had been heavily engaged in the actions to eliminate the MIR in the south of the country in the first weeks of military rule, and the secretive Joint Command had pursued the central committee of the Communist party in the mid-1970s. But the service was not implicated in any crimes after Mattei took over from the ousted Gustavo Leigh in 1978. "As Commander-in-Chief, I reiterate that I am responsible for what took place in my institution," he told the National Security Council, "as the law indicates and my honor as a soldier demands." "I respect that we, the broad majority of Chileans, have acknowledged the effort of President Aylwin to seek the reconciliation that would permit Chile to project itself into a better future . . . I am convinced that only representative democracy, with its balance of powers and its full vigilance of the rule of law, offers guarantees that there will never again be repeated in Chile an experience such as the one described in the Report."[15] It was as if the old tensions between Gustavo Leigh and Augusto Pinochet had resurfaced in the air force's terse statement in reply to the Report of the National Commission on Truth and Reconciliation. If representative democracy was indeed the only guarantee for a better future without the recurrence of political violence, then Pinochet's bid to remain in office until nearly the end of the twentieth century surely had been a bad thing.

The armed forces' categorical rejection of the Rettig Report came as no surprise. The reaction of the Chilean high court was another matter. Too many lawyers had served eagerly as prosecutors, and too many judges had applied unquestioningly the armed forces' laws or had routinely denied habeas corpus petitions. How would the magitrates of the Chilean high court react to the criticisms of the lawyers who chronicled the crimes and complained of the judicial system's complicity in them?

At the beginning of October 1989, only a month before Aylwin was elected president, Chilean judge José Cánovas published his *Memoirs of a Magistrate*.[16] Cánovas harshly criticized the regime's interference with the courts and the passivity of most judges. Prompted by the publication of the book, the Chilean news magazine *APSI* published an article revealing the results of a telephone survey of an unspecified number of Chilean lawyers. The lawyers were simply asked to identify judges who in their opinion had demonstrated independence in highly political cases. The lawyers consulted could name only a very few.[17] The named judges had distinguished themselves in some of the more infamous cases. Carlos Cerda, judge on the Court of Appeals, had exposed the violations of the air force Joint Command leading to the arrest of some forty air force officers, including Gustavo Leigh, once a member of the junta. Rubén Galacio had initially handled the explosive Case of the Thirteen disappeared members of the Communist party central committee before it was turned over to a military court and dismissed. Adolfo Bañados had been the magistrate who investigated the case of 15 bodies found in an abandoned lime kiln in Lonquén and proved the involvement of carabineros in the crime; he would later convict DINA chief Manuel Contreras and sentence him to prison. Marcos Libedinsky had been instrumental in tracking the issuance of false passports that ultimately proved the involvement of Michael Townley in the Letelier assassination in Washington. Alberto Chaigneau proved the involvement of soldiers in the torture and death of a university professor, and even blocked the execution of a man convicted in the assassination of an army intelligence officer.

René García, a judge on the XX Criminal Court in Santiago, was also mentioned. García too had written a book on the subject of the courts and human rights. García documented numerous cases of torture at the CNI station located at Borgoño, Santiago. His own memoir, *I am a Witness*, is an eloquent denunciation of the "torments" CNI agents routinely inflicted on those in their custody.[18] García was forced from the bench in 1990, on the very eve of the transfer of power to the democratic government, but not before he became a tireless defender of the human right not to be tortured. Because the CNI facility located on Borgoño Street fell within his jurisdiction, García was in a position to document countless cases if he so chose. He did. García's book details numerous cases of torture and disappearance, and contains incisive criticisms of the reservations the Pinochet regime attached to the UN and OAS conventions against torture. It also provides a glimpse of how, even in the second decade of the regime, the courts could not intervene to save those the secret police had arrested from torture.

The case of Yuri Guerrero is illustrative. In 1985, CNI agents moved to arrest Guerrero and a companion. The companion was shot to death in the process. Guerrero was arrested and taken to the CNI location at Borgoño street and tortured. His family immediately filed a habeas corpus action, and in one of the rare cases, the intelligence agency complied. Guerrero was examined by a government physician at the Medical-Legal Institute who found signs of torture. The physician took the extraordinary step of publicly reporting that the CNI had tortured Guerrero.[19] The court then ordered Guerrero to be taken to a local hospital, where x-rays revealed the full extent of his injuries. He required prolonged hospitalization.

Guerrero had the courage to file a criminal complaint, at which point García became involved. After a preliminary investigation, Judge García ordered two agents who had brought Guerrero to court in connection with his habeas corpus appeal to appear before his court. They appeared, but refused to present their identity cards. Further investigation almost led García to the identity of Guerrero's torturers, despite interference by the CNI. The judge, in fact, indicted eight unnamed agents. At that point, the military stepped in to block the civilian court's actions. The military courts brought the matter before the Supreme Court, arguing that only military courts were competent to hear the case. The Supreme Court ruled in favor of the military. Five hundred pages of evidence were forwarded to the military tribunal, but nothing came of the criminal complaint.

García publicly decried this and other acts of torture, and his openness earned him the hostility of the military prosecutor, the military courts, and finally the Supreme Court of Justice. The end came when within the span of a few short weeks García gave an interview to a Spanish radio station, and then attended a public commemoration of the death of Sebastian Acevedo, the man from Concepción who immolated himself in front of the cathedral in that small city in protest of the arrest of two of his children. The Sebastian Acevedo Movement Against Torture had invited the judge to participate in the brief ceremony marking the death on the National Day Against Torture. The Supreme Court, in its decision to sanction García and eventually to remove him from his position on the XX Criminal Court of Santiago, cited him for making public statements about matters before his court and for his participation in political activities. The judge vigorously protested that his public statements that there was torture in Chile, a fact verified by international missions of the United Nations, Inter-American Human Rights Commission, and Amnesty International, were no different than if he had said that there were robberies, homicides, and extortion taking place in the country. The Sebastian Acevedo Movement Against Torture, in a letter addressed to the Supreme Court, buttressed García's claim that the public ceremony commemorating Sebastian Acevedo was not political. All to no avail. René García was forced from the bench in January 1990, only a month after Patricio Aylwin was elected president. García's separation from the bench was portentous. The fact that a judge who dared to investigate and denounce torture could be separated from the court on the eve of a democratic transition did not bode well for the rule of law in Chile. A favorable reception of the conclusions and recommendations of the Rettig Commission by the Supreme Court of Justice, therefore, became all the more important.

The Rettig Commission severely criticized the Chilean high court in a chapter drafted by former Supreme Court justice Ricardo Martín.[20] The report noted that the military did not dissolve the judicial branch, and quoted the Supreme Court president Enrique Urrutia's emphatic assertion that "the courts under our supervision have functioned in the normal fashion as established by the law."[21] The commission cited this as proof that the Supreme Court of Justice could have done more to protect the lives of Chileans. The Rettig Commission fully acknowledged that the court was hampered by "restrictions imposed by an array of special laws, and the general lack of resources, particularly help from the police," but did not believe this excused the court's inaction.[22] The fact was that the courts possessed two indispensable instruments, habeas corpus and the power to sanction the guilty, but neglected to employ them. Indeed, the Vicariate of Solidarity reported that the courts granted only ten of the habeas corpus petitions of the 8,700 filed by the Vicariate between 1973 and 1988. Consequently, wrote the commission, "whatever qualifications might be made, the judicial branch as a whole proved ineffective both in protecting human rights and punishing their violation during the period in question." The ineffectiveness of the courts, concluded the Rettig Commission, "was partly due to serious shortcomings in the legal system as well as to the weakness and lack of vigor on the part of many judges in fully carrying out their obligation to assure that the essential rights of persons are truly respected."[23]

The Supreme Court of Justice waited until May 13 to respond publicly to the Report of the National Commission on Truth and Reconciliation. The so-called "Accord of the Supreme Court" was nearly as contentious as the "Responses of the Armed Forces." "Impassioned, reckless, biased," was how the court characterized the Report of the National Commission on Truth and Reconciliation.[24] "Its judgment against the courts was the result of an irregular investigation, and probably political prejudices, which has the effect of placing judges almost on par with the very ones responsible for the violations of human rights." Fifteen members of the court signed the document protesting what was essentially the Rettig Commission's indictment of their competence as judges and commitment to the rule of law.[25] The Chilean congress would move to impeach three of them at the beginning of

1994, for voting to place a controversial human rights case involving the notorious Osvaldo Romo in the jurisdiction of courts martial, thereby insuring that nothing would come of it. One judge, Hernán Cereceda, would actually be expelled from the court for "gross abandonment" of duties.[26]

The Chilean Supreme Court of Justice voiced a number of complaints by way of rejection of the Rettig Report. Seizing on a point the Rettig Commission itself had made, that the regime had imposed an array of special laws intended to marginalize the judicial system, the court accused the Rettig Commission of contradicting itself. How could the court be responsible for human rights violations, almost on a par with those who committed the crimes, under such conditions? The court protested that Chile had been ruled by "a government of a regime of exception," a regime that took power in reaction to the "excesses of the previous government."[27] The signatories of the accord apparently believed this absolved the court for its sins of omission.

The high court also protested that the judicial system had done its duty and stood up to the military government. The accord enumerated thirteen such instances, the first coming on March 10, 1975, when the Supreme Court of Justice adopted a number of measures to counteract the junta's efforts to weaken the remedy of habeas corpus. But by then the military dictatorship was halfway through its second year in power. The Rettig Commission documented 1,261 human rights violations resulting in death during the first three and one-half months of the military regime alone, and another 309 in 1974. And, in 1974, the regime established the DINA to systematize the repression. Human rights groups were alerting the courts to what was happening in Chile. The court had waited a long time before it concerned itself with habeas corpus and other protections of basic rights.

The high court also complained that the Rettig Commission maligned its president at the time of the coup, Enrique Urrutia, simply by quoting him. "Contrary to what unworthy Chileans or foreigners operating with a particular political aim have said," exclaimed Urrutia in 1974, "Chile is not a land of barbarians; it has striven to give strict observance to these rights." These were words that would later come back to haunt him. "With regard to torture and other atrocities, I can state that here we have neither firing squads nor iron curtains, and any statement to the contrary is the product of a press that is trying to propagate ideas that could not and will not prosper in our country." In fact, some fifty-nine Chileans had already been executed by firing squad by the date of the speech, and many more had been summarily executed. As far as habeas corpus petitions were concerned, said the president of the high court, "the Appeals Court in Santiago and this Supreme Court have been overwhelmed with a large number of habeas corpus actions that have been introduced, alleging arrests made by the executive branch. The administration of justice has thereby been impeded, since the higher courts, particularly in Santiago, have been prevented from attending to urgent matters entrusted to them."[28] The Commission on Truth and Reconciliation published those remarks without commentary to illustrate a sad truth about the past.

The signatories of the accord considered the Rettig Commission's publication of Urrutia's remarks to be "malicious," because at the time they were made neither Urrutia nor the other members of the court were aware of the abuses. The Supreme Court of Justice was attempting vindicate itself by defending Urrutia on the plea of ignorance. The argument is unconvincing. Judge Urrutia may not have known about the repression, but he did not care to know. Urrutia had earned a reputation for his unconditional support of the Pinochet regime and his willingness to overlook its abuses. Amnesty International had noted this after an AI delgation visited Chile in 1974, stating with alarm that Urrutia "consistently expressed his desire to cooperate with the military junta," and that he "questioned neither the legitimacy of an extended state of war, nor that the prisoners had inadequate guarantees for defense."[29]

The charge leveled by the Rettig Commission that jurists protested most bitterly was that Chilean judges "adhered too strictly to the law." That charge "merits the most categorical repudiation," said the accord. The Rettig Commission admonished judges not to "hew to the letter of the law if the actual result is its violation," and emphatically recommended that legal education be reformed to produce judges "willing to set aside their role of simply applying the law mechanically, at least in matters concerning human rights."[30] The justices of the Supreme Court reacted harshly to this. "Judges do not make the laws, they apply them," they explained, adding that when "the meaning of a law is clear it is the obligation of judges to put in practice the intent of the legislator."[31] This rebuttal ignored the fact that for almost the entire duration of the dictatorship the courts were silent as the junta acted above and outside the rule of law, with grave consequences for Chileans. In fact, the pattern continued. On the very eve of the transition, a judge who had spoken out against torture had been forced from the bench. And the Supreme Court of Justice's subsequent rulings about the 1978 amnesty law would effectively impede the search for the "disappeared."

The Search for the Disappeared

The publication of the Report of the National Commission on Truth and Reconciliation did not resolve the problem of human rights in Chile. Human rights remained a delicate issue intertwined with the politics of democratic transition. President Aylwin still had to meet the demands of hundreds of families and human rights organizations for the release of scores of political prisoners languishing in prisons. And he had to act on the Rettig Commission's recommendation that the investigation of past abuses be carried on by another agency. The Rettig Commission had not reached a moral conviction in hundreds of cases, and, as it turns out, hundreds more would be added to the case-load. Most dramatically, the fate and whereabouts of nearly one thousand disappeared remained to be clarified. The National Commission on Truth and Reconciliation had ably succeeded in painting a reasonably complete picture of the human rights abuses committed by the Pinochet regime. But it had neither the time nor the power to find the "disappeared."

The political prisoners presented a vexing problem. When Patricio Aylwin assumed office there were some 350 political prisoners serving time for offenses under the anti-terrorism, weapons control, or national security laws decreed by the dictatorship. Most belonged to the Manuel Rodríguez Patriotic Front (now split, with the emergence of an "autonomous" faction). Some had been involved in the assassination attempt on Pinochet. Depending on one's point of view, the prisoners were either the terrorists responsible for the political violence decried by the National Commission on Truth and Reconciliation, or freedom fighters who took up arms against an entrenched dictatorship. Notably, the wave of violence did not end with the dictatorship; another one hundred and fifty members of the FPMR and the more recent MAPU-Lautero group were taken into custody after Aylwin entered office.[32] This fact stiffened the resolve of the armed forces, the Carabineros, and the right-wing parties to keep those in custody behind bars and to punish them to the full extent of the law.

But, if all Chileans genuinely sought national reconciliation, movement on the issue of the political prisoners was crucial. A certain segment of the public was incensed by the fact that those who had resisted the dictatorship were incarcerated, while known torturers and murders remained free — indeed, the Rettig Commission had not even ventured to name them. The Commission for the Defense of the Rights of the People (CODEPU) took up the cause of the prisoners with considerable energy and tenacity. Aylwin had promised to do everything in his power to gain their release, but in the prevailing political circumstances simply pardoning them all was unthinkable. The military considered the release of these terrorists to be nearly as unacceptable as the prosecution of soldiers for past crimes. Aylwin pardoned a substantial number, some one hundred and forty by mid-March, 1994. But it took two long hunger strikes by a group of the prisoners to keep the issue in the public eye, and when Aylwin acted, his instinct for compromise was again apparent.

Richard Ledesma led the hunger strikes from his cell in the *Penitenciaria*, in central Santiago, a short walk from the Mapocho River in one direction and from the Moneda palace in the other. Ledesma, a Rodriguista, was captured by carabineros after the ill-fated operation that eventually cost Raúl Pellegrin, head of the FPMR, his life. In the last week of October 1988, after Pinochet had been defeated in the historic plebiscite, commandos of the FPMR staged an utterly senseless attack on a Carabinero checkpoint at

Los Queñes, killing a carabinero.[33] Although the details are uncertain, Pellegrin and his companion Cecilia Magni were almost immediately captured and killed. Ledesma was subsequently captured. Three years later, Ledesma still sat in the old central jail in a legal limbo, waiting for reluctant courts to pass sentence so Aylwin could act in his case and others like it. The first hunger strike left Ledesma emaciated and weakened, but he was as alert and militant as ever. And he was as unrepentant as the officers who were his mortal enemies. Asked whether the FPMR was responsible for the series of assassinations that culminated with the murder of Senator Jaime Guzmán, in April 1991, Ledesma was evasive.[34] Then the dialogue turned to the matter of justice "to the extent possible" after the publication of the Report of the National Commission on Truth and Reconciliation. The Manuel Rodríguez Patriotic Front would demonstrate forbearance for a time, he said assuredly, but if the Aylwin government did not bring the material — and above all, the intellectual — authors of the crimes to justice, the FPMR would exact vengeance. The most likely victim, he said, was Senator Sergio Onofre Jarpa, the stalwart of the right who had briefly served as Pinochet's minister of interior.

The second hunger strike was much longer and nearly cost Ledesma his life. The officials controlling the prison hospitalized him when his kidneys began to fail. But the tenacity of the hunger strikers forced Aylwin to hasten the judicial process. Aylwin could pardon prisoners or — as in the case of Ledesma and some of the more dangerous Rodriguistas — commute their sentences, but only after the courts had pronounced sentence. The courts, however, were deliberately slow in processing such cases to stave off a presidential pardon. The hunger strikes forced the issue. In May 1993 Ledesma was placed on a plane to Belgium for exile, where he joined a number of his former comrades in arms. The following March, four Rodriguistas serving life sentences for their involvement in Operation XX Century, the assassination attempt on Pinochet in 1986, followed Ledesma to Belgium, having had their sentences commuted from life imprisonment to exile.

The compromise chosen by Aylwin in these controversial cases was to commute their sentences to exile.[35] The solution was as good as could be hoped for under the circumstances: it was another measure of political rationality. But it was also another indication of the contradictions of Chile's democratic transition. Here was a democratic president sending Chileans into exile at the very time that he was setting up a government agency to process the return of thousands of Chileans who had sought refuge abroad or had been expelled by the regime. Paradoxically, amendments made to article 41 of Pinochet's 1980 constitution in 1989 forbade exile.[36] Seemingly, under the circumstances, to send these men abroad as a condition for their release was not to exile them, but something entirely different.

Aylwin also pledged that the investigation into past abuses would continue. To carry on with the investigation Aylwin created the Corporation on

Reparation and Reconciliation. In fact, this had been one of the Truth and Reconciliation Commission's recommendations. But it would be nearly two years before this public corporation would be fully functioning. And, somewhat like the Commission on Truth and Reconciliation whose unfinished business it was to complete, its existence would be brief, by law.

The corporation got off to a slow start. The Chilean congress did not pass the law creating the Corporation for Reparation and Reconciliation until the end of January 1992, more than ten months after Aylwin's televised address to the nation announcing the findings of the Rettig Commission. Administrative requirements and bureaucratic red tape prevented the corporation from moving from an inadequate, temporary location into its office on Avenida Vicuña Mackenna in Santiago until October 1992. The corporation did not take possession the archives of the Commission on Truth and Reconciliation until mid-January 1993. The legislation creating the corporation limited its legal existence to only twenty-four months, but it was extended another year. The corporation went out of existence at the end of 1994.[37]

The corporation's most urgent tasks were to classify cases, and to find the disappeared and the executed. Beginning with the classification of cases, the corporation's responsibilities were really threefold. The corporation had to reach a "conviction" with respect to the hundreds of cases about which the commission had not reached a conclusion, it had to consider hundreds of other cases that the commission had registered but had not begun to investigate, and it had to consider new cases. All of this involved reopening the commission's case files or developing new ones, and then determining whether the evidence supported the "conviction" that an identified individual was a victim of a human rights violation, political violence, or violence committed by private individuals for political reasons. The corporation began its life with a substantial back-log of cases, and was soon buried by an avalanche of new ones. Those privy to the corporation's continuing investigation soon learned what the victims' families knew all too well — when the tallying was done, the criminality of the Pinochet regime would take on larger proportions than had been reported by the Rettig Commission.

The Corporation for Reparation and Reconciliation inherited 989 unresolved cases.[38] It registered new cases during a 90-day period ending in mid-October 1992. Another 640 new cases were added to its list of likely victims. But so many Chileans were coming forward with new denunciations that the corporation was forced to reopen registration. The following year, the corporation registered cases for another 90-day period ending in mid-June 1993. Notably, the rate of denunciations did not taper off significantly; another 562 were registered during the second phase. So, by the time the Corporation on Reparation and Reconciliation issued an interim report in March 1994, the corporation was working on 2,119 cases. Of those, 1,210 cases—a full 55 percent — were entirely new. The Commission for Truth and Reconciliation had not even known of these cases, much less reported them.[39]

The disappeared constituted a searing problem. There were two different situations, that of the arrested-disappeared who are presumed dead, and that of persons known to have been executed but whose bodies had not been returned to the families. The corporation began its investigation with a list of 978, all corresponding to cases identified by the Truth and Reconciliation Commission. By January 1994, the corporation had taken up another 140 cases, for a total of 1,118 cases of arrested-disappeared.[40] The corporation had not arrived at an exact number of known dead whose bodies had not been delivered to their families by the time of the publication of its interim report. But it was working on as many as 435 such cases; 208 already identified by the Truth and Reconciliation Commission, another 40 identified by the corporation itself, and another 187 pending further study. So, as of January 1994, the corporation found itself confronted with the grim task of finding the mortal remains of 1,553 Chileans, 1,118 detained-disappeared, and 435 known dead — with less than a year of legal existence remaining.

This grim reality prompted the congress to extend the corporation's legal existence from 24 to 36 months, both to allow it to classify victims, and to find them. But even an additional year proved inadequate. The corporation was slow in reaching "moral convictions" about the cases it had registered. The corporation ran up against the same insurmountable obstacle that impeded the commission — the conspiracy of silence of the armed forces. Both the commission and the corporation have been most successful in the cases of those killed in the very first months of the dictatorship; after that the regime's methods of repression and concealment became too "sophisticated."

There were some spectacular discoveries, but they were not always the work of the corporation. Clandestine graves were discovered even prior to the transfer of power. In 1978, the Vicariate of Solidarity discovered fifteen of the "disappeared" in an abandoned lime kiln in Lonquén. The victims had been arrested in early October 1973, during the crackdown ordered from Santiago. But the largest and most dramatic discovery was made in August 1991, a few short months after the publication of the Rettig Report and on the eve of the anniversary of the September 11 coup, when 126 bodies were found in 108 coffins in Lot 29 of Santiago's General Cemetery. The grisly fact that, in some instances, there were two bodies placed inside a single coffin caused special outrage. General Pinochet, caught off guard by a young reporter's question while leaving a meeting in the Moneda, only made matters worse. When asked if he were aware that two bodies had been buried together, Pinochet quipped callously, "que economía más grande!" roughly translated, "How very economical!"

The military protested that the revelation of the discovery was timed to sully yet again the reputation of the armed forces. Rosemarie Bordard of the Legal Department of the Vicariate of Solidarity denied that the discovery had been staged for effect. From her office in the Vicariate it is possible to see Raúl Rettig's law office on Phillips Street, across the Plaza de Armas in Santiago. The Vicariate was in the processing of closing down operations when she consented to an interview about the discovery and the Rettig Report.[41] It was mere coincidence, she asserted a few weeks after the gruesome discovery, that the discovery of the truth about Lot 29 came so close to the anniversary of the coup. The fact was that the rare discovery was the result of the Vicariate's meticulous work. The Vicariate had been able to correlate reports of disappearances, for the most part dating to the first months after the coup, to hospital records and to burial registries. Most of the graves bore the inscription NN, ningún nombre, "No Name." The victims had disappeared between September and December 1993, further attesting to the sad fact that the remains of the regime's earliest victims would be the easiest to discover.

The corporation's interim report is remarkably frank about the limited time afforded it, especially with regard to the fact that the corporation was also created to implement the dozens of constructive recommendations for reform carefully drawn up by the Truth and Reconciliation Commission. "The scope of the recommendations," said the preliminary report of an entity whose time was quickly running out, "exceeds the human and material resources [of the corporation], and many of them, by their very nature, require a time to develop that obviously goes beyond the legal duration of its existence."[42] Members of the Rettig Commission, cognizant of the commission's limitations, had expressed confidence in the corporation, and even saw its existence as a vindication of their own work and their fidelity to a restrictive mandate. Raúl Rettig repeatedly mentioned the corporation in the context of what the commission was unable to accomplish. "We established the official truth. And that resulted in the enactment of a law creating the [corporation] that is presently studying the cases we gave it, and studying the indemnization of the families, primarily those of the disappeared, on the merits of the case which we established." Jaime Castillo was likewise confident. "At least the commission left the field open for the Corporation for Reconciliation that is functioning now," he said, taking some consolation in the fact. "They investigated a great deal and are conducting a lot of inquiries about the disappeared, and they have found quite a few. Andrés Domínguez, who works there, has told me that they have done pretty well and that there are going to be plenty of revelations. This would be also a follow-up of, a continuation, of the work of the Commission, let's say a consequence of it."

Some who worked at the corporation were less sanguine. One of them, Fernando Escobar, was an assistant to Andrés Domínguez, the executive secretary of the Corporation for Reparation and Reconciliation. With a few short months remaining, Escobar left a different impression from the one Andrés Domínguez evidently gave Jaime Castillo. He expressed great concern about the corporation's limitations and the possible consequences of its passing out of existence.[43]

For one thing, the corporation lacked the resources to conduct a thorough investigation, especially outside metropolitan Santiago. "It is extraordinarily difficult for us to investigate what happened in the regions," Escobar explained. Even travel to and in the regions was problematic. "According to the law that created the corporation, the provincial governments should help us, so when we go to investigate cases in the regions what we do is ask everyone we can if they will help us. In practice what happens is that the Ministry of Government will normally provide us a vehicle, and sometimes the Investigations Police will also lend us a vehicle and help us with logistics. Then, too, there is what I call the remnant of the human rights movement. In other words, what was once the active human rights movement in the country, where it still exists, it helps us. People who live in the regions who are disposed to collaborate with us in this work help us, but they do not have great capabilities."

"It is strange that you would have to request help from them when you ought to be helping them."

"Yes it's strange, but that is precisely it. That is the reality."

When the discussion turned to the great number of pending cases and the many disappeared who remain unaccounted for, Escobar focused on politics.

"How can the Corporation go out of existence if the mission is to find the bodies and there are still so many?"

"That is the question that undoubtedly worries us too. What can be hoped is that before the Corporation is terminated, the board of directors will have to tell the president, 'Look, we have not progressed very far and somebody has to continue this work'." But hopes often turn on political realities, and Escobar quickly noted that "the Corporation is administered by a politically diverse board of directors, it has people from the Chilean right."

Escobar, like many involved in human rights, hoped that Aylwin would be successful in enacting legislation creating a human rights ombudsman, but that initiative died in congress. He was concerned about the consequences of that. "The concern is that once the Corporation is closed, the only state entity that is concerned with human rights is closed. The rule of law is imperfect in Chile, it has all the limitations you know about, so the possibility of human rights violations is latent. In that sense, the question becomes, 'How much more likely is that possibility once the only body of this kind disappears?' "

The Corporation for Reparation and Reconciliation quietly went out of existence on the last day of 1994. At the beginning of December, at the closure of the Summit of the Americas in Miami, Chile had been invited to join the North American Free Trade Agreement with considerably more fanfare. The Chilean government, now led by Aylwin's successor, fellow

Christian Democrat Eduardo Frei, would focus on Chile's bright economic future rather than on its dark authoritarian past.

For the families of the disappeared, ignoring the past is not an option. The spouses and children of the disappeared, who are collectively the Association of the Families of the Detained-Disappeared, work out of a cramped and drafty building on the grounds of FASIC, the Foundation for Social Assistance of Christian Churches. It is located on Manuel Rodríguez Street, just a few blocks from the Moneda palace. The walls are covered with some of the association's many posters. One reads: "A country that does not close the wounds of the past has neither a present nor a future." Another shows the photos of members of the junta, the director of the DINA, judges of the Supreme Court of Justice, and some of the disappeared. "The Guilty, the Accomplices, the Victims" is how it reads. Sola Sierra, the Association's soft-spoken but hard-driven president, speaks poignantly about the victims, and reproachfully of the others.

She speaks most poignantly about her husband, Waldo Pizarro Molina. Sola Sierra's husband was one of the thirteen high-ranking Communist party leaders, who according to the Rettig Commission were arrested and disappeared by the Joint Command at the end of 1976. Seven of the thirteen, including Waldo Pizarro Molina, were disappeared on December 15, 1976.[44] "From the very day of the coup, they began to look for him, but as we always knew that we hadn't done anything wrong, we did not hide, and we didn't leave the country together as a family because we always told ourselves we don't have anything to fear. Having an ideology, belonging to a party, being Catholic, being protestant — that is not a crime anywhere in the world. But in Chile, during the military regime, yes, it was a crime, and they arrested him on 15 December, 1976." Sola Sierra went to the place where he was abducted the night before, carrying a photo of her husband. Someone in a nearby bakery described to her how two men had been arrested, how hoods were forced over their heads, and how one of them was struck in the head with the butt of a machine gun. The next day, she said, "the blood was still there as proof of how brutally they acted, I even saw the blood myself, the black stain from the day before."

So, what was the reaction to the Rettig Report of this woman, whose life had become a search for the missing, the truth, and justice? "We are dissatisfied" she said frankly, "because most of 'the truth' contained in the Report is a truth that — during all these years, ever since they started arresting people, ever since we have been an organization — we have been denouncing." That said, her assessment was unambiguous: "the Rettig Commission did not even manage to establish what happened to the Arrested-Disappeared, much less to do justice." Her complaints about the report are that simple, it is a matter of knowing the complete truth, and of justice.

From her perspective, the publication of the report "in effect, made official the truth," but all that the country might have been told about the disappearances, and about who was responsible for them, based on the information brought to the commission by the families, was never revealed. "This was the commission's little secret," she said "because when the commission was created, it was stipulated that the identities of people who appeared involved in the human rights violations would not be made public." Because the commission did not possess the power to subpoena, the testimony of soldiers was voluntary. "Those who all these years have denied their responsibility for the arrest and disappearances of members of our families managed to keep the secret—no, actually, they managed to preserve their impunity." This was intolerable to her. "Not being obliged to testify actually gave them impunity, and they did not deliver any information." She lamented the consequences of the Rettig Commission's restricted powers. "The Report did not help us very much with respect to the clarification of the fate suffered by our family members, and to this day, we are in the same situation as before."

The commission could not publicly identify the guilty, but could forward the information it obtained or developed to the courts of law for action. This did not satisfy Sola Sierra either. "Insofar as the possibility of justice is concerned," she commented, "the commission did not help us either, because it did not even have investigative authority. So it was limited to forwarding information to the courts. Sometimes that helped to reopen cases, but in the vast majority of cases in which information was forwarded to the courts, the cases were opened through the efforts of the families together with their lawyers, the Vicariate of Solidarity, FASIC and CODEPU."

She expressed still more serious concerns. One related to the number of disappeared persons published by the Commission on Truth and Reconciliation and taken up by its successor, the Corporation for Reparation and Reconciliation. "The Rettig Commission says that there were less than three thousand. Of the five thousand we are speaking about, the Corporation for Truth and Reconciliation has two thousand of them, but it has not reached a conviction in those two thousand cases because it does not want to publish a new report that could increase the number of human rights victims of the past." The politics of human rights had now become the politics of counting. Sola Sierra's figures far exceed even those released by the corporation. "There are tremendous discrepancies in the work of the corporation in classifying new cases," she said. "There are situations in which two people were arrested by the same unit, on the same day, in the same place, but the Corporation does not classify them as human rights violations, or as disappearances. It simply says that there are cases where there are no facts that prove them to be violations."

Another concern was that the publication of the Rettig Report had the unfortunate effect of creating the impression among Chileans that the country's human rights problem was solved. The very fact that the commission published a conservative figure of the disappeared was partly to blame.

"Would you say, then, that it would have been better if there had been no Commission at all, because this Commission published a report and created the impression that the problem of human rights is a thing of the past?"

Yes. In that sense it has made us worse off in our struggle because as a result of the report everybody believes that everything is solved. The [report] was important because the country, which did not know about the human rights violations, became conscious of the fact that human rights were violated in the past. But because there were not any proposals to solve the problem, and it was thought that the commission, together with the families, had the problem [of the disappeared] resolved, as a practical matter, everyone thinks that the problem is solved — everybody, international organizations, international human rights agencies, even human rights organizations in our own country. And, what makes things worse, is that both the government of Aylwin and now the government of Frei consider the situation overcome. As a consequence, for us, especially the families of the detained-disappeared, we still do not know the destiny in nearly all the cases. And we have not seen justice done. Not a single human rights violator who participated in disappearances has been sentenced.

The torment is great. The human rights organizations that emerged during the dictatorship learned a great deal about the physical harm done by repression, and they are just beginning to learn about the psychological destruction. Studies have been made of "the culture of fear" created by the Southern Cone military regimes. Activists like Elizabeth Lira, formerly of FASIC, have documented the profound, mysterious psychological harm extensively.[45] Clinical experience has left deep impressions on Lira and on her colleagues about the complex psychological effects of the many techniques of repression practiced by the regime: house search, arrests, torture, disappearances, executions, exile.

Sola Sierra explains with sadness and concern that many of the survivors are tormented to death by a disappearance. "In recent years we have been able to prove that almost 300 relatives who have been active in the Association have been dying from different, unknown illnesses and all the grief and sense of impotence that they have been living with." More alarming are the inexplicable effects on many of the children of the disappeared.

Our children appeared to be overcoming the problem, they managed to study and they contributed to society. But they come to the stage of their life between twenty-five and thirty years old, that just now we are becoming aware of. A depression comes on them, some psychological disorder. We have nearly twenty cases of irrecoverable schizophrenia in children of the disappeared. The doctors cannot explain it. Some of them had managed to start homes, they were working well, and all of a sudden they suffer some crisis as a result of this abnormal situation they have been living, a crisis that causes them a psychological disturbance so great that they become schizophrenic, and many of them are institutionalized and many others are about to be institutionalized.

The official response of the Association of the Families of the Detained-Disappeared to the Report of the National Commission on Truth and Reconciliation was released in November 1990. Nearly eight months had elapsed since President Aylwin personally handed Sola Sierra a copy of the sad report before appearing on television. The association's response was eloquent and powerful. The United Nations Rapporteur on Enforced and Involuntary Disappearances could not have made a more cogent case for the designation of disappearances as a crime against humanity. "The forced disappearance of persons is an opprobrious technique, which is, in itself, an assault on each and every one of the rights of the person. In this inhuman process, the rights harmed are, first of all, those of the detained-disappeared person; then ours, their families, and then those of all Chileans who must live permanently with the insecurity that this might happen again."[46] The association left no doubt that it would not rest until the fate and whereabouts of the disappeared was disclosed. Aylwin's dilemma vis-à-vis both the familes of the victims and the armed forces remained.

Aylwin did offer a proposal to resolve the problem, a proposal quickly dubbed "la ley Aylwin." The phrase was a misnomer because the Aylwin Law was never enacted. The Aylwin Law was a serious proposal that offered the military everything a penitent could hope for: a means to confess in anonymity and without fear of punishment. But the armed forces were not inclined toward penitence. Aylwin proposed to assign as many as fifteen special investigating judges (*ministros en visita*) to the cases of the missing. The Supreme Court would provide the president with the list of candidates. The judges would hear the testimony of armed forces officers, soldiers, and carabineros in absolute confidentiality, outside the court room if necessary, in order to ascertain detailed information about the fate and whereabouts of the more than one thousand Chileans who had vanished into the night and fog. Although those who were responsible for the disappearances, even as accessories, would be shielded from prosecution, any officer of the court who leaked the confidential statements of the penitents would be subject to sanctions including imprisonment.[47] Aylwin had the unwavering support of his Christian Democratic Party and the Catholic Church, but that is all. The military did not see any advantage in cooperating; the right was largely unsympathetic to the plight of the families; the left could not make yet another concession on an issue dear to it; and, most pertinently, the families of the disappeared could not be fooled into believing that yet another grant of immunity would convince criminals to admit the truth.[48]

Justice to the Extent Possible

On November 12, 1993, Judge Adolfo Bañados sentenced General Manuel Contreras, the once powerful director of the Directorate for National Intelligence, to seven years in prison for his complicity in the assassination of Orlando Letelier and Ronnie Moffitt in Washington, D.C., in September 1976. Contreras's subordinate and chief of operations, Brigadier Pedro Espinoza was given a sentence of six years. It was twenty years, nearly to the week, after then-Colonel Contreras briefed General Augusto Pinochet and the other members of the newly installed junta on his plans for a new intelligence agency, the DINA.

This long and arduous legal — and political — process began in March of 1978, when the Chilean Supreme Court appointed a special investigating judge to look into a perplexing case involving the issuance of false passports to Michael Townley, the man who fabricated and planted the bomb that killed Letelier and Moffitt. The man the Chilean high court appointed, Marcos Libedinsky, was one of the few Chilean judges known for his independence in politically charged cases. Libedinsky's investigation uncovered evidence that led from Townley to Espinoza and finally all the way to Contreras, although apparently not to Pinochet himself. Because the murders were committed in Washington, D.C., the 1978 amnesty law decreed by the junta did not extend to Contreras and Espinoza. So, if pursued, the case was certain to have serious political repercussions.

For that very reason, nothing came of the case until after the democratic transition. The Letelier crime had been a constant irritant in U.S.-Chilean relations, but Contreras was too powerful, knew too much, and was too close to Pinochet. "I believe in Contreras," Pinochet told reporters as the case reached its final stages, "I have always believed in Contreras."[49] In July 1991, some months after the publication of the Rettig Report, Patricio Aylwin petitioned the Supreme Court to name another judge to try Contreras and Espinoza for the Letelier crime. The Court assigned Adolfo Bañados to the case, another judge known for his courage.

Bañados eventually pronounced guilt on the engineers of the repression, but that did not end the matter. Chileans now lived in democracy, and Contreras and Espinoza had the right to appeal. The process took months. Then, at the end of May 1994, the Fourth Chamber of the Supreme Court of Justice upheld the conviction and the sentence. It seemed that "Mamo," as Contreras is called, would finally be held accountable for his crimes. But Contreras engineered his own disappearance, and plunged the country into the most serious crisis in civil-military relations since the return of democracy. In an operation that involved intelligence units from two of the army's most important divisions, Contreras disappeared from his ranch far to the south of Santiago. Even the highest ranking cabinet ministers acknowledged that Contreras' actions had taken them by surprise, and that for some hours at least, they had no knowledge of his whereabouts. Contreras reappeared in the naval hospital at the sprawling naval base in Talcahuano, near Concepción. Contreras had defiantly refused to accept the courts' judgment against him, and defiantly refused to go to jail.

The episode prompted a series of high-level meetings within the army high command, and between the army and the Aylwin government. Among those involved in the army's deliberations was Brigadier Miguel Krasnoff

Marchenko, who had served loyally under Contreras in the DINA. Indeed, Krasnoff, who was by then attached to the General Staff, had commanded the DINA's ruthless Halcón Brigade that had effectively decimated the MIR during the darkest phase of the repression. The crisis surrounding Contreras's refusal to surrender himself to authorities highlighted the tenuousness of civilian control of the armed forces. The fact that men like Krasnoff remained on active duty and had been promoted up the chain of command highlighted the awful reality of impunity.

But Contreras, who had been forced into retirement soon after Pinochet disbanded the DINA in 1977, was by now expendable. After tense deliberations the army announced publicly that it would respect the courts' ruling, even though this disturbed many in the service who had served under Contreras and who frankly believed he had done no wrong. Pinochet himself told a reporter that Contreras had been unjustly treated. "Contreras was subjected to an *ad hoc* tribunal, similar to the Nuremberg tribunal, for political reasons," he said.[50] Pinochet, whose comments so often had the opposite effect to that he intended, had inadvertently struck upon the truth again. Contreras was directly responsible for the campaign to "disappear" Chileans, like the one hundred and twenty-six missing Chileans found in Lot 29 of Santiago's General Cemetery in August 1991. So the reference to Nuremburg had a particular—if unintended—relevance. The Nuremburg Tribunal condemned German Field Marshal Wilhelm Keitel to death for issuing the "Nacht und Nabel" order, the command to disappear French partisans into the night and fog. Now, Contreras was finally convicted of a crime committed in an invented war.

The conviction of Contreras and Espinoza, who eventually surrendered themselves for confinement in military facilities, was symbolic. But it did not remotely satisfy the demands of justice. These men are guilty of far more crimes than the assassination of Letelier and Moffitt. Incredibly, Contreras, the engineer of disappearances in Chile, was never even charged in a case involving a disappeared person. This was the extent of possible justice in Chile. Nor did the conviction accomplish anything in the way of the recovery of the truth. Sola Sierra expresses the matter poignantly. "Those who all these years have denied their responsibility for the arrest and disappearances of members of our families managed to keep the secret—no, actually, they managed to preserve their impunity."

The Politics of Human Rights

The generals who seized power on September 11, 1973 were on a mission to transform Chile. In the junta's very public appearance on the evening of the eleventh, air force commander Gustavo Leigh's explained that the transformation of Chile would involve, first and foremost, the extirpation of Marxism. From that moment on, repression became policy. When Pinochet ceded power to Patricio Aylwin seventeen years later, he could confidently boast "mission completed."

The regime over which Augusto Pinochet presided was inherently repressive. The Chilean state was militarized, the courts were marginalized, and the armed forces and the DINA committed human rights violations in a massive and systematic manner. State terrorism became policy, and the regime amassed victims.

The politics of transition were inevitably dominated by the terrible legacy of the repression. Politics and human rights were inextricably intertwined. The democratic government could not ignore the moral imperative to confront the truth about the horrors of past, but neither could it risk precipitating a crisis with the military that would imperil the transition. President Aylwin's dilemma vis-à-vis the families of the victims—who were victims themselves—and the guardians of the old order could not have been more acute. The president and his advisors searched for a viable human rights policy, cognizant of the stark political realities of a negotiated transition. "Justice to the extent possible" summarized the policy, and captured the political reality that determined it.

The categorical rejection of the Report of the National Commission on Truth and Reconciliation by the armed forces and Carabineros and the Supreme Court of Justice sent an ominous signal to a democratic government and a traumatized society. Two of the country's most important institutions had dismissed an honest effort to recover the truth, emptying the celebrated phrase "Never Again" of its potency. The armed forces and Carabineros proclaimed that they had no reason to seek pardon. The Supreme Court of Justice refused to apologize for its failure to protect Chileans from violations of their most basic rights.

Human rights organizations in Chile and abroad were understandably dismayed that justice was not possible to any significant extent. The National Commission on Truth and Reconciliation could neither name the culpable nor find the disappeared. The prosecution of Contreras and Espinoza ironically served as a bitter reminder that everyone else involved in the repression escaped punishment. The members of Association of Families of the Detained-Disappeared were the most deeply aggrieved. But the voices of Sola Sierra and the other grieving widows, widowers, sons, and daughters would inevitably fade from political discourse as time passed. Their efforts to remind the rest of Chilean society that a terrible injustice had gone unpunished would become increasingly futile.

The question for students of Chile's democratic transition—and by extrapolation all democratic transitions—goes directly to Patricio Aylwin's good faith effort to reconcile the virtue of truth with the virtue of prudence: should the transitional government have risked more? The politics of democratic transition is fraught with dangerous risks: the risk of sacrificing justice at the expense of the rule of law, and the risk of imperiling a transition with terrible consequences for human rights. The politics of democratic transition and the politics of human rights are inseparable.

Shortly after the transition, General Pinochet commented that "the moment they touch one of my boys, the rule of law is over."[51] For those averse to the risk of imperiling the transition, this threat was more than enough to act with all due caution. They will remind their critics that the general had staged two dramatic shows of force in the years after the transition. For those averse to sacrificing justice, Pinochet's threats were empty. They will recall that Pinochet did nothing to forestall Contreras's encarceration.

In August 1991, the world was transfixed by Boris Yeltsin's courage, as he climbed upon a tank and faced down soldiers staging a coup against Mikhail Gorbachev's reformist government. The international community repudiated the action of the old Soviet hardliners, and the coup failed. The episode sparked conversations on the campus of the University of Concepción, the birthplace of the disappeared MIR. Did the international repudiation of the Soviet coup-plotters, and world leaders' vocal suport of Yeltsin, indicate that it might be possible to arrest Pinochet and face down a coup attempt in Chile? Those who suggested that it might be possible never spoke above a whisper. The consensus on the campus was that such a thing was too dangerous even to contemplate.

After retiring from active duty in 1998, General Augusto Pinochet became senator for life, as allowed by his 1980 "constitution of liberty." Nearly two thousand Chileans were "disappeared" into the night and fog during General Pinochet's uprecedented tenure as president. As senator, Pinochet continues to have a voice in national politics. Sola Sierra continues the search for her husband, Waldo Pizzaro, and the other disappeared from the drafty office of the Association of the Families of the Detained-Disappeared. Her voice has been muted.

Notes

Chapter 1

1. See generally Paul E. Sigmund, *The Overthrow of Allende and the Politics of Chile, 1964–1976* (Pittsburgh: University of Pittsburgh Press, 1977); Lois Hecht Oppenheim, *Politics in Chile: Democracy, Authoritarianism and the Search for Development* (Boulder, Colo.: Westview Press, 1993); Nathaniel Davis, *The Last Two Years of Salvador Allende* (Ithaca, N.Y.: Cornell University Press, 1985); Arturo Valenzuela, *The Breakdown of Democratic Regimes: Chile* (Baltimore: Johns Hopkins University Press, 1978).

2. International Commission of Jurists, *Chile: A Time of Reckoning, Human Rights, and the Judiciary* (Geneva: ICJ, 1992), 77.

3. Sigmund, *The Overthrow of Allende*, 223–25.

4. The president had done this the previous year after the October *paro*, but named a civilian cabinet after the March elections.

5. Sigmund, *The Overthrow of Allende*, 233.

6. Eugenio Ahumada et al., *Chile: la memoria prohibida*, 3 vols. (Santiago: Pehuén, 1989), 1: 95.

7. Ibid., 100.

8. Ibid., 111.

9. Ibid., 179–82. In attendance were members of the junta, and former presidents Videla, Alessandri and Frei. Frei had to be convinced to attend, and made the public gesture of not shaking the hands of the junta members.

10. Ibid., 182.

11. Oppenheim, *Politics in Chile*, 40.

12. Kenneth Roberts, "Renovation in the Revolution? Democracy, and Political Change in the Chilean Left," Kellogg Institute for International Studies Working Paper 203 (Notre Dame, Ind., March 1994), 22.

13. Ibid., 22.

14. Allende backed Altamirano in an effort to control the party's left wing. Valenzuela, *The Breakdown of Democratic Regimes*, 119 n.36.

15. Carmelo Furci, *The Chilean Communist Party and the Road to Socialism* (London: Zed Books, 1984), 109, 111.

16. Roberts, "Renovation in the Revolution," 29 n.61.

17. Furci, *The Chilean Communist Party*, 107.

18. Allende had also headed those coalitions, known as the Popular Action Front or FRAP.

19. Furci, *The Chilean Communist Party*, 110.

20. Oppenheim, *Politics in Chile*, 78.

21. Roberts, "Renovation in the Revolution," 8.

22. Jorge Castañeda, *Utopia Unarmed: The Latin American Left After the Cold War* (New York: Alfred Knopf, 1993).

23. *Rebelde* 28 (September 1964): 4. The remark is a distortion of the Chilean national motto "By reason or by force."

24. The material on the MIR is from Michel Lowy, *El Marxismo en América latina: antologia desde 1900 hasta nuestros dias* (Mexico City: Ediciones Era, 1980); Carlos Sandoval Ambiado, *MIR: una historia*, vol. 1 (Santiago: Sociedad Editorial Trabajadores, 1990); León Gómez Araneda, *Tras la huella de los desaparecidos* (Santiago: Ediciones Caleuche, 1990).

25. Sandoval, *MIR: una historia*, 1: 131–32.

26. Furci, *The Chilean Communist Party*, 99.

27. Davis, *The Last Two Years of Salvador Allende*, 185.

28. Furci argues that the MIR "was originally founded as an underground organization." *The Chilean Communist Party*, 99. Others suggest that the MIR went underground only in 1967, midway through President Eduardo Frei's term in office. At any rate, the MIR remained underground until Allende took power.

29. The MIR was composed of the Revolutionary Workers Front (FTR), the Revolutionary Student Front (FER), the Movement of Revolutionary Peasants (MCR), and the Movement of Revolutionary Shanty-Town Dwellers (MPR). It also set out to create a "Central Force."

30. José Del Pozo, *Rebeldes, reformistas y revolucionarios: una historia oral de la izquierda chilena en la epoca de la Unidad Popular* (Santiago: Ediciones Documentas, 1992), 113.

31. Ibid., 127.

32. Ibid., 113 n.19.

33. Sandoval, *MIR: una historia*, 46.

34. *Punto final* 99 (March 3, 1970): 5.

35. Sandoval, *MIR: una historia*, 135.

36. Ibid., 52.

37. Grupo de Amigos del Presidente. The group's actual name was the Depositivo de Seguridad Presidencial. Not all were MIRistas; others were recruited from the Socialist Party's armed Elmo Catalán Brigades. See Gómez Araneda, *Tras la huella de los desaparecidos*, 52; and Davis, *The Last Two Years of Salvador Allende*, 88.

38. Interview with Nelson Gutierrez, one of the few surviving members of the MIR's Political Commission, in the documentary *El Once veinte años después*.

39. Davis, *The Last Two Years of Salvador Allende*, 185.

40. Brian Loveman, "The Transformation of the Chilean Countryside," in Arturo Valenzuela, and J. Samuel Valenzuela, eds., *Chile: Politics and Society* (New Brunswick, N.J.: Transaction Books, 1976), 264.

41. Ibid., 256.

42. After Chile's democratic transition in 1990, President Patricio Aywlin established a presidential commission of inquiry, the National Commission on Truth and Reconciliation. The work of the commission is described in chapters 8 and 9.

43. The reference is to a title of one of Che Guevara's books.

44. See generally, Sigmund, *The Overthrow of Allende*; Sigmund, "The 'Invisible Blockade' and the Overthrow of Allende," *Foreign Affairs* 52, 2 (January 1974): 322–40; Sigmund, "Less Than Charged," *Foreign Policy* 16 (Fall 1974): 142–56; Elizabeth Farnworth, "More Than Admitted," *Foreign Policy* 16 (Fall 1974), 127–41. The official U.S. investigation is contained in U.S. Senate, *Covert Action in Chile, 1963–1973* (Washington, D.C.: U.S. Government Printing Office, 1975).

45. Schneider was succeeded by another constitutionalist, General Carlos Prats, who would also be assassinated the year following the coup.

46. Brian Loveman, *Chile: The Legacy of Hispanic Capitalism*, 2nd ed. (New York: Oxford University Press, 1988), 275.

47. Ibid., 276.

48. Furci, *The Chilean Communist Party*, 118.

49. Davis, *The Last Two Years of Salvador Allende*, 15. Valenzuela, *The Breakdown of Democratic Regimes*, 49.

50. Renán Fuentealba, one of the drafters of the Statute of Guarantees, became president of the PDC. Fuentealba was among the first to charge publicly that Allende had violated it as early as September 1971. Valenzuela, *The Breakdown of Democratic Regimes*, 73.

51. The murder was committed by the Organized Vanguard of the People (VOP), a breakaway group from the MIR. Davis, *The Last Two Years of Salvador Allende*, 20. Pérez, Frei's Interior Minister in 1969, had ordered carabineros to dislodge squatters from a settlement in Puerto Montt. Seven were killed, scores injured. Sigmund, *The Overthrow of Salvador Allende*, 77.

52. "As we had imagined, the initial triumph that made Chileans so happy was considered by the leaders of the Christian Democratic Party as an opportunity to regain power and to place the president of the Senate, don Eduardo Frei, at the head of the government." Augusto Pinochet, *Camino recorrido: memorias de un soldado*, 2 vols. (Santiago: Instituto Geográfico Militar de Chile, 1991), 2: 23, 26.

53. Pamela Constable and Arturo Valenzuela, *A Nation of Enemies: Chile Under Pinochet* (New York: Norton, 1991), 282.

54. Guillermo Campero, "Entrepreneurs Under the Military Regime," in Paul W. Drake and Iván Jaksić, eds., *The Struggle for Democracy in Chile, 1982–1990* (Lincoln: University of Nebraska Press, 1991), 128–58.

55. Davis, *The Last Two Years of Salvador Allende*, 151. The president of the CPC was Jorge Fontaine Adulante. His brother Arturo was assistant director of *El Mercurio*, Santiago's largest and most influential daily newspaper. *El Mercurio* was a vocal opponent of Allende. The U.S. Senate investigation revealed that the paper had received substantial sums of money from the CIA, some paid directly to Augustín Edwards, the publisher.

56. Campero, "Entrepreneurs Under the Military Regime," 131–32.

57. Constable and Valenzuela, *A Nation of Enemies*, 37.

58. Constable and Valenzuela (*A Nation of Enemies*, chap. 2) provide an excellent discussion of the social isolation of soldiers.

59. "Respuestos de las fuerzas armadas y de orden al informe de la Comisión Nacional de Verdad y Reconciliación," *Estudios Públicos* 38 (Autumn 1990): 450.

60. Total expenditures increased by 32 percent between 1973 and 1974 alone. Augusto Varas, *Los militares en el poder: régimen y gobierno militar en Chile, 1973–1986* (Santiago: FLASCO, 1987), especially chapter 4.

61. Augusto Varas, "The Crisis of Legitimacy of Military Rule in the 1980s," in Drake and Jaksić, eds., *The Struggle for Democracy in Chile*, 73–97.

Chapter 2

1. Pinochet, *Camino recorrido*, 28, 108. Each volume carries an appendix entitled "Irregular War," with an annual summary of the threat confronted by the armed forces.

2. "Very soon after September 11, 1973 the armed forces and police accomplished their most immediate objective, to bring the country under their control and to eliminate any pockets of armed resistance on the part of supporters of the deposed regime. Such resistance actions can truly be said to have been minimal." *Report of the*

Chilean National Commission on Truth and Reconciliation (Notre Dame, Ind.: University of Notre Dame Press, 1993), 1: 129. Former U.S. ambassador Nathaniel Davis described the fighting as "one-sided military operations." *The Last Two Years of Salvador Allende*, 235–36.

3. Pinochet refers to the radio communications in his book *El Dia decisivo: 11 de septiembre de 1973*, 5th ed. (Santiago: Andrés Bello, 1984), in a chapter entitled "La Batalla de Santiago." Excerpts translated and reproduced here are from Eugenio Ahumada et al., *Chile: la memoria prohibida*, 3, 1: chaps. 5 and 6.

4. Pinochet's version of this exchange differs in that the adjective "mugrientos" (filthy or scummy) is replaced by "marxistas" in describing Tohá, Almeyda, and the others. Compare Pinochet, *El Dia decisivo*, 139 and Ahumada et al., *Memoria prohibida*, 118.

5. John Dinges and Saul Landau, *Assassination on Embassy Row* (New York: Pantheon, 1980), 154.

6. *Report of the Chilean National Commission*, 1: 155–56.

7. The junta claimed that the "bombing of the Moneda would save lives," according to Davis, *The Last Two Years of Salvador Allende*, 369. Pinochet after the June 29 Tancazo reportedly said that "when the army comes out, it is to kill." Sigmund, *The Overthrow of Allende*, 215.

8. Pinochet, *El Dia decisivo*, 71.

9. Pinochet was most concerned about armed resistance in Calama and Antofagasta, in the north, and in Talca and Valdivia, in the south. He admitted later that leftist groups "did not constitute a serious threat in those moments." *El Dia decisivo*, 141. In October he would send a delegation to each of those cities to execute leftists.

10. Davis, *The Last Two Years of Salvador Allende*, 233.

11. Ahumada et al., *Chile: la memoria prohibida*, 162. Davis, *The Last Two Years of Salvador Allende*, 272. The military and police suffered casualties on the campus.

12. Pinochet commented that "we did not receive from the industrial belts any of the reactions we feared," and that after a few days the "hard work of cleaning-up began." *El Dia decisivo*, 145.

13. The following paragraphs are based on *Report of the Chilean National Commission*, 1: 193, 158–99, 902 (Table 6).

14. Interview with the author, Santiago, June 1993. Maira was considered by the secret police to be one of five "principal agitators" whom the regime would have to silence. The most dangerous of the five, Orlando Letelier, was assassinated in Washington in September 1976. See Manuel Salazar, *Contreras: historia de un intocable* (Santiago: Grijalbo, 1995), 127.

15. Amnesty International, *Chile: An Amnesty International Report* (London: Amnesty International Publications, September 1974), 67–8.

16. Ibid., 16. That figure does not include brief (24-hour) detentions.

17. Ibid., 24.

18. Ibid., 25.

19. Gómez lists ten criteria: ideological preparation, level of leadership responsibilities, military instruction, special war courses, guerrilla training, degree of participation in the Popular Unity government, degree of participation in everyday political activities, attempts to resist arrest, degree of cooperation during interrogation, degree of future dangerousness. He does not cite a source. León Gómez Araneda, *Tras la huella de los desaparecidos*, 212.

20. Geneva Convention (I) for the Amelioration of the Condition of the Wounded and Sick in Armed Forces in the Field, article 17: Parties to the Convention "shall further ensure that the dead are honourably interred," and that graves be marked "so that they may always be found." Geneva Convention (III) Relative to the Treatment of Prisoners of War (1949), article 120: "The burial or cremation of a prisoner

of war shall be preceded by a medical examination of a body with a view to confirming death and enabling a report to be made and, where necessary, establishing identity." Geneva Convention (IV) Relative to the Protection of Civilian Persons in Time of War (1949), article 16: "As far as military considerations allow, each Party to the conflict shall facilitate the steps taken to search for the killed and wounded." Michael W. Reisman and Chris T. Antoniou, eds., *The Laws of War: A Comprehensive Collection of Primary Documents on International Laws Governing Armed Conflict* (New York: Vintage, 1994), 169, 213, 236.

21. The following paragraphs are based on the *Report of the Chilean National Commission*, 1: 164–69.

22. Ibid., 430–31.

23. Amnesty International, *Chile: An Amnesty International Report*, 19.

24. In January 1974 the ICRC began to provide meals, clothing, and medicine to 3,000 families (estimated at between 12,000 and 15,000 persons). Inter-American Commission on Human Rights, "Report on the Status of Human Rights in Chile: Findings of the 'On-the-Spot' Observations in the Republic of Chile, July 22–August 2, 1974" OEA/Ser.L/V/II.34 doc. 21 corr. 1 (25 October 1974), 67–8.

25. Amnesty International, *Chile: An Amnesty International Report*, 17, 50.

26. Ibid., 66.

27. The following paragraphs are based on the *Report of the Chilean National Commission*, 1: 238–49.

28. The following paragraphs are based on the *Report of the Chilean National Commission*, 1: 342–47, 460.

29. Davis, *The Last Two Years of Salvador Allende*, 156, 203.

30. Information in the following paragraphs is based on Patricia Verdugo, *Los Zarpazos del puma* (Santiago: Ediciones CESOC, 1989); Eugenio Ahumada et al., *Chile: la memoria prohibida* (1989), and *Report of the Chilean National Commission*, 1: 143ff, 258ff.

31. Verdugo mistakenly reported the date as 30 October, but subsequently indicates that the arrival date was 30 September, as do other sources. *Los Zarpazos del puma*, 26.

32. Constable and Valenzuela, *A Nation of Enemies: Chile Under Pinochet*, 15.

33. If the executions in Cauquenes are counted, the final toll rises to 72.

34. Verdugo, *Los Zarpazos del puma*, 136; *Report of the Chilean National Commission*, 1: 303.

35. Verdugo, *Los Zarpazos del puma*, pp. 175–6.

36. Arellano Stark's son, Sergio Arellano Iturriaga, has consistently stated that his father was not aware of the acts committed by members of his entourage on their own authority. Constable and Valenzuela, *A Nation of Enemies*, 38.

37. Salazar, *Contreras: historia de un intocable*, 124.

38. Amnesty International, *Chile: An Amnesty International Report*, 13–14.

39. Thomas Hauser, *Missing: The Execution of Charles Horman* (New York: Simon and Schuster, 1978), 96.

40. Dinges and Landau, *Assassination on Embassy Row*, 70–71.

41. Davis, *The Last Two Years of Salvador Allende*, 368–69.

42. Amnesty International, *Chile: An Amnesty International Report*, 31.

43. *Report of the Chilean National Commission*, 2: appendix II, 903. Amnesty International's estimate of "more than 2,000" came closest to the mark.

Chapter 3

1. Davis, *The Last Two Years of Salvador Allende*, 228.

2. Ibid., 195.

3. Pinochet, *El Día decisivo: 11 de Septiembre de 1973.*

4. Arturo Valenzuela, "The Military in Power," in Drake and Jaksić, eds., *The Struggle for Democracy in Chile,* 27. The remarks of the other junta members are translated from Pinochet's memoir entitled *Camino recorrido,* 2: 18–19.

5. Pinochet, *El Día decisivo,* 162.

6. "An entire network of jurisdictional, procedural and administrative subtleties and differences separates each one of these systems from the other, leaving a common element which is the predominance of special legislation over permanent and regular institutions, or the primacy of the power of the head of state over written law." Inter-American Commission on Human Rights, "Third Report on the Situation of Human Rights in Chile," OEA/Ser.L/V/II.40 (11 February 1977), 8.

7. *Report of the Chilean National Commission,* 1: 79.

8. Roberto Garretón, "Leyes secretas en Chile," *Revista Chilena de Derechos Humanos* (1st trimester 1985).

9. Pinochet, *Camino recorrido,* 27.

10. International Commission of Jurists, *Chile: A Time of Reckoning,* 81.

11. "Pocos, sumamente pocos," *APSI* 325 (October 1989): 17–19.

12. Jorge Correa, "Dealing with Past Human Rights Violations: The Chilean Case After the Dictatorship," *Notre Dame Law Review* 67 (1992), 89, 92.

13. Brian Loveman, *Chile: The Legacy of Hispanic Capitalism,* 322.

14. Arturo Valenzuela, "The Military in Power"; Varas, *Los Militares en el poder: régimen y gobierno militar en Chile 1973–1986* and Genero Arriagada, *Pinochet: The Politics of Power* (Boston: Unwin Hyman, 1988).

15. Valenzuela, "The Military in Power," 37; *Report of the Chilean National Commission,* 1: 74.

16. Arriagada, *Pinochet: The Politics of Power,* 16.

17. Ibid., 123.

18. Valenzuela, "The Military in Power," 37.

19. Ascanio Cavallo Castro et al., *La Historia oculta del regimen militar: Chile, 1973–1988* (Mexico City: Editorial DIANA, 1990), 44.

20. *Report of the Chilean National Commission,* 1: 473.

21. The biographical information is from Salazar, *Contreras: historia de un intocable,* 1995.

22. Ahumada et al., *Chile: la memoria prohibida,* 1: 390.

23. Salazar, *Contreras,* 52; Constable and Valenzuela, *A Nation of Enemies: Chile Under Pinochet,* 102.

24. Principal sources are Eugenio Ahumada et al., *Chile: la memoria prohibida,* 1: esp. chapter 16; Cavallo Castro et al., *La Historia oculta,* especially chaps. 5 and 14; María Eugenia Rojas, *La Represión política en Chile: los hechos* (Madrid: IEPALA Editorial, 1988); Gómez Araneda, *Tras la huella de los desaparecidos*; Dinges and Landau, *Assassination on Embassy Row.*

25. Davis, *The Last Two Years of Salvador Allende,* 153.

26. Constable and Valenzuela, *A Nation of Enemies,* 93.

27. Gómez (*Tras la huella,* 203–8) provides the fullest picture of the structure of the Metropolitan Brigade. Cavallo et al. (*La Historia oculta,* 50) were only able to identify Purén and Cuapolicán. María Rojas (*La Represión en Chile,* 33) designates groups by letter instead of name. Neither the human rights organizations that documented the violations of the DINA over the years, nor the National Commission on Truth and Reconciliation, provide details of the agency's structure.

28. Salazar, *Contreras,* chapters 5, 7; Keith Slack, "Operation Condor and Human Rights: A Report from Paraguay's Archive of Terror," *Human Rights Quarterly* 18, 2 (1996): 502, 505–6. Dinges and Landau discuss the U.S. connection and the assis-

tance provided to the DINA by U.S. army General Vernon Walters. *Assassination on Embassy Row*, 126.

29. Salazar, *Contreras*, chapter 5.

30. Paul E. Sigmund, *The United States and Democracy in Chile* (Baltimore: Johns Hopkins University Press, 1993), 110.

31. Patricio Orellana, "Los Organismos de derechos humanos en Chile hacia 1985," in Orellana and Elizabeth Q. Hutchison, *El Movimiento de derechos humanos en Chile, 1973–1990* (Santiago: Centro de Estudios Políticos Latinoamericanos Simón Bolívar, 1991), 7–68; and Nubia Becker and Oswaldo Torres, *Sistematización de la experiencia de defensa de los derechos humanos en Chile* (Santiago: Asociación Latino-americana para los Derechos Humanos, 1993).

32. Ahumada et al., *Chile: la memoria prohibida*, 317–19; Cavallo et al., *La Historia oculta*, 94.

33. Ahumada et al., *Chile: la memoria prohibida*, 376.

34. Gary MacEóin, ed., *Chile Under Military Rule* (New York: IDOC/North America, 1974), 126–129.

35. Cynthia Brown, *The Vicaría de la Solidaridad in Chile* (New York: Americas Watch, 1987), 8.

36. Ibid., 20.

37. Ibid., 20.

38. Jaime Esponda, "Objetivos y criterios estratégicos aplicados por la Vicaría de la Solidaridad del Arzobispado de Santiago en su tarea en defensa de los derechos humanos," in Hugo Fruhling, ed., *Represión política y defensa de los derechos humanos* (Santiago: Ediciones Chile y América, 1986), 117.

39. Author's interview with Rosemarie Bornard, Juridical Department of Vicariate, Santiago, November 1991. Vicaría de la Solidaridad, *Vicaría de la Solidaridad: Historia de su trabajo social* (Santiago: Ediciones Paulinas, 1991).

40. Hugo Fruhling, Gloria Alberti, and Felipe Portales, *Organizaciones de derechos humanos de América sur* (San José: Instituto Interamericano de Derechos Humanos, 1989), 152; Patricio Orellana, "La Lucha silenciosa por derechos humanos: el caso de FASIC," in Orellana and Hutchison, *El Movimiento de derechos humanos en Chile*, 143–98.

41. Orellana, "La Lucha silenciosa."

42. Sofia Salimovich, Elizabeth Lira, and Eugenia Weinstein, "Victims of Fear: The Social Psychology of Repression," in Juan Corradi et al., eds., *Fear at the Edge: State Terror and Resistance in Latin America* (Berkeley: University of California Press, 1992), 89.

43. Patricia Chuchryk, "Subversive Mothers: The Opposition to the Military Regime in Chile," in Marjorie Agosín, ed., *Surviving Beyond Fear: Women, Children, and Human Rights in Latin America* (Fredonia, N.H.: White Pines Press, 1993), 86–97.

44. Author's interview with Marcel Young, Chilean Human Rights Commission, Santiago, June 1993.

45. Fruhling et al., *Organizaciones de derechos humanos*, 148.

46. Eric Stover, *The Open Secret: Torture and the Medical Profession in Chile* (Washington, D.C.: American Association for the Advancement of Science, 1987), 48.

47. Fruhling et al., *Organizaciones de derechos humanos*, 141.

48. Author's interview with Miguel Urbina, Sebastian Acevedo Movement against Torture, Concepción, Chile, December 1991.

49. Constable and Valenzuela, *A Nation of Enemies*, p. 284.

50. Ibid., 120–22; Alfred Hennelly and John Langan, eds., *Human Rights in the Americas: The Struggle for Consensus* (Washington, D.C.: Georgetown University Press, 1982), 291.

51. Hernán Montealegre, "The Security of the State and Human Rights," in Hennelly and Langan, eds., *Human Rights in the Americas*, 187–210.

Chapter 4

1. *Chile hoy* 57 (July 1973): 5; Arturo Valenzuela, *The Breakdown of Democratic Regimes: Chile*, 101.

2. "La Tactica del MIR en la actual período" ("The Tactic of the MIR at the Present Moment") (mimeograph, December 19, 1973), 281.

3. Military intelligence estimates were that the MIR had 4,735 members and 8,000 weapons in 1973, half of them automatic weapons. *Camino recorrido*, 2: 230, 300. See also José del Pozo, *Rebeldes, reformistas y revolucionarios*, 113 n. 19.

4. Nathaniel Davis, *The Last Two Years of Salvador Allende*, 161; Pinochet, *El Dia decisivo*, 78.

5. "Ahora le toca a Miguel," in Cavallo Castro et al., *La Historia oculta*, 52. "Dile a Miguel que llegó su hora," Gómez Araneda *Tras la huella de los desaparecidos*, 51.

6. Gómez, *Tras la huella*, 36. The MIR secretary general was third on the list, after Carlos Altamirano and Luis Corvalán, the secretaries general of the Socialist and Communist parties respectively. Altamirano managed to flee the country; Corvalán was captured on September 27, and exchanged for a Soviet dissident in December 1976.

7. *Report of the Chilean National Commission*, 1: 232–33; Gómez, *Tras la huella*, 62–63.

8. *Report of the Chilean National Commission*, 1: 233.

9. Amnesty International, *Chile: An Amnesty International Report*, 35.

10. "Pauta del MIR para unir fuerzas dispuestas a impulsar la lucha contra la dictadura" ("The MIR's Guiding Principle to Unify Forces Disposed to Impel the Struggle against the Dictatorship"), February 17, 1974 (mimeograph).

11. "Los Golpes recientes, algunas lecciones y la reorganización de las direcciones" (The Recent Blows: Some Lessons and the Reorganization of the Directorates), June, 1974 (mimeograph).

12. Gómez, *Tras la huella*, 118; Cavallo et al., *La Historia oculta*, 57.

13. Amnesty International identified Calle Londres 38 as "an interrogation center in Santiago under FACH [Air Force of Chile] control." *Chile: An Amnesty International Report*, 61. In fact, it was the initial headquarters of DINA's Cuapolicán group.

14. The figures on the number of prisoners disappeared from Londres 38 are from the *Report of the Chilean National Commission* 2: 525–34. The estimated number of victims of the MIR given in the appendix of the report is 384. The DINA was responsible for approximately 220 of those.

15. Salazar, *Contreras*, 92; Verdugo, *Los Zarpazos del puma*, 254; Ahumada et al., *La Memoria prohibida*, 393.

16. Cavallo et al., *La Historia oculta*, 54.

17. There is evidence to connect Romo to some twenty disappearances. Romo was extradited to Chile from Brazil in late 1992, after the transition to democracy. But Romo would never face prosecution for his crimes because of a 1978 amnesty law. "La Prisión de los ex-agentes de inteligencia," *La Epoca* 14 (March, 1994): 21. In a written deposition given to the First Criminal Court in late 1991, Contreras said of Romo "he was . . . a repentant extremist, an informer of a DINA agent, and a very effective collaborator. Thanks to him Miguel Enríquez fell, and that is the reason the MIR condemned him to death." Salazar, *Contreras*, 175.

18. Cavallo et al., *La Historia oculta*, 56; *Report of the Chilean National Commission*, 2: 529.

19. Two witnesses identified Marcelo Moren Brito as her torturer. Rojas, *La Represión política en Chile: los hechos*, 56.

20. Gómez provides a first-hand account of the transfer from Londres 38 to José Domingos Cañas. *Tras la huella*, 157.

21. *Report of the Chilean National Commission*, 2: 537. The Italian ambassador granted asylum to Humberto Sotomayor and his wife on October 6, the day after Miguel Enríquez was killed in a firefight. The treatment of Lumi Videla was the DINA's way of exacting revenge on the Italian government. Salazar, *Contreras*, 92.

22. Salazar, *Contreras*, 92; Gómez, *Tras la huella*, 231–32.

23. Mónica González and Héctor Contreras, *Los Secretos del comando conjunto* (Santiago: Ornitorrinco, 1991), chap. 2.

24. *Report of the Chilean National Commission*, 2: 554.

25. Ahumada et al., *Chile: la memoria prohibida*, 3, chap. 8; Pinochet, *Camino recorrido*, 2: 332–33.

26. *Report of the Chilean National Commission*, 2: 612–13.

27. Pinochet, *Camino recorrido*, 2: 333.

28. The following quotations are from Becker and Torres, *Sistematización de la experiencia de defensa de los derechos humanos en Chile*, 58–59.

29. Keith Slack, "Operation Condor and Human Rights," 492–506.

30. *Report of the Chilean National Commission*, 2: 614; Iain Guest, *Behind the Disappearances: Argentina's Dirty War Against Human Rights and the United Nations* (Philadelphia: University of Pennsylvania Press, 1990), chap. 3.

31. González and Contreras, *Los Secretos del comando conjunto*, 32.

32. "Respuesta del MIR a los gorilas" ("The MIR's Response to the Gorillas"), September 10, 1974 (mimeograph).

33. Gómez, *Tras la huella*, 118.

34. "Convertir el odio e indignación en organización de la resistencia" ("Converting Hatred and Indignation into an Organization of the Resistance"). *El Rebelde* 99 (August 16, 1974) (mimeograph).

35. González and Contreras, *Los Secretos del comando conjunto*, 32.

36. Joseph Persico, *Nuremberg: Infamy on Trial* (New York: Penguin Books, 1994), 187.

37. Ibid., 214.

38. Pinochet, *El Dia decisivo*, 136.

39. The estimates are based on the case summaries in the *Report of the Chilean National Commission*, and include murders for which both the DINA and undetermined agencies were involved.

40. *Report of the Chilean National Commission*, 2: 593–95; Gómez, *Tras la huella*, chap. 10.

41. *Report of the Chilean National Commission*, 2: 565–68, 579. One of the men disappeared by the DINA may have been a CIA operative who was killed before discreet CIA communications with DINA could save him. Dinges and Landau, *Assassination on Embassy Row*, 167–70.

42. The DINA was reorganized about this time. The Cuapolicán group continued to pursue the MIR, but the operations of the Tucapel, Lautero, and Purén groups were concentrated in Purén. *Report of the Chilean National Commission*, 2: 474.

43. On June 8 the air force murdered Guillermo Bratti, an airman, and Carol Flores, a communist informant, on the suspicion that they had passed information to the DINA.

44. *Report of the Chilean National Commission*, 2: 469–95; González and Contreras, *Los Secretos del comando conjunto*, 37–40, 97–103.

45. *Report of the Chilean National Commission*, 2: 482.

46. The very existence of the Joint Command was made known by Andrés Valenzuela, who first told his story to Mónica González, an investigative reporter for *Cauce*. She in turn arranged for Valenzuela to give a detailed account to Héctor Contreras, an attorney with the Vicariate of Solidarity. Valenzuela entered the air force in 1974 and was assigned to the Air War Academy to guard political prisoners. Subsequently he became heavily involved in covert operations, including those resulting in the murders. The story is told in González and Contreros, *Los Secretos del comando conjunto*, published in 1991. In December 1984 the Association of the Families of the Detained-Disappeared published a pamphlet containing Valenzuela's admissions entitled "Confesiones de un agente de seguridad" (Confessions of a Security Agent). That same year Valenzuela told his story in a documentary produced for the Public Broadcasting System program *International Dispatch.*

47. Amnesty International, *"Disappearance" and Political Killings: A Manual for Action* (Amsterdam: Amnesty International Publications, 1994).

48. *Report of the Chilean National Commission*, 2: 592–93; Gómez, *Tras la huella*, 369–70; Inter-American Commission on Human Rights, *Third Report on the Situation of Human Rights in Chile* (Washington, D.C.: General Secretariat of the OAS, 1977), 25–32.

49. *Report of the Chilean National Commission*, 2: 570–71; IACHR, *Third Report on the Situation of Human Rights in Chile*, 17–19.

50. *Report of the Chilean National Commission*, 2: 578; González and Contreras, *Los Secretos del comando conjunto*, 172–76.

51. *Report of the Chilean National Commission*, 2: 567; Ahumada et al., *Chile: la memoria prohibida*, 2: 272–76.

52. *Report of the Chilean National Commission*, 2: 566–67; Gómez, *Tras la huella*, chap. 11.

53. *Report of the Chilean National Commission*, 2: 581; González and Contreras, *Los Secretos del comando conjunto*, 234–43; Constable and Valenzuela, *A Nation of Enemies*, 94.

54. *Report of the Chilean National Commission*, 2: 573; author's interview with Sola Sierra, president of the Association of the Families of the Detained-Disappeared, and wife of Waldo Pizarro, Santiago, 1994.

55. In January 1977 the Chilean government replied tersely that "the investigations conducted to date as to the status of this individual [Carlos Lorca] indicate that he was not arrested by any security organization." IACHR, *Third Report on the Situation of Human Rights*, 25–26.

56. Ibid., 29–32.

57. "Las Declaraciones del procurador de la República de Chile" (Santiago: March 22, 1988) (mimeograph). The categories of abuse listed are sexual; privations; immobilization; electricity; blows or fractures; cuts, puncture, extirpation, and wounding; ingestion; dangling, hurling, and stretching; beatings; drugs; burns; submersion and affixation; unnerving and terrifying noises; situations provoking terror; insults and ill-treatment; psychological; and obligation to sign declarations.

58. IACHR, "Report on the Status of Human Rights in Chile: Findings of 'on-the-spot' Observations in the Republic of Chile, July 22–August 2, 1974," 118–19.

59. Ibid., 116.

60. They recounted their story in a documentary, *In Women's Hands*, first aired in 1993 as part of the Public Broadcasting System's *Americas* series.

61. See Stover, *The Open Secret.*

62. Constable and Valenzuela, *A Nation of Enemies*, 96.

63. *Report of the Chilean National Commission*, 2: 579.

64. The National Commission on Truth and Reconciliation concluded that the

DINA is responsible for the disappearance of these men. *Report of the Chilean National Commission*, 2: 573. Sola Sierra, Pizarro's wife, believes the Joint Command disappeared him.

65. González and Contreras, *Los Secretos del comando conjunto*, 126.

66. Ibid., 122.

67. See especially, Sofia Salimovich, Elizabeth Lira, and Eugenia Weinstein, "Victims of Fear: the Social Psychology of Repression," in Corradi et al., eds., *Fear at the Edge*.

68. Author's interview with Sola Sierra, Santiago, June 1994.

Chapter 5

1. Inter-American Commission on Human Rights, *Ten Years of Activities, 1971–1981* (Washington, D.C.: General Secretariat OAS, 1982), 251.

2. Inter-American Commission on Human Rights, "Report on the Status of Human Rights in Chile," 7.

3. Ibid., 7.

4. Carlos Camus, "La Experiencia de la iglesia chilena en la defensa de los derechos humanos," in Fruhling, ed., *Represión política y defensa de los derechos*, 55. It was Carlos Camus who, in mid-1974, accompanied Laura Allende to the Air War Academy on behalf of the MIR to ascertain the condition of imprisoned MIRistas.

5. Constable and Valenzuela, *A Nation of Enemies*, 101, 281.

6. IACHR, "Report on the Status of Human Rights in Chile," 22.

7. The number of complaints received by the IACHR doubled between 1973 and 1974 (from 31 to 73). Between 1975 and 1980, the number of complaints doubled each year until the commission was receiving 3402 complains in 1980. IACHR, *Ten Years of Activities*, 99.

8. Ibid., 147–50. A number of physicians were killed after the coup, apparently because the military believed that they would staff clandestine clinics in the event of a civil war. Stover, *The Open Secret*, 42.

9. IACHR, *Ten Years of Activities*, 148.

10. Ibid., 150.

11. The resolution is contained in OEA/Ser.L/V/II.35. doc.33, rev.1.

12. Amnesty International, *Chile: An Amnesty International Report*, 79.

13. The following paragraphs are based on U.S., House of Representatives Committee on Foreign Affairs, *Human Rights in Chile*, Hearings before the Subcommittees on Inter-American Affairs and on International Organizations and Movements of the Committee on Foreign Affairs, House of Representatives, 93rd Congress, 2nd Sess., December 7, 1973; May 7, 23; June 11, 12, 18, 1974 (Washington, D.C.: U.S. Government Printing Office, 1974), 12, 14, 17, 25, 173.

14. Ibid., 12. The U.S. ambassador at the time responded to the charges this way: "The United States never signed the various Latin American conventions on asylum, and the U.S. prohibitions were generally known in political and informed circles throughout the hemisphere. . . . The fact that U.S. policy was longstanding did not, of course, make it right, as it deprived the United States of the ability to carry out acts of compassion." As to the murder of Charles Horman and Frank Terruggi, the former ambassador writes that "neither had registered with the consulate . . . I find it some consolation in terms of the embassy's efforts to think that we might have succeeded in saving them if we had known about their detention when they were still alive." Davis, *The Last Two Years of Salvador Allende*, 376–77, 378–79. The Chilean government did not respond until the end of March 1974, some five months later.

Charles Horman: Was found shot to death on a public thoroughfare on the morning of September 18, 1973. It has not been possible to determine whether his death was caused by a military curfew patrol, which was obliged to fire because he did not obey the order to halt, or whether his death occurred at the hands of extremists who, under cover of night, fired against the armed forces, the police, and the civil population in desperate and suicidal attacks. IACHR, "Report on the Status of Human Rights in Chile," 48.

15. Bascuñán, a Christian Democrat, was later appointed by Pinochet to the commission to draft a new constitution. Ahumada et al., *Chile: la memoria prohibida*, 387 n2.

16. Committee on Foreign Affairs, *Human Rights in Chile*, 9, 169–70.

17. The ICJ published two reports in Chile on 1974, the first in September, the second in October. Lars Schoultz, *Human Rights and United States Policy Toward Latin America* (Princeton, N.J.: Princeton University Press, 1981), 85–86.

18. Genaro Arriagada, "The Legal and Institutional Framework of the Armed Forces in Chile," in Valenzuela and J. Samuel Valenzuela, eds., *Military Rule in Chile: Dictatorship and Opposition* (Baltimore: Johns Hopkins University Press, 1986), 121.

19. MacEóin, ed., *Chile Under Military Rule*, 123.

20. Ibid., 123.

21. Statement of Convey Oliver, Hearings before the House Committee on Foreign Affairs, *Human Rights in Chile*, 57.

22. Ibid., 63.

23. Ibid.

24. Howard Tolley, *The International Commission of Jurists: Global Advocates for Human Rights* (Philadelphia: University of Pennsylvania Press, 1994), 201–2.

25. Schoultz, *Human Rights and United States Policy Toward Latin America*, 54.

26. Tolley, *The International Commission of Jurists*, xvi.

27. Amnesty International's September 1974 report noted the existence of the DINA, and its origin in the SENDET, but that was based on information forthcoming after AI's visit to Chile.

28. IACHR, "Report on the Status of Human Rights in Chile," 53.

29. Ibid., 55.

30. Ibid., 56.

31. Ibid., 57.

32. Ibid., 58.

33. Gómez, *Tras la huella de los desaparecidos*, chap. 5. Gómez provides a first-hand account of the transfer. The commission had learned of Londres 38 and mentioned it in its report, but it did not know about the facility at José Domingos Cañas.

34. IACHR, "Report on the Status of Human Rights in Chile," 100, 118.

35. Ibid., 1.

36. Ibid., 2.

37. IACHR, *Ten Years of Activities*, 252.

38. Ibid., 253.

39. AG/RES. 190 (V-0/75) adopted on May 19, 1975.

40. The text of the letter and the other documents quoted in the following paragraphs are reproduced in Centro de Información, Documentación y Analisis Latinoamericano, *Los Derechos humanos, la OEA y Chile* (Caracas: CIDAL, 1977). The authors were Jaime Castillo Velasco, Eugenio Velasco Letelier, Héctor Valenzuela Valderrama, Andrés Aylwin Azócar, and Fernando Guzmán Zañartu.

41. Constable and Valenzuela, *A Nation of Enemies*, 102.

42. Ahumada et al., *Chile: la memoria prohibida*, 2: 353–55.

43. *Report of the Chilean National Commission* 2: 555.

44. Organization of American States, AG/RES. 243 (VI-0/76). The Second Report covered the period from its August 1974 on-site inspection to the second week of March 1976. The wave of arrests and disappearances of Communist party leaders began in April and culminated in December. See also IACHR, *Ten Years of Activities*, 257.

Chapter 6

1. Loveman, *Chile: The Legacy of Hispanic Capitalism*.
2. Arriagada, *Pinochet: The Politics of Power*, 22.
3. Ibid., 37.
4. Constable and Valenzuela, *A Nation of Enemies*, 190, 340 n.62.
5. Arriagada, *Pinochet*, 20.
6. Pinochet, *Camino recorrido*, 2: 145.
7. Ibid., 145.
8. Ibid., 146.
9. Valenzuela, "The Military in Power," in Drake and Jaksić, eds., *The Struggle for Democracy in Chile*, 49.
10. United Nations Economic and Social Council, "Study of Reported Violations of Human Rights in Chile, with Particular Reference to Torture and Other Cruel, Inhuman or Degrading Treatment or Punishment," Report of the Ad Hoc Working Group (E/CN.4/1266 1 February 1978, Annex V), 16.
11. General Assembly resolution 32/118 of 16 December 1977, E/CN.4/1266 (1 February 1978) at Annex I. The resolution passed by a vote of 94 to 16 with 24 abstentions.
12. International Commission of the Latin American Studies Association to Observe the Chilean Plebiscite, "The Chilean Plebiscite: A First Step Toward Redemocratization," *LASA Forum* 19, 4 (Winter 1989): 18.
13. *Report of the Chilean National Commission*, 1: 89.
14. Hugo Fruhling, *Justicia por violación de derechos humanos y redemocratización en Chile* (Santiago: Centro de Estudios del Desarrollo, 1988), 10.
15. Report of the Ad Hoc Working Group (E/CN.4/1266 1 February 1978, Annex VII), 1–4.
16. Silvia Borzutsky, "The Pinochet Regime: Crisis and Consolidation," in James Malloy and Mitchell A. Seligson, eds., *Authoritarians and Democrats: Regime Transition in Latin America* (Pittsburgh: University of Pittsburgh Press, 1987), 70.
17. Valenzuela, "The Military in Power," in Drake and Jaksić, eds., *The Struggle for Democracy in Chile*, 50. Admiral Merino was the other junta member who had opposed the January plebiscite, but he did not resist the ouster of Leigh in July.
18. Office of International Justice and Peace of the United States Catholic Conference, *LADOC* 9.5 (May–June 1979): 31–32.
19. *LADOC* 9.1 (September/October 1979): 13–16.
20. Pinochet, *Camino recorrido*, 2: 362.
21. Luis Alvarez Baltierra, "Alessandri y la Constitución de '80," *Alternativa* (16 April 1986): 5–6.
22. Mark Ensalaco, "In with the New, Out with the Old? The Democratising Impact of Constitutional Reform in Chile," *Journal of Latin American Studies* 26 Part II (1994): 409.
23. Interview with the author, Santiago, June, 1993. See Luis Maira, *La Constitución de 1980 y la ruptura democrática* (Santiago: Editorial Emissión, 1988). The military had cited pronouncements by the congress and the Supreme Court asserting that Allende had violated the Statute of Guarantees as justification for the coup. But,

notably, as the regime entered its second decade in power, Luis Maira, Renán Fuentealba, and Jaime Castillo, three of the men who had drafted the statute, had been banished by the dictatorship.

24. Rhoda Rabkin, "The Aylwin Government and 'Tutelary' Democracy: A Concept in Search of a Case?" *Journal of Inter-American Studies and World Affairs* (1994): 154.

25. Eduardo Silva, "The Political Economy of Chile's Regime Transition: From Radical to 'Pragmatic' Neo-Liberal Policies," in Drake and Jaksić, eds., *The Struggle for Democracy in Chile*, 107; and Jeffrey M. Puryear, *Thinking Politics: Intellectuals and Democracy in Chile, 1973–88* (Baltimore: Johns Hopkins University Press, 1994), chap. 4.

26. Arriagada, *Pinochet*, chap. 7; Manuel Antonio Garretón, "The Political Opposition and the Party System Under the Military Regime," in Drake and Jaksić, eds., *The Struggle for Democracy in Chile*, 211–50.

27. Arriagada, *Pinochet*, 69.

28. *Report of the Chilean National Commission*, 2: 723.

29. Pinochet, *Camino recorrido*, 2: 90.

30. Amnesty International, *Chile Under the State of Siege* (London: Amnesty International Publications), AMR 22/53/84; Americas Watch/Lawyers Committee for International Human Rights report, untitled (mimeograph, 1985), 2.

31. U.S. House of Representatives, Committee on Foreign Affairs, Subcommittees on Human Rights and International Organizations and on Western Hemisphere Affairs, 99th Congress, 1st Session (March 20, 1985), 114.

32. Americas Watch Committee/Lawyers Committee, untitled (1985), 2, 16. Citing information from the Chilean Commission on Human Rights, the report lists 15,077 arrests in 1983 the year the protests began; 39,429 the following year, most after the imposition of the state of siege. According to a follow-up report by Americas Watch/Lawyers Committee for Human Rights released in September 1985, during the 17 months the state of siege was in effect, 39,500 were arrested, 621 were "relegated" (sentenced to internal exile), and that on average 2 cases of torture and 1 death were reported each week.

33. Americas Watch Committee/Lawyers Committee, Untitled (1985), 7.

34. Lawyers Committee for Human Rights and Americas Watch, "Report on Human Rights in Chile: February–March–April 1985" (June 1985), 20. The crime is described below.

35. Americas Watch/Lawyers Committee, "Report on Human Rights in Chile: May–July 1985 (September 1985), 15, 21–22.

36. Lawyers Committee on Human Rights/Americas Watch, "Report on Human Rights in Chile: February–March–April 1985" (June 1985), 19. Author's interview with staff members of CODEPU, June 1993.

37. Americas Watch/Lawyers Committee for Human Rights, "Report on the Human Rights Situation in Chile: May–July 1985," 9.

38. Ibid., 7–8.

39. *Report of the Chilean National Commission*, 2: 639.

40. Ibid., 693–94.

41. The following paragraphs are based on Nelson Caucoto Pereira and Héctor Salazar Ardiles, *Un Verde manto de impunidad* (Santiago: Ediciones Academia, 1994), chapter 7. Their account, in turn, is based on Miguel Estay's testimony before a special prosecuting judge in 1992.

42. Pinochet, *Camino recorrido*, 3: 255.

43. González and Contreras. *Los Secretos del comando conjunto*. Several men who were either directly involved in the crime or worked with DICOMAR had been with the Joint Command.

44. *Report of the Chilean National Commission* 2: 666.

45. *Camino recorrido*, 3: 255. This volume of his memoir was published in 1993, when evidence of DICOMAR complicity was unquestionable, much less unknown. Miguel Estay Reyna, Fanta, confessed his involvement before a court of law in December 1992.

46. "Human Rights in Chile: Time for United States Action," Hearing before the Subcommittee on International Development Institutions and Finance of the Committee on Banking, Finance, and Urban Affairs, House of Representatives, 99th Congress, Second Session (July 30, 1986), 8.

47. "Memorial de la dictadura: cronología de 14 años de pesadilla," *Análisis* (September 1987): 81–83.

48. Ascanio Cavallo Castro et al., *La Historia oculta*, esp. chapters 28 and 33.

49. Pinochet, *Camino recorrido*, 2: 363.

50. Cavallo et al., *La Historia oculta*, 293, 351.

51. Ibid., 350–51; *Report of the Chilean National Commission*, 2: 648–49; Pinochet, *Camino recorrido*, 276–77.

52. *Report of the Chilean National Commission*, 2: 653–54.

53. Pinochet, *Camino recorrido*, 2: 354, 365, 375–76; 3: 278–82, 295–97, 313–15, 329–36.

54. *Report of the Chilean National Commission*, 2: 686–712.

55. Ibid., 641–42, 667. Ahumada et al., *Chile: la memoria prohibida*, 3; chap. 7.

56. Cavallo et al., *La Historia oculta*, 300, 413; *Report of the Chilean National Commission*, 2: 688, 690, 651–52.

57. Kenneth Roberts, "Renovation in the Revolution?" 7; Hernán Vidal, *Frente Patriótico Manuel Rodríguez: el tabu del conflicto armado en Chile* (Santiago: Mosquito Editores, 1995), 105.

58. Vidal, *El Frente patriótico*, 110–11.

59. Information on the campaign of bombings and assassinations is from Pinochet, *Camino recorrido*, 3: 327–28; and the *Report of the Chilean National Commission*, 2: 696, 698, 709.

60. Pinochet, *Camino recorrido*, 3: 63–74.

61. *Report of the Chilean National Commission*, 2: 664; Mary Helen Spooner, *Soldiers in a Narrow Land: The Pinochet Regime in Chile* (Berkeley: University of California Press, 1994), 220–23. Pinochet, *Camino recorrido*, 3: 73.

62. *Report of the Chilean National Commission*, 2: 657–58; and Adriana Pohorecky, *Ignacio Valenzuela: fundador del Frente Patriótico Manuel Rodríguez* (Santiago, no publisher), 1995.

63. Imprisoned Rodriguistas testified that CNI interrogators were showing photographs of Valenzuela as early as September, 1986. Pohorecky, *Ignacio Valenzuela*, 183.

64. Pinochet, *Camino recorrido*, 3; 73; *Report of the Chilean National Commission*, 2: 664.

Chapter 7

1. Schoultz, *Human Rights and United States Policy*, 185–86; Sigmund, *The Overthrow of Allende*, 260.

2. Sigmund, *The Overthrow of Allende*, 261.

3. Schoultz, *Human Rights and United States Policy*, 198.

4. U.S. House of Representatives, Committee on Foreign Affairs, *Human Rights in Chile*.

5. Davis, *The Last Two Years of Salvador Allende*, 383.

6. *Human Rights in Chile*, 113–14.

7. Ibid., 118–19.

8. Ibid., 121.

9. U.S. House of Representatives, Committee on Foreign Affairs, Subcommittees on International Organizations and Movements and Inter-American Affairs, 93rd Congress, 2nd Sess. Human Rights in Chile: Part II (November 19, 1974), 21.

10. Ibid., 25.

11. Schoultz, *Human Rights and United States Policy*, 200.

12. Thomas Carothers, *In the Name of Democracy: U.S. Policy Toward Latin America in the Reagan Years* (Berkeley: University of California Press, 1991), 151.

13. Statement by Ambassador W. Tapley Bennett, Jr., U.S. Representative in Committee III of the UN General Assembly, Before the Vote on Resolution on Human Rights in Chile, October 22, 1974, *Human Rights in Chile*, 17.

14. Ibid., 18. The following year, the United States voted with the majority on a resolution containing almost identical wording. Schoultz, *Human Rights and United States Policy*, 282.

15. Ibid., 131.

16. Dinges and Landau, *Assassination on Embassy Row*.

17. Inter-American Commission on Human Rights, *Third Report on the Situation of Human Rights in Chile*. The report documented the campaign to disappear communist leaders begun on the eve of the OAS regular session, and "Operation Colombo," a DINA disinformation campaign intended to convince the public that one hundred and nineteen leftists listed as "disappeared" had in fact been killed in internecine fighting in neighboring Argentina.

18. The FBI was able to construct a list of top DINA officers as a result of General Contreras's request for visas for members of Pinochet's security detail. Ahumada et al., *Chile: la memoria prohibida*, 3: 29–32.

19. The indictments were handed down in August, 1978. Also named in the indictments were Armando Fernando Larios and Michael Townley, the man who constructed and planted the bomb. Sigmund, *The United States and Democracy in Chile*, 112–15.

20. Carothers, *In the Name of Democracy*, 156, 280.

21. Iain Guest, *Behind the Disappearances*, 300.

22. Carothers, *In the Name of Democracy*, 151.

23. E/RES/1235 (XLII) 6 June 1967 and E/RES/1503 (XLVIII), 27 May 1970. Tom J. Farer, "The United Nations and Human Rights: More than a Whimper, Less than a Roar," in Richard Pierre Claude and Burns H. Weston, eds., *Human Rights in the World Community: Issues and Action*, 2nd ed. (Philadelphia: University of Pennsylvania Press, 1992), 227–44.

24. Howard Tolley, Jr., *The UN Commission on Human Rights* (Boulder, Colo.: Westview Press, 1987), 63 and 81.

25. Ibid., 64.

26. Human Rights Commission Resolution 8 (XXXI) of February 27, 1975. The mandate of the Ad Hoc Working Group was routinely extended until 1979, when a Special Rapporteur was appointed.

27. Resolution 13 (XXXIV), 1978. Tolley, *UN Commission on Human Rights*, 149.

28. Pinochet, *Camino recorrido*, 2: 87.

29. Pinochet, *Camino recorrido*, 2: 89, 107.

30. United Nations Economic and Social Council, "Study of Reported Violations of Human Rights in Chile, with Particular Reference to Torture and other Cruel, Inhuman, or Degrading Treatment or Punishment," E/CN.4/1266 (1 February 1978), 72.

31. Guest, *Behind the Disappearances*, 129.

32. Ibid., 487 n.16.

33. David Weissbrodt and James McCarthy, "Fact-Finding by International Non-

governmental Human Rights Organizations," *Virginia Journal of International Law* 22, 1 (1981): 22.

34. Guest, *Behind the Disappearances*, 487 n.16.

35. Ibid., 131; Weissbrodt and McCarthy, "Fact-Finding by International Non-governmental Human Rights Organizations," 71; Report of the Economic and Social Council "Protection of Human Rights in Chle" UN Doc. A/33/331 at Annexes I–V (1978).

36. Pinochet, *Camino recorrido*, 2: 199–201.

37. Arriagada, *Pinochet: The Politics of Power*, 68.

38. Ibid., 74–75.

39. *LADOC* 16, 8 (January/February 1986): 1–7.

40. Arriagada, *Pinochet*, 75.

41. *LADOC*, 2.

42. Pinochet, *Camino recorrido*, 3: 154.

43. "Protection of Human Rights in Chile," A/40/647 (17 September 1985), 4.

44. Ibid., 6–7.

45. Ibid., 12.

46 Ibid., 17, 19.

47. Americas Watch, "Comments on the Report Prepared for the UN General Assembly by Prof. Volio Jiménez of Costa Rica, Special Rapporteur on the Situation of Human Rights in Chile" (November 1985), 1.

48. Ibid., 3.

49. Ibid., 3.

50. Arriagada, *Pinochet*, 67; Constable and Valenzuela, *A Nation of Enemies*, 290.

51. U.S. House of Representatives Subcommittee on International Development Institutions and Finance, Committee on Banking, Finance and Urban Affairs, 99th Congress, 2nd Sess. (July 30, 1986), Serial No. 99–89, 2, 4.

52. Ibid., 34.

53. Ibid., 24–25, 32.

54. Sigmund, *The United States and Democracy in Chile*, 161; Pinochet, *Camino recorrido* 3: 314.

55. Howard Wiarda, *The Democratic Revolution in Latin America: History, Politics and U.S. Policy* (New York: Holmes and Meier, 1990), chap. 6.

56. Carothers, *In the Name of Democracy*, 158; Sigmund, *The United States and Democracy in Chile*, 180–81. However, these sums were relatively small in comparison with the monies poured into Nicaragua to defeat the Sandinistas at the polls in 1990. Congressional Record, vol. 135 (Tuesday, October 17, 1989), S 13522.

57. Pinochet, *Camino recorrido*, 3: 175.

58. Ibid., 179–80, 187. Pinochet fixes the amount of NED aid at $10 million, nearly ten times the actual amount.

59. Constable and Valenzuela, *A Nation of Enemies*, 298.

60. Constable and Valenzuela, *A Nation of Enemies*, 309–10; Sigmund, *The United States and Democracy in Chile*, 175–76.

61. Pinochet, *Camino recorrido*, 3: 290.

Chapter 8

1. Patricio Aylwin Azócar, *La Transición chilena: discursos escogidos, marzo 1990–1992* (Santiago: Editorial Andres Bello, 1992), 19.

2. Ibid., 86.

3. "National Agreement for the Transition to Full Democracy," reprinted and translated in *LADOC* 16, 18 (January/February, 1986): 2.

4. Correa Sutil, "Dealing with Past Human Rights Violations," 1460.

5. Ibid., 1461.

6. Aylwin, *La Transición chilena*, 21.

7. Raúl Alfonsín had created the National Commission on the Disappeared (CONADEP), or the Sábato Commission, in 1983. It issued its report, *Nunca más* (Never Again), the following year. Farrar Straus Giroux published an English translation in 1986.

8. Aylwin, *La Transición chilena*, 33.

9. Biographical material in this paragraph comes from interviews with commission members conducted in June, 1993, and David Weissbrodt and Paul W. Fraser, National Commission on Truth and Reconciliation (Rettig Commission), "Report of the Chilean National Commission on Truth and Reconciliation," *Human Rights Quarterly* 14, 4 (November 1992): 603.

10. José Zalaquett, "Confronting Human Rights Violations Committed by Former Governments: Principles Applicable and Political Constraints," in Justice and Society Program of the Aspen Institute, *State Crimes: Punishment or Pardon*, 1989.

11. Washington Office on Latin America. *The Ethics of Responsibility*, Paper 2, Human Rights: Truth and Reconciliation in Chile. Transcript of a seminar with José Zalaquett Daher, April 17, 1991. Washington, D.C.: WOLA, 1991, 12.

12. Jorge Correa Sutil, "The Judiciary and the Political System in Chile: The Dilemmas of Judicial Independence During the Transition to Democracy," in Irwin Stotzky, ed., *Transition to Democracy in Latin America: The Role of the Judiciary* (Boulder, Colo.: Westview Press, 1993), 89–106.

13. Daan Bronkhorst, *Truth and Reconciliation: Obstacles and Opportunities for Human Rights* (Amsterdam: Amnesty International Dutch Section, 1995), 20.

14. *Report of the Chilean National Commission*, 1: 6–8.

15. "According to information gathered by the Commission, the armed forces and security faced no organized rebel troops." *Report of the Chilean National Commission*, 1: 129.

16. Ibid., 1: 31.

17. Ibid., 2: 680.

18. Ibid., 1: 454.

19. Ibid., 1: 40, 154. Notably, it chose not to include President Salvador Allende in this category, although he took his own life during the final assault on the presidential palace.

20. The following paragraphs are based on the author's interviews with Rettig Commission members conducted in Santiago in June 1994.

21. Zalaquett, "Confronting Human Rights Violation Quotations are from the reproduced version appearing in *Persona y Sociedad* (Santiago) 56 (1993), 51–80.

22. Bronkhorst, *Truth and Reconciliation*, 20.

23. Zalaquett, "Confronting Human Rights Violations," 54.

24. *Report of the Chilean National Commission*, 2: 472.

25. Mark Ensalaco, "Truth Commissions for Chile and El Salvador: A Report and Assessment," *Human Rights Quarterly* 16, 4 (November 1994): 656–75.

26. Commission on the Truth for El Salvador, *From Madness to Hope: The 12-Year War in El Salvador* UN Doc. S/25500 (1 April 1993), 18.

27. Author's interview, Washington, D.C., October, 1994. See also Thomas Buergenthal, "The United Nations Truth Commission for El Salvador," *Vanderbilt Journal of Transnational Law* 27, 3 (1994): 497–554.

28. Bronkhorst, *Truth and Reconciliation*, 26. Bronkhorst says Zalaquett "refused to claim a direct link."

29. *Report of the Chilean National Commission*, 1: 430.

30. The Rettig Report does not name René Muñoz Alarcón as a victim, or mention

the death by stabbing of anyone on the date of Muñoz's death. Nor does the report list him among those persons whose cases were declared unresolved.

31. The army publicly acknowledged the contact in its official response to the report of the Rettig Commission. "Respuestas de las fuerzas armadas y de orden al informe de la Comisión Nacional de Verdad y Reconciliación," *Estudios Públicos* 38 (1990): 450.

32. Bronkhorst, *Truth and Reconciliation*, 22.

33. *Report of the Chilean National Committee*, 2: 552.

34. Ibid., 520.

35. *Report of the Chilean National Commission*, 2, 519. Bachelet was arrested by Commander Edgar Ceballos ("Inspector Cabezas"), who would later become a senior officer in the air force's murderous Joint Command. Ahumada et al., *Chile: la memoria prohibida*, 1: 290.

36. *Report of the Chilean National Commission*, 1: 42.

37. Ibid., 2: 804, 808, 811.

38. Ibid., 1: 459–60. The army also claimed that a soldier who was killed when a rifle discharged after falling from a weapons rack was a victim. The Commission sensibly rejected that claim. 2: 816.

39. The Enríquez and Bordas cases are described in *Report of the Chilean National Commission*, 2: 539, 558 respectively. The Commission inadvertently dates Bordas's death on 5 December 1975 instead of 1974.

40. *Report of the Chilean National Commission*, 2: 744–45.

41. From an interview aired in *The Eleventh Twenty Years Later.*

42. *Report of the Chilean National Commission*, 1: 153–54. Allende's death is the first case considered in the report. Two days after the coup, the Permanent Committee of the Catholic Bishops issued this statement: "The blood which has been shed on our streets saddens us immensely and oppresses us . . . We ask for respect for those who fell in the struggle and, first of all, for the man who was until Tuesday the eleventh of September, President of the Republic." Ahumada et al., *Chile: la memoria prohibida*, 178.

43. *Report of the Chilean National Commission*, 1: 204; Verdugo, *Los Zarpazos del puma*, chaps. 1–2.

44. *Report of the Chilean National Commission*, 2: 673.

45. 59 had been unjustly sentenced to death by war tribunals; 101 were murdered under the pretext that they were attempting escape; 815 were victims of extrajudicial execution or died as a result of torture; 93 were killed as a result of excessive force used to put down protests; 957 persons are disappeared, and the commission considers them deceased. Another 164 persons were pronounced victims of "political violence"; 132 of those were members of the armed forces or security forces.

Chapter 9

1. Aywlin, *La Transición chilena*, 131–32.

2. Ibid., 132.

3. Ibid., 132.

4. *Report of the Chilean National Commission*, 1: 29; 2: 869. Jaime Castillo went so far as to complain that the section of the report on "Situation in Chile leading up to 11 September, 1973," left the impression that the commission concluded that the coup was inevitable. Author's interview, Santiago, June, 1994.

5. Ibid., 1: 33.

6. Ibid., 2: 870.

7. Report of the International Commission of the Latin American Studies Associa-

tion to Observe the Chilean Plebiscite, "The Chilean Plebiscite: A First Step Towards Redemocratization," 34.

8. "Respuestas de las fuerzas armadas y de orden," 452.

9. Human Rights Watch/Americas Watch, "Unsettled Business: Human Rights in Chile at the Start of the Frei Presidency" (May 1994), 6–7.

10. "Respuestas de las fuerzas armadas y de orden," 469, 471.

11. Ibid., 457.

12. Ibid., 452. On Sherman and the logic of war, see Michael Walzer, *Just and Unjust Wars: A Moral Argument with Historical Illustrations*, 2nd ed. (New York: Basic Books, 1992), 32.

13. "Respuestas de las fuerzas armadas y de orden," 483.

14. Ibid., 495.

15. Ibid., 491.

16. Cánovas, *Memorias de un magistrado* (Santiago: Emisión, 1989).

17. "Pocos, sumamente pocos," *APSI* 325 (October 1989): 17–19.

18. René García Villegas, *Soy testigo: dictadura, tortura, injusticia* (Santiago: Amerindia, 1990).

19. Americas Watch/Lawyers Committee for Human Rights, "Report on Human Rights in Chile, May–July 1985" (September 1985), 26.

20. Washington Office on Latin America, *The Ethics of Responsibility* Paper 2, 12.

21. *Report of the Chilean National Commission*, 1: 119.

22. Ibid., 117.

23. Ibid., 119, 126.

24. "Acuerdo de la Corte Suprema," reproduced in *El Mercurio*, 16 May 1991. It contains eleven sections.

25. Ibid., section 11. Judge Adolfo Bañados, one of the magistrates cited in the APSI article as a defender of human rights, also signed the Acuerdo de la Corte Suprema.

26. Americas Watch, "Unsettled Business: Human Rights in Chile at the Start of the Frei Presidency," 8.

27. "Acuerdo de la Corte Suprema," section 11.

28. *Report of the Chilean National Commission*, 1: 118.

29. Amnesty International, "Chile: An Amnesty International Report," 45.

30. *Report of the Chilean National Commission*, 2: 859, 860. The Commission's Secretary used nearly identical language in his analysis of the Chilean judicial system. Correa Sutil, "The Judiciary and the Political System in Chile," 93.

31. "Acuerdo de la Corte Suprema," section 11.

32. Human Rights Watch/Americas, "Unsettled Business," 28.

33. *Report of the Chilean National Commission*, 2: 664, 706.

34. Author's interview, Santiago, November 1991.

35. Human Rights Watch/Americas Watch, "Unsettled Business," 28.

36. Brian Loveman, "The Transition to Civilian Government in Chile, 1990–1994," in Drake and Jaksić, eds., *The Struggle for Democracy in Chile*, 315.

37. Corporación Nacional de Reparación y Reconciliación, *Informe a Su Excelencia El Presidente de la Republica sobre las actividades desorrolladas al 31 de enero de 1994* (Santiago, March 1994), 14–15.

38. Ibid., 28. This figure includes 626 cases in which the commission could not reach a moral conviction and another 363 cases that the commission had registered but not investigated.

39. Ibid., 29.

40. Ibid., 35.

41. Author's interview, Santiago, November 1991.

42. Corporación Nacional, *Informe a su excelencia*, 14.

43. Author's interview, Santiago, June 1994.

44. Author's interview, Santiago, June 1994. "Juan Fernando ORTIZ LETELIER, a university professor, and Waldo Ulises PIZARRO MOLINA, a mining expert, both of whom were members of the CP Central Committee, were arrested in the presence of several witnesses near the intersection of Plaza Engaña and Avenida Larraín. They were arrested by several agents who put hoods over them. One of them managed to shout his name out, and was hit on the head for doing so. The agents violently forced them into a vehicle. They have been disappeared since that day. According to travel certificate No. 1082 dated April 20, 1977, Waldo Pizarro left the country on foot December 21, 1976, over Los Libertadores pass, but the court proved that document to be false." *Report of the Chilean National Commission*, 2: 573.

45. "Psicología de derechos humanos en una situación represiva: la experiencia de FASIC" in Fruhling, ed., *Represión política y defensa de los derechos humanos*, 269; Sali-movich et al., "Victims of Fear: The Social Psychology of Repression."

46. Agrupación de Familiares de Detenidos-Desaparecidos, "Respuesta de la Agru-pación de Familiares de Detenidos-Desaparecidos a la Comisión Nacional de Verdad y Reconciliación" (Santiago: AFDD, 1990), 13.

47. Human Rights Watch/Americas, "Unsettled Business," 9–10.

48. In late 1995 Eduardo Frei, Aywlin's successor, would offer a similar proposal. It met with a similar fate. "Organismos d DD.HH contra Proyecto de Ley," *El Mercurio* Edicion Internacional (January 11–17, 1996): 1.

49. Manuel Salazar, *Contreras: historia de un intocable*, 10.

50. Ibid., 11.

51. Correa Sutil, "Dealing with Past Human Rights Violations," 1461.

Bibliography

Agrupación de Familiares de Detenidos-Desaparecidos (Association of the Families of the Detained-Disappeared). "Respuesta de la Agrupación de Familiares de Detenidos-Desaparecidos a la Comisión Nacional de Verdad y Reconciliación." Santiago: AFDD, 1990.

———. "Confesiones de un agente de seguridad" (Confessions of a Security Agent). Santiago: AFDD, 1990.

Ahumada, Eugenio et al. *Chile: la memoria prohibida*. 3 vols. Santiago: Pehuén, 1989.

Alvarez Baltierra, Luis. "Alessandri y la Constitución de '80." *Alternativa* (16 April 1986): 5–6.

Americas Watch. *Comments on the Report Prepared for the UN General Assembly by Prof. Fernando Volio Jiménez of Costa Rica, Special Rapporteur on the Situation of Human Rights in Chile (A/40/647, 17 September 1985*. Washington, D.C.: Americas Watch Committee, November 1985.

———. "Human Rights Concerns in Chile March 1987." New York: Americas Watch, 1987.

———. *The Vicaría de la Solidaridad in Chile*. New York: Americas Watch, 1987.

Americas Watch and Lawyers Committee for International Human Rights. "Report on Human Rights in Chile December 1984–January 1985 From the Chilean Human Rights Commission." New York: Americas Watch/Lawyers Committee for International Human Rights, February 1985.

———. "Report on Human Rights in Chile February–March–April 1985 (from the Chilean Commission on Human Rights)." New York: Americas Watch/Lawyers Committee for International Human Rights, June 1985.

———. "Report on Human Rights in Chile May–July 1985." New York: Americas Watch/Lawyers Committee for International Human Rights, September 1985.

Amnesty International. *Chile: An Amnesty International Report*. London: Amnesty International Publications, September 1974.

———. *Chile: 50 Cases of Torture, February 1987 and March 1987 Update* . AI22/03/87. New York: Amnesty International, 1987.

———. *Chile Under the State of Siege*. AMR 22/53/84. London: Amnesty International Publications, 1984.

———. *"Disappearance" and Political Killings: A Manual for Action*. Amsterdam: Amnesty International Publications, 1994.

———. "March 1987 Update." AMR 22/10/87.

———. "50 Cases of Torture, February 1987." AMR 22/03/87.

Arriagada, Genero. "The Legal and Institutional Framework of the Armed Forces in Chile." In Valenzuela and Valenzuela, eds., *Military Rule in Chile: Dictatorship and Opposition*.

———. *Pinochet: The Politics of Power*. Trans. Nancy Morris, Vincent Ercolano, and Kristen Whitney. Boston: Unwin Hyman, 1988.

Aylwin Azócar, Patricio. *La Transición chilena: discursos escogidos, marzo 1990–1992*. Santiago: Editorial Andres Bello, 1992.

Becker, Nubia and Oswaldo Torres. *Sistematización de la experiencia de defensa de los derechos humanos en Chile*. Santiago: Asociación Latinoamericano para los Derechos Humanos, 1992.

Borzutsky, Silvia."The Pinochet Regime: Crisis and Consolidation." In Malloy and Seligson, eds., *Authoritarians and Democrats: Regime Transition in Latin America*.

Bronkhorst, Daan. *Truth and Reconciliation: Obstacles and Opportunities for Human Rights*. Amsterdam: Amnesty International Dutch Section, 1995.

Brown, Cynthia. *The Vicaría de la Solidaridad in Chile*. New York: Americas Watch, 1987.

Buergenthal, Thomas. "The United Nations Truth Commission for El Salvador." *Vanderbilt Journal of Transnational Law* 27, 3 (1994): 497–554.

Campero, Guillermo. "Entrepreneurs Under the Military Regime." In Drake and Jaksić, eds., *The Struggle for Democracy in Chile, 1982–1990*.

Camus, Carlos. "La Experiencia de la iglesia chilena en la defensa de los derechos humanos." In Fruhling, ed., *Represión política y defensa de los derechos humanos*.

Cánovas, José. *Memorias de un magistrado*. Santiago: Emisión, 1989.

Carothers, Thomas. *In the Name of Democracy: U.S. Policy Toward Latin America in the Reagan Years*. Berkeley: University of California Press, 1991.

Castañeda, Jorge G. *Utopia Unarmed: The Latin American Left After the Cold War*. New York: Alfred Knopf, 1993.

Castillo Velasco, Jaime, Eugenio Velasco Letelier, Héctor Valenzuela Valderrama, Andrés Aylwin Azócar, and Fernando Guzmán Zañartu. *Los Derechos humanos, la OEA y Chile*. Caracas: Centro de Información, Documentación y Analisis Latinoamericano, 1977.

Caucoto Pereira, Nelson and Héctor Salazar Ardiles. *Un Verde manto de impunidad*. Santiago: Ediciones Academia, 1994.

Cavallo Castro, Ascanio, Manuel Salazar Salvo, and Oscar Sepúlveda Pacheco, eds. *La Historia oculta del regimen militar: Chile, 1973–1988*. Mexico City: Editorial DIANA, 1990.

Chilean National Commission on Truth and Reconciliation. *Report of the Chilean National Commission on Truth and Reconciliation*. Trans. Philip E. Berryman. 2 vols. Notre Dame, Ind.: University of Notre Dame Press, 1993.

Chuchryk, Patricia. "Subversive Mothers: The Opposition to the Military Regime in Chile." In Marjorie Agosín, ed., *Surviving Beyond Fear: Women, Children and Human Rights in Latin America*. Fredonia, N. H.: White Pines Press, 1993. 86–97.

Claude, Richard P. and Burns H. Weston, eds. *Human Rights in the World Community: Issues and Action*. 2nd ed. Philadelphia: University of Pennsylvania Press, 1992.

Commission on the Truth for El Salvador. *From Madness to Hope: The 12-Year War in El Salvador*. UN Security Council UN Doc. S/25500, 1993.

CONADEP (Argentine National Commission on the Disappeared). *Nunca más (Never Again)*. Buenos Aires: Buenos Aires University Press, 1984. London: Farrar Straus Giroux, 1986.

Constable, Pamela and Arturo Valenzuela. *A Nation of Enemies: Chile Under Pinochet*. New York: W. W. Norton, 1991.

Corporación Nacional de Reparación y Reconciliación. *Informe a Su Excelencia El*

Presidente de la Republica sobre las actividades desorrolladas al 31 de enero de 1994. Santiago, March 1994.

Corradi, Juan E., Patricia Weiss Fagen, and Manuel Antonio Garretón, eds. *Fear at the Edge: State Terror and Resistance in Latin America.* Berkeley: University of California Press, 1992.

Correa Sutil, Jorge. "Dealing with Past Human Rights Violations: The Chilean Case After the Dictatorship." *Notre Dame Law Review* 67 (1992): 1455–85.

———. "The Judiciary and the Political System in Chile: The Dilemmas of Judicial Independence During the Transition to Democracy." In Stotzky, ed., *Transition to Democracy in Latin America,* 89–106.

Davis, Nathaniel. *The Last Two Years of Salvador Allende.* Ithaca, N.Y.: Cornell University Press, 1985.

"Las Declaraciones del Procurador de la Republica de Chile." Mimeograph. Santiago, March 22, 1988.

Del Pozo, José. *Rebeldes, reformistas, y revolucionarios: una historia oral de la izquierda chilena en la epoca de la Unidad Popular.* Santiago: Ediciones Documentas, 1992.

Dinges, John and Saul Landau. *Assassination on Embassy Row.* New York: Pantheon, 1980.

Drake, Paul W. and Iván Jaksić, eds. *The Struggle for Democracy in Chile, 1982–1990.* Lincoln: University of Nebraska Press, 1991.

———. *The Struggle for Democracy in Chile.* Rev. ed. Lincoln: University of Nebraska Press, 1995.

Ensalaco, Mark. "In with the New, Out with the Old? The Democratising Impact of Constitutional Reform in Chile." *Journal of Latin American Studies* 26, Part II (1994): 409–29.

———. "Military Prerogatives and the Stalemate of Chilean Civil-Military Relations." *Armed Forces and Society* 21, 2 (1995): 255–70.

———. "Truth Commissions for Chile and El Salvador: A Report and Assessment." *Human Rights Quarterly* 16, 4 (1994): 656–75.

Esponda, Jaime. "Objetivos y criterios estratégicos aplicados por la Vicaría de la Solidaridad del Arzobispado de Santiago en su tarea en defensa de los derechos humanos." In Fruhling, ed., *Represión política y defensa de los derechos humanos.*

Farer, Tom J. "The United Nations and Human Rights: More Than a Whimper, Less Than a Roar." In Claude and Weston, eds., *Human Rights in the World Community,* 227–44.

Farnworth, Elizabeth. "More Than Admitted." *Foreign Policy* 16 (1974): 127–41.

Fruhling, Hugo. *Justicia por violación de derechos humanos y redemocratización en Chile.* Santiago: Centro de Estudios del Desarrollo, 1988.

———, ed. *Represión política y defensa de los derechos humanos.* Santiago: Ediciones Chile y América, 1986.

Fruhling, Hugo, Gloria Alberti, and Felipe Portales. *Organizaciones de derechos humanos de America sur.* San José: Instituto Interamericano de Derechos Humanos, 1989.

Fuerzas Armadas y de Orden. "Respuestas de las Fuerzas Armadas y de Orden al informe de la Comisión Nacional de Verdad y Reconciliación." Reproduced in *Estudios Públicos* (Santiago) 38 (Autumn 1990).

Furci, Carmelo. *The Chilean Communist Party and the Road to Socialism.* London: Zed Books, 1984.

García Villegas, René. *Soy testigo: dictadura, tortura, injusticia.* Santiago: Editorial Amerindia, 1990.

Garretón, Manuel Antonio. "The Political Opposition and the Party System under the Military Regime," in Drake and Jaksić, eds., *The Struggle for Democracy,* rev. ed. 211–50.

Garretón, Roberto. "Leyes secretas en Chile." *Revista Chilena de Derechos Humanos* (1st trimester 1985).

General Secretariat, Organization of American States. *Inter-American Commission on Human Rights: Ten Years of Activities, 1971–1980*. Washington, D.C.: Secretariat of the Inter-American Commission on Human Rights, 1982.

Gómez Araneda, León. *Tras la huella de los desapracidos*. Santiago: Ediciones Caleuche, 1990.

González, Mónica and Héctor Contreras. *Los Secretos del comando conjunto*. Santiago: Ornitorrinco, 1991.

Guest, Iain. *Behind the Disappearances: Argentina's Dirty War Against Human Rights and the United Nations*. Philadelphia: University of Pennsylvania Press, 1990.

Hauser, Thomas. *Missing: The Execution of Charles Horman*. New York: Simon and Schuster, 1978.

Hennelly, Alfred and John Langan, eds. *Human Rights in the Americas: The Struggle for Consensus*. Washington, D.C.: Georgetown University Press, 1982.

Human Rights Watch/Americas Watch. "Unsettled Business: Human Rights in Chile at the Start of the Frei Presidency." May 1994.

Inter-American Commission on Human Rights. "Report on the Status of Human Rights in Chile: Findings of the 'On-The-Spot' Observations in the Republic of Chile, July 22–August 2, 1974." OEA/Ser. L/V/II.34 doc. 21 corr. 1 (25 October 1974).

———. *Ten Years of Activities, 1971–1981*. Washington, D.C.: General Secretariat OAS, 1982.

———. *Third Report on the Situation of Human Rights in Chile*. OEA/Ser. L/V/II.40 doc. 10 (11 February 1977). Washington, D.C.: General Secretariat of the OAS, 1977.

International Commission of Jurists. *Chile: A Time of Reckoning, Human Rights, and the Judiciary*. Geneva: ICJ, 1992.

International Commission of the Latin American Studies Association to Observe the Chilean Plebiscite. "The Chilean Plebiscite: A First Step Toward Redemocratization." *LASA Forum* 19, 4 (Winter 1989).

International League for Human Rights. "Analisis del Informe del Departmento de Estado sobre la Situación de los Derechos Humanos en Chile, Año 1981." (Estudio realizado por los señores Andrés Domínguez Vial y Gustavo Rayo Urrutia, del Departamento de Coordinación de la Comisión Chilena de Derechos Humanos. Santiago 26 de marzo de 1982.) New York: International League for Human Rights Human Rights Working Papers.

Lawyers Committee for International Human Rights. "Report on Human Rights in Chile October–November 1984." New York: Lawyers Committee for International Human Rights/Americas Watch, 1984.

Lira, Elizabeth. "Psicología de derechos humanos en una situación represiva: la experencia de FASIC." In Fruhling, ed., *Represión política y defensa de los derechos humanos*.

Lira, Elizabeth and María Isabel Castillo. *Psicologia de la amenaza política y del miedo*. Santiago: Instituto Latinoamericano de Salud Mental y Derechos Humanos, 1991.

Loveman, Brian. *Chile: The Legacy of Hispanic Capitalism*. 2nd ed. New York: Oxford University Press, 1988.

———. "The Transformation of the Chilean Countryside." In Valenzuela and Valenzuela, eds., *Chile: Politics and Society*.

———. "The Transition to Civilian Government in Chile, 1990–1994." In Drake and Jaksić, eds. *The Struggle for Democracy in Chile*.

Lowy, Michel. *El Marxismo en América Latina: antología desde 1900 hasta nuestros dias*. Mexico City: Ediciones Era, 1980.

MacEóin, Gary, ed. *Chile Under Military Rule*. New York: IDOC/North America, 1974.

Maira, Luis. *La Constitución de 1980 y la ruptura democrática.* Santiago: Editorial Emisión, 1988.
——. *Notas sobre la transición chilena* Santiago: CENAT, 1991.
Malloy, James and Mitchell A. Seligson, eds. *Authoritarians and Democrats: Regime Transition in Latin America.* Pittsburgh: University of Pittsburgh Press, 1987.
"Memorial de la dictadura: cronologia de 14 años de pesadilla. *Análisis* (September 1987): 81–83.
Montealegre, Hernán. "The Security of the State and Human Rights," In Hennelly and Langan, eds., *Human Rights in the Americas,* 187–210.
Movimiento de la Izquierda Revolucionaria (MIR). "Algunos antecedentes del Movimiento de Izquierda Revolucionaria (MIR)." Mimeograph. March 1970.
——. "Conferencia de prensa realizada el 8 de Octubre de 1973." Mimeograph.
——. "Discurso por cadena de radioemisoras." Mimeograph. 6 June, 1973.
——. "Los Golpes recientes, algunas lecciones y la reorganización de las dirreciones." Mimeograph. June 1974.
——. "Pauta del MIR para unir fuerzas dispuestas a impulsar la lucha contra la dictadura." Mimeograph. 17 February, 1974.
——. "La Resistencia popular triunfará." Mimeograph. 16 August, 1974.
——. "Respuesta del MIR a los gorilas." Mimeograph. September 1973.
——. "La Táctica del MIR en el actual período." Mimeograph. December, 1973.
Office of International Justice and Peace of the United States Catholic Conference. LADOC 9, 5 (May/June 1979): 31–32.
——. LADOC 10, 1 (September/October 1979): 13–16.
Oppenheim, Lois Hecht. *Politics in Chile: Democracy, Authoritarianism, and the Search for Development.* Boulder, Colo.: Westview Press, 1993.
Orellana, Patricio. "La Lucha silenciosa por derechos humanos: el caso de FASIC." In Orellana and Hutchison, eds., *El Movimiento de derechos humanos en Chile,* 143–98.
——. "Los Organismos de derechos humanos en Chile hacia 1985." In Orellano and Hutchison, eds., *El Movimiento de derechos humanos en Chile, 1973–1990.*
Orellana, Patricio and Elizabeth Q. Hutchison, eds., *El Movimiento de derechos humanos en Chile, 1973–1990.* Santiago: Centro de Estudios Políticos Latinoamericanos Simón Bolívar, 1991.
"Pauta del MIR para unir fuerzas dispuestas a impulsar la lucha contra la dictadura" (The MIR's Guiding Principle to Unify Forces Disposed to Impel the Struggle Against the Dictatorship). February 17, 1974. Mimeograph.
Persico, Joseph E. *Nuremberg: Infamy on Trial.* New York: Penguin Books, 1994.
Pinochet, Augusto. *Camino recorrido: memorias de un soldado.* 3 vols. Santiago: Instituto Geográfico Militar de Chile, 1991.
——. *El Dia decisivo: 11 de septiembre de 1973.* 5th ed. Santiago: Andrés Bello, 1984.
"Pocos, sumamente pocos." *APSI* 325 (October 1989): 17–19.
Pohorecky, Adriana. *Ignacio valenzuela: fundador del Frente Patriótico Manuel Rodríguez.* Santiago, 1995.
"La Prisión de los ex-agentes de inteligencia." *La Epoca* 14 (March 1994): 21.
Puryear, Jeffrey M. *Thinking Politics: Intellectuals and Democracy in Chile, 1973–1988.* Baltimore: Johns Hopkins University Press, 1994.
Rabkin, Rhoda. "The Aylwin Government and 'Tutelary' Democracy: A Concept in Search of a Case?" *Journal of Inter-American Studies and World Affairs* (1994).
Reisman, Michael W. and Chris T. Antoniou, eds. *The Laws of War: A Comprehensive Collection of Primary Documents on International Laws Governing Armed Conflict.* New York: Vintage, 1994.
Roberts, Kenneth. "Renovation in the Revolution? Democracy, and Political Change in the Chilean Left." Kellogg Institute for International Studies Working Paper 203, March 1994. Notre Dame, Ind., 1994.

Rojas, María Eugenia. *La Represión política en Chile: los hechos*. Madrid: IEPALA Editorial, 1988.

Salazar, Manuel. *Contreras: historia de un intocable*. Santiago: Grijalbo, 1995.

Salimovich, Sofia, Elizabeth Lira, and Eugenia Weinstein. "Victims of Fear: The Social Psychology of Repression." In Corradi, Fagen, and Garretón eds., *Fear at the Edge*.

Sandoval Ambiado, Carlos. *MIR: una historia*. Vol. 1. Santiago: Sociedad Editorial Trabajadores, 1990.

Schoultz, Lars. *Human Rights and United States Policy Toward Latin America*. Princeton, N.J.: Princeton University Press, 1981.

Sigmund, Paul E. "The 'Invisible Blockade' and the Overthrow of Allende." *Foreign Affairs* 52, 2 (January 1974): 322–40

——. "Less Than Charged." *Foreign Policy* 16 (Fall 1974): 142–56.

——. *The Overthrow of Allende and the Politics of Chile, 1964–1976*. Pittsburgh: University of Pittsburgh Press, 1977.

——. *The United States and Democracy in Chile*. Baltimore: Johns Hopkins University Press, 1993.

Silva, Eduardo. "The Political Economy of Chile's Regime Transition: From Radical to 'Pragmatic' Neo-Liberal Policies." In Drake and Jaksić, eds., *The Struggle for Democracy in Chile*.

Slack, Keith. "Operation Condor and Human Rights: A Report from Paraguay's Archive of Terror." *Human Rights Quarterly* 18, 2 (1996): 492–506.

Spooner, Mary Helen, *Soldiers in a Narrow Land: The Pinochet Regime in Chile*. Berkeley: University of California Press, 1994.

Stotzky, Irwin P., ed. *Transition to Democracy in Latin America: The Role of the Judiciary*. Boulder, Colo.: Westview Press, 1993.

Stover, Eric. *The Open Secret: Torture and the Medical Profession in Chile*. Washington, D. C.: American Association for the Advancement of Science, 1987.

Tolley, Howard Jr. *The International Commission of Jurists: Global Advocates for Human Rights* Philadelphia: University of Pennsylvania Press, 1994.

——. *The UN Commission on Human Rights* Boulder, Colo.: Westview Press, 1987.

United Nations Economic and Social Council. "Protection of Human Rights in Chile." UN Doc. A/10285 (1975).

——. "Protection of Human Rights in Chile." UN Doc. A/33/331 at Annexes I–V (1978).

——. Report of the UN Special Rapporteur for Chile. UN Doc. E/CN.4/1428 (1981).

——. Report of the UN Special Rapporteur for Chile. UN Doc. E/CN.4/1484 (1982).

——. Report of the UN Special Rapporteur for Chile. UN Doc. E/CN.4/1983/9 (1983).

——. Report of the UN Special Rapporteur for Chile. UN Doc. E/CN.4/1984/7 (1984).

——. Report of the UN Special Rapporteur for Chile. UN Doc. E/CN.4/1985/38 (1985).

——. Report of the UN Special Rapporteur for Chile. UN Doc. E/CN.4/1986/2 (1986).

——. Report of the UN Special Rapporteur for Chile. UN Doc. E/CN.4/1987/7 (1987).

——. Report of the UN Special Rapporteur for Chile. UN Doc. E/CN.4/1988/7 (1988).

———. Report of the UN Special Rapporteur for Chile. UN Doc. E/CN.4/1989/7 (1989).

———. Report of the UN Special Rapporteur for Chile. UN Doc. E/CN.4/1990/5 (1990).

———. "Study of Reported Violations of Human Rights in Chile, with Particular Reference to Torture and Other Cruel, Inhuman, or Degrading Treatment of Punishment." Report of the Ad Hoc Working Group. UN Doc. E/CN.4/1266 1 (February 1978), Annex V.

U.S. House of Representatives, Subcommittee on International Development Institutions and Finance of the Commission on Banking, finance, and Urban Affairs. "Human Rights in Chile: Time for United States Action." 99th Congress, Second Session (July 30, 1986).

U.S. House of Representatives, Committee on Foreign Affairs. *Human Rights in Chile* Hearings before the Subcommittees on Inter-American Affairs and on International Organizations and Movements of the Committee on Foreign Affairs, U.S. House of Representatives, 93rd Congress, Second Session, December 7, 1973; May 7, 23; June 11, 12, 18, 1974. Washington, D.C.: U.S. Government Printing Office, 1974.

U.S. Senate. *Alleged Assassination Plots Involving Foreign Leaders.* Washington, D.C.: U.S. Government Printing Office, 20 November 1975.

———. *Covert Action in Chile, 1963–1973.* Washington, D.C.: U.S. Government Printing Office, 1975.

Valenzuela, Arturo. *The Breakdown of Democratic Regimes: Chile.* Baltimore: Johns Hopkins University Press, 1978.

———. "The Military in Power." In Drake and Jaksić, eds., *The Struggle for Democracy in Chile.*

Valenzuela, Arturo and J. Samuel Valenzuela, eds. *Chile: Politics and Society.* New Brunswick, N. J.: Transaction Books, 1976.

Valenzuela, J. Samuel and Arturo Valenzuela, eds. *Military Rule in Chile: Dictatorship and Oppositions.* Baltimore: Johns Hopkins University Press, 1986.

Varas, Augusto. "The Crisis of Legitimacy of Military Rule in the 1980s." In Drake and Jaksić, eds., *The Struggle for Democracy in Chile,* 73–97.

———. *Los Militares en el poder: régimen y gobierno militar en Chile, 1973–1986.* Santiago: Pehuén: FLACSO, 1987.

Verdugo, Patricia. *Los Zarpazos del puma: caso arellano.* Santiago: Ediciones Chile y América — CESOC, 1989.

Vicaría de la Solidaridad. *Vicaría de la Solidaridad: historia de su trabajo social* Santiago: Ediciones Paulinas, 1991.

Vidal, Hernán. *Frente Patriótico Manuel Rodríguez: el tabu el conflicto armado en Chile.* Santiago: Mosquito Editores, 1995.

Walzer, Michael. *Just and Unjust Wars: A Moral Argument with Historical Illustrations.* 2nd ed. New York: Basic Books, 1992.

Washington Office on Latin America. *The Ethics of Responsibility.* Paper 2, Human Rights: Truth and Reconciliation in Chile. Transcript of a seminar with José Zalaquett Daher, April 17, 1991. Washington, D.C: WOLA, 1991.

Weissbrodt, David and Paul W. Fraser. "National Commission on Truth and Reconciliation (Rettig Commission), Report of the Chilean National Commission on Truth and Reconciliation." *Human Rights Quarterly* 14, 4 (November 1992).

Weissbrodt, David and James McCarthy. "Fact-Finding by International Nongovernmental Human Rights Organizations." *Virginia Journal of International Law* 22,1 (1981), 22.

Wiarda, Howard. *The Democratic Revolution in Latin America: History, Politics, and U.S. Policy.* New York: Holmes and Meier, 1990.

Zalaquett, José. "Balancing Ethical Imperatives and Political Constraints: The Dilemma of New Democracies Confronting Past Human Rights Violations." *Hastings Law Journal* 23 (August 1992): 1425–38.

———. "Confronting Human Rights Violations Committed by Former Governments: Principles Applicable and Political Constraints." In Justice and Society Program of the Aspen Institute, *State Crimes: Punishment or Pardon*. Aspen Institute, 1989.

Index

Acknowledgments

I owe a debt of gratitude to many persons for the various forms of support and assistance they have given to me and this project. The support and assistance of the University of Dayton was crucial. Frederick Inscho and David Ahern, as chairs of the Department of Political Science, supported the faculty exchange that enabled me to conduct research at the Facultad de Ciencias Jurídicas y Sociales of the Universidad de Concepción, Chile. The Dean of the College of Arts and Sciences, Dr. Paul Mormon, and above all, the Provost, Dr. John Geiger, likewise supported my leave — this after only three semesters at the University.

The faculty and students of the University of Concepción were immensely helpful. They helped me acclimate myself to a university that, as the birthplace of the Movement of the Revolutionary Left, managed to survive seventeen years of military intervention in its academic affairs. I owe Sergio Mancenelli and his wife, Gabriela, a special debt of gratitude for innumerable acts of kindness they displayed to me and my family.

My family, especially my son Adam and my daughters Monica and Nora, showed great patience as I labored in my study. I thank them all for their understanding.

Marcelo Julio arranged the vast majority of the interviews I conducted in connection with this research in Chile. He graciously shared his many contacts and, more importantly, convinced many of them that it was all right to speak to me. Beyond that, he made available to me his impressive collection of mimeographed documents and secondary sources, and I promise that one day soon I will return these to him.

Silvia Bortzutsky encouraged me to pursue this project when it was in its earliest stages, and shared her insights into Chile's democratic transition. Likewise, Elizabeth Lira shared with me her analysis of the repression and her first-hand experience of the inner workings of human rights organizations with which she was associated in several long conversations over dinner in the United States and Costa Rica. Brian Loveman gave me encouragement, guidance, and advice at various times over the past few years. He critiqued the original manuscript of this book, and I took his comments and criticisms very seriously, especially insofar as they touched on some controversial assertions I make in the book.

I have to thank Paula Braley who proofed the manuscript. Her attention to detail, her precision, and her hard work made it possible for me to complete the manuscript.

Two individuals deserve mention, although neither participated directly in this research. Gary Hoskin and Claude Welch, Jr., of the State University of New York at Buffalo, have my gratitude as the mentors who taught me my craft. I hold them in the highest esteem.

Sharon Conway has my most sincere gratitude for her support.

Finally, I want to thank María de los Angeles: ya lo sabes.

As always in these matters, the people I have acknowledged deserve much of the credit for what is good about this book. I alone am responsible for its deficiencies.